The Pauline Hanson Story ...

by the

Man Who Knows

The Pauline Hanson Story ...

by the **Man Who Knows**

John Pasquarelli

NEW HOLLAND

Produced and published in Australia by
New Holland Publishers Pty Ltd
3/2 Aquatic Drive
Frenchs Forest
NSW 2086 Australia

Sydney • Melbourne • London • Cape Town

Editor: Scharlaine Cairns, Charlie C. Editorial Pty Ltd
Typesetter: Midland Typesetters
Printer: Griffin Press, Adelaide

National Library of Australia Cataloguing-in-Publication Data:

Pasquarelli, John.
The Pauline Hanson story by the man who knows.

ISBN 1 86436 341 X.

1. Politicians – Australia – Biography. 2. Women
politicians – Australia – Biography. 3. Aborigines,
Australian – Government policy. 4. Australia – Emigration
and immigration – Government policy. 5. Australia –
Politics and government – 1990–   . I. Title.

994.065092

Cover photograph: Andrew Meares/The Fairfax Photo Library

For Joe, Marie and Leon Pasquarelli, and 'Dusty' and Maud Rhodes.

Foreword

Pauline Hanson and John Pasquarelli — what a double! Even the book-makers wouldn't lay odds on this combination!

I have known John Pasquarelli for years. There is certainly no-one else around like him — a huge-framed man with a fierce and ugly appearance and a round, bald head that has gained him the nickname of 'Kojak'. He was nothing short of the ideal person to look after Pauline Hanson.

Pasquarelli is a genuine political animal, and has been 'out there' in the real world. He spent half a lifetime in Papua New Guinea and was a Member of Parliament in that country for a number of years. John has been campaign director for the former senator John Stone, personal secretary to Graeme Campbell, Federal Member for Kalgoorlie, and has stood, unsuc-cessfully, for our Federal Parliament himself.

This book is the gripping story of a lady who owned a fish and chip shop, and her incredible rise to prominence and power as an elected member of the House of Representatives.

The phenomenon of Pauline Hanson and the avalanche of orchestrated attacks upon her by major political Parties and the press causes us to wonder whether we all do live in a free society after all.

I encountered similar experiences to Hanson myself, in the 1980s when the RSL spoke out on immigration. The mere raising of the subject brings 'grubs out of the woodwork' — the sort of 'grubs' that will do Pauline Hanson's cause no good.

John Pasquarelli was the right person to fill the role as Pauline Hanson's chief minder, so it was sad that they parted ways. John would have sorted 'the wheat from the chaff' when dealing with the people that came out in support of her.

Read this book — it certainly makes previous accounts of Australian politics mild reading in comparison to the phenomenon of Pauline Hanson as described by John Pasquarelli.

Bruce Ruxton
State President,
Returned Services League of Australia
(Victoria Branch)

Contents

CONTENTS

Acknowledgements

When Pauline Hanson sacked me just after 3:30 pm on Monday, December 9, 1996, she made it possible for me to write this book — so she must take credit for that.

I was given much advice and encouragement by many people during the writing of this book but to acknowledge them would necessitate changing their names 'to protect the innocent'. As the magnitude of the attacks on Hanson intensified, I was amazed at the number of prominent people who contacted me during the course of 1997 and asked me not to mention them in my book. Many of them had met Pauline in her office as well as socially but, with the benefit of hindsight, they obviously regretted even that simple act of social intercourse — so concerned were they about the possible repercussions to their business, political and employment prospects. The politically correct are still a force to be reckoned with.

Since my early days as a Parliamentarian in Papua New Guinea I have kept diaries. I acknowledge the advice and support of my regular East Melbourne morning tea companions, together with that of two of my regular racetrack associates, one of whom told me, 'Diarise everything that happens, as there may be a book in it.' How right he was! Pauline has warned One Nation members not to talk to me. 'Pasquarelli will write down everything you say,' she said.

Scharlaine Cairns as my patient editor must be named. Her other, much heavier cross in life is being a fanatical and totally committed supporter of the Footscray Football Club (now politically correctly named the Western Bulldogs).

Apart from Pauline Hanson, another woman is responsible for making possible this book. Averill Chase, the Publisher for New Holland Publishers took a punt and came to Melbourne to see me when she heard I was writing a book on Hanson. I trust that her faith in me will be rewarded at the cash register.

John Pasquarelli

List of Abbreviations

The following abbreviations are used throughout this book:

AAFI	Australians Against Further Immigration
ABC	Australian Broadcasting Commission
AEC	Australian Electoral Commission
ATSIC	Aboriginal and Torres Strait Islander Commission
ASIO	Australian Security Intelligence Organisation
ASIS	Australian Secret Intelligence Service
CBD	Central Business District
CEO	Chief Executive Officer
CGT	Capital Gains Tax
CPA	Commonwealth Parliamentary Association
DAS	Department of Administrative Services
DSS	Department of Social Security
GST	Goods and Services Tax
HREOC	Human Rights and Equal Opportunity Commission
ISD	International Subscriber Dialling
MLA	Member of the Legislative Assembly
MP	Member of Parliament
NSW	New South Wales
PM	Prime Minister
PNG	Papua New Guinea
QC	Queen's Counsel
RAAF	Royal Australian Air Force
SSAA	Sporting Shooters' Association of Australia
TKO	Technical knockout
VCR	Video Cassette Recorder
VIP	Very Important Person
WA	Western Australia

Preface

Australia becoming a republic and the arrival of a new century will not, even in combination, magically change the way Australians live and work — but that notion is being promoted by those men and women in politics, the media and public life who see themselves as opinion makers for the rest of us. The cherished dream of these people is for the two events to occur simultaneously — in an orgy of self-congratulation, multicultural celebration and stupendous fireworks displays that will illuminate Australia ever so briefly for the benefit of all those viewers in outer space!

The harsh reality is that nothing will change and there is the very real possibility that things will become worse. Young Australians look forward to very uncertain employment prospects, while a lot of their older compatriots have given up and dropped out of the race. If interest rates and inflation were currently running at high levels, our country would be in the grip of recession and would be sinking out of sight in economic quicksand. Taking into account the state of the teetering Asian economies, it would require little to push Australia off its present, precarious economic perch.

The drug plague is flourishing in an environment of corruption and lack of official and judicial will, combined with confusion on the part of those seeking solutions. The cost to the general community is enormous.

For decades, ordinary mainstream Australians have been paying billions of dollars in taxes to support a raft of minority lobby groups. These groups all demand much more than their fair share and hope to obtain it by exploiting gutless and shameless politicians well-versed in the art of trading votes for dollars. The legacy of Mabo and Native Title has been one of division and rancour, with white Australians rebelling against the threats and blackmail levelled at them by Aboriginal lobbyists — far too many of whom look as white as the rest of us.

Pervading these divisive and destabilising issues has been the theme of the 'Asianisation' of Australia, begun in 1983 by Australia's then Foreign Minister Bill Hayden. Hayden said, 'It is inevitable but indeed desirable that Australia becomes a Eurasian nation by intermarriage.' Australians have been bombarded with propaganda from all sides of politics exhorting them to 'Asianise or perish'.

On March 2, 1996, Australian politics was stood on its head by the sudden and unexpected arrival of Pauline Hanson, who added new meaning to the word 'maverick'. Breaking all the rules, she dared to speak out about the things many Australians were concerned about but could not adequately express. With Parliament as a forum, and with my encouragement and advice, Pauline took on the sacred cows of political correctness, well-established in the pastures of Parliament, the judiciary and academia — all propped up by an eager and compliant media industry that had achieved 'pet' status during thirteen years of Labor Party rule.

The many thousands of faxes, letters and telephone calls that flooded into Pauline Hanson's offices in Canberra and Ipswich supported and echoed her stand on immigration, multiculturalism and the Aboriginal issue. Underlying these basic support themes were clearly discernible concerns and grave doubts about the economic direction that Australia is taking under the bipartisan policy of economic rationalism. There are now signs that the Labor Party, so strong under Paul Keating on this issue, is beginning to retreat.

During mid-1997, Pauline's One Nation bandwagon started to develop serious wheel wobbles, gripped by factional in-fighting and administrative incompetence. Hanson herself stood back in silence and declined to take part in the debate about major issues on which her constituency had supported her. She started to drift downward in the polls — an alarmingly far cry from the 18 per cent Senate voting intention recorded by the *Bulletin-Morgan* poll in November, 1996, when I was still on board.

Politically, 1996 was Pauline Hanson's year, and her story needs to be told for the benefit of those interested in Australia and its politics, and for those who love her or hate her. As her speechwriter and adviser during that turbulent year, I am the person best positioned to tell the story — armed with copious diary notes and other documents.

The cynical defection of Cheryl Kernot from the Australian Democrats to the Labor Party has added a new dimension to the next Federal election. Two women, each the antithesis of the other, will be fighting for their political survival in Queensland Seats. If they were competing for the same Seat, it would surely be an election script written in media heaven. The nation will be forced to take a back seat, but I am determined to be there at ringside.

ONE

The Road to Ipswich and Pauline Hanson

T he road that led me to Pauline Hanson and to Ipswich, the major centre of the Federal Electorate of Oxley, was a tortuous one. It started in the Northern Italian village of Conzano when my grandfather, Luigi Pasquarelli, migrated to Australia to cut sugar cane and to fell timber in the off season. He disembarked at the Northern Queensland river port of Halifax where, today, a large sign warns unwary tourists about crocodiles. The road continued from the sugar town of Ingham and took my father, Guiseppe, to medical school at Melbourne University during which time he struck up a close and enduring friendship with the great 'Weary' Dunlop and married my mother, Marie. My uncle Palmo, the only child of my grandparents to be born in their new homeland, did not get the chance to travel far on life's road. Picking vegetables for his mother in the house garden one day, he was bitten by a Taipan snake and died ten hours later. He was just seven years of age. My grandmother, Raimonda, never recovered from the shock and tried to numb her grief by working in the canefields like a navvy.

My part of the road took me to country Victoria and boarding school at Ballarat Grammar, and then to Melbourne University, where I was a foundation resident at the newly-created International House — that still stands in Royal Parade, Parkville. International House catered for Asian students (some on Colombo Plan scholarships) and selected Australian students from country and metropolitan areas. During my time at university, where I studied law, I was a member of the Aboriginal Scholarships Committee.

Characters such as Barry Humphries helped to make life on campus bearable. In one moment of great weakness I agreed to act as a 'fall guy' in his brilliant student-staged revue, *Rock 'n Reel*, at the New Theatre in Flinders Street, Melbourne. Five evenings of sitting in the front row being berated mercilessly by the budding genius was too much and I threw in the towel.

Realising that my future did not lie in the law, or in a respectable house with a wife and family in leafy Camberwell, Hawthorn or Brighton, I detoured to the Coober Pedy opal fields in South Australia, which was a subterranean community of Greeks, Italians, Yugoslavs, other 'reffos' and Anglo-Australians. My mining partner was John Bennett who in later years was to generate considerable publicity over his views on the Holocaust.

An accident with a loaded Colt .45 automatic pistol in a South Yarra flat on the eve of our departure for Coober Pedy came within inches of having the former Geelong Grammarian on a morgue slab and myself in the Coroner's Court. I was relaxing on the lavatory reading a road map when control of my bodily functions was short-circuited by a sudden explosion as the flat filled with acrid cordite fumes and plaster dust. Trying to gather my wits and fight back panic, I heard myself croak, 'Are you all right?'

I stumbled into the bedroom, expecting to see blood and guts everywhere. Bennett was sitting on the single bed with my small fibre suitcase next to him. He was staring in dazed bewilderment at a large hole in the plastered brick wall some two to three metres away opposite him. Plaster dust was settling on his hair and shoulders. I had left my handgun on top of the suitcase after cleaning it. It was loaded and cocked but with the safety catch on and the hammer down. Bennett had taken the safety catch off, worked the hammer back and then pulled the trigger. He had no gun sense whatsoever and could easily have been looking down the barrel when the gun went off! The result of a frantic search for the bullet sent us both into shock. Ricochetting off the wall, it was found in the bottom of the suitcase, flattened out to the size of a twenty-cent piece. The former owner of the weapon, very well known in Australian business and literary circles, now knows how close he came to becoming involved in what would have been a very messy affair in 1959.

The flat in question had seen its fair share of 'characters' come and go.

It had been the venue for wild parties attended by members of the Melbourne 'Push', including Germaine Greer and the late Bill Collins, 'The Slaughterman' (not to be confused with the late, famous race caller).

After a stint of opal mining and more close shaves with guns and gelignite, a ruptured appendix, requiring the ministrations of 'Weary' Dunlop, brought me back to Melbourne.

My father had served in New Guinea during World War II, and he was contacted by an old wartime mate who was recruiting patrol officers for the Australian Administration. I was on the verge of sailing off to South America, with the Amazon River in mind. Instead I settled for New Guinea and, in 1960, found myself on the great, meandering, crocodile-infested Sepik River.

The public service quickly bored me and I turned my hand to crocodile shooting and general trading activities. My interest in Sepik primitive art led to me being appointed the Papua New Guinea (PNG) representative for the prestigious Basle Museum based in Switzerland. In 1964, at age twenty-seven, the Sepik people elected me to the PNG House of Assembly as the youngest member of a Commonwealth Parliament. I completed my term in 1968, retiring without contesting the next election — I had seen the writing on the wall, and the message was not encouraging. I did stay on in Papua New Guinea to build the world famous wilderness tourist resort Karawari Lodge but it never realised its full economic potential. It still stands, a monument to my youthful enthusiasm and the hard-earned money poured into it.

I found myself in Sydney in the early 1980s, working as a 'private eye' with an old New Guinea mate, John Stuntz. A chance reunion with Ann Knappett from my Melbourne University days brought me back to Melbourne and to marriage for the first time, in 1984 at the age of forty-eight. Tim Burstall, the film director, married Neela Dey in a shared ceremony with Ann and myself. The *Australian* in one of its gossip columns cheekily dubbed the event 'the double wedding of the century'.

A caring wife and comfortable home in fast-becoming-trendy Fitzroy could not anchor me — so I packed up and, in late 1989, moved to the Sunshine Coast in Queensland, where I worked for a time for National

Party Senator and former Secretary of the Treasury, John Stone. Disillusioned by the Coalition's effort in the 1990 Federal Election, I returned to PNG to work on the Kutubu Oil Pipeline. I viewed, with disbelief, the devastating destruction of the soundly working infrastructure passed on to an independent PNG in 1975 by the Australian Government.

In late 1990, I was at John Senior's trading post at Kikori on the Kikori River in the Papuan Gulf when I was suddenly felled by overpowering waves of nausea, dizziness and disorientation. I could not stand up and, as I lay hunched on the floor, I was convinced I was suffering from a stroke and was dying. I cried for help in the Police Motu language, but Senior's female domestic staff ignored me with much laughter, accusing me of wanting to 'play around'. The settlement of Kikori is straight out of a Somerset Maugham script and seemed a suitably dramatic backdrop for my demise.

It was later revealed that the episode was my first attack of Ménière's Disease. After a barrage of subsequent episodes, I stumbled off a plane at Brisbane Airport on March 15, 1991, still not diagnosed and not caring much about anything.

The search for a confirmed diagnosis brought me back to Melbourne, where Mr Jack Kennedy — eminent ear, nose and throat specialist, survivor of a terrifying aeroplane accident and fanatical Collingwood supporter — told me I was suffering from Ménière's. Ménière's will not kill you, but it can destroy your life.

Down and out, and perilously close to bankruptcy, I decided to stay in Melbourne where I had a support base and was close to Jack Kennedy. I was living in the back room of John Bennett's house in Carlton. It was during this period when my medical condition fluctuated between attack and remission that John Bennett introduced me to Graeme Campbell, the then Labor Member for the Western Australian Federal Electorate of Kalgoorlie — so, without the involvement of Bennett, I would never have worked for Pauline Hanson.

Bennett had swung at either end of the political pendulum. When being caned in a lavatory block at Geelong Grammar by a Prefect (the son of a Governor-General) only a year older than himself, the pyjama-clad Bennett was given as the reason for his punishment, 'It's nothing specific Bennett, it's just your general attitude,' which at that time included a belief in Communism. It was also this belief that led my father to tell me that he didn't want Bennett in his house.

His introduction of Graeme Campbell to me was not the first time that Bennett had participated in political chess movements. By the late 1960s, influenced by the late Dr Frank Knopfelmacher, who at one stage described Bennett as a 'foxy lion', Bennett had become an anti-Communist. He became a researcher for 'The Participants', a group of Labor Party members that included former Victorian Governor Richard McGarvie, former Victorian Premier John Cain, and present Labor MP and former quiz whiz Barry Jones. Bennett was the only member of the group expelled from the ALP for publicly calling for Federal intervention to remove the State executive of the Victorian ALP. The eventual removal of the executive paved the way for Whitlam's Federal victory in 1972.

With Beatrice Faust, Bennett formed the Victorian Council for Civil Liberties in 1966 and was its Secretary until 1980, when he was summarily expelled for questioning the extent of the Jewish Holocaust. Organiser of the rival Australian Civil Liberties Union in 1980 (which still functions), he is also the author of *Your Rights*, the best selling layman's guide to the law, now in its twenty-third year.

I had opposed the John Howard led Liberal Party's policies on immigration and multiculturalism when I won Liberal pre-selection for the Victorian Federal Seat of Jagajaga in the 1987 Federal Election — so I was pretty well in tune with Campbell. In this respect, I was following in my late father's footsteps. In the late 1960s he was talking publicly about the need for new settlers to assimilate.

My relationship with Graeme Campbell developed to the point where I did a small amount of paid, part-time work for him and met with him whenever he was passing through Melbourne. Late in 1995, Paul Keating finally cut the traces, with Graeme losing his endorsement for Kalgoorlie and facing the forthcoming Federal Election as an independent. As such, Graeme was entitled to an extra staff member, a 'Private Secretary Grade 1' which was a staff position normally allotted to ministers. The job description included unlimited travel within Australia, the travelling allowance so beloved by Senator Colston and most of his Parliamentary colleagues, and a Cabcharge card. This extra staff position was allocated to independents to compensate them in some way for their not having access to a Party structure (that provides so much assistance in the performance of electoral and Parliamentary matters). Graeme offered me the position and on December 20, 1995, I flew from Melbourne to Kalgoorlie to help him in his battle to hold the seat of Kalgoorlie as an independent.

Graeme Campbell's wife, Michele, met me at the Kalgoorlie Airport where she kissed me for the first and last time. Michele is a continental socialist and, with her attractive French accent and obvious culture, she seemed at odds with the admittedly beautiful but dramatically harsh Australian desert that surrounds the last-frontier mining town of Kalgoorlie.

The Campbell campaign for Kalgoorlie was a hard fought, bitter brawl that split the local Labor Party. It was conducted against a backdrop of the bustling mining industry, where new-breed miners ride Harley-Davidsons and have their drinks served by topless barmaids. These miners are also drug tested as part of their job application and random testing is carried out in the workplace. Amphetamines are currently the go. Drug dealers follow the money, even into the desert.

Most political offices are pressure cookers but, during an election campaign, the safety valves blow. Graeme's office was a female one working under Michele Campbell, the office manager. Graeme and I were in agreement that the election campaign would be an anti-Keating one. The same card was to be played by the Coalition, but getting that message across to Graeme's staff was another matter. The three women, all Keating fans, fought tooth and nail to oppose any anti-Keating press releases, advertising or speeches. For his part, Graeme was loath to dump on Hawke in any shape or form. Fifteen years a Labor man, Graeme had developed ingrained habits too deep to cast off lightly.

The campaign was directed from behind the scenes by some of Graeme's Labor mates, and the rear door to his office, opening on to a back lane, got plenty of use. I took care of press releases, speech writing, advertising, liaising with the media and, most importantly, converting Liberal voters to the Campbell cause. Graeme saw advantage in the fact that I was a long-standing member of the Liberal Party.

The Liberal Party, with the best of intentions, gave Graeme a big head start by fielding an Aboriginal candidate, Cedric Wyatt, who had been a member of Graeme's local Labor Party branch when he had been working in Kalgoorlie. Wyatt took leave from his job as Director of Aboriginal Affairs in Perth to fight the election.

It is a small world. I had known Wyatt when he was 'Ricky' Wyatt the happy-go-lucky, popular schoolteacher, working in village schools on the Sepik River in PNG. When he was in PNG, most people assumed that he was of Lebanese extraction — his nickname was 'The Arab'. Now he was fighting his old Labor mate for the prize of Kalgoorlie. 'Ricky' Wyatt, 'The Arab', was in fact Cedric Wyatt, an Aborigine from Meekathara.

Wyatt and I met in the Palace Hotel in Kalgoorlie and spent a couple of hours over coffee, catching up on old times. I found I could still warm to him but, unfortunately for him, many Liberal voters could not. More than once, Liberals told me, 'I can't vote for that Abo'. Some of them were much more uncharitable. With the pressures of Mabo, Native Title, a one-sided view of our colonial history and now Wik, the gulf between white and black sadly continues to grow wider. 'Reconciliation' is a failed and doomed concept, not helped by individuals in the Aboriginal 'industry' and their lickspittles in the media who try and ram the concept down the throats of mainstream Australia. The strategy used by radical Aboriginal leaders in promoting their cause has backfired badly.

Graeme Campbell reached the peak of his political Everest on the evening of March 2, 1996, with a resounding win. The local Labor Party was shattered and its election night party was reminiscent of Miss Haversham's tragic wedding reception. Ian Taylor, the defeated Labor Party candidate and former Deputy Premier of WA, said almost seriously that he was going off to coach his daughter's basketball team. Cedric Wyatt returned to his government sinecure in Perth. The scene was set for a bitter return bout come next election.

During the evening's celebrations, I was watching the TV coverage of the election results when I noted that Pauline Hanson, a political novice, a fish and chip shop proprietor and an independent, had won the prized

7

Queensland Labor Seat of Oxley in the most dramatic circumstances. She had been very publicly disendorsed by the Liberal Party very close to polling day for making allegedly racist comments about Aborigines — and that was all I knew about her. Oxley was the seat that had survived the Malcolm Fraser anti-Whitlam landslide of 1975. This was the seat held for so long by Bill Hayden, former Governor-General and the man who should have been Prime Minister in 1983. As the TV cameras zoomed in on their newly-elected target, my impression was of a slim, pleasant looking, red-headed woman looking frazzled and slightly bewildered, trying to fend off a media barrage. My attention was diverted by a well-lubricated Campbell supporter urging me to have another drink, but the germ of an idea had been sown.

Graeme and I had agreed that I should cease my employment with him at the end of June 1996, when he would offer my position to Peter Mc-Kerrow, a lawyer and ex-staffer of Graeme's. McKerrow knew the electorate of Kalgoorlie well and was an expert on Aboriginal affairs and industrial relations. I would fill in the remainder of my time doing research and writing. As it turned out, McKerrow did not take the position.

It was Sunday, the day after polling day, and I was having lunch at Graeme's house when Pauline Hanson again appeared on TV. On this occasion she looked extremely strained and had almost lost her voice. The media were all over the top of her and had her hemmed in like a witness in a sensational criminal trial. I drew Graeme's attention to what was happening and we sat in his lounge and discussed the impact and value of this political newcomer's win in Oxley. I told Graeme that he would need an independent ally in Parliament to second motions and private members' bills, and that Hanson seemed to be generally in tune with him on the Aboriginal issue. I put to Graeme that it would be chivalrous and politically sensible to offer Pauline Hanson advice and support during a particularly stressful time. Graeme could see the value in this and told me to make contact with Hanson. My germ of an idea was starting to sprout.

That afternoon I was able to make contact with Pauline Hanson and spoke to her and her campaign manager, Morrie Marsden. I told Pauline that Graeme offered support and was prepared to send me to Queensland to help her with the media and the very important job of setting up her electorate office. Pauline seemed thankful for the offer but Morrie Marsden seemed more than a little suspicious of this help coming from thousands of kilometres away. I told Pauline I would call her back on the following Tuesday. I advised her to stop talking to the media until I got to Ipswich.

Melbourne winters were starting to get me down, and my two nieces and nephew living in Brisbane and on the Gold Coast are the only family I have. Their father, my only sibling, died tragically when he was only thirty-eight, leaving a big hole in my life. The more I thought about it, the prospect of working for Pauline Hanson was exciting and challenging. I could sense, even from a distance, that dull and boring it would *not* be!

On Tuesday, March 5, 1996, I telephoned Pauline Hanson and arranged to fly to Ipswich as soon as possible. I left Kalgoorlie in style. Graeme's staff were still carousing in one of the local taverns and the part-Aboriginal boy-friend of one of them, well primed, decided to make a fool of himself. Bur-dened by the huge chip on his shoulder, he let go with some wild swings but ended up head butting the bar rail and then in typical fashion cried 'copper'. A friend drove me away to the airport just as the police arrived.

On Thursday, March 7, 1996, I flew to Brisbane from Melbourne, then taxied to Ipswich. My first port of call was Morrie Marsden's house. Marsden walked down his driveway to meet me. A single man in his mid-forties and of medium build, he was possessed of the gestures and speech of a genuine Queenslander. He was reserved and gave me very clear signs of his being guarded and wary of me — which was not surprising. After all, he had run Pauline Hanson's campaign and now here I was, a complete stranger, dropping in from Kalgoorlie to play what role? After a brief exchange of pleasantries, Morrie drove me to Pauline's house in Doyle Street, Silkstone, a suburb of Ipswich.

What greeted me at Pauline's house was a media contingent reminiscent of the ones that pawed the ground outside an Alan Bond trial. Morrie and I pushed our way through the media pack that was lined up to the wire gates of the low wire fence at the front of Pauline's very modest, in-need-of-painting, small Queensland bungalow. Two TV journalists, emboldened by our arrival and a change in the stalemate, attempted to follow us to the front door. I turned on them, reminding them of the laws of trespass, and they quickly retreated, camera whirring.

Morrie Marsden ushered me into a small kitchen where I was introduced to Sue Wykes, sitting at a laminex table. Moments later, Hanson herself walked in from the adjoining loungeroom and I introduced myself, shaking her hand. I was facing a youngish, slim woman of medium height with carroty-red, short hair that would, in time, become one of her trademarks and the most talked about and parodied coiffure in the land. 'This slip of a woman' as she would later be described, was dressed in faded blue jeans and a white T-shirt. She was not wearing lipstick but I noticed the too-bright scarlet of her fingernails. Her hoarse voice masked her decidedly Queensland 'twang'. Despite her obvious fatigue, her blue-green eyes were large and focused, giving her a feline appearance, reinforced by her dropped-shoulder, hip-swishing walk.

The telephone at the front of the house was keening like a jammed car horn and I felt, strangely, as if I was in a house where a police siege was being played out. I could hear noises at the front door and, upon opening it, found the same TV journos that I had told to stay off the property. They were very keen to know who I was — but I kept them guessing. After advising Pauline and Marsden, I returned to the baying throng that was lined up at Pauline's front gate like a football crowd waiting for the gates to open at the MCG on Grand Final day.

I walked towards them wearing my 'ugly' mask. Lane Calcutt from Channel 9 Brisbane told me later that he thought I was going to head-butt someone. For my part, I was wondering how many of the journos had black-belts in karate! I told the assembly that Pauline, for the time being, would not be giving any more interviews as she had to start representing the people of Oxley. 'It is a nice warm Queensland day and the beer down at the local pub is nice and cold. Go and have a few drinks and calm down,' I urged. My message provoked a barrage of questions amid frantic gargling yelps from the more frustrated scribes. I turned and walked back to the house. My road had finally brought me to Ipswich and Pauline Hanson, and I had not the slightest inkling of the rollercoaster ride that lay ahead.

Early Days in Ipswich

Ipswich is a genuine 'struggletown' — through no fault of its own. It was almost the capital of Queensland, but lost out to Brisbane. As a young-ster growing up in Brisbane, I remembered Ipswich as a country town, just outside Brisbane on the way to the Darling Downs. Since World War II, Ipswich has lost its woollen mills, coal mines, railway workshops and the ancillary businesses those industries supported. Fire robbed the city of its only traditional, family-owned department store and 'for lease' signs are displayed in many shop fronts. Being so close to Brisbane is an advantage for those Ipswichites who are lucky enough to find work in the big city. Those less fortunate must keep their places in the local unemployment queues. High levels of unemployment, especially among the young, have sapped morale and have helped to increase drug and crime levels. Despite its increasing absorption by the greater metropolis of Brisbane, Ipswich is still very parochial — a place where strangers are viewed with suspicion.

The electorate office of Les Scott, the defeated Labor Member for Oxley, had been on the ground floor of the W. G. Hayden Building on the corner of South and East Streets in central Ipswich. One side of the office was opposite the local movie house and the other was opposite the politically-correctly entitled 'Global Information Centre' (or in ordinary, mainstream Australian language, the 'Public Library'). Pauline was not able to shift into the office until the declaration of the poll and, until that occurred, we were forced to operate out of her house. Under the circumstances, this was extremely trying and stressful, with only one phone and boxes of letters and telephone messages stacked up on the floor of the cramped, built-in verandah.

On Friday, March 8, 1996, Pauline drove me out to her other house at Coleyville, about half-an-hour's drive from Ipswich and outside the electorate of Oxley. Pauline had built a very comfortable, ranch-style timber dwelling on 150 acres and had shared the property with Rick Gluyas, her former de facto and a current Ipswich Councillor. We sat on the verandah enjoying the view and talking about the tasks that lay ahead. I told Pauline about my arrangement with Graeme Campbell and said that, if she felt comfortable with me, I was prepared to work for her. Pauline was obviously relieved at my availability and offered me the position as her Senior Adviser, which I accepted, telling her we would need to seek ministerial approval for my appointment from David Jull, the Minister for Administrative Services.

Tactfully, during this conversation, I mentioned the role of Morrie ·Marsden — not wishing to tread on too many toes at this early stage. But Pauline said that Morrie had his job with Suncorp Insurance in Ipswich and, besides, he was not qualified for a senior advisory position. I even suggested that it would be quite in order to give Morrie a short-term consultancy role until we filled the three positions in the Ipswich office. This would in some way compensate him for all the hard, unpaid work he had done for Pauline. Pauline quite firmly rejected this proposal, making some brusque comments about her past intimate relationship with Marsden, so I decided to quickly drop the matter. I had absolutely no desire to become involved in any domestic situations. I had come to Ipswich to wage political war, not to become a human relations counsellor!

Despite this, I made a mental note to make sure I kept Morrie Marsden on side. As the man who had once had a de facto relationship with Pauline, he had been responsible for encouraging and directing her political career and had run her campaigns for her election to the Ipswich Council in 1994 and then for the Federal Election. He was a local identity, Ipswich born and bred, and later I was to drive along 'Marsden Parade' and past a 'Marsden Park'.

Until I arrived on the scene, Pauline Hanson had never been to Canberra — a bit surprising for a woman of forty-two who had been overseas. I thought it essential for Pauline to visit Canberra well before the new members' orientation course, scheduled for March 28 and 29, 1996, so I organised a day trip for Saturday, March 9.

As the jet lined up on its final approach to Canberra's Fairbairn Airport, I mused that the last time I had been there was during the pilots' strike, when John Stone and I had 'hitched' a ride back to Brisbane on a RAAF VIP Falcon jet.

I gave Pauline a quick guided tour of Canberra, including Black Mountain and other tourist attractions. She was very impressed by the War Memorial, saying she could have spent a day there. She was obviously in awe of what she had seen but time was running out, so I had to take her away from the Honour Roll where she was engrossed, reading the names of our fallen. I regretted not having my camera with me as I framed Pauline with my fingers. It would have been a fine shot of this hitherto unknown woman who had been catapulted into national prominence, coming to grips with a dramatic and poignant part of the history of her country. Before we left, I introduced her to the very fine statue of Sir Edward 'Weary' Dunlop, standing in the forecourt.

Next stop was the Yowani Lawn Bowling Club to meet Doug Blake. Doug was in his retirement, having served the nation and Parliament well as one of its most respected and well regarded Clerks of the House of Representatives. Doug was a no-nonsense ex-Navy man, and I had first met him when he was sent to Port Moresby in 1964 by the Australian Government to drum some sense into PNG's new politicians. While Doug Blake taught my colleagues and me about the Westminster System and the rules of debate, we introduced him to the delights of Rugby League PNG style and South Pacific Lager.

Over drinks, Doug told Pauline that she would be a big fish in a little pond back in Oxley but would be the reverse in Canberra. He stressed to her that if she could keep her head the same size, she had a chance of not becoming 'just another politician'. Over the years, Doug Blake had seen countless politicians come and go — most of them without trace. At the time he spoke to Pauline, neither Doug nor I had any idea what the future held for her.

Being a Saturday, Parliament House was host to the usual bus loads of tourists coming to see just what their tax dollars had paid for. After one of the attendants kindly showed us over the House of Representatives, we walked to the Senate side of the building and, quite by chance, met Gerard McManus from the Melbourne *Herald Sun* who had recently transferred to the Parliamentary press gallery. He invited us to have a coffee with him in the public cafeteria. He was to remark months later that Pauline had improved '1000 per cent' on that first meeting. After a hectic day, Pauline and I returned to Ipswich. The Member for Oxley had, for the first time, visited the colosseum where she would become, in the not too distant future, one of the major gladiators.

The next few days were hectic — organising a government-provided car for Pauline's public and private use, organising which office she would have in Parliament House, connecting government-paid phone and fax lines to her house, and performing a myriad of other housekeeping tasks.

Apart from Pauline and myself, we still had no staff. There were three Electorate Officer positions available at A, B and C levels — C being the highest paid. These support staffing positions are provided for all back-benchers and carry salaries in the $35 000 to $40 000 range, plus limited airfares, travelling allowance and the opportunity to work overtime. The qualifications are general but, in this day of the communication highway, a high level of computer literacy is expected along with those interpersonal skills required to look after the needs of constituents.

I realised that, with the quite obvious local distrust of 'outsiders', it was important that, if at all possible, the three office positions be taken by Ipswich people. To this end Pauline and I interviewed Pam Payne, a pleasant Ipswich City Council executive with good qualifications who had worked with Pauline during her time as a Councillor. Unfortunately for me, Pam Payne declined the offer and my failure to find a compatible, local office manager would eventually cost me dearly. Pauline told me that Heidi Lewis, a young local woman who had worked in what was to become the best known fish and chip shop in Australia, was a university student but was prepared to come and work in the electorate office. She was a junior and totally without political experience, but she had some computer skills and that was a start. Most importantly, she was an Ipswich girl.

Federal MPs are supplied with a vehicle fuelled and serviced by the taxpayer. At a certain point, they have the option of buying out the lease and obtaining full title. Pauline chose a burgundy Fairmont for her government-provided vehicle but there was a delay in its delivery so, in an ironic twist, she was provided with an interim Holden Acclaim that was surrendered by Michael Lavarch, the former Labor Attorney-General, when he lost his Queensland Seat of Dickson.

David Elder, the Serjeant-at-Arms for the House of Representatives offered Pauline the choice between Ted Mack's old Parliamentary office and that of Phil Cleary. Mack is Australia's most famous independent having held elected office at Council, State and Federal levels. He had never belonged to a political Party and had resigned from Parliament when Paul Keating called the 1996 election. I suspect that Ted Mack left office a frustrated and disillusioned man, sick and tired of the artifice and hypocrisy of Party politics. He confirmed this in a media interview when, in reply to a question about his achievements as a Federal independent, he said, 'Bugger all'.

Cleary, on the other hand, had been affiliated with the Labor Party, won the seat of Wills as an independent and then lost it to Labor's Kelvin Thompson, with a degree of acrimony. I advised Pauline to take Mack's office. He had left Parliament undefeated and that was a good omen.

I went shopping with Pauline in one of the Ipswich supermarkets and was amazed at the support she received, much of it verging on the emotional. Her election had certainly struck a nerve. On Monday, March 11, I was brought back to earth when my mobile phone began its annoying burble. A friendly voice told me that journos in the Canberra press gallery had vowed to 'get that bitch and that big, bald bastard' and that they were going to try and gain access to our Department of Social Security (DSS) and tax files. In the battle to come, neither side would be prepared to take prisoners.

The media was on the rampage again. A Brisbane Channel 7 TV crew had laid siege to her house in Doyle Street and her fish and chip shop. It was a hot Ipswich day and I had forgotten to wear a hat. Pauline slipped away through the front of the shop while I kept the TV crew entertained at the rear. They wasted a couple of hours, and I got a sunburnt skull.

That Fish and Chip Shop

After two failed marriages, Pauline Hanson found herself a single mother with three sons and a daughter. In media interviews, she has consistently refused to discuss whether she received any sort of benefits. While working as a barmaid at the local Ipswich Booval Lawn Bowling Club in 1987, she met Morrie Marsden, a bachelor and member of a well-established Ipswich family. A de facto relationship developed, with Marsden prepared to marry Pauline. But his commitment was rejected, leaving emotional wounds that are still easily reopened today. Pauline was finding it hard to survive on her pay with four dependent children, and it was Marsden who came to her rescue with a business proposition. A local fish and chip shop just around the corner from Pauline's Doyle Street home had been owned by a Marsden relative, had been on-sold and then had started to trade poorly. Morrie Marsden could see the potential for rebuilding the business and advised Pauline to buy it, which she did for a reported $28 000.

According to Marsden, when Pauline told him she had bought the shop, she was in tears. It had been a big decision for the single mother and battling barmaid. Marsden put his arms around her, telling her that everything would be all right and that he would help her. Pauline cleaned up the business and worked hard at it, justifying Marsden's business judgment and his faith in her capabilities. She did have some early family experience to draw on. Her parents had operated a successful food outlet near Brisbane's famous Woolloongabba cricket ground and Pauline had worked there after school. During Pauline's early days of running the shop, Morrie would come in at the end of his working day to help out, looking after her children, keeping her company in the shop and serving customers when there was a rush on. On most Thursdays, Pauline would drive down to the Brisbane Fish Markets for stock and would engage in banter with the mostly ethnic traders there.

Pauline ran that business for almost ten years and, when she sold it in early 1997 for a reported $104 000, 'Marsden's Seafoods' was still the name officially displayed on the shopfront. The most famous fish and chip shop in Australian history helped to send the media into bursts of frenzy from time to time and provided cartoonists with a subject well beyond their wildest dreams.

During Pauline's operation of the shop, she had broken off her relationship with Morrie Marsden, briefly renewed her relationship with her first ex-husband Walter, and then embarked on a brand new liaison with Rick Gluyas who would go on to be an Ipswich City Councillor with her.

Marsden had lived in a house directly opposite the fish and chip shop but, after his rift with Pauline, he could no longer bear living that close to her, so he sold out and moved to the nearby suburb of Ripley. The expense and time involved in such a move is testimony to just how devastated he was by his parting of the ways with Pauline. I came to know Morrie well, and it was obvious that Pauline Hanson had greatly affected his life. He wore his heart on his sleeve, which was not always to his advantage in a community such as Ipswich, where private lives very quickly become public.

During my first few weeks in Ipswich, discussing with Pauline how she should be portrayed, I told her, 'You are a fish and chip shop lady, and that's what we want Australians to see'. But her response was lukewarm, insisting that the shop was really a 'take-away-seafood' shop. I detected just a whiff of unexpected snobbery, or maybe it was just that Pauline thought my suggested title for her did not sit comfortably with her view of what the public expected of a politician. I had quite a vigorous battle with Pauline and Morrie Marsden but, in the end, I won out. Pauline actually seemed to warm to the label as time went by and it was included in her maiden speech. It helped to firmly establish her place in the Australian political firmament and I had taken the first step in creating an anti-politician who would send salvos of convulsion and revulsion into the ranks of the establishment on both sides of the political fence.

I went with Pauline to the Brisbane Fish Markets a couple of times and it was obvious that she was accepted as 'one of the boys'. The traders and retailers there were predominantly of European extraction. There were some Vietnamese, but I detected tension between them and the others and, as far as I could see, Pauline had no rapport at all with them. Pauline told me that she got a lot of political feedback and anecdotal evidence from her mates at the market and from customers over the counter at her shop. In that sort of environment people say what they think and, to a real politician, that sort of polling is pure gold. The problem is that too many of our politicians have totally lost all contact with mainstream Australia.

When Pauline worked in the shop she went flat-out and a twelve-hour shift was not unusual. The shop had a high turnover and the displayed seafood presented well. There was always a steady stream of customers and a lot of interaction between them and Pauline. I made one grave error when I questioned the quality of Pauline's chips. For me they were too short. Pauline took genuine exception to my very much tongue-in-cheek criticism and I realised then that her sense of humour didn't extend to any jokes at her own expense. I made a mental note to try and remedy this flaw down the track, when I got to know her better. Pauline was going to be an obvious target for the cartoonists and the comedy industry, so a keen sense of humour would be her only antidote against the poisoned barbs that would come raining down on her.

On more than one occasion I had reason to adopt the role of security guard at the shop as, from time to time, there were warnings of impending vandalism. But, during my time with Pauline, there were no serious incidents. I was on good terms with the local taxi drivers and they told me they always checked the shop out when driving by. It was good for Pauline to have that sort of support.

Pauline continued working stints in the shop and I told her that this was all right as long as it did not clash with her Parliamentary duties. It was great public relations and, from initially advising her to sell the shop, I ended up telling her that maybe it would be better to keep it. I suggested that she enter a profit sharing arrangement with one of the women who ran the shop most of the time, but this idea did not appeal to Pauline and in the end the shop was sold. Pauline working in the shop would have been a wonderful backdrop for election campaign advertisements, but maybe that can still happen. Images of her serving up fish and chips have been deeply etched into the psyche of every TV viewer in Australia as well as abroad.

The Ides of March

March 1996, was a month of frantic activity and a month in which my ultimate fate was sealed. In that month, the course was plotted that would eventually lead me to crash onto the reefs of dismissal at the end of the year.

Barbara Hazelton had worked for Queensland National Party Senator John Stone and left his employ before I arrived at his office in late 1989. Before working for John Stone, she had been an Electorate Officer with Peter Slipper, the then National Party Member for the Queensland Federal Seat of Fisher. In the 1987 election, Slipper had been defeated by Michael Lavarch who went on to be Labor's Attorney-General. Peter Slipper is now back in Federal Parliament as the Liberal MP for Fisher. Later in the year, Peter Slipper would give me information about Barbara Hazelton that would confirm my worst fears.

In the first week I was with Pauline in Ipswich, Barbara Hazelton contacted me by obtaining my mobile phone number from Graeme Campbell's office in Kalgoorlie. She told me that she had just returned from Hong Kong, where she had been with her husband who was employed by an international airline. She said that Pauline sounded like a person for whom she would like to work and she asked me what positions were available. She drove up from the Gold Coast and had a meeting with me at Pauline's house. Barbara Hazelton is a shortish, bouncy woman, with a gushy manner that colours her body language and speech.

I was still desperate to find a local person to run Pauline's electorate office. Heidi Lewis who had worked for Pauline in the fish and chip shop had agreed to throw her lot in with us, but she was inexperienced and would start off in the lowest of the three available positions. John Stone told me that he thought Barbara Hazelton could handle the position, based on her performance with him in his Senate office. But, as time progressed, two things would negate that recommendation. First, I was not John Stone, the proper and very correct former Treasury bureaucrat and, second, Pauline's office would soon become a pressure cooker, always on the verge of blowing its safety valve — so much busier than a Senate office could ever be. In time, Pauline's office would become much busier than the average government minister's office but would have only one-third of the staff. I was in a quandary. Barbara Hazelton lived at Runaway Bay on the Gold Coast, over one hour's drive from Ipswich. This was a very serious disadvantage — particularly for the office manager of a highly-charged political office, where people needed to be on call in times of crisis. I discussed the situation with Pauline and Barbara, conveying to them that the job was not set in concrete and could be just a six month job setting up the office until a more appropriate candidate appeared. Barbara Hazelton started work on Monday, March 18, 1996.

I was living out of a suitcase in Ipswich during the first few weeks, moving from an up-market motel down to one with a reasonable tariff. I put thoughts of renting a flat to one side as events threatened to overtake us. I decided to swim with the undertow until things calmed down and I settled myself into a pleasant period guesthouse operated by Bruce and Elaine Glass, who coincidentally had been missionary workers in PNG. Their premises were an easy walk from Pauline's office and I needed the exercise to keep myself on the pace. I am a non-smoker and, these days, virtually a teetotaller due to my Ménière's Disease. An absence of vices can lead to boredom but working for Pauline Hanson would make sure that could never be the case.

We were still waiting for the declaration of the poll and it was as if there was a conspiracy to keep Pauline and her embryo office frustrated and disorganised. On Thursday, March 14, twelve days after polling day, Jeff Barrett the Australian Electoral Office Returning Officer for Oxley told me that the declaration of the poll might be the following Tuesday. Oxley was one of the last electorates to have its poll declared. I got on well with Jeff Barrett and he was only doing his job.

The 'friendly voice' who had earlier warned me about press gallery bastardry spoke to me again. This time, Brisbane journos were checking me out to see if I had an ASIS file and if I had any questionable business dealing skeletons in my cupboard. I told the 'voice' that I had never been involved in a conspiracy to overthrow the government and I had no concern about the other issue. At this stage I considered it prudent to report to the Federal Police all that the 'voice' had told me.

After a number of false starts, Jeff Barrett advised me that the declaration of the poll for Oxley would take place in his office on the third floor of the W. G. Hayden building on Thursday, March 21. What a relief. We would finally have access to a proper office and have the facilities to better fend off our enemies, who seemed to be growing in number rapidly day by day.

I wrote a short, sharp acceptance speech for Pauline and distributed it to the media. The gathering in Jeff Barrett's office was an anticlimax after all the media hullabaloo of the past couple of weeks. Pauline and I were there, along with Morrie Marsden, Barbara Hazelton and Heidi Lewis. Les Scott, the defeated Labor member stood to one side. There was one TV camera crew and a reporter from the *Queensland Times*, the local paper. Jeff Barrett gave Pauline the nod to speak first and this is what she said:

Mr Jeff Barrett and staff, ladies and gentlemen. I thank, with all my heart, the men and women of Oxley who elected me to be their representative in Canberra. I thank Mr Barrett and his staff for their professional conduct of the poll in Oxley.

I thank Morrie Marsden, my campaign manager and his small but dedicated team. They kept their heads up when the going got tough and gave me tremendous support when I came under intense media pressure.

I thank all those people from the electorate of Oxley and from all over Australia who have phoned, faxed and written me messages of encouragement. Their support has been magnificent and as soon as my office is up and running, I will be replying to them.

I thank Graeme Campbell, the Independent Member for Kalgoorlie for his advice and support when it was most needed. More than ever, Australia needs politicians who are not frightened to speak out.

The events of the past few weeks have taught me a lot. I have been disgusted at the way a large section of the media have acted. These people have harassed me at my home and business and have tried to set me up. They have taken my words out of context to suit their purpose and agenda.

I have been told that some journalists are out to get me, whatever that means, but I must remind members of the media that they are not the people of Australia, they are not the people of Oxley. I am answerable to all my constituents, I repeat, all my constituents of Oxley, not to a minority who act as a law unto themselves.

I will not be apologising for, or retracting anything I have said before the media put their spin on it.

My success in Oxley was a win for the silent majority of ordinary Australians. For far too long, too many governments have fallen into the trap of listening to, then governing for, a whole hotchpotch of minority lobby groups who have become very powerful because they have been extremely well funded by taxpayers who have had no say in the matter. Now the people of Oxley at least, have had their say.

Governments must look after all the people and not play favourites. It goes without saying that the rights and concerns of minority groups must be recognised but I stress that with rights come responsibilities.

I believe that all Australians should be treated equally, I repeat equally. Once some sections of society are seen as being treated more equally than others, divisions are created.

My electorate office will shortly be open for business and it will be an open office, accessible to all, I repeat, accessible to all. I invite those with concerns and problems to come and see me and my staff. I will be concentrating on Oxley, not Canberra, and trust that I will be a worthy representative of this electorate. I thank you all.

Pauline was done in three minutes. She was incredibly nervous and Morrie Marsden remarked later that she was shaking. This acceptance speech did not receive wide coverage and that is a pity, as sensible media treatment of it may have defused a lot of the hysteria and nonsense that occurred in subsequent weeks.

What came next was comical but sad. It was Les Scott's turn to respond and, after referring to a prepared speech, promising not to impose on the time of his indifferent audience, he launched into a boring monologue that lasted an incredible twenty minutes. Scott, a lean, bespectacled and earnest looking man, was obviously taking his loss very badly and would confirm this with his subsequent whingeing 'letters to the editor' and a number of public appearances. As Scott droned mercilessly on, I yawned in a most extravagant fashion and pointedly looked at my watch. Morrie Marsden and Jeff Barrett, acknowledging my actions, raised their eyebrows. The TV cameraman gave up and turned off his camera. As Scott ground to a halt, we took our leave, still shaking our heads in disbelief. It was one of the worst performances I had ever witnessed.

We immediately shifted into Les Scott's old office, ushered in by Jeff Barrett who gave us the keys and explained the security system to us. The office was substantial and impressive — with a reception foyer and glassed-in counter, a large open-plan main office, the member's office, and a room to house the photocopier, letter-folding machine and other office equipment. There was also a small kitchen and a small conference room. One thing was very noticeable. The office was absolutely bare, with not one piece of notepaper left behind — not one biro, not one paper clip. It took days to get the fax going again, as it seemed to be possessed by electronic gremlins. I was told by an employee of the Department of Administrative Services (the organisation that looks after Parliamentarians and their offices) that the majority of defeated members took their loss with good grace and usually left some stationery and other basic material behind.

I laid claim to the conference room for my office, because it would give me respite from the hurly-burly of the main office and allow me to concentrate on my main brief — that of providing Pauline with advice on political strategy, writing speeches and press releases, and teaching her how to deal with the media. There would also be a benefit for those in the main office. Ménière's Disease had totally destroyed the hearing in my left ear and, like a lot of deaf people, I speak very loudly — to such a degree that Pauline would often remind me of the fact in no uncertain manner!

On Thursday, March 28, 1996, Pauline and I flew to Canberra for her attendance at an orientation course for new MPs. She was briefed on all aspects of a new member's job including, most importantly: her salary and other allowances; the procedures for organising travel and Commonwealth cars; the use of facilities at Parliament House, such as the all important reference library; and the guidelines for employing staff — particularly the industrial relations aspect of that function. Pauline's failure to appreciate and understand the latter, would be a contributing factor to the circumstances surrounding my sacking on December 9, 1996.

On the evening of Thursday, March 28, 1996, Pauline and I had dinner with Ted Mack and Peter Andren. Peter Andren was the newly-elected independent MP for the NSW Seat of Calare. He had never belonged to a political Party and was to later display a certain lack of courage and generosity when he refused to join a group photograph of independents, in an attempt to distance himself from Pauline. In June 1997, he finally bit the bullet and changed seats in Parliament so that he no longer sat next to Pauline. Our Parliament is full of heroes.

Ted Mack, the Godfather of independents, would in a very short time have the title of 'Australia's most famous independent' snatched from him by Pauline. At the dinner table, on the pavement outside the Santa Lucia restaurant in Kingston, Ted Mack gave Pauline a lot of advice in a short time. He told her that she had two options, with the first being to enjoy being the Member for Oxley, going on the odd committee, and doing what she could for her constituents, but preserving and enjoying her private life and then going to the election on the basis she would only be a one-termer with no regrets.

The second option was to determine to hold the Seat by kissing every baby, opening everything that had to be opened, being seen at every major function, working relentless hours and having absolutely no private life or real leisure time. I was watching Pauline as Ted Mack made his pitch. Everything had happened so quickly, and had so overwhelmed her, that I don't think she realised the significance of Ted's advice at the time. I would remind her many times of it. On more than one occasion, Pauline would set my alarm bells ringing by giving me good reason to think that she would resign. My unease was confirmed by Morrie Marsden.

That evening, Pauline and I stayed in the same suite at the Sundown Village motel in Canberra. I had not booked into a motel so Pauline invited me to stay for the night. She slept in the main bedroom and I told her to keep her door closed because I know I snore. The rumour mills would later have me sleeping with Pauline but, as with most rumours, they were groundless. Pauline did not sexually appeal to me, but it was a different story for a lot of other men. When we got to know each other better, Pauline would laughingly tell me that knowing me had cured her of ever thinking of marriage again. On that night in Canberra, Pauline, in strange surroundings and feeling alone and a little lost, simply wanted company.

The following day, Pauline flew back to Queensland and I took off for Melbourne to help Bernie Finn, the Victorian State Liberal backbencher for Tullamarine, hold his Seat in the March 30 election. I handed out his how to vote cards at several booths and it was soon clear that Bernie would hold his Seat well and send his Labor arch foe David White off to political oblivion. My day was further brightened by having a brief confrontation with the excited, diminutive, left-wing Federal Labor MP, Andrew Theophanous who was barely decipherable as he sputtered and spattered on about Graeme Campbell and myself being racists.

The Ides of March had passed, but their legacy would remain. During the month, issues and new battles to be fought had swirled and tumbled around Pauline's office like flotsam in the eye of a whirlpool. The office was undermanned by one position and the media were circling like sharks with their blood lust far from sated. Pauline was being stridently attacked. The Human Rights Commission was threatening to have her thrown out of Parliament for allegedly saying that she would not represent Aborigines. Pauline on my advice had 'banned' the ABC over what would become known as 'the Purga Mission affair', and the Queensland Liberal Party had refused to refund her share of the government-provided election funding monies. Her enemies were coming, with equal ferocity, from both sides of the political fence. The sacrosanct Seat of Oxley, nurtured so carefully by Labor for thirty-five years, had been painfully wrenched from the Party's grasp by a raw, poorly educated political novice.

How Pauline Hanson won Oxley

The Federal Seat of Oxley had been held from 1949 to 1961 by a Liberal, D. A. Cameron. Labor's local son, W. G. Hayden held it from 1961 to 1988, when the baton was passed on to Les Scott, a former Westpac Bank clerk. The Seat had even survived the disaster of 1975 when Whitlam and Labor were comprehensively routed by Malcolm Fraser.

The electorate and its major centre, Ipswich, with its economic woes, was ripe for an act of rebellion by the usually compliant and loyal Labor voters who had continued to send their representatives to Canberra, election after election. Its young people faced the bleak prospect of being able only to dream of prosperity and a secure future — two goals, once guaranteed realities, achievable by all hardworking Australians.

Working away in Ipswich, in her fish and chip shop, was Pauline Hanson. She approached the operation of her business in a most determined and singular way — ten hours or more a day, seven days a week. Her life in Ipswich during this period has been described as 'insular'. She had absolutely no political background, or experience in politics at any level, and had no active involvement with any community-based organisations. Her social life was virtually non-existent and she had no close friends to speak of. In her life before the media meltdown that engulfed her, Pauline Hanson was a loner.

Pauline's de facto, Rick Gluyas, a former public servant and consultant to the then mayor of Ipswich, introduced Pauline Hanson to politics at the local government level when he decided to stand for the Ipswich Council on an independent ticket and encouraged Pauline to stand with him. She was never formally approached to join the ticket. Her relationship with Gluyas degenerated into an 'on-again, off-again' affair and it was during one of the 'off' phases that she approached Morrie Marsden to run her campaign as an independent for Ipswich Council. It was as if her only motive for standing for Council was simply that the man she had been living with intended trying his hand and she didn't want to be left out of the process. There appear to have been no pressing local issues that may have prompted Pauline Hanson to put up her hand — no obvious stirring of political ambition.

Pauline Hanson was elected to the Ipswich Council in 1994 but was to face the voters again in 1995 when a Council amalgamation brought on an early election. She was surprisingly beaten, which prompted her political enemies to refer to her as the shortest-termed Councillor in the history of the Council. This attack was not warranted, because she would have served out her three-year term but for the premature amalgamation process.

According to Morrie Marsden, Pauline performed well in the first six months of her term as Councillor, then followed a series of policy backflips, the creation of some enemies and, then, defeat. Pauline took this defeat in her stride and, at Marsden's urging, joined the local Bremer branch of the Liberal Party in late 1995. When I asked her why she had joined the Liberals, Pauline said that she was attracted to the Party because it supported small business, and that seemed to be her only reason. Her involvement at local branch level was minimal but, despite this, she told Marsden that she wanted to stand for Liberal Party preselection as a candidate in the forthcoming Queensland State election.

Morrie Marsden would be the first to agree that he is not an experienced or professional political operator, but his advice to Pauline in the circumstances was extraordinary and prophetic. He told her that she would not have a chance at the State level but could win the Federal Seat of Oxley. Marsden with his wide range of grass-roots contacts in the local insurance industry had a strong gut feeling that the trend of voter intention in Oxley had been turning away from Labor in recent years. Despite this, his advice was a bit like betting on a '5000 to one' country maiden galloper to win the Melbourne Cup ten months before entries closed for the big race.

Pauline took Marsden's advice and, on election day, the longshot of all longshots won, running away!

At the preselection for Oxley, Pauline stood against two forgettable candidates and became the Liberal candidate for Oxley. There was no fanfare or media excitement, and even the Queensland Liberals hardly noticed the event. For them, winning Oxley was in the realms of fantasy. This was the seat that had survived the 1975 massacre of Labor but, inexorably and as if preordained by some mysterious force, a series of events would conspire to send shock waves through the Australian political landscape.

On January 6, 1996, three weeks before Paul Keating announced the election, the local Ipswich paper the *Queensland Times* published a letter to the editor from Pauline. The letter read as follows:

Black deaths in custody seem to be Robert Tickner's latest outcry. Pity that as much media coverage or political grandstanding is not shown for white deaths in custody. As for Mr Tickner's statement that Aborigines should not go to jail because apparently it is not working: imagine what type of country this would be to live in if Aborigines didn't go to jail for their crimes. One of these men was serving a 12-year sentence and it wasn't just for a speeding fine.

Can you imagine then if we had equality, then we would have no prisoners at all. The indigenous people of this country are as much responsible for their actions as any other colour or race in this country. The problem is that politicians in all their profound wisdom have and are causing a racism problem.

I would be the first to admit that, not that many years ago the Aborigines were treated wrongly but in trying to correct this they have gone too far. I don't feel responsible for the treatment of Aboriginal people in the past because I had no say but my concern is now and for the future. How can we expect this race to help themselves when governments shower them with money, facilities and opportunities that only these people can obtain no matter how minute the indigenous blood is that flows through their veins and that is what is causing racism.

> Until governments wake up to themselves and start looking at equality not colour then we might start to work together as one.

This letter was clumsily constructed but totally innocuous — and repeated, careful reading of it fails to identify any element in it that satisfies the standard definition of 'racism'. It reflects what Pauline was no doubt hearing as she served out flake and chips in her shop. It also provides evidence of the first stirrings of her awareness regarding the increasing resentment of mainstream white Australians towards the 'black armband' view of our colonial history and the efforts of those in the 'guilt industry' to force present generations of white Australians to accept responsibility and pay compensation for what happened two hundred years ago.

This letter should have gone unnoticed — and it would have but for the almost hysterical intervention of Paul Tully, an Ipswich Labor Councillor and Pauline's most vocal and vehement local foe. Tully made a great song and dance about the letter, accusing the Liberals of endorsing and supporting a racist candidate, and this in turn excited the interest of the Brisbane *Courier-Mail*, which generated more publicity and propelled the story into the national media spotlight. The local Laborites then called on the Queensland Liberals to apologise on behalf of Pauline which, stupidly, they then did. The Liberals then demanded that Pauline also apologise, but she threw a spanner into the works by refusing to do so. The matter was referred to the Federal Liberals and John Howard, and the rest is history. Pauline Hanson was disendorsed in a blaze of publicity, ensuring that every voter in Oxley — and Australia — knew who she was.

Her sacking was too late to allow the Australian Electoral Office to withdraw the ballot papers and put 'Independent' next to Pauline's name — the 'Liberal' label remained. Pauline stuck to her guns and went to the election as a last-minute independent, winning the seat with a 22.76 per cent swing that catapulted her into national and international prominence.

The allegations of racism against the Liberal-endorsed Hanson, triggered by her critical letter about Aborigines, created panic and near hysteria in a Liberal Party facing what it thought was going to be a closely-fought election campaign.

31

This virus of fear infected John Howard — the man who had refused to believe that he would never become Prime Minister, despite being knocked down, time and time again. Howard needed to try to destroy Pauline Hanson in order to send a clear message to the Asians and other ethnic minorities expunging the memories of what he had said about Asian immigration in 1988. He failed, and the ghost of the 1988 statements directed at the same constituency that would rise up to support Hanson had returned to haunt him.

On election night, Pauline celebrated with a barbecue at the house of the ever-faithful Morrie Marsden. The women scheduled to do the catering cancelled at the last moment and it was left to Morrie's sister to fill the breach. Pauline financed the food and drink. There were about fifty people at the gathering, plus the media, and the phones were gridlocked. When the results came through, the response was noisy jubilation.

Pauline responded in a very undemonstrative way. She did not make a fuss of her helpers and summon them to her side to thank them as one may have expected. Her almost silent, unidentified 'Thank you' to Morrie Marsden on the other side of the room could have been directed at a picture on the wall. Marsden told one of Pauline's workers from the fish and chip shop that he felt Pauline's win marked the absolute end of his relationship with her. He was right.

I came to know Morrie Marsden well during my time in Ipswich and, after Pauline sacked me, we stayed in touch. He kept me advised about what was happening on the ground in Oxley. Morrie is a real Ipswich boy — part of the local furniture — and he has no pretensions. He goes to the races and plays the pokies at the local Brothers' Club. He is your typical Queenslander — open, truthful and without real malice and, therefore, totally unsuited to playing the grubby and deceitful game of politics. Plagued by the onset of panic attacks during his bumpy relationship with Pauline and by a pathological fear of flying, he told me she had, 'Cost me ten years of my life.' Morrie Marsden deserves better and I hope that one day he can recapture those 'lost' years.

Pauline had spent just on $12 000 of her own money on the campaign, with the Queensland Liberals having put in about $1500 up to the point when she was disendorsed. Again, Morrie Marsden had been her campaign manager. There was no professional campaign, no clever advertising, no public rallies. There was just one letterbox drop before polling day. The newspaper advertisements were simple slogans, such as 'Equality for all' and 'Equal justice for all'. The letterboxed pamphlets were basic and simple. Pauline's campaign broke almost all the rules of conventional electioneering. Major political parties, please take note!

During the campaign, Pauline had displayed breathtaking political naivety while she was still the Liberal candidate. She submitted a Liberal Party generic press release to her local paper the *Queensland Times*, and she forgot to write her name and other details in the spaces provided. When contacted by an inquisitive *Queensland Times* reporter about the missing information, she responded that she had been pushed for time, saying, 'I thought you [the *Queensland Times*] could fill it in.' Morrie Marsden was furious.

Why did Pauline Hanson win Oxley in such spectacular fashion? The starting point is, without doubt, the involvement of Morrie Marsden and the advice he gave Pauline (which, luckily for her, she accepted — from buying the fish and chip shop, to standing for the Federal instead of the State Seat). Paul Tully, Pauline's Ipswich tormenter, played a star role worthy of an 'Oscar' for, without his grandstanding and intervention over her January letter to the editor of the *Queensland Times*, which turned it into a *cause célèbre*, Pauline would have remained a Liberal and would not have won the Seat. At best, she would have only seriously frightened her Labor opponent by registering a strong anti-Keating vote against him and then have simply disappeared forever into that political 'black hole' that is the graveyard of most defeated candidates.

If Pauline had remained a Liberal, that 'tag' would have deterred those Labor voters who at their moment of truth, in the polling booth, are unable to kick their old habits and vote 'Liberal'.

Les Scott was the Labor man Pauline Hanson had thrashed in Oxley. He had been a poor replacement for Bill Hayden and I was told that he was perceived to be too smug and had not performed all that well in the eyes of a lot of constituents — emphasising the powerful anti-Keating emotion running throughout Oxley as it ran through most electorates. He also proved to be a very bad loser.

After her disendorsement, Pauline became the epitome of the underdog — a battling single mother and fish and chip shop lady, taking on all the big parties and saying things about Aborigines with which many mainstream Australians agreed. At this stage, Pauline had not broken ground on the immigration and multiculturalism questions. That was to come later when she and I sat down and discussed the direction she would take. Pauline's known lack of any longstanding political Party involvement, coupled with her hugely publicised disendorsement, made it very easy for disenchanted blue-collar Labor voters in Oxley to support her. They were the key to her success. Pauline Hanson's political future now rests with those same people.

Whose Rights Anyway?

O n Monday, March 4, 1996, just two days after Pauline Hanson was elected, the *Australian* newspaper ran an article headlined 'Liberal reject proclaims a victory for the "white community".' At that time, I was yet to arrive in Ipswich and Pauline had given a telephone interview to journalist Christopher Dore who tape-recorded the conversation with her on Sunday, March 3 — the day after polling day. Pauline was in a state of exhaustion following the massive publicity fallout after election day and Morrie Marsden was furious at her giving a media interview without first consulting him. Dore has told me that he cannot remember whether he told Pauline he was recording her. In the article she was quoted as saying she was fighting for:

> . . . the white community, the immigrants, Italians, Greeks, whoever, it really doesn't matter — anyone apart from the Aboriginals and Torres Strait Islanders.

This quote, as it stands, is clearly and blatantly discriminatory against indigenous Australians and it was seized on immediately by the Human Rights and Equal Opportunity Commission — their Brisbane commissioner John Britton becoming quite agitated and going public.

The Aboriginal 'industry' immediately rose up fulminating, saying it would petition the Speaker of the House of Representatives, seeking to have Pauline stripped of her Parliamentary Seat. From the day I arrived in Pauline's office until the day I was thrown out of it, there was a barrage of correspondence from the Human Rights Commission demanding that Pauline attend at their Sydney headquarters to enter into a process of reconciliation with the aggrieved parties. After seeking advice from several quarters, I advised Pauline very early in the exchange to totally ignore the Commission. It was furious that Pauline would not attend its 'kangaroo court'. I am pleased to note that the 1997 Budget saw a significant reduction in spending on the Commission. Hopefully there will continue to be more cuts.

Of course there are always two sides to every story and this case is no exception. The Human Rights Commission subpoenaed the audio tape from the *Australian* and was obliged to release a copy to Pauline — which it did. In his article, Christopher Dore failed to publish Pauline's full response. In the verified transcript, a full stop did not follow after 'Aboriginals and Torres Strait Islanders'. There was a comma, and then further comment by Pauline. What follows here is the proper and correct response transcribed from the original tape.

[Christopher Dore from *The Australian* asks:]

So you're fighting for the white community generally?

[Pauline Hanson responds:]

Yeah, look, the white community, the immigrants, the Italians, Greeks, whoever, it really doesn't matter, you know, anyone apart from Aboriginals and Torres Strait Islanders, you know. I just want everyone to be equal and I think then we could get rid of this umm, I think there's a racial discrimination out in the community and we might start to get on to work together as one.

This statement was classic 'Hansonese' — poorly constructed, barely fluent and convoluted in the extreme — providing wonderful ammunition for the social engineers in the Human Rights Commission and, of course, her friends in the media.

It is obvious from reading the 'undoctored' version of Pauline's response, that realising she had got herself tangled up, she qualified herself immediately after making reference to 'Aboriginals and Torres Strait Islanders'. She was putting the view that Aborigines receive more benefits than non-Aborigines and that the latter needed to catch up in the 'hand-out' stakes before equality was achieved. She was also drawing attention to the reverse racism complained of by many Australians with good reason. Her plea for 'everyone to be equal' and her desire for everyone 'to work together as one' puts an entirely different interpretation on the very damaging, selective quote used by the journalist.

An interesting postscript to this story occurred over a year later when David Armstrong, the new Editor in Chief of the *Australian* newspaper, saw fit to write a letter to the editor of the Brisbane *Courier-Mail*. On May 9, 1997, Mr Armstrong wrote:

> Pauline Hanson, in her interview with the *Courier-Mail* (May 8), denies having said she would not represent Aboriginal people. Further, she accuses the *Australian* of misreporting her. A transcript of the relevant interview with Ms Hanson, conducted by the *Australian*, shows she has no interest in representing Aboriginal people.

Mr Armstrong then went on in his letter to repeat the selective quote used by Chris Dore a year earlier. Pauline Hanson was foolish to use the language she originally did but, having done so, quite obviously sought to correct herself. On the other hand, Mr Armstrong's letter has quite clearly also selectively quoted the transcript. For a man who is the Editor in Chief of Australia's national newspaper that is clearly inexcusable. Just as inexcusable, from Pauline's recollection of events, is the way she was interviewed on the telephone. She maintains that Chris Dore did not warn her he was taping her conversation. Dore says he cannot remember whether he warned her or not. If Pauline's recollection is correct, then the law was broken and the *Australian* should never have used the piece. When the media behaves in this manner, it is little wonder journalists are down on the bottom rungs of the ladder of public acceptance, along with politicians. The two groups deserve each other.

The final act in this mini-drama between Pauline Hanson and the Human Rights and Equal Opportunity Commission (HREOC) was played out on Friday, October 24, 1997, when Commissioner Sir Ronald Wilson found that Hanson's comments about 'Aborigines and Torres Strait Islanders', taken in the context of the entire interview, did not constitute racial discrimination as defined by the Racial Discrimination Act. This finding, which took a long, drawn-out eighteen months to reach, is an indictment of every journalist who selectively quoted Pauline out of context. We should not hold our breath waiting for the published apologies. The report of the finding by HREOC was relegated to a minuscule 16 cm single column buried on page 17 in the Melbourne *Herald Sun*. Equally disappointing was the total lack of response from Pauline's office, which should have made great capital out of the favourable result.

SEVEN

The Purga Mission and 'White Trash'

Purga Mission is on the outskirts of Ipswich and was once an operating Aboriginal mission station. On the Tuesday after election day, and two days before I arrived in Ipswich, Pauline had arranged to meet with Aboriginal elders at Purga in an attempt to resolve the perceived differences between her and them, mainly emanating from the article in the *Australian* newspaper. During a telephone call from Kalgoorlie, I told Pauline to only meet with the elders on the proviso that there would be no media present. She stated her terms and these were accepted by the Aborigines at Purga.

Pauline was accompanied by two men — John Ranizowski an Ipswich JP, and Jarrod Stewart an engineering student — but, on their arrival at Purga, they were ambushed by the Australian Broadcasting Commission's *7.30 Report* team and a female journalist from the Brisbane *Courier-Mail*. Pauline told the people that they had broken their agreement about the media and she was not going to stay at Purga. As Pauline and her companions started to withdraw, she was abused by all and sundry, but in particular by one Aboriginal woman who called her a 'white cow' and 'white trash'.

Ranizowski and Stewart heard the offending words as they walked back with Pauline to their car. The TV crew and the *Courier-Mail's* female journalist were all very close to the action. In that evening's *7.30 Report*, it was obvious that editing had deleted the 'white trash' abuse. When I investigated the matter and spoke with local taxi drivers who viewed a video of the incident, I was told that the woman who had abused Pauline had been part of a group that had come from Brisbane. The drivers knew most of the Aborigines in the Ipswich area because taxis are used a lot on pension days.

When I later spoke to the female print journalist about the matter, she admitted to hearing some of the abuse directed at Pauline. However, she went so far as to say, 'But what's so bad about white trash?' This incredible comment bowled me out like a Shane Warne 'mystery ball'. I could just imagine the headlines if Pauline had called the Aborigines at Purga 'black trash'. I told Pauline to place a personal ban on the ABC, which she did. She also placed a ban on that female journalist. The ABC and the then producer of the *7.30 Report*, David Margan, have steadfastly denied the abuse ever occurred.

Banning the ABC proved a very effective strategy and helped to feed the Pauline Hanson phenomenon. The 'white trash' slur struck a vibrant chord with mainstream Australia. Here was Pauline, battling against the big political parties and the high priests of political correctness and, at the same time, fighting off the media — particularly the ABC and its mates, who do not rate at all well with ordinary Australians. The 'blackballing' of the ABC obviously hurt, because the organisation tried hard to have the ban lifted all through 1996. I received letters and faxes from senior ABC executives, and Pru Goward from Radio National's breakfast show (now a well chosen adviser to the Prime Minister on women's affairs) tried very hard to secure an interview with Pauline. In obvious desperation, the ABC sent in its bigger guns when Monica Attard, one of its most prestigious and respected award-winning journalists rang me at least six times attempting to effect a rapprochement. I told Monica to give up, which she did.

On one occasion, a female ABC journalist called me from Darwin and made an impassioned plea for an interview with Pauline, setting out in great detail all the advantages to be gained. I had already taken about forty media calls and was in no mood to be hounded. In response to my bluntness, the woman from Darwin burst into tears and told me I was a nasty man. 'No, you are wrong,' I told her. 'I am a *very* nasty man!'

The commercial media took great delight in the ABC's obvious discomfort at being frozen out, and I am told the ABC broke out the 'bubbly' when Pauline sacked me. Why didn't they invite me to the party?

Not long after the Purga Mission affair, Pauline was fiercely attacked in the Letters to the Editor column of her local paper, the *Queensland Times*. I told her that she would need to defend herself, and she agreed. I wrote the following letter for her. It was a precursor to Pauline's material on reconciliation. The letter is Pauline very much on the offensive:

Dear Sir,

History tells us where we have been and teaches us to learn from our mistakes.

History can also be selectively quoted to suit a particular agenda and accurate history can be twisted by those who attempt to rewrite it to suit their own purpose.

Shane Lewis of Bribie Island attacked me in a letter to the *Queensland Times* dated April 3, 1996. He mentioned white people kicking the heads of Aboriginal babies and other atrocities. In her letter to the *Queensland Times* dated April 6, 1996, Patricia Thompson of Silkstone also mentioned the massacring of Aboriginals by non-Aboriginals.

It is a pity Shane Lewis and Patricia Thompson were so selective in their treatment of history.

T. G. H. Strehlow is probably the highest authority on Aboriginal culture and customs. He was an internationally respected anthropologist and his memory is revered by black and white alike. In one of his works entitled *Journey to Horseshoe Bend*, Strehlow describes the terrible massacre of one group of blacks by another. The event took place in 1875 in the Finke River area of Central Australia. The massacre was triggered by an act of sacrilege committed by a respected ceremonial chief.

In Strehlow's words, 'the warriors turned their murderous attention to the women and older children and either speared or clubbed them to death. Finally, according to the grim custom of warriors and avengers, they broke the limbs of the infants, leaving them to die "natural deaths". The final number of the dead could well have reached the high figure of from eighty to a hundred men, women and children.' This massacre described by Strehlow is just one of many instances of brutality by black against black.

In the *Queensland Times* on February 22, 1996, an article was published, entitled 'Elders: Hanson ignorant'. In that article, an Aboriginal elder, Gladys Graham, said and I quote, 'Mrs Hanson should receive a traditional Urgarapul punishment; having her hands and feet crippled.' It is a sad indictment that such savage and primitive sentiments still exist. Inciting violence is a criminal offence. If a white Australian had made such comments, the response from the politically correct would have been deafening.

The greater Aboriginal community is not well served by many of those who claim to be its leaders. Their actions and words only create increased resentment and disaffection in the wider community. The growing scandal of ATSIC [The Aboriginal and Torres Strait Islander Commission] is just one example. ATSIC is a disgrace and should be abolished. It has helped create two Australias and has failed dismally to help those it was meant to serve. Senator Herron must allow it to be exposed to public scrutiny so that ordinary taxpayers know how billions of their dollars have been squandered on the whole Aboriginal industry.

It does not serve any good purpose to continually dredge up the past. In the long run, nobody profits. We should look to the future but many activists find this impossible.

There can only be one united Australia if we are to survive as a viable, sovereign nation. At present, there are divisive forces in our society that put their self interest ahead of the national interest. Governments cannot continue to listen to noisy, taxpayer funded minority groups at the expense of mainstream Australia.

P.S. Dear Editor

Due to the nature of the attacks on me through your Letters to the Editor column, I would appreciate my response being published without editing. If there is a problem with space please contact me.

The letter was published in the *Queensland Times* on April 10, in its original form. It was written twelve days before I started on the first draft of the maiden speech, the basic themes of which appear in this letter in embryonic form. I was starting to warm up.

Beware! No Refunds!

Long-suffering Australian taxpayers should realise that, besides paying the wages and other benefits for their politicians, they also pay for much of their election campaign expenses. Electoral funding was agreed to by Parliament and is paid out at the rate of $1.57 per primary vote to every candidate who polls over 4 per cent of the vote, irrespective of whether they win or lose. The major Parties are the chief beneficiaries because their candidates never see the money, which is paid directly to the Parties' treasurers by the Australian Electoral Commission (AEC). Independents, on the other hand, do see the money, and if they want to spend it at the races they can! The accountability guidelines for this are very liberal.

When Pauline Hanson won Oxley as an independent, she polled 33 960 primary votes and should have received a cheque from the Australian Electoral Commission for $33\,960 \times \$1.57594 = \$53\,518.92$. However, when I left her office on December 9, 1996, that money was still in the coffers of the Queensland Liberal Party. This story of one of Pauline's many battles gives an insight into one of the grubby and most unattractive aspects of a big Party machine. It is this type of behaviour that helps turn ordinary Australians off conventional political Parties and the people who run them.

Pauline had scant knowledge of the electoral funding benefit when she was still a Liberal candidate but became more aware of it after her disendorsement — so much so, she told the voters that if she won the Seat of Oxley, after reimbursing herself for the $12 000 of her own money that she had spent on her campaign, she would return the balance to the electorate in the form of increased car parking areas at the local hospital or a much needed extra police vehicle. As well as being an honourable and generous gesture on Pauline's part, it was also wonderful politics.

Pauline made all this very clear well before polling day, but she also told me that she disagreed entirely with the public funding of elections — and more credit to her for this. Hers was an offer not likely to be matched by any other independent and it was the sort of gesture that would help to strengthen her growing appeal as an anti-politician.

When I started with Pauline, one of my first jobs was to try and recover the monies due to her from the Queensland Liberal Party. In the end, after a lot of work, I made very little headway.

I have already mentioned that, due to the closeness to polling day of Pauline's disendorsement, the Australian Electoral Commission had no time to withdraw the ballot papers for Oxley and reprint them with Pauline identified as an 'Independent'. So she went to the election with 'Liberal Party' still next to her name. Under the provisions of the Act, the AEC were, therefore, legally bound to forward to the Queensland Liberal Party what should have been Pauline's entitlement. I was told by an AEC official that there was nothing in the Act to cover Pauline's situation and she was purely a victim of a loophole that had ended up favouring the Liberals. I suggested to Pauline that she introduce a Private Member's Bill to amend the Electoral Act accordingly.

Pauline had never enjoyed good relations with the Liberal Party machine in Brisbane and it was obvious that they regarded her as an aberration that would hopefully fade away. She told me that, at the time of her disendorsement, she was roundly abused on the telephone by Jim Barron, the then director of the Queensland Liberals. She and Morrie Marsden had then driven to Brisbane to see Barron and Bob Tucker, the State President, and they had not been extended a cordial reception. Marsden threatened to walk out of the meeting if Barron and Tucker did not tone down their abusive language.

On March 14, 1996, I telephoned Bob Tucker about the refunding of Pauline's monies, but made no progress. When Tucker told me that David Jull 'is a mate of mine', I knew that Pauline was going to have problems getting her money. David Jull was the Minister for Administrative Services responsible for, among other things, administering the Electoral Act.

On April 16, 1996, Pauline and I went to Brisbane to see Jim Barron and Bob Tucker. Bob Tucker, on meeting me in the office reception area, told me in a suitably pompous and condescending way that he did not want me to be present at Pauline's meeting with himself and Barron. Pauline dug in and told Tucker that 'all bets were off' and that she and I would go straight back to Ipswich.

In the end the meeting took place. It was strained and unproductive and it was obvious that the Liberals were going to play hard ball.

The Queensland Liberals have always been the weaker, poorer cousins of their southern counterparts and the ungracious way Barron and Tucker treated Pauline only served to confirm this.

The matter was simple. Pauline wanted the Liberals to refund to her the electoral funding they had taken from the AEC due to the loophole in the Act. She was prepared to reimburse the Liberals for their 'on ground expenses' up to the time she was disendorsed and, by her reckoning, this was about $1500. She would take out her own expenses, which amounted to about $12 000, and then she would return the balance to the electorate.

At the request of Jim Barron and Bob Tucker, Pauline instructed me to prepare her submission to the Liberals for her refund, and copies were sent out to John Howard, David Jull, Tony Staley the Federal Liberal President, and Andrew Robb the Federal Director.

Incredibly, up until the time I left Pauline's office, the Queensland Liberals never formally acknowledged her submission. We were forced to rely on 'back door' information to keep up with what was going on. According to sources, Pauline's submission was received and voted on at a meeting of the Management Committee, but was defeated. We were told that Joan Sheldon, the Queensland Deputy Premier, had voted in favour of Pauline but the outcome was inevitable because the committee was allegedly controlled by David Jull's and Bob Tucker's people.

I told Pauline that her only chance for recovery from the Liberal Party lay with the law and, after a few false starts, I was referred to Watkins Stokes

Templeton, a firm of lawyers in Brisbane, who were brave enough to take on Pauline as a client. When I left Pauline's employ her solicitor was negotiating a settlement with his counterpart representing the Liberal Party.

This battle between Pauline and the Liberal Party over the spoils of election funding should never have happened. It showed the Liberals in the worst possible light. All of Australia knew that Pauline had won the seat as an independent and the Liberal Party should have accepted this in good grace but, instead, it applied the strict letter of the law to obtain a benefit it did not deserve. I tried to enlist the help of the Federal Liberals but they duck-shoved, saying that they could not intervene. It was a gutless response from people for whom I no longer had much respect. There were no winners from this grubby and demeaning exercise — only losers. It made a mockery of John Howard's election appeal to the 'battlers', because the real losers (besides the Liberals) were the 'battlers' of Oxley.

Bob Tucker also became a loser on Saturday, June 7, 1997, when he was voted out as State President of the Queensland Liberal Party. As I read details of Tucker's come-uppance in the *Australian, schadenfreude* swept over me as I acknowledged that there is such a thing as poetic justice. Pauline Hanson now shares just one thing with Bob Tucker — he and she were both sacked by the same organisation.

More of Pauline's Liberal Party enemies were to bite the dust in 1997. David Jull the Minister for Administrative Services and one of the key power brokers of the Queensland Liberal Party was forced, to resign in September over the 'Travelgate' scandal. In mid-1996, I had a meeting with Grahame Morris, John Howard's right-hand man, about the impact of Pauline Hanson. Morris told me that he had seen 'Messiahs come and go'. Ironically, it was Grahame Morris who went when John Howard sacked him on Friday, September 26, after a close twenty-year relationship.

The eighteen-month stalemate in Pauline's legal sparring with the Queensland Liberals was finally broken when, on September 15, 1997, Watkins Stokes Templeton launched legal proceedings in the Brisbane District Court on behalf of Pauline against the Queensland Liberal Party, claiming $53 518.92 plus costs and interest. The Liberals may yet rue the day they were so nasty, mean and uncharitable to Pauline Hanson.

NINE

The Office

It is vitally important to understand the politics of Pauline's office and the flow-on effect this would have during 1996 and beyond. Silly, inane office politics that had nothing to do with the vital political issues bogged us all down and cost a huge amount in productivity and lost opportunity. Bitchiness, pettiness and overweening ego ruled the day.

My first advice to Pauline when we moved into her Ipswich office after the declaration of the poll was that she needed to establish an efficient, professional office — its prime purpose being to service her constituents and lay the groundwork for her re-election. During my time with her, I was unable to come anywhere near achieving this objective and, after my sacking, Pauline's office remained the object of much media comment and criticism fuelled by some considerable public dissatisfaction in Oxley. This dissatisfaction was expressed in the 'Letters to the Editor' column in the local newspaper. Some of these letters complained about the tardiness of Pauline's office. One man said that he had written four times with no reply. Other letters complained about Pauline's absence from the electorate when she was promoting her new One Nation Party. These letters, some of which admittedly could have come from political opponents, created damaging perceptions that could then be given more weight by genuine examples of inefficiency in processing constituency matters or other questionable decisions such as Pauline cancelling her fortnightly (and very successful) visits to the local shopping malls.

When we moved into the office on Monday, March 21, 1996, Barbara Hazelton was holding the top 'C' position and Heidi Lewis, the junior 'A' one. The 'B', or middle position, was yet to be filled. The chain of command was Pauline, me, and then Barbara Hazelton, whose job it was to manage the office. I was Pauline's delegate and could approve overtime, travel allowance and other job-related entitlements. Heidi Lewis was the only person in the Ipswich office with better than basic computer skills and she told me she wished to take advantage of the government provided and paid for improvement courses offered to all electorate office staffers. I had been led to believe that Barbara Hazelton was fully computer literate — in fact a 'whiz' in all areas — but, during my time in the office, that proved not to be the case. She had been away from the Parliamentary office scene for some time, in fact about five years, while she was living in Hong Kong (where her husband was working).

By the beginning of April, I was having serious doubts about Barbara's capacity to do the job at the level required, even though she had only been in the job for a couple of weeks. After all the outcry over Pauline's alleged comments about not representing the Aborigines, I was taken aback that, when sorting out invitations for Pauline to appear at various functions, Barbara seriously suggested Pauline might like to attend a 'Black Deaths in Custody' seminar being held in Brisbane. This would have been a stupid and insensitive thing to do, and would have been totally unproductive. Barbara was later to indicate she did not know who Ted Drane was, at the height of the gun debate, and she thought that Cheryl Kernot was a Western Australian Senator. I had expected someone with a little more political savvy.

A senior industrial relations expert advised me to have all Pauline's staff sign ninety-day probationary employment agreements in order to protect her against the danger of frivolous unfair dismissal claims.

With the best of intentions I did this, and Heidi Lewis and myself signed up — but Barbara declined, taking the matter up with Pauline who told me that, although she had told Barbara to sign the document, it would not have any relevance in her case. In a very short time, Barbara Hazelton had insinuated herself very firmly into Pauline's confidence. I don't think she realised it at the time, but Pauline had taken the first step in dividing her office into two camps.

At this stage, Pauline's office was, if anything, less busy than some of its metropolitan counterparts but I attributed this to the fact that she was a new Member and it would take a little time for her constituents to establish contact so soon after an election. There is always that post-election malaise when everyone seems to just want to forget about politics and politicians. Little did I realise that Pauline's office would soon resemble an active volcano, ready to blow its top.

For a short period of time, Pauline took on a female 'temp' to fill the 'B' position, but she proved to be unsuitable — more so as I gained the distinct impression that her political views were very contrary to Pauline's. She was selected by Barbara Hazelton, who then started to promote her as a permanent appointee to the position, despite the fact that I was in sole charge of interviewing applicants and preparing a short list for Pauline. I had told Barbara that I did not consider this person at all suitable but, despite this, her curriculum vitae was placed very prominently on Pauline's desk.

On May 7, 1996, the female 'temp' walked off the job, alleging that Morrie Marsden had sworn at her during a telephone conversation. For the time being I had one less problem to worry about — but there were plenty to replace it.

Before my relationship with Barbara Hazelton deteriorated completely, she was quite vitriolic in her comments about Morrie Marsden saying on one occasion that he was, '. . . just a jumped up little twit who couldn't forget his brief moment of glory'. This reference was to Morrie's role as Pauline's very successful campaign manager, and the attack on Morrie told me how confident Barbara must have been of her developing relationship with Pauline. I hoped that Pauline had not in any way encouraged this 'bagging' of Marsden who had played such a significant role in her rise to public prominence. Barbara's relationship with Pauline would be even more substantially reinforced by Pauline in a subsequent media interview.

Heidi Lewis, the young girl in the office, had worked in Pauline's fish and chip shop since her mid-teens and had enrolled in a university course when Pauline won the election. Fiercely loyal to Pauline, Heidi had deferred her course to come and work in the electorate office. At twenty, Heidi was helping care for her gravely ill mother at home, so she was constantly under pressure from day one. She had a pleasant manner but she was, on her own admission, totally apolitical and had a lot to learn. I was sure that she would develop if properly trained and I did my best, in the time I had, to encourage her to develop views on the political issues that were quickly starting to become part of the everyday business of Pauline's office.

I told Pauline that I wanted Barbara to teach Heidi the comparatively simple task of keeping Pauline's appointments diary, but I was unable to achieve even that simple goal. Barbara managed to spend a substantial amount of time as Pauline's personal assistant and was soon acting as her companion at functions, even staying overnight at Pauline's house. She also began to accompany Pauline to Canberra, leaving the Ipswich office under-manned and, therefore, less able to efficiently service constituents.

Even Heidi was not immune from Barbara, who complained more than once to me that Heidi was not performing in her job. Invariably her criticism was prefaced by telling me how 'delightful' Heidi was, but then launching into an attack on her. On more than one occasion I asked Heidi if her workload was too much but she stoically said that things were okay. She was very much under the combined influence of Pauline and Barbara and had no idea of how to stand up for herself. As she told me later, she felt that she was 'the ham in the sandwich' between Barbara and myself. She would later qualify her position.

I told Barbara that she was responsible for Heidi's training and left it at that, as I needed to concentrate on more pressing matters. Barbara's carping hastened my efforts to find someone to fill the other position in the office as soon as possible.

Right up until the day of my dismissal, the operation of the Ipswich office was a large and deeply imbedded thorn under my saddle. On numerous occasions I had my personal mail, including my tax returns and other confidential letters, opened in error. On returning from Canberra I would find my opened letters resealed, along with little notes bemoaning the errors. It was just a case of no-one in the office being able to simply sort the mail before opening it.

There were incorrectly made appointments and, more seriously, complaints from staff from other offices that invitations to Pauline had not been acknowledged. At one particular time, the office was contacted by supporters who had received 'thank you' letters from Pauline. They advised that they had also received, in error, correspondence meant for Pauline and other people. I questioned Heidi about this particular problem and she laid the blame squarely at Barbara Hazelton's feet.

After considerable research, seeking to streamline the job of the staff dealing with constituents, I introduced a constituent enquiry form tailored for entering information into the computer database and also for providing a compact and coherent manual file. For reasons known only to her, Barbara Hazelton vehemently opposed the move. Even Pauline could see the advantage of my suggestion over the wholly inadequate and messy manual system being used by Barbara. After a lot of wasted time and useless argument, I finally managed to win the day. Barbara did in fact, at public expense, eventually complete a computer training course on Access which is the program used for the all-important task of establishing data bases. Even after this, I noticed that she was going to Heidi all the time for help. It should have been the other way around.

Pauline and I hardly ever argued on political policy or strategy and we were very much in tune in those areas. Once I knew where her sympathies and direction lay on a particular issue, I would expand and explain the background and detail to her. She acknowledged my role during a *Witness* interview in 1996, saying about me, 'He's been a tremendous help . . . He's been a real learning experience . . . He's been my back-up . . . He's been my teacher in a lot of ways.' This was all lavish praise from a person who was later to sack me, refusing to give any reasons for doing so. We did have our differences on the Goods and Services Tax (GST), she saying that it would be a good thing, but my position being that small business would only end up being the unpaid collector for the tax. I said we would discuss the matter if and when it raised its head again, which did not happen during 1996.

Pauline and I certainly had many heated exchanges about the running of her office and Barbara Hazelton's role, but these arguments never became really nasty. She said that she would never sack Barbara, and I would say that Pauline didn't know how to run a political office, which she would rebut by saying that, if one could run a fish and chip shop, running an office was just an extension of that operation. As a solution to my problem with Barbara, Pauline suggested that she be responsible for Barbara and I for the rest of the staff. I told Pauline that such a system was unworkable.

Pauline's office never operated as an effective unit during my time with her, simply because she would not take my advice on what was required to get it up and running properly. Long after I had gone, I was told that Paul Filing, the former Liberal WA independent, had sent his senior staffer to Ipswich to help get Pauline's office operating more smoothly.

When I first discussed my role with Pauline, I told her that I wanted nothing more than a professional working relationship and that I didn't want to invade her after-hours life any more than was necessary. I realised she needed that precious time for herself and the two teenage children still living with her. I stressed to her that, at the end of the day, it would be fatal to take the office home with her in the form of one of her staff. It can become an impossible situation living with, then working with someone. It becomes very difficult for the other staffers. The end result is that the office becomes divided into two camps — the boss and her mates versus the rest, and that is exactly what happened in Pauline's office.

TEN

Bring Back 'Nasho'!

A nzac Day, 1996, was Pauline Hanson's first public engagement and her 'blooding' as the new Federal Member for Oxley. She was to give an address at the Bundamba Honour Stone, at Bundamba on the outskirts of Ipswich, and then had other functions to attend during the day. The weather forecast said a good day, and it was. Pauline and I had a general discussion about the significance of Anzac Day and its increasing popularity with young people in recent years — which is a slap in the face for those who have been desperately trying to do their best to remove the day from our national calendar. Pauline referred to her visit to the War Memorial in Canberra that had so impressed her, and said how important it was for school children to visit there.

I told Pauline that her Anzac Day speech should be traditional and should not venture too far into the political arena. I wrote her a short, to-the-point address, in plain language but striking the right note. As Pauline's public speaking skills at this stage were very basic, I did not want to burden her with anything too long or complicated.

During my discussions with Pauline, we spoke about the high level of youth unemployment in Australia and the flow-on effect of that on the general community by way of the drug problem, homelessness and increased crime rates. The electorate of Oxley had very high levels of unemployment affecting all age groups, so the subject was topical.

The re-introduction of National Service has continued to pop up from time to time, but governments conveniently brush any moves in this direction aside. The fact that eighteen year olds vote may have something to do with this. Millions of dollars are shovelled out on trying to correct the results of the problem of high youth unemployment, instead of trying to reduce it at its starting point — the dole queues.

I suggested to Pauline that she call for the reintroduction of National Service on the basis that basic military training be combined with civil works, such as the construction of the Alice Springs to Darwin railway line, reafforestation and water conservation projects. She warmed to this idea and it obviously struck a chord. At this early stage of being with Pauline, I gained the impression that she was eager to learn but, as time went by, she would give me plenty of reasons to change my mind.

In a subsequent *60 Minutes* programme, Pauline's mother claimed the credit for her daughter's National Service policy and I defer to her. Great minds think alike!

Pauline delivered her speech in front of a good and appreciative crowd at the Bundamba Honour Stone, Brisbane Road, Bundamba, about 9 km from Ipswich — and she was well received. She spoke slowly with traces of nervousness, but managed quite well. She took about six minutes to read the prepared speech. Here is what she said, after dealing with the formalities:

I recently visited Canberra for the first time and was taken to visit The Australian War Memorial. I was on a day visit and ran out of time. I promised myself that I would return to the Memorial and spend the necessary time to take it all in.

The approaches to the Memorial are impressive, more so that they are now overlooked by the statue of one of Australia's greatest heroes, Sir Edward 'Weary' Dunlop, who gave hope and comfort to so many of his countrymen during a time of evil and despair.

The Australian War Memorial should be compulsory visiting for all Australians, especially the young. The day I was there I saw many young Australians and it was obvious they were fascinated by what they saw. Many of the exhibits bear testimony to the marvellous feats men and women are capable of, under terrible circumstances.

Wars have been with us since the beginning of history and we wish, of course, that they would become extinct. We must, however, be practical and be on constant guard against threats to our national sovereignty. In 1996, the world continues to be wracked by the blight of war and all the misery it brings.

The terrible conflicts in Bosnia, the Middle East and much of the African continent remind us all that there is no beast like the human beast. There are other trouble spots all over the world where men, women and children are being butchered as I speak. Our closest neighbour, Papua New Guinea seems unable to resolve humanely, the troubles on Bougainville.

This Anzac Day in 1996 is as always, a time for reflection, a time for all Australians to share a quiet moment together, remembering those who gave their lives to keep this country safe and those who survived and returned to their loved ones. Anzac Day has become firmly established in the Australian identity and culture.

It annoys me greatly that there are those amongst us that constantly denigrate our Australian identity and culture. There is a clearly defined Australian identity and culture and it is vital that we resist efforts to downgrade or smother these important elements of our society. I call on all our new settlers to enter mainstream Australia with conviction and good will, without sacrificing their cultural heritage. I ask them to pledge their loyalty and allegiance to this great country.

The greatest debt owed by Australians today, is to those Australians who gave their lives for this country, that still provides today, a safe haven for those less fortunate, from far and abroad, who have been forced to flee their homeland and for those seeking a better life.

Having said this I, of course, pay great homage to those men and women from other backgrounds who fought and died for their new homeland. Their sacrifice was the ultimate act of assimilation.

The 'Australia Remembers' programme was a wonderful success

for its organisers and all Australians. Young Australians embraced the concept with energy and vigour which augurs well for the future. It was heart-warming to see different generations applauding each other. Each year it is obvious that more and more young people are attending Anzac Day ceremonies, especially in the major centres.

I am sure I speak for the majority of Australians when I say how happy I am to see Vietnam veterans take their rightful place on Anzac Day. I ask you to join me in saluting them.

Our enemies need not come from abroad. The great American General, Douglas MacArthur warned 'not only of the enemy without but within'.

We must be sensible about the defence of this nation and make sure that our armed forces are properly equipped and funded. We must make sure that we can continue to offer good employment to young Australians wishing to make a career of the armed services.

We have too many of our young people on the streets, many of them in self-destruct mode. Youth unemployment is at an all time high and affects us all. Perhaps the reintroduction of National Service would be appropriate.

National Service would provide employment and direction for young Australians. The opportunity to take up trades and professions would return them to civilian life better prepared to cope with adult life. The present generation needs to be economically secure in order to face the future.

I am very proud to have been able to speak to you all on this Anzac Day and join with you in remembering all those to who we all owe so much.

During the course of the day we attended several other functions and I noticed one common denominator — the presence of Les Scott, the defeated Labor ex-Member for Oxley. Everywhere Pauline went, there was Les Scott, standing in the crowd looking suitably crestfallen and shattered, like a man who had lost his faithful dog. He would repeat this behaviour throughout most of 1996, and it was plain for all to see that he had been one of the reasons why Labor had lost the seat to Pauline. There is no reason to feel sorry for Scott, especially since his indexed annual retiring allowance of about $40 000 for life will no doubt help to make his existence a little less miserable.

On Friday, May 17, 1996, twelve senior students from Ipswich schools came to Pauline's office at her invitation to put their views on National Service. They ended up being featured on Channel 7's *Witness* show which happened to be filming Pauline at work that day. I was more than surprised when five of the students declared that they were in favour of some sort of National Service.

Pauline's matter-of-fact call for National Service generated a lot of media attention as well as good public reaction that started to come into the office from all over Australia. The first signs were emerging of a public response to her that would soon have the media referring to her as a 'phenomenon'.

ELEVEN

The Member for Oxley Raises her Hand

Sunday, April 28, 1996, was the day Australia froze in horror when a grinning madman slaughtered his way into history at Port Arthur. I arrived in Canberra that day to begin preparing for Pauline's big day — her swearing-in ceremony for the 38th Parliament of Australia, scheduled to take place on Tuesday, April 30, 1996. The moment would be overshadowed and marred by the terrible stories that continued to blaze forth from Tasmania.

The new Coalition government would start its term with the gutting and emotional 'Gun Debate'. A debate that would create deep divisions in the Australian electorate, and may be resolved at the next Federal Election. At Sale, in Victoria, Australians would see, for the first time in their country's history, their Prime Minister wearing a bullet-proof vest. A photograph taken from behind John Howard by Ray Strange of the *Australian* depicts the PM, clearly wearing the vest, addressing an open-air crowd with his arms raised in the 'I surrender' position. It is a dramatic photograph that will have an increased impact with the passing of time.

Pauline and her children by her second husband, Adam fifteen and Lee thirteen, were staying at the Garden City Motel with her mother, Mrs Hannorah Seccombe. I think I blotted my copybook for not asking Pauline's mother's permission to call her by her Christian name.

Chris Blackburn from Channel 7 Brisbane and Lane Calcutt from Channel 9 Brisbane were also staying at the motel, having flown down with Pauline to record her swearing-in for the Brisbane TV news. The pall from Port Arthur hung heavily over the national capital and it was obviously impossible at that time for the media to concentrate too hard on anything else.

On Monday, April 29, 1996, Pauline met Graeme Campbell for the first time, in her Canberra office. Further down the track, Graeme would regret ever having allowed me to go to Ipswich to help Pauline, but that is what politics is all about — the missed opportunities, the botched deals and the friendships made so easily and then just as easily broken. It is a grubby, wretched business.

Pauline Hanson was sworn-in to the 38th Parliament of Australia on the morning of Tuesday, April 30, 1996. Pauline was seated in the House of Representatives with the other independents. Graeme Campbell was on her right and, until he moved away from her, Peter Andren was on her left which was in keeping with his brand of 'soft' politics. Directly in front of Pauline were Alan Rocher and Paul Filing, the two Western Australian ex-Liberals. All the sanctimonious puff and wind from her motley assortment of enemies who had said they would stop her taking her seat in Parliament had been in vain. The first of many battles had been fought and won.

That evening Pauline and I had dinner at Roberto's in Manuka. I could not interest her in anything different from the run-of-the-mill menu items and she settled for lasagne. We went 'Dutch' as was always the case on the very few occasions that we dined out together.

Waiting for me in Pauline's office was Jackie McKimmie, a documentary maker from Brisbane, who had previously contacted me by telephone. She was with a male associate, and a hectic day was about to become just a little more so. McKimmie wanted to make a documentary film on Pauline's Parliamentary term, right up to and including the next election. She wanted the *whole* shooting match. Pauline in the Parliament, in her Parliamentary and electorate offices, at functions, electioneering, socialising, at home with the kids, at the kitchen sink, walking along the beach at Surfers Paradise, down at the Brisbane Fish Markets — McKimmie was waxing enthusiastically and, the more she did, the more I started to feel a great rush of scepticism, suspicion and doubt overtaking me. All my worst doubts were confirmed when I asked where the funding for such a project would be coming from. My blood started turning to battery acid when the ABC was finally mentioned!

Barbara Hazelton became very enthusiastic about the project and was quickly recruited by McKimmie to help convince Pauline, who was consequently subjected to a heady and seductive 'hard sell' along the lines of how important the film would be to Australian women, how it would become a vital part of the nation's political history and how it would help to enhance Pauline's image.

My barely contained thoughts were running in the opposite direction at a thousand miles an hour. The first reaction from any politician was sure to be one of wild enthusiasm about such great publicity. It is the stuff that most ministers would kill for. A mere backbencher presented with the opportunity for such publicity would ask, 'How many people do you want me to kill?'

I could see the treacherous quicksands that clearly lay ahead. The ABC's involvement was my best card to trump McKimmie's pitch. Pauline had 'banned' the ABC and, for obvious reasons, it would be witless and just plain stupid to let the ABC fund a documentary about her. I had visions of selected clips, showing Pauline in a bad light, being released to be aired at election time. Then there were all the other obvious debits — the added disruption to an office that was not running at all smoothly, the constant interruption of discussion when matters of confidentiality arose, undue pressure on Pauline in the office and at home (particularly when she was not in the best of moods), gaffes that would be impossible to correct, and the effect of all this on staff. After three years of that kind of orchestrated hell, Pauline and her office would be in absolute ruins. Well done, ABC!

I told Pauline that, for starters, I would leave the office every time the camera appeared. I told her about the enormous down-side of such an adventure and drove home very hard the fact that the funding for this project would be coming from the taxpayers through an organisation that we refused to speak to. Pauline had started talking about accountability with respect to ATSIC and other areas of government spending, so I thought I would use one of her own arguments against her.

I finally convinced Pauline to scrap the idea but McKimmie, not to be denied, then made another run on her — again with Barbara Hazelton's help. By this stage I was really gnashing my teeth at the persistent stupidity of people who had little idea of the mechanics of politics.

It took me from April 30 until June 6 to kill off the project well and truly. I was starting to have doubts about Pauline's basic political skills, but gave her the benefit of the doubt on this occasion. She was green and naïve and I could understand her being overwhelmed by someone wanting to make a film about her. It was high-octane, ego-boosting fuel. As for me, I had wasted a lot of valuable time and energy fighting a brushfire that should have been stamped out while it was just a flicker of flame. My pulse rate gave a healthy jump as I shredded the McKimmie file.

Brett Heffernan

Brett Heffernan, although only briefly in Pauline's employ, played a significant and pivotal role in her rise to political stardom.

Desperate to fill the 'B' position in Pauline's office, we advertised and were surprised at the large number of applications that came in — I thought, even in those early days, that working in Pauline Hanson's office would be off-limits for those looking for any sort of a career in mainstream politics.

I was hoping to be able to appoint someone from the Ipswich area so as to 'localise' the office. I was an 'outsider' and so was Barbara Hazelton, so it was important to correct the imbalance. Despite the fact that Ipswich and its environs are being rapidly gobbled up by metropolitan Brisbane, the long-term residents in the Ipswich area are decidedly parochial — dare I say xenophobic!

Try as I may, I could not get a local applicant 'up'. The ones I short-listed lacked even a glimmer of the hard political edge I was looking for. I finally settled on a young man who had previously worked in a senior National Party minister's office in Brisbane but, at the last moment, I was given an unfavourable reference for him. I discussed this with Pauline and we both agreed not to take the risk and appoint him, so it was back to the drawing board. Fate had raised its finger.

Next in line was Brett Heffernan, a twenty-six-year-old single journalist who was from Melbourne but living and working on the Gold Coast. He had worked for a time for an old PNG contact of mine, Denis Williams who is currently a senior writer for the *Aussie Post*. Williams spoke favourably of Brett, so we took the plunge and put him on. He had a degree in Journalism and Political Studies from Deakin University in Victoria. His political experience was limited, but he knew his way around a computer and seemed to have good communication and writing skills. I was prepared to compromise on the basis that Brett looked as if he would be a quick learner. I was right but I still had serious misgivings about now having two staffers who were over one hour's drive away from Ipswich. In times of crisis and work overload, you need people closer to the office than that. It was a handicap I had to bear but one that finally prevented me from lasting the distance.

Brett Heffernan started working for Pauline on Monday, May 20, 1996. He came to the position full of enthusiasm and confidence — telling me that he was looking forward to working for Pauline and doing his very best for her. He understood the challenges that lay ahead and knew that the going was likely to get tough. I told him that the road ahead would be pretty bumpy but, if we all supported each other, we would get through. It was a good start and, at last, I felt that I had a chance to stabilise the office and get it running more efficiently. I told Pauline that we would need to use Brett as a combined researcher and constituent advocate.

Pauline was quite rightly aware that she would need hard facts and figures to back up her general statements on issues. I was starting to fight too many battles on different fronts to be able to sit down and properly research all the issues, so Brett Heffernan was thrown into the deep end. As Pauline had ridden into the political arena on the back of the Aboriginal issue, it seemed appropriate that this be the starting point for some in-depth research.

Pauline had called for government benefits to be allocated on the basis of need, not the colour of one's skin, so I told Pauline that we would get Brett to do a comparative study of benefits paid to Aborigines versus those paid to non-Aborigines.

Brett got stuck into the project with great gusto and ended up working weekends on his home computer. In just twenty-four days he produced a twenty-eight page document, completely sourced from official government records. The research document was set out in two columns with the differences in benefits listed under headings. I stressed to Brett that he carefully double-check all his sources and reminded him that, if Pauline's critics could expose any flaws, I would cop the flak. I left it to him to work out where he would stand in the scheme of things in the event of such a disaster.

On Thursday, June 13, 1996, Brett Heffernan brought the completed research into the office. He was forty-five minutes late and he and I were to look back on that day as the start of the countdown to his planned resignation.

While I was waiting for Brett to turn up that morning, Barbara Hazelton announced, 'Brett's always late.' I had noticed that Brett managed to get into the office consistently after the starting time of 9:00 am, but usually no more than fifteen minutes late. Until Barbara started to make an issue of it, I was not going to. When Barbara and Brett started car pooling for a while, the problem was solved, but only temporarily.

Political offices are not your usual run-of-the-mill nine-to-five work-places. There must be a lot of give and take, and clockwatching is a petty and pointless exercise that serves no end. When Pauline, obviously alerted to Brett's lack of punctuality by Barbara, commented on the matter, I told her that getting the job done was the main objective. When I said, tongue-in-cheek, that Brett's research had been worth his year's salary, Pauline went 'ballistic'. She could not help but apply her rules and standards from the fish and chip shop to the running of her electorate office. Making her properly appreciate the difference was impossible during my time with her.

Barbara Hazelton then tried another tack. It was vital for Pauline to keep abreast with the print media and, to this end, I had organised Heidi Lewis to clip those newspapers not dealt with by the Parliamentary Library in Canberra, which does provide an excellent service with respect to the major dailies. The local papers were very important to us, especially the 'Letters to the Editor' columns. As Pauline attracted more media attention, the task was becoming very time-consuming and Heidi was required for work on the all-important computer. Barbara commented that Brett should be doing the clipping and she prattled on about what other offices did. For someone who had been out of the political loop for five years, Barbara should have been polishing her own skills. Wanting to release Heidi from this chore anyway, I told Brett Heffernan to take over, and to also read the important items and keep Pauline briefed.

It was obvious to me that any chance of a sound working relationship between Pauline and Brett had evaporated completely, almost before it even existed. In a bad mood, which was not that uncommon for her, particularly in the morning, Pauline made a catty, nasty and unnecessary remark about Brett 'spending most of his time reading the papers'. That was just too much and in a rush of frustration and exasperation I lost my temper, yelling at Pauline, 'Thank Christ someone is reading the papers, Pauline! Brett's a researcher, for Christ's sake! Of course he's reading the newspapers! He's looking for things that might concern you!'

When Brett Heffernan asked me what all the fuss had been about and I told him, his look of sheer incredulity and disappointment told me that he wouldn't be qualifying for long-service leave.

On Friday, June 14, 1996, I sent Brett Heffernan's research paper, covered by a press release, to all the media as well as to every State and Federal Parliamentarian in Australia. It was also mailed out Australia-wide to Pauline's ever-increasing support base. The research identified very clear differences in benefits, favouring Aborigines over non-Aborigines and, when presented in one document, the effect was emotive and powerful. Brett and I explained to Pauline that there existed a separate argument as to whether the extra benefits to Aborigines, in some instances, were justified because of their apparent particular disadvantage in those areas. Pauline insisted that everyone should be treated equally, particularly in metropolitan areas and it was reverse discrimination, for example, to grant cheap housing loans to Aborigines over working class non-Aborigines and to deny Austudy to non-Aboriginal prisoners while granting Abstudy to their Aboriginal counterparts.

The response to the research paper was immediate and spirited. Some conservative politicians applauded it, while those from the left faxed and mailed emotional and impassioned denunciations. One could just imagine the breast-beating and anguish of the authors. The Human Rights Commission redoubled its efforts to get Pauline to its 'kangaroo court' in

Sydney. Her supporters contacted her office for more copies of the research and, over a period of months, thousands went out.

It was obvious that the research had struck an already exposed nerve out there in mainstream Australia. Well may the Aboriginal 'industry' bemoan that its cause is not being applauded by the majority of Australians and that its extravagant plans are not being realised overnight. It only has itself to blame. Billions of taxpayers' dollars have been squandered to promote the views and ambitions of only 1.6 per cent of the overall population. The 1996 National Census figures, published in 1997, have increased that figure to 2 per cent. Ordinary, hard-working Aboriginal Australians have been betrayed by most of their self-appointed leaders who constantly appear on TV as sleek 'fat cats', all giving a good impression of trying to outdo Senator Colston.

The politicians can pander as much as they like to the 'chattering classes' and the 'pointyheads' drifting through academia. They can pass lofty and puffed-up resolutions, and make sombre and concerned 'apologies', but they will do so on their own while the majority of Australians look on, bemused and wondering, and becoming more and more resentful.

Trish Worth, the vapid Liberal MP for Adelaide who told me so pompously that she didn't 'speak to staffers', launched an attack on Pauline's research paper. But Brett Heffernan's swift and concise rebuttal, again quoting official sources, quickly silenced her. Worth later supported a Labor-sponsored motion in Parliament which, in typical gutless politician fashion, was directed at Pauline but failed to name her. The motion was moved by the formidable, over-coiffed, over made-up Janice Crosio, Labor MP for the NSW Seat of Prospect.

The final straw for Brett Heffernan came when Barbara boasted to him that, when things had been quiet while they were canvassing Harrisville, a semi-rural shopping centre on the western boundary of the electorate, she and Pauline had taken an afternoon off to go shopping in Brisbane. Pauline rang Brett from Brisbane to cancel an appointment with a person who had come from Townsville. After all the pettiness over his lack of punctuality, an enraged Brett told me there and then that he wanted to resign immediately, but there was more to come.

I was sitting with Pauline in her office one morning when she suddenly launched into Brett in a very spiteful and petulant way. 'Brett is a socialist!' she said. Due to my hearing problem, I asked Pauline to repeat herself, which she did. A video camera focused on my face would have shown rare perplexity and slack-jawed amazement. Quickly composing myself, I asked Pauline the reason for her outburst. 'Because he didn't agree with my National Service policy,' was her answer. I asked Pauline did she know the definition of 'socialist' and I didn't even get a 'Please explain!'

I was angry at Pauline's irrational treatment of Brett Heffernan. I would have expected most twenty-six year olds to be a bit wary of National Service anyway, and I told Pauline that a political office would be a very dull place without vigorous argument and debate. Barbara Hazelton had told me quite forcefully that she also opposed the policy. I wondered if she had taken this up with Pauline. It interested me that she spoke with such concern, as if Pauline actually had the political power to implement such a policy.

After that episode, I realised that I would need to get Brett out of the office before Pauline sacked him unfairly and blotted his good employment record. I was exasperated and disappointed. Brett wanted to resign immediately, but I prevailed on him to stay because I wanted time to plan and an undermanned electorate office was something I could do without. I decided not to tell Pauline of Brett's impending resignation because I was convinced that she would pre-empt his intention by sacking him. She at least understood that the office needed its full complement to operate, especially when Barbara left Ipswich to go to Canberra with her, so Brett was safe for the time being.

I had a good relationship with Bob Katter, the National Party MP for the Queensland Seat of Kennedy. David Thomas, who was to replace me briefly in Pauline's office in February 1997, was working for Katter while Brett was working for Pauline. Politics is an incestuous business. I told Bob Katter about my problem and, as chance would have it, he happened to be looking for a staffer for his Innisfail office, so Brett put in his application. Bob, quite rightly, did not want to do the wrong thing by Pauline, but I told him I would square off with her the best I could when the time came.

On Friday, September 20, 1996, Brett Heffernan resigned after his application with Bob Katter was successful. I was in Melbourne at the time but, on my return to Ipswich on the following Monday, Pauline had plenty to say. She was very vindictive about Brett and proved my fears correct when she said that she would have sacked him if she had known he intended resigning. She took his departure very personally and I think her pride and ego were dented. Slowly but surely, I was starting to see more and more of the real Pauline Hanson.

I told Pauline that Brett had strengthened her position immensely with his research paper. But she was very dismissive of his efforts and got cranky when I reminded her that I had to cajole her into thanking Brett for his excellent work. She then went on to say that she would tell Bob Katter that she had not been happy with Brett — and ended up doing so. But I beat her to the punch by getting in first and forewarning Brett and Bob. I tried to explain to Pauline that it was bad tactics declaring war on one's staff or ex-staff, that it served no good purpose and was totally non-productive. I was wasting my breath — I could have been talking to the cars passing in the street outside.

Brett Heffernan started his job with Pauline full of enthusiasm and determination to perform well. He resigned almost four months later to the day, unhappy and resentful at the treatment he had received. He had produced a piece of research that had defied a concerted attack by the Aboriginal 'industry', its 'chattering' supporters and wishy-washy politicians. Pauline rode on the back of this research — it gave factual credibility and emphasis to her argument. My mobile number was on the press release and, in 1997, I was still receiving calls inquiring about the research. Brett Heffernan joined a long list of men who, after falling out with Pauline, went away to become active or potential enemies. None remained friends. Brett's departure was a great blow to me but, after my much-chequered career, it took a lot to unsettle me. It was back to the drawing board.

THIRTEEN

Those Blasted Plants

All Federal Members of Parliament receive a one-off grant of $600 from the Department of Administrative Services, to be used for beautification of their electorate offices. Whatever is purchased with this grant remains the property of DAS and is not for the personal use of the members. The grant is usually spent on such items as framed prints, dried flower arrangements and the like and, in many offices, indoor plants are purchased.

In July 1996, Barbara Hazelton announced that she intended to smarten up the Ipswich office, using the $600 from DAS. It was necessary 'housekeeping', but not something with which I wished to become involved. I could see the point in having some sort of decor in the public reception area and, of course, in Pauline's office, as these were the two areas frequented by constituents and other visitors. A bit of sensible decoration would be in order, and it would brighten up the place a bit.

On returning to the office mid-morning one day, I was confronted by a veritable jungle of indoor potted plants of all shapes and sizes, lined up in the main office between the desks of Heidi Lewis and Brett Heffernan. I looked at Brett who looked back at me and then at the plants. He didn't need to say anything. 'The only thing missing here', I said, 'is Tarzan and Jane!' There were just too many plants and I could see, apart from anything else, that it would be a job just keeping them watered. Pauline seemed to be looking forward to working in this botanical garden and she ribbed me about putting some of the plants in my office. I would have none of that, telling her that there were just far too many of them and it would be a good idea to return some and use the money for other, more useful, items.

In the end, the plants were spread around the main office and Pauline's office. I managed to repel the green invasion and kept them out of my working space. In Pauline's office they were lined around the top of her bookshelves like soldiers on guard, shoulder to shoulder, down on the floor and flanking the entrance door.

Life in the jungle went on. Pauline was viciously attacked by Malcolm McGregor in the *Financial Review* on Monday, July 8, 1996, when he called her 'a lumpenproletariat hag'. I drafted a reply for Pauline, which was published and, on Wednesday, July 10, 1996, the thick-skinned McGregor telephoned her. I was amazed that Pauline even spoke to him, but was more amazed when she did so civilly. I thought that she would get stuck right into him, but she didn't. That afternoon, Pauline asked me to help her take some of the plants out of the office and down to her car which was parked in the underground carpark, one floor below. She had obviously realised that the 'greening' of her office had been a case of overkill. We made two trips, filling the boot, and then placed some smaller plants on the rear floor of her car. I told her that she should keep a few plants for her office and give the rest to one of the local nursing homes. Pauline and I were the last to leave the office that evening. She gave me a lift back to the Parkview Homestay where I lived when I was in Ipswich.

The following day Pauline and Barbara Hazelton went to the local shopping malls for 'meet and greet' sessions. I had suggested to Pauline that she do this every Thursday fortnight payday when she was in the electorate. These visits proved highly successful and provided good photo opportunities for the local papers.

That afternoon, Pauline asked me again to help her take some more plants out of the office to her car. This time we made just one trip. The indoor jungle was starting to thin out. Pauline said that a couple of the plants were dying and she thought that the air conditioning may have been affecting them. I wasn't particularly interested.

On Monday, August 26, 1996, Pauline took two more of the plants out of the office. This told me that the novelty had finally worn off. The 'plants' episode was just another trivial event that had nothing at all to do with politics but ended up causing political damage to Pauline. It was this sort of 'lead in the saddle bags' that was continually hampering me during my time with Pauline, as I tried in vain to establish a professionally run office with high levels of morale.

On November 22, 1996, Pauline featured on Channel 9's *Burke's Backyard* show as Don Burke's celebrity gardener. The backdrop was her 'farm' outside Ipswich. The potted plants that came into camera range certainly looked as if they could have been the same ones that Pauline had taken from her office. Pauline held her own on the show. At that stage, the last thing I was interested in was potted plants.

I became interested much later when I read the front page of the December 16, 1996, edition of the Brisbane *Courier-Mail* that had been faxed to me. The article dealt with a range of matters from Pauline's spending of her electorate allowance, to former Attorney General Michael Lavarch's allegations that Barbara Hazelton was 'a Labor sympathiser'. The article quoted 'former members of Ms Hanson's staff' who alleged removal of the by-now-becoming-famous pot plants. One of my Ipswich contacts told me that Pauline was blaming me for these leaks to the media, but she was wrong. At this stage five staffers, including myself, had left Pauline's office and four of them had left under very acrimonious circumstances. The story was interesting in that, apart from revealing details of Barbara Hazelton's alleged disloyalty to her ex-employer Peter Slipper, doubts were being raised by the journalist about Pauline Hanson's integrity. Perceptions are everything in politics and here was Pauline Hanson, the anti-politician, possibly behaving just like all the other mostly-despised politicians in the land. A person who constantly calls for accountability and honesty has a reputation to guard.

Shortly after the *Courier-Mail* article, Pauline Hanson was interviewed by Ron Casey on Sydney Radio Station 2GB. The transcript makes for interesting reading. In response to Casey asking, 'Could you tell me what the heck is going on?', Pauline replied, 'There's talk about these blasted plants I'm supposed to have taken home. I admit I took three home because they were dying with the air conditioning — my staff told me.' Casey then asked, 'Well plants, we're down to accusing you of taking plants?' Pauline then went into more detail about the plants by saying, 'Oh for crying out loud, you know, the fact is that if the media runs through some of their old footage they will see that all the plants have been here all the time. So yes, there is this, you know, to pull me down, to discredit me whatever way they possibly can and anyway.'

I read through the transcript again, just to clearly understand what Pauline had said.

The story of Pauline and the plants is peripheral to the real story underlying the whole sorry saga. It is a story of silliness and pettiness. The plants were, at some stage, brought back into the office. Brett Heffernan saw many more than three plants removed and other staff members would have noticed that most of the plants were missing. In retrospect I gave Pauline bad advice when I told her to give the plants to a local nursing home because, under the DAS guidelines, the plants were not her's to give away. I don't particularly care for indoor plants any more.

FOURTEEN

Reconciliation is a Dirty Word

Monday, May 27, 1996, saw the launch of Reconciliation Week and, after discussing with me the repercussions of this for her stand on the Aboriginal issue, Pauline decided to go on the attack. The following day I issued a press release and it took off like a rocket. The media response was like a pack of starved greyhounds running down a hare. The release stated:

'Reconciliation is a failed concept and should be abandoned. It is the creation of black activists and the "Aboriginal industry" and is designed to force present generations of mainly white Australians to acknowledge and accept guilt for what happened in the past,' said Pauline Hanson, the Independent Member for Oxley, commenting on the Prime Minister's launching of National Reconciliation Week.

'World history is full of man's inhumanity to man and Australian history is no exception. There are those, however, who are trying to rewrite or ignore our history. There are many well documented examples of horrific acts committed by blacks against blacks. Will the descendants of those blacks who cannibalised Chinese miners on the Palmer River in 1875 be required to bear the guilt of their forefathers?' she said.

'Mabo and the Native Title Act have set black against white and black against black. Apartheid is taking place before our eyes. A process of reconciliation forced down mainstream Australia's throat will be bitterly resented and dredging up the past serves no end. Aborigines who support me say that all they want is to be treated like ordinary Australians, with the opportunity to get a job and enjoy good health, education and housing,' Pauline Hanson said.

On Wednesday, May 29, Kerry-Anne Walsh from the *Bulletin* magazine contacted me at Pauline's Canberra office and asked for a 750 word article from Pauline on 'reconciliation' to be published in 'The Last Word', a one page opinion piece by a guest commentator appearing in the back pages of the magazine and sponsored by the National Australia Bank. I gave Pauline a briefing on the history of reconciliation and the lopsided view of our colonial history being pushed by the new wave of historical revisionists. She told me to write the piece and, after she checked it out, it was published in the June 11 edition of the *Bulletin*.

My comments on reconciliation, the day after the launch of Reconciliation Week, certainly spurred the Aboriginal Industry into action. It has developed over the years into a culture, feeding off the taxes of ordinary, hard working Australians. It has attracted a mix of black and white activists, politicians, academics, ex-politicians and people who see themselves as community leaders.

These people formulate policies that are largely at odds with mainstream Australia and they hold office by virtue of appointment by compliant governments. If criticised, they enlist the services of the pedlars of political correctness and reverse racism.

Since my election, I have been called 'white trash,' 'white cow,' a 'pig in the mud,' a 'dingo' and [one] female Aboriginal elder called for my hands and feet to be crippled! These insults have saddened rather than offended me, more so as they came from Aborigines.

There is a movement to create more than one Australia. We have a separate Aboriginal flag and it has been suggested that there should be 'protected' Aboriginal seats in our Parliaments. Mabo and the Native Title Act have created serious divisions in our society, particularly in rural areas. Black has been set against black and against white. It is a sorry state of affairs that has been created by politicians and judges, without reference to the people.

I have said that the concept of reconciliation is tarnished and should be abandoned and I do not retreat from this position. Reconciliation was designed to make today's white Australians plead guilty for what happened in the distant past and to pay compensation.

Before Captain Cook came to Australia, Aborigines were conducting tribal wars with horrific consequences. White settlement did not bring immediate peace to warring Aborigines and brought its own problems which are well documented elsewhere. But anthropologist T. G. H. Strehlow described in his 1969 work, *Journey to Horseshoe Bend*, a terrible massacre of blacks by blacks in 1875 in Central Australia, where infants had their limbs broken and were left to die 'natural deaths'. James Flett, a Victorian goldfields historian, describes the virtual genocide of one tribe by another prior to the arrival of white settlers. Manning Clark tells of the massacre and cannibalism of Chinese miners on the Palmer River in 1875. The list goes on and on.

It is because of this historical background that reconciliation as proposed by the Aboriginal 'industry' must fail. It is a biased, one-sided policy, which has absolutely no credibility with ordinary Australians. The past tells us what we have been and some of our history is not palatable but it is pointless to continually dredge up that past as, in the long run, this does not serve either side of the argument. Far better for all Australians to consider the past without acrimony and concentrate on ensuring that the future is worth looking to.

The other problem with reconciliation is that while some politicians share my views in varying degrees, the Party system denies them freedom of expression. This means that a lot of Australians are not being properly represented and that is bad for democracy. A process of reconciliation forced down mainstream Australia's throat will be bitterly resented and will ensure that divisions already

76

evident in our society remain. I speak with authority on this matter as, since my press release on reconciliation, the phones at my electorate office have been running hot from all over Australia. From past experience, I will get hundreds of letters of support. This is the best polling politicians can get.

Australia cannot afford to let itself be divided by the actions of a noisy, taxpayer funded minority. I am receiving support from Aboriginal people who take the view that their future lies in being treated just like other Australians, with the opportunity to get a job and enjoy good health, housing and a sound education for their children.

Aboriginal people have been poorly served in the main by those of their kind who were meant to serve them. The excesses of organisations like the Aboriginal and Torres Strait Islander Commission are under scrutiny and the real shame lies in the billions of dollars that have been squandered, failing to reach those really in need. The government must not buckle under to those forces within its ranks who have neither the courage nor the vision to correct the mistakes of the past while there is still time.

Australians can put the past behind them if they can see that they are being treated equally. We owe it to future generations to make sure this happens.

Pauline's *Bulletin* article triggered off another shock wave of media indignation and emotional attacks from the Aboriginal 'industry' and its conglomerates, including her continuing sparring partner, the Human Rights Commission. The National Australia Bank withdrew its sponsorship of 'The Last Word' column, obviously not considering those thousands of Hansonites who banked with it.

Pauline received a $500 fee from the *Bulletin* and I told her I would go her halves for having written the article. She gave me cash but then realised later that she would be required to pay tax on the full amount. She was not very happy. I must make sure my accountant declares my share.

'Reconciliation' has been discounted like a lot of other words in our vocabulary. 'Gay' has been stolen by the homosexuals. 'Racist' has been used so many times in the wrong context that it is now totally valueless. 'Reconciliation' is rapidly heading down the same track. Billions of taxpayer's dollars have been spent on Aborigines who represent only 2 per cent of the Australian population. More and more the question is asked, 'How many of this number are "real" Aborigines?' The perception is fast growing that 'Aboriginality' is becoming yet another rort directed at the taxpayers of Australia by a mushrooming group of 'pretenders', eager to jump on board the gravy train.

Against a backdrop of Mabo, Native Title and now Wik, genuine reconciliation seems an impossible dream that should never have been conjured up in the first place. Totally unrealistic expectations have been raised in the ranks of the Aboriginal 'industry' — beginning with Hawke promising a treaty to be written into the Constitution, supported by a gaggle of self-serving devotees in academia and the media, arriving at the Reconciliation Convention meeting in Melbourne in May 1997 calling for a 'People's Movement' to be funded, of course, out of the public purse. Mainstream Australia gives the distinct impression of being singularly 'turned off', the more it is assailed and moralised at by self-righteous unctuous ex-judges, judges, big business and big mining mouthpieces, Aboriginal demagogues and even the Governor-General playing to an audience stacked with a kaleidoscope of multiculturalists, apologists for the rest of us, and a veritable pot-pourri of whingers and breast beaters.

'Real' Aboriginal Australians have been poorly served by their mainly self-promoted and appointed leaders who, during most of 1997, have seemed to spend most of their time blackmailing ordinary Australians over the 2000 Olympics and threatening to call on their ragtag mates in the United Nations for international trade sanctions against their own country. The white backlash against these crazy and primitive threats will ferment like pus in a boil until it is released by the lancing effect of a related election issue such as Wik.

Kim Beasley and Gareth Evans, the new politically-correct crybabies of the Labor Party, stifling their sobs during the May 1997 Parliamentary debate on reconciliation, were received with the embarrassed silence afforded them by the majority of ordinary Australians. Kim Beasley speaking in Parliament choked back his sobs on the 'Stolen Children' issue and repeated the performance on the death of Princess Diana. Where are his tears for our unemployed youth and older Australians? Where are his tears for the small businessman gone broke, or the farmer thrown off his farm by a bank? Mr Beasley I assume, wants to be PM. If he were and missiles were raining down on Darwin, would he be able to offer calm, dry-eyed leadership? Australians want Prime Ministers and leaders who can be compassionate and generous without losing control. Hawke ended up a laughing stock for his repeated and boring doses of crocodile tears.

The politicians can apologise as many times as they like. They can pass bipartisan motions and shovel out more money to those with their hands out. 'No reconciliation without monetary compensation' was the cry of one not-so-black leader in May 1997 when contributing to the debate on the 'Stolen Children' issue. Any parties with a grievance in this area will need to do what the rest of us must do — go and give a lot of money to those people that wear wigs.

The one missing part of this equation is the most important — the majority of mainstream Australians who have had their patience so sorely tested that, many of their number, angry and frustrated, have defected to the Hanson camp where they will remain, surly and brooding until the next election. The politicians have no hope of obtaining their freely-given support and cooperation in a process long discredited and out of control. It is like a puny dentist trying to shift a deeply imbedded and stubborn wisdom tooth.

If there were to be a double dissolution over John Howard's Ten Point Plan on Wik, the result would be crushing for the Labor Party, but the hopes and aspirations of decent, Australian Aborigines would be smashed to smithereens forever. The Left of the Labor Party acknowledge the devastation that could occur, but say that they would be able to 'sleep with a clear conscience'. How precious and smug. Some sleep.

FIFTEEN

Pistol Packing Pauline

As John Howard approached the halfway mark of his government, his only really decisive and positive action was his stand during the so-called 'Gun Debate'. Like the so-called 'Race Debate' there was never any sensible and proper debate, just uncontrolled emotion and anger on both sides, with the Howard Government coming down hard on a couple of vacillating State premiers. It was an ugly and un-Australian time, brought about when a biological time bomb exploded in Martin Bryant's brain. That was one of those events that prompt commentators to say things like, 'This was the day Australia lost its innocence.' It was certainly a day that most of us will never forget and a lot of us quite correctly ask, 'Where has the Australia gone that we once knew?'

It is just not good enough for some among us to say that we must change with the times, if changing means replacing tried and tested systems and values with models that fail and break down. When John Howard wore a bullet proof vest to address an open-air crowd at Sale in Victoria, it was another milestone in Australian history. The Prime Minister's safety is paramount but John Howard, the man, was telling his fellow Australians that he didn't trust them. He was poorly advised.

Ted Drane was the president of The Sporting Shooters' Association of Australia (SSAA) at the time of the 'Gun Debate'. He is based in Melbourne and, over the past few years, as public concern over guns has developed and increased, Ted Drane has appeared in the media and on TV and radio talkback, putting the case for sensible and responsible firearm use.

I had spoken to Ted Drane when I had been working on Graeme

Campbell's campaign in Kalgoorlie. I re-established contact with him from Pauline's office and he said that he was interested in getting Pauline and Graeme together to talk about general strategy on the gun issue. Pauline was basically sympathetic to Ted Drane's line and I told her that with the very high number of gun licence holders in her electorate she would need to tread carefully. When I checked with the Firearms Licensing Registry in Brisbane I found that, in Pauline's electorate of Oxley, 22.5 per cent of people over fifteen years of age had licences. In the Toowoomba area, which is to the south of Ipswich, the figure ran close to 40 per cent. It looked as if there were people out there getting ready for World War III!

Pauline flew to Melbourne on Sunday, May 19, 1996, and linked up with Graeme Campbell and Ted Drane. Ted took them both to his association's firing range at Little River near Geelong, where they were given a demonstration of various firearms. Pauline and Graeme then had some practice with various weapons. Pauline fired a .22 rifle but I was told she was no 'Annie Oakley'. On Saturday, June 1, 1996, the pro-gun lobby held a rally in Melbourne. According to Ted Drane over 100 000 people attended. Aerial photos were taken of the crowd and then gridded to arrive at a crowd count. A lot of country people travelled to the city to lodge their protest against what they saw as the severity of the proposed new gun laws. It was, as much as anything else, a protest by country people against the 'city slickers' who controlled their lives from the comfort of Federal and State Parliament houses and from the boardrooms of big business.

On Wednesday, June 5, 1996, I asked Brett Heffernan to do a street poll in Ipswich on the proposed new gun laws. He asked a simple question: 'Are you in favour or not of the proposed new gun laws?' He received an almost 50–50 result, which surprised me a little as I thought the negative response would have prevailed. John Howard's proposal seemed to have struck a chord with the younger voters (30s and lower), particularly women. Older voters (the 40s-plus, who make up the overwhelming bulk of the electorate of Oxley) were against the new laws, on the basis of everything from freedom of choice to the need for self-defence. I showed the results to Pauline and advised her that she would need to perform a fine political balancing act in order not to lose too many voters from either side of the argument.

On Thursday, July 4, 1996, Ted Drane came to Ipswich to see Pauline. He had an ABC reporter with him who was forced to cool his heels for three hours while Ted and Pauline talked, due to Pauline's ban on his employer. Ted and Pauline got on well together and Ted said that he had no desire to put any pressure at all on Pauline to join his Australia Reform Party. He also said that, come election time, his organisation would help her with some advertising bills and, more importantly, with manpower to assist at her polling booths. There were over one thousand Sporting Shooters' Association members in Pauline's electorate before the Port Arthur massacre and this number increased during the fallout after the event, as sporting shooters started to organise themselves. Ted Drane's offer was generous and I was pleased that his meeting with Pauline had been so productive.

The only movie theatre in Ipswich is directly opposite Pauline's office. After Ted Drane had left to drive back to Brisbane, I felt like relaxing and walked across the road to switch off for a couple of hours. As I sat in the darkness, I mused about the bumpy and difficult road that lay ahead. The feature film was *Mission Impossible* and I wondered if there was a message for me in that.

When he returned to Melbourne, Ted Drane kindly offered Pauline space to state her views in the September issue of the SSAA *Australian Shooter's Journal*. I seized on the opportunity because the magazine, which has a circulation of 65 000, would be the vehicle for the precursor to the maiden speech. It would also give Pauline a chance to air her policy on guns. I wrote the article, checked it out with Pauline and then faxed it to South Australia where the magazine is printed. The article was entitled 'An Independent Speaks':

The horror of Port Arthur has blotted Australia's history and the relatives of the victims will have to live with the terrible memories until the day they die. It serves no purpose to pretend Port Arthur did not happen. However, we must be sensible and deal with its

effects in a rational and balanced way. I am now more firmly of
the opinion that the Federal government could have handled the
problem differently.

The question of gun control embraces many complex issues and
must be considered in the light of informed public opinion. Debate
on such an important matter should not become the property of a
particular lobby group. Many of the issues have not been properly
debated, given the action taken by Canberra against a backdrop of
public emotion and revulsion at the alleged criminal deeds of one
person. The issues that stand out are the ownership of guns, the
persistent erosion of community values, Canberra's rights over
those of the States, the intrusion into the leisure time of its citizens
by Government, and fair and just compensation.

The world we live in is not a Utopian fairyland, nor is it ever
likely to be. The world today is a dangerous place with international terrorists wreaking their vengeance side by side with
tribal, political and religious wars on most of the major conti-
nents. Australia has managed to remain sovereign and free from
the horrors that have beset many other countries and we owe
it to future generations to ensure we pass on a united and strong
nation. We can only do that if we resist the pressures from
various minority groups that are seeking to create more than one
Australia.

Australians have always had a relationship with firearms. We
have used them in times of war and may have to do so again. We
have used them for recreation and sport and our first Gold Medal
in Atlanta was won by a young trapshooter, closely followed by
another Gold and Bronze in the Double Trap events.

It would not seem unreasonable to allow law-abiding citizens to
own certain types of firearms simply because they want to. It is a
measure of how dramatically times have changed to consider that
after World War II the Australian government dumped thousands
of military .303 calibre rifles on the market at the equivalent of $5
each and ammunition was freely available. At that time there were

no licensing requirements and there were no horrific shootings involving these firearms.

One alarming aspect of the present so-called debate is that a large cross-section of the ordinary Australian community has been vilified by journalists and cartoonists as bloodthirsty, murderous killers. Sensible, law-abiding men and women risk the prospect of being treated like criminals, facing sentences more severe than some of those handed out to rapists and armed thugs. Given the changed times, I acknowledge the need for change in firearm ownership requirements. Anyone convicted of crimes involving serious violence should never be allowed to own a firearm, nor should those with a history of mental illness. There should be a cooling-off period of one month before possession could be effected. I can see no reason why semi-automatic, conventional firearms should be prohibited.

Why have terrible serial killings, many involving female victims raped, beaten and strangled, become more evident in recent years? Why has thoughtless, brutal violence spread into our streets and homes? There is no doubt in my mind that the shocking violence on our movie and television screens has increased dramatically over the past thirty years, together with the violence that the family can view during the evening news. To this element must be linked the erosion of traditional family values and soaring unemployment. Add the government policies that create suspicion and instability in the general community and one has the ingredients for a potent cocktail leaving a devastating hangover.

There is increasing evidence that young people especially can be heavily affected by continued exposure to graphic violence which is often combined with explicit pornography. They become callous and insensitive and resort to violence to solve their problems. So-called amusement venues attract youngsters to play video games that leave nothing to the imagination and for the really young there are violent cartoons to watch. Sensible censorship would seem to be part of the solution but there is still a noisy,

trendy, politically-correct group that says censorship is old fash-
ioned and a contravention of civil liberties. One must also remember that the movie and video industry is a very powerful lobby
group with friends in high places. I feel that Canberra is not doing
what it should in this area. The V-chip is not the answer. Part of
the answer is to set up a censorship board, better able to tap into
mainstream Australian sentiment and then to act accordingly.

Economic and political policies can contribute to the erosion of
community values. The bipartisan support of economic theories has
resulted in the loss of many Australian jobs to our overseas competitors and our manufacturing base has been seriously reduced.
Many of our once prosperous rural areas are now economic waste-
lands with young people drifting to the cities where they only find
more problems. It seems crazy that we are importing chicken, fish,
fruit and vegetables. Deregulation has destroyed many small businesses which find themselves being crushed between big business
and big government.

It may be hidden by the way statistics are compiled these days
but there is reason to believe the unemployment queue is in reality
about one-and-a-half million people long and that is reason for
grave concern. High youth unemployment is a cancer that attacks
the future prosperity of this country and there is a ratio between
it, drugs and an increase in crime. The saddest and most revolting
crimes are those where our senior citizens are attacked by young
criminals.

Other bipartisan policies of immigration and multiculturalism
have helped to create fear and uncertainty in the general community. Mainstream Australians find themselves competing for jobs
with migrants, many of whom are unskilled and lack fluency in
English. Multiculturalism and the policy of separatism in respect of
Aborigines are creating more than one Australia where the majority
can see taxpayer funded ghettoes being established.

It is often productive to look back at history. In 1961, the Prime
Minister, Robert Menzies, almost lost the Federal Election because

unemployment was running at 2 per cent! Australians tolerated unemployment at 10 to 12 per cent for years under a Labor Government, so we have all changed a lot. In those days of high employment and low interest rates, the general community was much more stable and secure.

It is vital that small business be freed from incentive-killing taxes like Capital Gains Tax, so it can expand and start employing more people. Governments have to decide whether or not to encourage the manufacturing sector, and rural policy has to be changed to stop country centres becoming ghost towns. Australians must shoulder much of the responsibility for our present predicament. Militant unionists helped give us a bad reputation as unreliable producers and suppliers and Australian workers in many areas of industry let their production rates decline, thus giving the advantage to our competitors. A busy, industrious community is usually a happy one and that is far from the situation today.

It is difficult to challenge the Government's rush to claim the high ground over Port Arthur. Things could have been done differently however, in the sense that more consultation and discussion should have taken place after the initial rush of emotion and anguish had subsided. Canberra has resorted to intimidating the States with the threat of a referendum on the gun issue and that is unfortunate. It is a little like the bullyboy tactics employed by Hawke and Gareth Evans over the Franklin River, on the basis that right was on their side. In the present debate, ordinary law-abiding Australians have been cast in the role of villains and their cause has not been helped by the ratbag antics of a few.

In the present economic and political climate, the Howard Government has serious problems with its real enemies in the Senate, the Democrats and the Greens, who must be welcoming with a degree of relief the problems being encountered by the Coalition with many of its supporters. The Government would be reckless in the extreme if it were to run a $52 million referendum on firearms, followed by an equally expensive double dissolution.

Canberra's attack on recreational and sporting shooters is the first time a government has seriously intruded on the leisure time of its citizens and this is of great concern. It is an essential element of democracy that law-abiding citizens be allowed to spend their leisure time as they see fit, provided they do not interfere with others. Under proposed legislation, many restrictions will be imposed which will have the effect of limiting the enjoyment of their leisure time by many Australians.

The implementation of new gun legislation brings attention to the question of compensation. Under draft proposals, planned compensation is a joke and will result in severe loss to those involved. Apart from firearms, shooters like fishermen spend a lot of money on accessories ranging from reloading gear and clothing through to camping gear, airfares, accommodation and motor vehicles. Arbitrary and unfair compensation will result in serious financial loss not only to gun owners but to the mainly small business community who serve them. These are facts obviously overlooked by the Prime Minister's advisers. If compensation was fair and based on market value and included all those accessories that complement sporting shooters, Mr Costello's black hole would become bottomless.

The State Governments have buckled under to Canberra's threat of a referendum and the scene is now set for a protracted political battle leading up to the next election. New laws will only affect the overwhelming majority of law-abiding citizens. Criminals and those with other sinister motives will never give up their guns. From all reports, there is already a flourishing black market and just as large quantities of illegal drugs are smuggled into Australia with apparent ease, what will stop the illegal entry of firearms?

The lopsided debate on the issue and Canberra's threat of a referendum have set Australians against each other and sent the clear message that the Government no longer trusts a large number of

its citizens nor its State Governments. Those Coalition Parliamentarians who were so vocal in the past about States' rights are now
so silent. I would have supported a referendum on firearms laws
if it had been expanded to include questions on immigration, multiculturalism and Aboriginal funding — divisive issues that again
threaten to create more than one Australia.

As an Independent MP who has been described as 'controversial'
(I prefer to call myself just an ordinary Australian), I receive letters,
faxes and phone calls from all over Australia and the impression I
get is that the Coalition could suffer losses in many rural and maybe
a few metropolitan Seats at the next election. One thing is certain.
The Government's conduct will be greatly resented and never
forgotten.

The article was received very favourably and we got good feedback in
the office. It helped set the tone for the forthcoming maiden speech and I
hoped that those sporting shooters in Pauline's electorate would remember
her stand when the next election came around.

I think I had positioned Pauline, as well as I could, in the middle of the
road on the gun issue. She was not being extremist one way or the other
but she would not be able to appease the strident anti-gun lobby and,
hopefully, there were not too many of its members in Oxley.

Pauline's delicately poised balancing act on the gun issue was almost
upset later with the publication of the book, *Pauline Hanson — The Truth*
which appeared at the launch of One Nation on April 11, 1997. The words
were not from the mouth of Pauline Hanson but, in a chapter dealing with
the gun debate, an argument was mounted for the return of semi-automatic
rifles to the Australian marketplace. 'It will be good to see the latest Colt
AR-15 on our gun shelves again,' the article said. This was the weapon
used by the mass-murderer Martin Bryant at Port Arthur. I found it amazing
that the people around Pauline had obviously not vetted the book that
bore her name.

In late August 1996, Pauline and I drove down to Brisbane to attend a
briefing on the new Queensland gun laws, held in Police Minister Russell

Cooper's office. Pauline quickly established a rapport with a couple of the hard-headed police officers there and, by the end of the meeting, had been fully advised as to how to apply for a firearms licence. She told me that she would be obtaining a weapon as soon as possible and I later accompanied her to the Ipswich Police Station to fill in the relevant forms. Journalists, protesters and political opponents beware!

TV or not TV

Federal backbenchers each receive a $26 076 per annum electorate allowance in addition to their salaries, to assist them in the performance of their duties in their electorates. The guidelines governing this allowance are extremely liberal and open to generous interpretation. According to the Department of Administrative Services, while there is an expectation that the allowance will be used in the service of the electorate, there is no clear rule that says this. The tax man is the ultimate arbiter of the electorate allowance come tax-return time. If the monies are expended on items or services that assist in the member's performance in the electorate, those expenditures are not taxed. If a member cares to, he or she can take the whole amount to the racetrack and give it to the 'bagmen' but, come tax time, will pay the top tax rate.

Politicians who apply the allowance properly and appropriately, use the money in a variety of ways. Some members use it to help needy causes in the electorate, to provide plaques and awards for sporting and other competitions, to create modest scholarships and do other good works.

It is amazing that, in this age of technology and communications, Federal backbenchers do not have TVs and video recorders provided in their electorate offices as they have in their Canberra offices. It is essential that members keep abreast of all the news and current affairs shows if they want to keep on the political pace.

It was August, 1996, when I told Pauline that we needed a TV and a video recorder (VCR) for her Ipswich office. It would be useful for both of us, especially when we were working back late — which I did all the time when I was in town. The Parliamentary Library provides a video-taping facility for members, which is a valuable research tool and, as Pauline became more embroiled in controversy, it was vital to see what was being said about her. I told Pauline that it would be in order to buy a TV and a VCR for the office, using her electorate allowance. For reasons of economy, I suggested that second-hand units be bought.

Opposite Pauline's Ipswich office is an outlet for R. T. Edwards, Ipswich's largest whitegoods retailer. The store has a section set aside for second-hand items and I was quoted $400, after a discount, for a colour TV with a built-in VCR. The item was compact and could be carried by one person. It was ideal for what I had in mind. I told Pauline about the deal and she said that she would think about it. I put the matter to one side while I concentrated on some minor legal problems concerning the electorate that Pauline was required to deal with. A solicitor had been briefed and I felt comfortable with paying his fees from Pauline's electorate allowance. To this end, I asked Barbara Hazelton what the balance of the electorate allowance account was, as the account was her responsibility. The allowance was paid in monthly instalments so needed to be budgeted reasonably carefully. When I asked Barbara how much money was in the account her reply surprised me. She told me that there wouldn't be that much left in credit, '. . . after Pauline has paid for that TV.' Wondering what that meant, I went back to what I was doing.

That afternoon there was a knock on the rear door of the office, adjacent to where I was working. On opening the door, I saw two R. T. Edwards employees standing there with a trolley carrying a very large, wide-screen TV set — one of those that is installed in its own cabinet with space for a VCR and video storage. Somewhat taken aback, I made room for the two men. Barbara Hazelton told them to put the TV set down between her desk and that of Brett Heffernan. Pauline was not in the office when the TV arrived but, when she did appear, my enquiries about it didn't get very far. That afternoon, I left the office before dark.

The next day, the TV set that had been sitting in the middle of the main office like an imposing, glossy robot from a *Star Wars* movie had gone. Its presence in Pauline's office had been fleeting, to say the least. It had obviously been removed sometime the previous evening and all I could do was wonder why it had come to the office in the first place. I later noticed that a small, almost portable-size colour TV and accompanying VCR had appeared in Pauline's office. These units were obviously second-hand.

The new TV had been purchased out of Pauline's electorate allowance, together with a VCR, and had now been taken to Pauline's farm. A TV and VCR from Pauline's home had been brought back into the office to satisfy the need for this equipment that I had drawn to Pauline's attention. I was mystified as to all the sleight-of-hand that had taken place with the TV sets and felt it was in order to ask Pauline what had been going on. When I broached the subject with her she didn't want to talk about it. Her body language and her hard-set jaw and eyes told me I was straying into dangerous territory.

It was obvious what had happened. Pauline had upgraded her TV and VCR with her electorate allowance which, to my way of thinking, contravened the spirit and expectation behind the granting of it. Having the TV delivered to her office and then removed the same day to her out-of-the-electorate residence was unusual and unnecessary to say the least. Why didn't R. T. Edwards just make the delivery direct from the store to Pauline's farm? Had R. T. Edwards been told that the TV was for Pauline's office because it was paid for with a cheque drawn on her office account? Did this make it important that the set be delivered to her office? Why was the TV removed under the cover of darkness and who transported it to the farm? It was becoming increasingly clear to me that the person who preached so fervently and frequently about the necessity for accountability in politics had, herself, quickly fallen victim to the insidious virus of double standards.

Reports in Pauline's local paper, the *Queensland Times* on April 4, 1997, were to place the value of the TV and VCR at $2500. This has not been disputed by her. Over one month's electoral allowance had been wiped out by one indulgent purchase that had not one skerrick of political merit in it.

SEVENTEEN

The Maiden Speech — Conception and Gestation

Peter Wilkinson of *60 Minutes*, described Pauline Hanson's maiden speech as '. . . this beautifully crafted speech.' Tracey Curro of *60 Minutes* said on screen that, 'The maiden speech that inflamed Australia was a masterpiece of headline grabbing and rare eloquence'. Michelle Grattan of the *Australian Financial Review*, described it as 'inflammatory'. The *Australian/Israel Review* said it '. . . was anti-Asian, anti-Aboriginal, anti-United Nations and until the last minute anti-homosexual'. In a letter to the *Australian*, Tricia Caswell of the international aid agency PLAN International was beside herself. 'Whatever we think, whatever we do, the demons unleashed by Pauline Hanson's maiden speech in Parliament are with us. It seems they are not going to go away. As an Australian I am shocked. I am ashamed,' she said. Peter Robinson of the Murdoch press referred to the speech as 'famous, if not notorious'. Virginia Trioli of the *Age* drew attention to 'the meaty sound-bites' in the speech. Gerard McManus, the Canberra press gallery man for the Melbourne *Sunday Herald Sun* advised that, 'People should read it,' and went on to say that Pauline Hanson's maiden speech was, 'The most widely discussed but least read speech in the history of the Australian Parliament.' Philip Adams, the oft caftanned ABC and media *enfant terrible*, labelled the speech 'wildly eccentric'. Frank Devine of the *Australian* referred to it as '. . . her feather-headed populist speech'. Geoff Kitney of the *Sydney Morning Herald* had this to say, 'Yet it was an extraordinary first speech. A maiden speech the likes of which the Australian Parliament has not heard before.' Many sub-editors called the speech 'famous and controversial'.

Depending on who one listens to, Pauline's maiden speech is most famous or infamous speech in Australia's political history. In this age of communication, the speech travelled on the international information highway at breakneck speed, attracting attention wherever it beamed down to Earth. If there are aliens out there, their security forces must have been on 'red alert'!

The media response to Pauline Hanson's maiden speech was like a swarm of blowflies trapped in a very large, not long empty, pickle bottle sitting in the midday sun. The expletives and invectives rained down like shrapnel at the front line of an artillery barrage. Many journalists and commentators fed off each other in a way not unlike a pack of rabid curs snapping and cutting at each other. It was obvious from much of their often hysterical reporting that most of them had not read the speech. The onslaught continued into 1997 with little respite, battle lines clearly drawn between supporters and detractors.

During discussions with Pauline in the first week of April 1996 about what her political priorities would be, I had told her that her first and most important job as a new politician would be the preparation and delivery of her maiden speech. To better acquaint her with what lay ahead, I went to the Parliamentary Library and obtained the maiden speeches of Graeme Campbell, John Howard, Paul Keating and Ted Mack. I gave Pauline copies of the speeches to read and then discuss with me, but that never happened — simply because she never got around to reading them. I was disappointed by this first evidence of Pauline's lack of capacity to concentrate, read and absorb knowledge. I was expecting more from a person who obviously had a lot of learning to do in a very short time.

I read all four of those maiden speeches and found them interesting. I noted Keating's very important comments about immigration where he said in March 1970:

It is time we considered the enormous cost of bringing migrants to this country.

[Keating then went on to suggest a system of subsidies to encourage larger Australian families by saying:]

After all, the best migrant is the infant Australian.

Those who bleat the loudest in blind and unthinking support for our present multicultural and immigration policies get decidedly uncomfortable when these Keating lines are dusted off and quoted. The Roman Catholic Keating of 1970 was far removed from the 1997 model. He was entitled to change his views but, in this case, he changed his whole philosophy. Did he really intend to, or was he putting on a show for the multicultural elitists who have so much disproportionate control over all politicians?

John Howard's maiden speech is what one would expect of a young Liberal suburban solicitor eager to get on. I graded the speeches: Campbell, Mack, Keating then Howard. Somehow, I don't think the Prime Minister will lose much sleep as a result of being marked down by me.

I started writing Pauline's maiden speech in her Ipswich office on Sunday, April 21, 1996. I had, as references, my PNG Parliamentary *Hansards* from 1964 to 1968, speeches I had written for others and myself, plus letters to the editors of various newspapers and published and unpublished newspaper articles — all spanning the period from 1964 to 1995. In 1964, when I gave my maiden speech, Pauline Hanson was just ten years old.

I told Pauline that maiden speeches were usually boring, mundane affairs that were necessary but needed to be got rid of quickly — a little bit like drinking castor oil to relieve constipation. Newly-elected politicians still feeling grateful towards their electorates for having been chosen to wallow in the golden Parliamentary trough, filled their maiden speeches with boring trivial detail and statistics about their electorates — quoting how many schools, churches and hospitals there are and almost quoting the number of street crossings controlled by traffic lights. These speeches quickly disappeared without trace into that great void of *Hansard*, the Parliamentary reference library, to be dredged up from the verbose ooze now and again by the odd PhD student. Being an independent, Pauline had the opportunity for a freedom of speech not available to many others in the public eye. She did not 'owe' anyone in the political sense and she could not be restricted in any way by policies or other constraints imposed on members of political Parties. I stressed to her that she only had one shot at her maiden speech and it had to be a good one. I told her she would need to be controversial in order to build on her stand regarding the Aboriginal issue and her call for National Service. It had been only recently that I had started talking to her about the history of Australia's immigration policy and the taxpayer funded policy of multiculturalism — issues in which Pauline clearly had no real backgrounding.

When I sat down at the word processor on that Sunday in April 1996, I knew pretty well what I was going to write. The basic themes were all there in my files, together with a lot of the actual language. It all just needed developing and to be adapted to Pauline's appreciation of the issues while keeping the language plain and simple, in tune with her vocabulary. I wanted to get a first draft out quickly so that she could start reading the speech and practising her delivery, which needed dramatic improvement.

Pauline was aware of her problem. She told me how nervous she became when speaking in public and that clearly worried and annoyed her. When she gave her Anzac Day speech, I told her that I would stand in front of her and she was to imagine I was naked. Pauline cracked up about that and I told her that me *au naturel* would bring the house down!

Pauline has a decided Queensland vocal 'twang' and, when she spoke publicly, she became much more nasal. The comedians have had a field-day at her expense. At times she sounded very whining indeed and, on these occasions, gave the impression that she was about to cry. I think, at these times, she would start to become frustrated and angry with herself and this would bring a telltale teary sparkle to her eyes. When she was telling me about this problem, I felt sorry for her predicament — it obviously caused her a lot of distress.

The week before I started writing the maiden speech, I organised a 250-word weekly column for Pauline, entitled 'Speaking Out', with her photo-portrait as the logo. This important vehicle was in the *Advertiser*, a local Ipswich free paper with a very high circulation. The column excited a lot of interest and allowed Pauline to stay in touch with the electorate. I wrote the inaugural column with small business, farmers and blue-collar workers in mind — Pauline's base constituency. The first column went to print on Wednesday, April 24, 1996, and carried the following message:

Small business, farmers and the men and women who work with these sectors are the real heroes of the Australian economy.

The unemployment queues in Australia are now over one million people long and youth unemployment has reached national crisis level. Politicians and economists seem unable to find positive solutions.

Business activity is geared to incentive and people will invest and work hard if they can see positive results at the end of all the hard grind. The Hawke Government robbed small business and the farmers in one fell swoop at the 1985 Tax Summit when he imposed a Capital Gains Tax [CGT]. [Capital Gains Tax] collections grew from $89 million in 1988 to $631 million in 1991.

In 1994–1995 the government took a massive $1.8 billion. [Capital Gains Tax] now affects a broad cross section of taxpayers including those who contribute to superannuation funds.

[Capital Gains Tax] taken by the government is really capital taken away mainly from small business and the farmers. This means less investment and less job opportunities.

The total abolition of CGT would result in a huge surge of activity in the private sector. Incentive would be restored to a sector which has the capacity to go out and employ more Australians.

Abolition of CGT would mean spending cuts but just look at some of the scandalous waste during the past thirteen years.

John Howard once said he would abolish CGT but then changed his mind. It is now time that he reviewed his position.

That column broke new ground in the once safe Labor Seat of Oxley and gave Pauline some political 'muscle', pushing a line radically opposed to Labor's anti-small-business stand. The introduction of the CGT by Hawke and his big business mates in 1985 dealt small business, and small farmers in particular, a near mortal wound that can only be healed by total repeal. None of the current crop of coalition politicians seem to want to talk about it because they have their feet well and truly nailed to the floor by their party bosses. I tried to make 'Speaking Out' as hard hitting as possible and the feedback gave it the 'thumbs up'.

Towards the end of May 1996, I had completed the first draft of the maiden speech and gave it to Pauline, telling her to practise reading it in front of a mirror. I told her to just try and get the words flowing to see if she was comfortable, and not to worry too much about the content at that stage. I impressed on her that she should have the speech completed and polished well ahead of time. I hate rushing things at the last moment as so much can go wrong. It did!

The production of the completed maiden speech, in fact, almost became a monumental miscarriage. If that had been the case, Pauline most certainly would never have had that spectacular, jet-propelled launch into the polit- ical stratosphere. While I was busily occupied fighting battles on different fronts, it escaped my notice for a while that there were a lot of distractions coming from different quarters.

I was finding it very difficult to get Pauline to concentrate on appreciating the draft speech and then discussing it with me. She accused me of nagging her about it, until one morning she said, 'It's not *me.*' She went on to say that she felt uncomfortable with some of the language, but I felt she was using this as a smokescreen. Right from the first draft I used the plainest of language. She did say that she got tongue-tied over the word 'hotch- potch', so I deleted it even though it had been used in her acceptance speech at the declaration of the poll.

I quickly realised that, 'It's not me' was another way of Pauline saying, 'People are telling me that I should be writing the speech personally.' I could have, right there and then, told Pauline to go off and write the speech, but then I would have had to try and cajole and wheedle a copy out of her to 'edit'. I am convinced that Pauline's lack of discipline in not being able to sit down quietly and research a broad range of issues would have resulted in a disorganised mess. I would have lost control of the situation, and Pauline's maiden speech would have joined all those others at the bottom of the *Hansard* harbour.

I had come to realise that this maiden speech was just as important to me as it was to her. I had some sort of reputation as a writer and a political operator to defend. But, then there was my real motivation — a deep-seated contempt and disdain for most of the Liberal Party at the machine and Parliamentary level, which had developed over the years, even when I was in PNG. For me, I think it all started with Malcolm Fraser during his eight years as PM from 1975 to 1983, when I came to realise he was nothing more than a Western Victorian grazier who should have been looking after the trusting people who gave him, not once but twice, record mandates to govern. He seemed to spend far too much time dabbling in African politics in an attempt to establish himself as some sort of revered international statesman while Australia, with problems that desperately needed solving, waited in vain.

After the Vietnam War, it was Malcolm Fraser who, more than anyone, threw the lever that changed Australia's immigration mix. Australia's racial and cultural stability suffered shock waves after the end of the dirty Vietnam War, when two million Vietnamese Catholics finally lost their battle against Communism. Many of them sought refuge in Asian countries close to them only, in many cases, to be pirated, murdered, raped and driven back out to sea. So much for the Keating-Asian version of 'mateship' and the brotherhood of man!

Malcolm Fraser, without any consultation, forced the majority of Australians to share his guilt as we started to take the first waves of 'boat people' from Vietnam. As always, the voters were being told what was going to be good for them.

This arrogant and selfish man who so desperately wanted to be revered by some of the wackiest voodoo politicians in the rapidly unravelling Commonwealth cried, not for us but for himself, when with trembling jaw he conceded to another well known histrionic weeper, Bob Hawke, on election night 1983. Malcolm Fraser, the clone of Easter Island monoliths and the squire of Nareen, promised so much but delivered so little. In October

1986, Malcolm Fraser went off to the Admiral Benbow motel in Memphis, USA, and lost his pants!

I knew that Pauline had been talking about the maiden speech to Barbara Hazelton, Morrie Marsden and her family — including her mother and father who lived on the Gold Coast. That was a perfectly natural thing to do and I am sure that more than a few suggestions came across the counter at the fish and chip shop and from the fish markets in Brisbane. What it really meant though, was that there were far too many cooks, however well-intentioned they were, and it all helped to make my job that much more difficult.

I redrafted the speech with an eye out for any more 'tongue twisters' and gave a more forceful treatment to some of the issues such as Aborigines, immigration and multiculturalism. At this stage, I had made no specific mention of Asian immigration. I took back the first draft from Pauline and gave her the new one with the same suggestions — 'Please practise this and come back with comment and any new ideas.' I timed Pauline at reading an A4 page and she came in at 1.12 minutes without rushing it. Maiden speeches have a time limit of twenty minutes and I wanted Pauline to finish sooner rather than later.

At the end of May 1996, I started talking to her about the history of immigration and the policy of multiculturalism which had always been promoted by the major parties on a bipartisan basis. I told her about the Whitlam and Fraser years and the involvement in these issues of some of the then main players, such as Labor's Al Grassby, who has been called the 'father of multiculturalism', and the Liberal's Immigration Minister under Fraser, Ian McPhee. It is these issues that will greatly affect Australia's future and that of our great-grandchildren.

I still shudder when I conjure up images of Grassby, pirouetting on the political stage like some Cockney costermonger, sputtering like a human sparkler. McPhee's bland persona and mealy-mouthed opportunism was complemented by his boring choice of bow ties.

Pauline had never heard of Professor Geoffrey Blainey or Bob Santamaria. She knew that Andrew Peacock 'had something to do with politics', a revelation that would sorely dent the ego of the dilettantish 'ex-colt from

Kooyong' and Australian Ambassador to Washington.

As a starting point, I took Pauline back to Bill Hayden's interview with *Asiaweek* magazine in September, 1983, when he was our Foreign Affairs Minister. He said:

> Australia is changing. We're an anomaly as a European country in this part of the world. There's already a large and growing Asian population in Australia.
>
> . . . It is inevitable and desirable that Australia becomes a Eurasian country and this will be achieved by intermarriage.

These comments by Bill Hayden, at the time, were the first real attack by a senior politician on the concept held by mainstream Australia for the past almost two hundred years — that its country would continue to be what had always been comfortable and secure — a society based firmly on Anglo-European roots, with the values and culture that flowed on from that heritage. Hayden's comments were as sensible and as relevant as saying that Japan is part of China.

I briefed Pauline about Professor Geoffrey Blainey's 1984 speech at a Rotary meeting in the Western Victorian town of Warnambool, when he called for the consideration of reduced Asian immigration. Pauline would quickly learn first-hand, in the aftermath of her maiden speech, what Blainey had been forced to endure back in the early 1980s, when he was pilloried and vilified by the media, politicians as well as many of his fellow academics.

I told Pauline about the long-standing involvement of Graeme Campbell on the immigration and multicultural issues and his call for zero nett immigration — 'One out, one in' was the way I explained it to Pauline. I told her about the contributions of Bruce Ruxton, John Stone (ex-Secretary of the Australian Treasury and former National Party Senator), former Labor Senator Peter Walsh and others, to the ongoing debate on immigration and multiculturalism over recent years.

In 1988, John Howard had tentatively tested the waters on a reduction in Asian immigration, but hastily scurried back up the beach when the politically correct stingrays and media sharks chased him out of the shallows. On August 1, 1988, John Howard said:

It would be in our immediate term interests and supportive of social cohesion if it [Asian immigration] was slowed down a little so that the capacity of the community to absorb [it] were greater.

. . . I'm not saying that I would end Asian immigration. I would never do that. But what I am saying is that it is a legitimate concern of any community and any government to say that the rate of migration from one particular area is so great that it is imposing social tensions and that it is imposing a lack of social cohesion.

When that occurs it is in our interests and the interests of people who have come here from all around the world that there be some alteration made.

John Howard called for a concept of 'one Australia', that was based less on multiculturalism and more on achieving a peculiarly Australian identity. This could have been a better educated and a more articulate Pauline Hanson talking.

John Howard was immediately assailed furiously by the media, the multiculturalists, Jeff Kennett and a host of assorted breast-beaters. It was too much. Unlike Pauline Hanson, he backed off at a rapid rate, but more was to come.

Senator John Stone in an appearance on Channel 10's programme *Face to Face*, confirmed his remarks made a month earlier that the Coalition would slow the level of Asian immigration. Senator Peter Baume called on Howard to repudiate Stone who was the Shadow Minister for Finance as well as being the National Party Leader in the Senate. Pressure was brought on John Stone to bow down and recant. His lightweight opponents should have known better. He dug his foxhole deeper and refused to budge. Boxed into a corner, John Howard threw up his arms in surrender and dumped John Stone from the Shadow Cabinet.

The John Howard versus John Stone confrontation in 1988 was, in a way, a full dress rehearsal for the events of 1996 when John Howard and his Party, stupidly and without thinking, forced Pauline Hanson out of their organisation only to watch her become their worst nightmare. If she had remained as the Liberal candidate for Oxley, John Howard would have still won the election handsomely, but Pauline Hanson would have still been serving up fish and chips in Ipswich.

Pauline was familiar with Paul Keating's strident and frenetic, almost urgent badgering of Australians about their role and involvement in Asia. Keating, possibly inspired by his speech writer and svengali, Don Watson, waxed lyrical, going right over the top.

On October 12, 1995, at the Australia-Chinese Forum in Sydney, Paul Keating said all the right things to a more than sympathetic audience:

Asia is emphatically where this country's security and prosperity lie. It is where an increasing number of our people come from and — unambiguously and wholeheartedly — it is where we want to be. Our efforts on free trade, multiculturalism, and education and training are all part of the same strategy.

Speaking to the Institute of South-East Asian Studies in Singapore, Keating was reported in the Melbourne *Herald Sun* on January 18, 1996, under the headline that must have displeased more than a few Australians: 'The ways we are Asians.' Obviously running hot in Singapore, Keating defined 'mateship' in an Asian context.

Keating was egged on, by some mainstream journalists who yearned for the day when Australians are 'honey coloured' and those academics who preached 'Asianise or perish'. A mischievous Prime Minister Mahathir of Malaysia said that Australia could not become part of Asia until 70 per cent of Australians were Asians!

There is no doubt that when the Australian people finally turned on Paul Keating at the polls, his pro-Asian ranting was a big factor. The people had quite simply decided 'enough was enough'.

After my oral briefings and tutorials on immigration and multiculturalism, Pauline was starting to get the message.

Simon Kelly was an eager young reporter on the *Queensland Times* in

Ipswich. I had been encouraging him in the habit of coming to talk to Pauline on a reasonably regular basis, and he seemed to be reporting her fairly.

On Wednesday, June 5, 1996, I was sitting at the back of Pauline's Ipswich office while she was talking to Simon. She had completed her first 100 days in office and the interview was dealing with that milestone. I was filling in time reading a paper, not particularly taking notice of what was being said. I started to look at the results of some local street polling that Brett Heffernan had done on the gun debate, when I heard Pauline say something. At the same time, I saw Simon Kelly's ears colour and twitch quite visibly.

'I think all Asian immigration should be stopped,' Pauline had said.

I tensed and caught Pauline's eye. I made furious cutting motions across my throat with my right hand as a signal to wind the interview up. I then pretended to be laid back and casual and produced a rather exaggerated yawn, more for Simon's benefit.

After Simon Kelly left, obviously going back to his office elated at the scoop he had just acquired, I started to sort things out with Pauline. 'Why did you go and say that?' I said, with disbelief. Pauline instantly disarmed me with her infectious smile and giggle. Armed with the new knowledge I had imparted to her, she had decided to try herself out, but had broken through the starting gates well and truly. It was not *what* Pauline said that threw me, but her timing and the place. Politics is all about preparation and timing, and Pauline was demonstrating just how new she was to the game. I was going to have to try and keep a tight rein on her. Morrie Marsden had warned me of Pauline's propensity for putting her foot in her mouth at the most inopportune of times. I had just had a practical demonstration.

I told Pauline that all hell would break loose and I started to immediately work out how to best hose things down. I knew that we couldn't retract what Pauline had said about Asian immigration but we could qualify it, and it had to be done quickly. I gave Simon Kelly time to get back to his office then rang him. I told him that Pauline would fax through a brief qualifying statement. The statement was as follows.

I must stress at this stage, that I do not consider those people from [other] ethnic backgrounds currently living in Australia, anything but first class citizens, provided of course that they give this country their full undivided loyalty.

Simon Kelly justified my faith in him as a fair journalist by printing Pauline's qualification along with the rest of his story.

The headlines I was dreading failed to appear in Thursday's *Queensland Times* but the thumbscrews were tightened a bit more when I was told the article would be in the Saturday edition, which had the highest circulation.

On the Friday, I travelled to Melbourne and Pauline went on to Adelaide to attend a conference of the Samuel Griffith Society. The Society's slogan for its publications, 'Upholding The Australian Constitution', says it all.

I told Pauline to come back through Melbourne and stay overnight at my house in Yarraville in the inner-west of Melbourne, as I wanted her to meet some contacts of mine. I would stay in Melbourne, holding my breath, waiting for the *Queensland Times* headline that was sure to come. I was absolutely sure that, when it did, Pauline would be overrun by a media avalanche.

I was up well before my usual rising time of 5:00 am, waiting for the paper which I had arranged to have expressed from Ipswich to Melbourne. It arrived mid-morning and there was the headline that I expected but it still hit me between the eyes like a brass knuckle-duster:

'HANSON SAYS NO TO ASIA.'

I assumed that the *Queensland Times* story would quickly flow out into the mainstream media and then the hounds would start baying. I had a bit of time up my sleeve and my Melbourne address and home phone number were secure for the time being.

I rang Pauline a few times on her mobile and she reported no unusual media attention in Adelaide. She had enjoyed the first day of the Samuel Griffith Society conference but, from her response, I gauged that she was getting more than a little bored. She told me that she would arrive in Melbourne late Sunday afternoon.

That evening, Pauline, myself and 'Gunsynd,' a senior Labor Party operative and the only man I know who doesn't own a refrigerator, went out for dinner at Tiamo in Lygon Street, Carlton. Pauline was in good spirits and shouted us gelati as we strolled up the street after our meal. On the way back to Yarraville I drove Pauline down the heavily Vietnamese-populated Barkly Street, Footscray, which is known by the retreating Anglos and Europeans as 'Little Hanoi'. I took her for a tour of the general area and we then dropped in on a friend and his wife who live not far from me in Yarraville.

That night Pauline Hanson and I slept under the same roof again, but nothing had changed. Pauline slept on a sofa bed in the lounge room. I was not going to give up my very comfortable king-size bed — not even for the Independent Member for Oxley!

On Monday, June 10, 1996, I drove Pauline to Victoria Street Richmond, which is a clone of Barkly Street, Footscray. On the way back to my house, we called in on John Bennett, my old opal mining partner. I could see Pauline looking askance at the jumble of thousands of books and files that line the walls of his very unrenovated Victorian terrace. Bennett who dresses out of 'op-shops' is himself very unrenovated. 'He's very strange,' said Pauline as we drove away. I think Pauline Hanson had just met her first eccentric. Even so, Pauline's comment was considerably milder than some of the attacks on Bennett made by people offended by his views on the Holocaust. Professor Bill Rubenstein, then of Deakin University, described him as 'an unpleasant eccentric', a 'squalid nuisance', a 'lone wolf malcontent', a 'freak of nature', and 'possibly more evil than Himmler and Pol Pot', while Phillip Adams said he hoped that the CSIRO could find a cure for Bennett's dissident thoughts.

We flew back to Brisbane that evening and I was fully expecting that Pauline would be ambushed by the media at Brisbane Airport but, apart from well-wishers acknowledging her, there was not a journalist in sight. I couldn't understand what was going on and wondered if the media had decided that Pauline was no longer news.

I spent the rest of the week working on a third draft of the maiden speech, waiting for the media barrage that I thought must surely come. It never did. It was a classic 'phoney war' scenario where the expected battle never eventuates. The provocative and sensational headline, 'Hanson says no to Asia', had simply disappeared into some sort of media 'black hole' where other great forgotten and unreported stories orbit, like rusting abandoned spaceships.

My original strategy for the presentation of the maiden speech was to get it over and done with as is done by a lot of new members, but I was becoming aware that Pauline was getting very tense and 'wound-up' about the whole deal. She told me that the prospect of getting up in the chamber and delivering the speech was really starting to get to her. She used the word 'terrified'.

On Thursday, June 20, 1996, I ruled out an early maiden speech for Pauline and made a tentative booking for her to give it during the three-day Budget sitting starting on Tuesday, August 20. With Pauline becoming increasingly fragile, I wanted to buy as much time as possible for her. Extra pressure was being placed on Pauline as the media increasingly pestered her about when she was going to give her speech and what she was going to say.

On several occasions, Pauline and I spoke about trying to combat the feelings of panic she was starting to develop about giving the speech. I suggested she could take some public speaking lessons to help build up her confidence. I actually organised an appointment with a woman in Canberra. Pauline and I went and met her but that was as far as it went. Pauline said she preferred to deal with somebody in the Ipswich area, so I got Morrie Marsden to try and organise something, but nothing ever came of that idea either. I was starting to run out of ideas and was getting cranky. I felt like a gun horse-breaker unable to get a bridle on a flighty and stubborn filly. I tried to make light of the situation with Pauline, telling her that one day we would all look back at ourselves and have a good laugh — which pretty well turned out to be the case but, for the time being, things were deadly serious.

I encouraged Pauline to start doing some radio interviews from the safety of her Canberra and Ipswich offices without opening the floodgates to every airwave Johnny. She performed reasonably well, despite some hiccups. I briefed her as well as I could before she went on air and I hoped that her confidence would start to build. I had to keep reminding myself that Pauline was new to all this and that I needed to be patient with her. The big problem was all the media flak coming at her from all directions, combined with the distractions and confusion created by a disorganised office. In a calmer, more professional environment things would have been different, but patience is not one of my virtues.

The pressure was getting to all of us and I hit a hurdle on Tuesday, June 25, when I was stricken with severe stomach and chest pain. Pauline took me to the Woden Hospital in Canberra, where I stayed under observation for most of the day. I was subsequently diagnosed as suffering from spasms of the oesophagus, in association with gastric reflux, and I continued to feel off colour for a few weeks. Long hours, too much of the wrong food at the wrong times, and not enough physical exercise were clearly telling me something.

Now that I can sit quietly and go back through my copious diary notes, it is very clear that Pauline Hanson was undergoing great strain and stress during the lead up to her maiden speech. We were in the Ipswich office on Thursday, July 25, when I realised it was Queensland Senior Citizens' Week. I suggested to Pauline that Barbara Hazelton prepare some tea and scones so that she could host a very informal morning or afternoon tea for some local seniors. I was not prepared for Pauline's response which rapidly became an outburst. She was obviously in a bad mood and retorted, not very graciously, 'Why should I have those people in my office? — I don't want them here.' Taken by surprise, I told her and Barbara I was sorry for raising the matter. Pauline's response was mean-spirited and totally unwarranted. Even taking into account the stress that I knew she was experiencing, she was showing me facets of the 'real' Pauline Hanson.

On Monday, July 29, Barabara Hazelton, like a bolt from the blue, told me that Pauline had asked her to organise the maiden speech. After telling her, sarcastically, that I thought that I had things under control, and advising her to concentrate on her own duties, I felt like a class tittle-tat going to Pauline to clarify what Barbara had said. Pauline was nonplussed and wondered what I was on about, saying that she had never told Barbara any such thing. I walked out of the office feeling like a dill and headed down to the Ipswich Mall to have a cup of tea with Morrie Marsden.

On Wednesday, July 31, I had been in the Ipswich office since 7:30 am when Pauline came in about 10:00 am. I went into her office and started talking with her when, obviously upset, she started to cry — not sobs but visible tears. It was the same story — fear of giving the maiden speech. I couldn't offer her much in the way of comfort because I am no good at handling weeping women.

During those many times Pauline was feeling 'down' she would say that she felt like resigning and, at first, I thought she was just over-reacting and trying to stir me up. But I started to pay serious attention when Morrie Marsden spoke to me on Thursday, August 1, from Ipswich when I was in Canberra. He had lunch with Pauline that day and she told him she was seriously thinking of resigning. It was Morrie's considered opinion that she was deadly serious.

There was one question that I often asked Pauline when I was having absolutely no success in getting her to do her 'homework'. It was, 'Do you like this job?' She would look down at the desk, put the tips of her fingers to her temples and remain stonily silent. She never said 'yes' and she never said 'no'. It really looked to me as if this wayward filly was thinking of jumping the fence.

I finally broke down Pauline's resistance against taking public speaking training when she agreed to see a young woman whom I had organised in Melbourne. There was still one hurdle to clear and that was the question of fees, which were quoted at $100 per hour. I learnt that the going rate was closer to $150. Pauline really reacted to the cost, saying that it was outrageous. 'Nobody's worth that sort of money,' she said. Without trying to be smart-arsed I reminded her that neurosurgeons charged a lot more than that! Pauline receives a substantial electorate allowance that allows her to pay for situations related to her electoral performance. I had taken advice that it would be in order for her to pay for public speaking training out of these funds, so I could not understand her objection. I had to conclude that she was just being very mean. I told her that, if voice training helped solve her problem, it would be money well spent. She took five hours training and that was that.

Pauline took no more lessons during the time I was with her, which annoyed me immensely given what the voice trainer told me. She said that Pauline had very good potential to become a competent public speaker but that she would need to work at it. I did not want to do a 'Professor Higgins' on Pauline, changing her style and accent — I just wanted to develop her confidence. The trainer said Pauline's chief attribute was that she passionately believed in what she was saying, irrespective of whether what she said was considered to be right or wrong. I had worked hard to lead the filly to water but she didn't want to drink that much.

After the *Queensland Times* headline false alarm, I asked Brett Heffernan to do some research on Asian immigration figures for the period 1984–1985 to 1994–1995. The figures were sourced from the Australian Bureau of Statistics and the Bureau of Immigration Multicultural and Population research. It showed that, for the indicated period, 40 per cent of all migrants coming into Australia came from Asian regions. At the bottom of the first page of this research, I had indicated with a black marking pen the 40 per cent figure and had written the words: 'If we keep this up we will be swamped.' (This research has been reproduced as artwork in the pictorial section in this book.)

I showed Pauline the briefing note and told her that, since she had 'outed' herself in the *Queensland Times* article, she may as well go for broke on Asian immigration in the maiden speech. She didn't take long to make up her mind. 'Let's go with it,' she said. That evening I worked late on the fourth draft of the maiden speech. The die had been cast.

Back in Canberra, getting ready for the August Budget sitting, I realised that it was simply impracticable and unrealistic to try and get Pauline on to the list of speakers to give her maiden speech, so I cancelled the arrangements with the Opposition Whip's office and rang Pauline, who was still in Ipswich, and told her the news. She was positively relieved and sounded like someone on 'death row' who had just received a stay of execution at one minute to midnight. She would now be one of the last new members to deliver their maiden speech. This would ensure maximum media attention and all eyes would be on Pauline. I went up to the press gallery and put the word out, telling a few selected journalists that there were a few surprises worth waiting for in the speech. Little did they know.

During this time in Canberra, I took a trip to Belconnen and visited The Old Bookroom bookshop, just to browse and see if anything attracted my interest. I am always on the lookout for any PNG books and those dealing with Australian political history. Two disastrous fires have savagely depleted my library, costing time and money to replace. I picked up, with interest, Arthur Calwell's autobiography *Be Just and Fear Not* — my copy of the book had been a casualty of one of my fires. As I thumbed the pages, the title of Chapter 14 'Black power and a multi-racial society' caught my eye. I walked out of the shop with the Calwell book and the Australian National University research on the 1964 PNG elections. Calwell's book was an easy read and I told Pauline that I would include a Calwell quote in her maiden speech. It appears in the second last paragraph on page 127 of his book. Pauline did not know who Calwell was, so I gave her a quick 'potted' briefing, telling her to at least read the relevant chapter, but she never did. The Paul Hasluck quote in the speech comes from my files.

Arthur Calwell was Australia's first and best Minister for Immigration and his autobiography is very pertinent to today's so-called 'Race Debate'. All sides of politics should read it, but we know they won't. If Arthur Calwell were to return to us today, he could well become the leader of the One Nation party!

Budget night came and went. I had obtained sets of Budget Papers for our Canberra and Ipswich offices and for Pauline personally. She looked at the intimidating stack with flat eyes. I told her to check the treasurer's speech for two, or maybe three points that she could relate to her electorate, and then we could make a response. At that stage I was only interested in getting Pauline to 'feed' her local papers. The Canberra press gallery was playing with Pauline as a lazy, smug cat plays with a wounded sparrow. She was good for the odd 'filler' stories but nothing much else. Later, of course, it would be a much different story.

On August 21, I went to the Parliamentary Library and brought some briefing papers on the Budget back to the office. I put them on Pauline's desk together with some other material for her to read so that she would be conversant with the Budget and its aftermath. I showed her the comprehensive Budget supplement in the *Australian* and said that she should commence her briefing with that. Pauline showed an almost indolent indifference which annoyed me, and we had words. I told Pauline that she was letting the side down by not backgrounding the important political issues and not doing all the other study that was required of her. I told her that she needed to lead by example. 'You are the Member for Oxley for God's sake,' I said. 'Well start acting like it and start leading from the front instead of having to be dragged along.'

She had not read the two books on Australian history by Professor Geoffrey Blainey that I had lent her when I first started working for her, or Marlene Goldsmith's excellent book on political correctness that I had given her as a present. When I speak to Pauline again, which I will undoubtedly do now that my unfair dismissal case is resolved, I will ask her to return Blainey's books. I need them more than she does.

In response to my criticism of her slackness Pauline, in a fit of pique, swept some of the briefing notes on to the floor saying, 'I can't retain, I can't retain.' She then went into the bathroom. I could hear her crying. I felt a bastard — but, of course, I am!

On Monday, August 26, we were back in Ipswich and I advised Pauline to wind down, take some time off and freshen up. I was starting to wonder whether I was pushing her too hard, but her obvious lack of enthusiasm for getting involved in the 'hard grind' side of the job stopped me from feeling too sorry for her. In her eyes the maiden speech had become a monster that threatened to consume her and I am sure that she had changed her mind about becoming too involved in the construction of it.

On the evening of August 28, Pauline and I drove to the Brisbane Exhibition Ground to hear Bob Santamaria celebrate the 50th anniversary of his movement, as guest speaker before a crowd of over 500 people. Pauline had never met Bob Santamaria. It is no dark secret that I have, over the years, written articles for his *News Weekly* magazine and that I support a lot of his views. Bob Santamaria delivered a stirring oration with Pauline obviously very impressed. We waited our turn after the address and I intro-duced Pauline Hanson to Bob Santamaria on the floor of the hall. She spoke to him briefly while I renewed acquaintances with Sir Jim Killen, Defence Minister in the Malcolm Fraser Government. We drove back to Ipswich with all the Santamaria material that Pauline was able to collect. She was in good spirits and told me that she wanted to include some of Santamaria's ideas and figures in her maiden speech. I told her that some of his themes were already in the speech. For those who will foam at the mouth and see shadowy figures lurking everywhere in the wings behind Pauline Hanson, Bob Santamaria has, admittedly, been very critical of some of her views but has also said that her sudden prominence provides clear warning signs that the major parties have comprehensively failed to deliver on even the most modest expectations of mainstream Australia.

On Wednesday, September 4, I contacted the Opposition Whip's office in Canberra and put Pauline on the speakers' list for Tuesday the 10th or Wednesday the 11th. I spent the rest of the day working on the fifth draft of Pauline's speech and could almost recite it by heart. It was a beast stirring in the bowels of the computer, straining to be unleashed, and it was running our lives.

That day Pauline came into the Ipswich office with some handwritten notes that she wanted to have incorporated into the speech. Exactly what I had feared was starting to happen — a mad, last minute scramble that would surely produce mistakes. I retreated to my office to study what Pauline had given me. There was obviously plenty of material extracted from Bob Santamaria's Brisbane speech, an attack on single mothers and a call to reform the Family Law Act and revise how the Child Support Scheme was administered. The suggested ending for the speech was a Frank Sinatra style 'I did it my way' wind-up. I detected Barbara's possible influence here as she had actually referred to that theme when we had been discussing Pauline's general political performance.

While I was working out what to do, I filled in time by checking Pauline's spelling and highlighting any errors. She was running at about ten to fifteen mistakes per A4 page and she could not construct sentences properly. Leaving school far too early had cost her dearly.

I will not forget that day easily. I was out in the main office working at the computer with a print-out of the speech laid out on the floor beside me, together with Pauline's notes. At one stage, Morrie Marsden turned up and it was while he was there that I noticed Barbara Hazelton typing away to my left on another computer. I refused to believe it but, when I inquired what she was doing, she said she was typing the maiden speech! In a barely controlled fury I told her to butt out. I just couldn't imagine what she was up to and I didn't want to talk about it any more. She stopped doing what she was doing and that was the end of that. While all this was going on, Pauline was walking in and out of her office, sometimes talking to me, sometimes not. I could see the tension building up in her like mercury rising in a thermometer on Ash Wednesday. I was getting ready to turn nasty, she was getting ready to spit the dummy!

I had been in the office since 6:00 am and was on the verge of losing my temper well and truly. I told Pauline that all this nonsense had to cease before the men in white coats came to take us away! I told her that I would not include her attack on single mothers in the speech, because I considered it incredibly illogical and politically suicidal, particularly as she had been one herself. Nor would I contemplate the 'Sinatra-like' ending which I managed to convince her was corny and arrogant. The line in the maiden speech which says, 'If you give a man a fish you feed him for a day. If you teach him how to fish, you feed him for a lifetime,' was heard by Pauline in a TV advertisement for an overseas aid agency and I had heard it myself. She was very impressed by this piece of homespun philosophy and I saw no harm in writing it in, although I considered it a bit trite. I conceded to her on the Family Law Court and Child Support material. Her office, as do all other political offices, had a large complaint base in these areas, reflecting that the lives and well-being of a large number of Australians from all social strata continue to be seriously affected. It is a very emotive and sensitive issue.

It was during this mad and bizarre session that I typed in the wrong population figures for the Asian nations, copying straight from Pauline's longhand notes extracted from Bob Santamaria's speech in Brisbane. She had the figures all wrong and she subsequently accepted the blame, but it

1. *Above:* Where were you when JFK was shot? Here I am with two Papua New Guineans at the headwaters of the Sepik River, PNG.

2 & 3. *Left and following page:* Crocodile skin makes wonderful handbags! Here's the tanned skin of a crocodile I shot for my mother. Mark Knight's cartoon, on the next page, speaks for itself.

4. A fair deal for all. Me bartering for a shield with a PNG native.

5. *Top left:* The youngest member of a Commonwealth Parliament in 1964. Here I am with the Speaker of the PNG Parliament, Horace Niall.

6. *Top right:* 'Andrew Peacock had something to do with Australian politics.' Peacock and me on his 1972 visit to the Sepik River, PNG.

7. *Above:* Me with family friend and great Australian hero, Sir Edward 'Weary' Dunlop.

8. *Above:* Once a Liberal . . .
February 1996, and Pauline
Hanson campaigns as a Liberal
candidate in Oxley assisted by the
Federal Member for Macpherson,
John Bradfield.

9. *Right:* Anyone for fish and
chips? Pauline at work in her fish
and chip shop after being elected
the independent Member for Oxley.

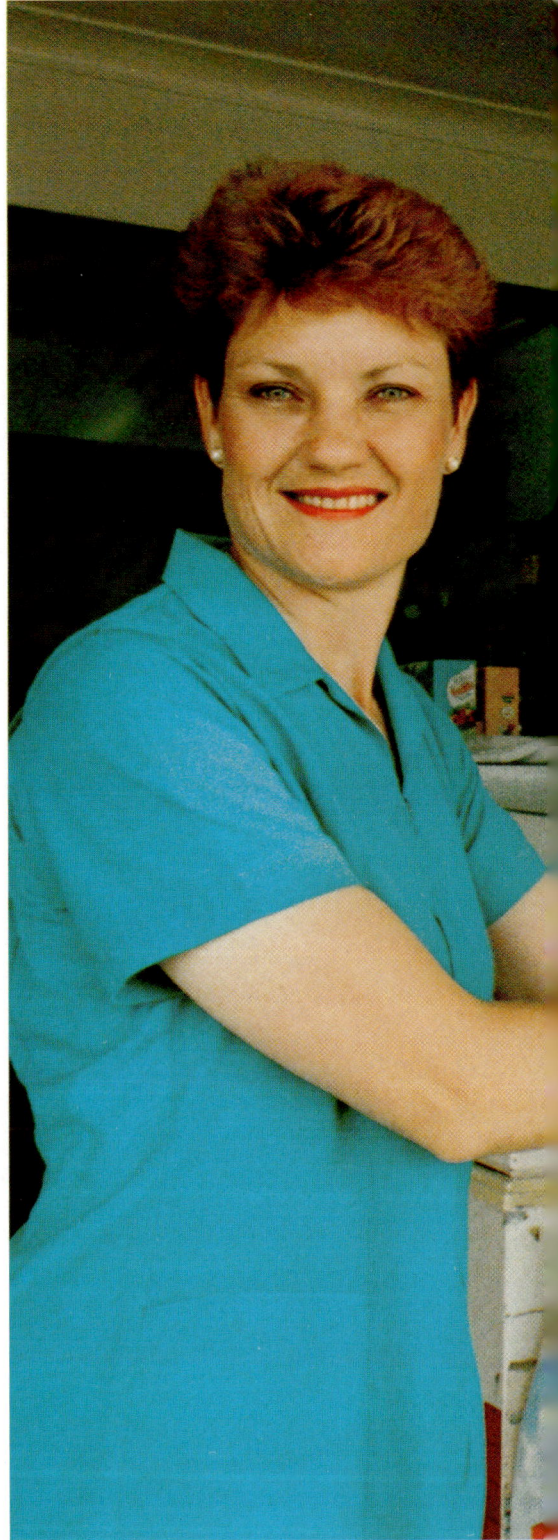

10. Swearing in–the phenomenon begins. The opening of Parliament, April 30, 1996.

11.

URGENT
CONFIDENTIAL (1)

Asian Immigration Influx 1984-85 to 1994-95

Figures incorporate immigration numbers from Southeast Asian, Northeast Asian and
Southern Asian regional countries.

Year	Intake	% of total immigration	
84-85	30,890	39.6%	(78,087)
85-86	30,583	33.1%	(92,410)
86-87	38,183	33.7%	(113,309)
87-88	48,889	34.1%	(143,490)
88-89	54,601	37.8%	(145,316)
89-90	50,607	41.7%	(121,227)
90-91	60,906	50.1%	(121,688)
91-92	54,392	50.6%	(107,391)
92-93	32,989	43.2%	(76,330)
93-94	27,766	40.0%	(69,768)
94-95	32,376	37.0%	(87,428)
Total	462,182	40.0%	(1,156,444)

Statistics: Bureau of Immigration, Multicultural and Population Research.

IF WE KEEP THIS UP ✳
WE WILL BE SWAMPED

12. 'I believe we are in danger of being swamped by Asians.' The research that led to
that statement in Pauline Hanson's maiden speech, with my handwritten comments.

13. The speech that started it all. Graeme Campbell looks on as Pauline Hanson delivers her maiden speech.

14. After the maiden speech. Pauline is congratulated by National Party MP De-Anne Kelly.

THE REST OF THE WORLD DOESN'T LIKE US... AND SOME OF THEM HAVEN'T EVEN HEARD OF PAULINE HANSON

TANDBERG

15.

I'D PREFER WE DIDN'T HAVE ANY ASIANS OR ABORIGINES!

I'D LIKE TO HAVE HER PREFERENCES

TANDBERG

16.

Oley, 25/10/96

My dear Pauline.

I am a Mainstream Aussie. I agree 100% with your opinions. But you disappoint me. Your voice is too soft. No action has happened till now. I will support you 100%. I will rape your mother and your kids and blame the Asians. I want action now. I hope you'll agree with me and support me 100%.

You are my favourite. I want blood.

17. *Above and opposite:* Anonymous fax filth. Some of the vile faxes received in Pauline Hanson's Ipswich office.

hanson...
YOU ARE A F█████G C██T

EVERYONE IN THIS COUNTRY
HAS RIGHTS AND I'M TELLING
YOU YOU F███████ WHORE THAT
I WILL MARRY WHO I WANT BE
THEY BLACK OR YELLOW OR
GREEN OR PINK AND IF I EVER
HEAR THAT MY KIDS ARE
CALLED MONGRELS,
YOU'LL BE DEAD
YOU BLOODY IDIOT FISH SHOP
OWNER.

Hanson blamed as magnet for bigotry

PM, HANSON TO MEDIA LIST R

Message to Asia ignore Hanson

PM FENI ON JAKA

Fishmonger

Secret Lib poll boosts Hanson

Ex-PMs blast Hanso

Hayden hails outspo

Costello swipes at Hanson

Hanson hurts Asian pro

China shru off Hanson

A crusade fo

Kernot: unseat the wicked witch of the North

Hanson party in turmoil

Medi

Hans

Kennett batters Hans

Antidote for the Hanson

Hanson slippi

SM COMPLAINTS SOAR

Crush Hanson, big parties urged

FF HANSON ATTACK
AID

ag wrapper

LP to put one
tion last

Pauline police cost $300, 000

MP

Police hurt at rowdy Hanson

Hayden out to stop Hanson

PM rails at Hanson after Asian criticism

Nationals may support Hanson

Howard hidin behind Hanson

Big guns turned on Hanson

med for
enzy

Hanson Moronic says Mahathir

so Hanson still makin headlines overseas

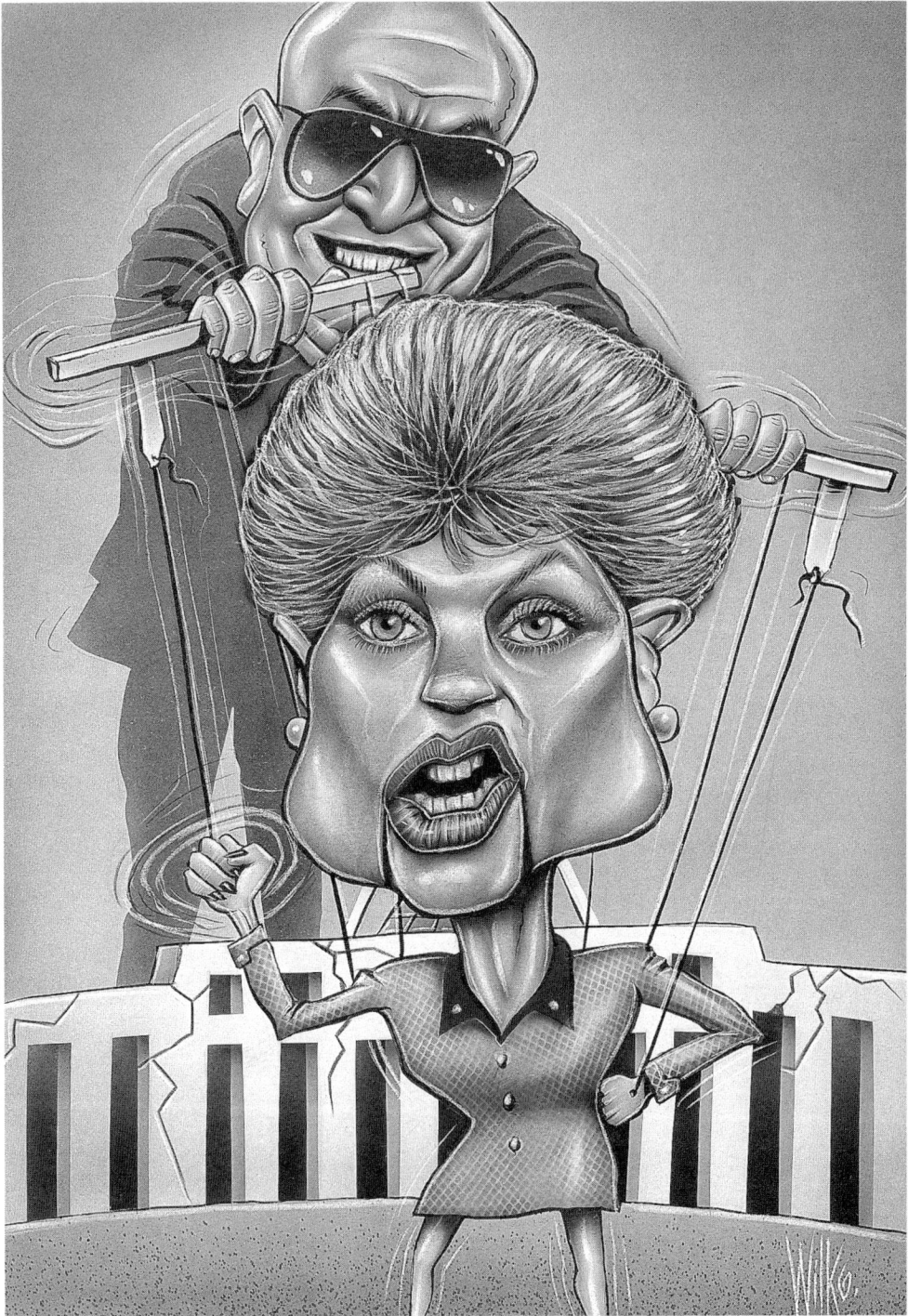

18.

was my fault alone — as simple as that. I was the worldly-wise adviser who had lived in South-east Asia for a year in the late 1970s. Pauline Hanson was the unsophisticated, poorly-educated battler who, against all the odds, had been thrown in at the deep end of the political pool. I made a stupid mistake. After a lifetime of self-delusion I realised that, after all, I was not invincible!

At the end of that absurd and ratty Wednesday that I will never forget, I told Pauline that the maiden speech was finished once and for all — *finito, finis,* all-done, the end, going, going, gone!

I printed off hard copies of the fifth and final draft for Pauline and myself and left a couple of master copies in the office file. The speech ran to sixteen A4 pages of Times New Roman text, in 16 point font, at double spacing. I reckoned that Pauline would take seventeen to eighteen minutes to read it. I copied off plenty of floppy disks to give me back-up.

Next day, I mailed disks by express bag to Pauline's Canberra office and kept a couple in my briefcase. I then packed up all the previous drafts stored on disks, together with my notes, and those of Pauline and mailed them to my Melbourne address. I had provided myself with plenty of insurance against any possible disaster.

Pauline's Anzac Day speech and the controversy that followed her pronouncements on reconciliation and the Aboriginal issue, kept her office fairly buzzing along with letters, faxes and telephone calls. It was very obvious, right from the start, that the majority of the support was coming from outside the electorate. This created a situation that might yet have serious electoral repercussions for Pauline. It made it very difficult for the office to properly cater for the needs of every politician's 'very important persons' — their constituents. In the last few weeks before Pauline's maiden speech however, her Ipswich office became strangely quiet — almost as if the people out there had a premonition of the occurrence of some extraordinary event.

On Friday, September 6, I packed my bags and flew to Canberra. Arriving there at 9:00 pm, feeling pretty flat and tired, I found myself wondering how Pauline was bearing up as her moment drew closer. The monster, the maiden speech, was about to snap its chain.

115

EIGHTEEN

The Maiden Speech — Birth

Pauline Hanson, Barbara Hazelton and Morrie Marsden arrived in Canberra on the evening of Sunday, September 8, 1996, on a direct flight from Brisbane. They all stayed in the one accommodation unit at the Sundowner Motel. Pauline had asked Morrie to come to Canberra for her maiden speech and I interpreted that invitation as some sort of attempt by Pauline to acknowledge in some small way the very significant role played by him in her election to Oxley.

I was in the office very early Monday morning and skimmed through the newspapers. I could sense a 'phoney war' atmosphere as I cruised through the press gallery but it was still a bit early in the day. It takes a little while for the purveyors of truth, honesty and objective opinion to stir from their lairs.

I went down to the Opposition Whip's office and confirmed that Pauline would be the last new member to give her maiden speech on Tuesday, September 10, late in the afternoon. The person preceding her would be the new MP for North Sydney, Joe Hockey, who won the Seat for the Liberals after that doyen of independents, Ted Mack resigned from politics. Hockey's only claim to political fame to date is that he was, until recently, the employer of Roxanne Cameron, the ex-mistress and careful diarist of disgraced former Liberal Senator Bob Woods.

On returning to Pauline's office, I found Barbara and Morrie there with glum looks on their faces. Pauline was not feeling well and would not be coming in to the office that day. My bald scalp tingled. They said that she thought she might be getting the flu, but I knew better. There was no doubt in my mind that Pauline Hanson was suffering from high levels of stress and anxiety brought on by the mounting pressure as the queue of new members giving their maiden speeches became shorter and shorter. Each day brought her closer to what she had convinced herself was her Nemesis. From Pauline's perspective it was probably not dissimilar to being on death row and waiting for the priest to arrive. Whenever I had told Pauline that the date of her speech had been postponed, the expression of her relief had been palpable. For my part, I told Morrie and Barbara that I would not try and contact Pauline. I hoped that the rest would help her compose herself. I was already switching into emergency mode in case the unthinkable happened and Pauline spat the dummy. I prepared a press release stating that stress and the flu had made Pauline a late scratching. If the worst happened, I was confident that it would only be a temporary set back. Seven months of a close working relationship with Pauline had allowed me to gain valuable insight into the best and worst points of her character. She was possessed of an almost pig-headed courage that enabled her to confront situations others, better equipped, would not dare contemplate. It was this quality that, in the end, would never have allowed her to throw in the towel and resign. I left the office at 6:30 pm, wondering what the next day would bring. Working with Pauline Hanson was never boring.

Next day, 'the' day, I was at the office at 7:00 am. There was nothing much to do except wait for Pauline to appear. She duly arrived mid-morning, with Barbara and Morrie, and I said nothing to her about the previous day. I told her to quietly sit in her office, go through the speech and practise deep breathing to help relax her. I told her that, when the time came to stand up and speak, she could afford to slow her speaking rate right down. On my estimation she would finish a minute or two ahead of time but, if she ran over by the same margin, the Speaker would be most unlikely to penalise her.

It was getting close to countdown time when Pauline asked me to come into her office. All afternoon, I had been getting copies of her speech ready to distribute to the press gallery as soon as she had finished speaking. There are about one hundred pigeonholes located in an alcove in the middle of the gallery and they are like informal post office boxes.

Morrie and Barbara were with Pauline, and they were looking concerned. The following quote is from the third paragraph of the speech.

We now have a situation where a type of reverse racism is applied to mainstream Australians by those who promote political correctness and those who control the various taxpayer funded 'industries' that flourish in our society, servicing Aboriginals, multiculturalists, homosexuals and a host of other minority groups.

The word 'homosexuals' was causing a problem. From what I could work out, Morrie Marsden had raised the question of Pauline being quizzed by the media about it, and she was saying that she was ignorant of the 'facts and figures'. I told her that there was plenty of available evidence and quoted the ABC's heavy involvement with the televising of the Sydney Gay and Lesbian Mardi Gras, and the many instances of government funding for homosexual organisations and publications over the years. I told Pauline we could handle the problem when it arose, just as we had done in the past with other issues. She became angry and adamant about deleting the reference and I had no option but to 'black' out the offending word with a felt pen. I think that Pauline was trying to even the score in some way over my refusal to include some of her last minute material in the speech. I was furious at this 'eleventh hour' change because I was running out of time and now needed to correct the one hundred copies I wanted to distribute to the media. I gave Pauline, Morrie and Barbara a 'serve' about stupid last-minute interference. This vigorous exchange, in fact, 'warmed' Pauline up and helped take off a fair bit of the nervous edge she was teetering on.

Time was ticking away as Pauline prepared to walk down to the House of Representatives chamber. Morrie and Barbara were going to sit in the public gallery and I was planning to watch on TV, in the safety and silence of the office, where I would be protected from silly people. The labour pains had well and truly begun.

At 5:15 pm on Tuesday, September 10, 1996, The Deputy Speaker of the House of Representatives, Garry Nehl, the National Party MP for the NSW seat of Cowper, gave the 'nod' to Pauline Hanson the independent Member for Oxley, to give her maiden speech. Pauline was dressed in a black, one-piece dress with gold buttons down the front. She looked very smart. On her right was Graeme Campbell, the independent Member for Kalgoorlie. On her left, looking a bit out of place and as if he really didn't want to be there because he didn't like her, was Peter Andren, the independent Member for Calare in NSW. To the front of her was Alan Rocher, the former Liberal and now independent Member for the WA Seat of Curtin. Paul Filing, the independent Member for the WA Seat of Moore was absent.

Pauline looked pretty feisty, as if she was still stirred up after our set-to in the office. She was hard-eyed and her mouth was set — the bright scarlet lipstick making her top lip appear more lop-sided than ever. The Labor party had boycotted Pauline's speech, leaving just a bare sprinkling of Liberals and Nationals. After months of turbulence, intransigence, stupid interference, petty wrangling and childish office politics, the moment had arrived. An Australian political phenomenon was about to be born. Pauline Hanson rose to her feet and started speaking:

Mr Deputy Speaker, in making my first speech in this place, I congratulate you on your election and wish to say how proud I am to be here as the Independent Member for Oxley.

I come here, not as a polished politician but as a woman who has had her fair share of life's knocks. My view on issues is based on common sense and my experience as a mother of four children, a sole parent and a businesswoman running a fish and chip shop.

I won the seat of Oxley largely on an issue that has resulted in me being called a racist. That issue related to my comment that Aboriginals received more benefits than non-Aboriginals.

We now have a situation where a type of reverse racism is applied to mainstream Australians by those who promote political correctness and those who control the various taxpayer funded 'industries' that flourish in our society, servicing Aboriginals, multiculturalists and a host of other minority groups.

In response to my call for equality for ALL Australians, the most noisy criticism came from the 'fat cats,' bureaucrats and the 'do-gooders'. They screamed the loudest because they stand to lose the most — their power, money and position, all funded by ordinary taxpayers.

Present governments are encouraging separatism in Australia by providing opportunities, land, monies and facilities, only available to Aboriginals. Along with millions of Australians, I am fed up to the back teeth with the inequalities that are being promoted by the government and paid for by the taxpayer under the assumption that Aboriginals are the most disadvantaged people in Australia.

I do not believe that the colour of one's skin determines whether you are disadvantaged.

Mr Deputy Speaker, as Paul Hasluck said in Parliament, in October 1955 (when he was Minister for Territories):

'The distinction I make is this. A social problem is one that concerns the way in which people live together in one society. A racial problem is a problem which confronts two different races who live in two separate societies, even if those societies are side by side. We do not want a society in Australia in which one group enjoy[s] one set of privileges and another group enjoy[s] another set of privileges.'

Hasluck's vision was of a single society in which racial emphases were rejected and social issues addressed.

I totally agree with him and so would the majority of Australians.

But remember, when he gave his speech, he was talking about the privileges white Australians were seen to be enjoying over Aboriginals.

Today, 41 years later, I talk about the exact opposite — the privileges Aboriginals enjoy over other Australians. I have done research on benefits only available to Aboriginals and challenge anyone to tell me how Aboriginals are disadvantaged when they can obtain 3 and 5 per cent housing loans denied to non-Aboriginals.

Mr Deputy Speaker, this nation is being divided into black and white and the present system encourages this. I am fed up with being told, 'This is our land.' Well, where the hell do I go? I was born here and so were my parents and children. I will work beside anyone and they will be my equal but I draw the line when told I must pay and continue paying for something that happened over 200 years ago. Like most Australians, I worked for my land — no one gave it to me.

Apart from the $40 million spent so far since Mabo, on Native Title claims, the Government has made available $1 billion for Aborigines and Torres Strait Islanders as compensation for land they cannot claim under Native Title. Bear in mind that the $40 million spent so far on Native Title has gone into the pockets of grateful lawyers and consultants. Not one Native Title has been granted as I speak.

Mr Deputy Speaker, the majority of Aboriginals don't want hand-outs because they realise that WELFARE IS KILLING THEM. This quote says it all: 'If you give a man a fish, you feed him for a day. If you teach him how to fish, you feed him for a lifetime.' Those who feed off the Aboriginal 'industry' don't want to see things changed. Look at the Council for Reconciliation. Members receive $290 a day sitting allowance, $320 a day travelling allowance and most of these people also hold other very well paid positions. No wonder they didn't want to resign recently!

Reconciliation is everyone recognising and treating each other as equals and everyone must be responsible for their own actions. This is why I am calling for ATSIC to be abolished. It is a failed, hypocritical and discriminatory organisation that has failed dismally the people it was meant to serve. It will take more than Senator Herron's surgical skills to correct the terminal mess it is in. Anyone with a criminal record can, and does, hold a position with ATSIC. I cannot hold my position as a politician if I have a criminal record. Once again — two sets of rules.

If politicians continue to promote separatism in Australia, then they should not continue to hold their seats in this Parliament. They are not truly representing ALL Australians and I call on the people to throw them out!

TO SURVIVE IN PEACE AND HARMONY, UNITED AND STRONG, WE MUST HAVE ONE PEOPLE, ONE NATION, ONE FLAG!

Mr Deputy Speaker, the greatest cause of family breakdown is unemployment. This country of ours has the richest mineral deposits in the world, vast rich lands for agriculture and is surrounded by oceans that provide a wealth of seafood and yet, we are $190 billion in debt with an interest bill that is strangling us.

Youth unemployment between the ages of 15–24 runs at 24 per cent and even higher in my electorate of Oxley. Statistics (by cooking the books), say that Australia's unemployment is at 8.6 per cent or just under one million people. If we disregard that one hour's work a week classifies a person as employed, then the figure is really between 1.5 and 1.9 million unemployed. This is a crisis that recent governments have ignored because of a lack of will. We are regarded as a third world country with first world living conditions. We have one of the highest interest rates in the world and we owe more money per capita than any other country. All we need is a nail hole in the bottom of the boat and we're sunk.

In real dollar terms, our standard of living has dropped over the past ten years. In the 1960s our wages increase ran at 3 per cent and unemployment at 2 per cent. Today, not only is there no wage increase — we have gone backwards and unemployment is officially 8.6 per cent. The real figure must be close to 12 or 13 per cent.

Mr Deputy Speaker, I wish to speak briefly on some social and legal problems encountered by many of my constituents — problems not restricted just to my electorate of Oxley. I refer to the social and family upheaval created by the Family Law Act and the ramifications of that Act embodied in the Child Support Scheme. The Family Law Act, which was the child of the disgraceful Senator

Lionel Murphy should be repealed. It has brought death, misery and heartache to countless thousands of Australians. Children are treated like pawns in some crazy game of chess. The Child Support Scheme has become unworkable, very unfair and one sided. Custodial parents can often profit handsomely at the expense of the parent paying child support and in many cases the non-custodial parent simply gives up employment to escape, in many cases, the heavy and punitive financial demands.

Governments must give to ALL those who have hit life's hurdles, the chance to rebuild and have a future.

Mr Deputy Speaker, we have lost all our big Australian industries and icons including Qantas when it sold off 25 per cent of its shares and a controlling interest to British Airways. Now this government wants to sell Telstra — a company that made $1.2 billion profit last year and will make $2 billion profit this year but first, they want to sack 54 000 employees to show better profits and share prices. Anyone with business sense knows that you don't sell off your assets, especially when they are making money. I may only be a 'fish and chip shop lady' but some of these economists need to get their heads out of the text books and get a real job in the real world. I wouldn't even let one of them handle my grocery shopping!

Mr Deputy Speaker, immigration and multiculturalism are issues that this government is trying to address but, for far too long, ordinary Australians have been kept out of any debate by the major Parties. I and most Australians want our immigration policy radically reviewed and that of multiculturalism abolished. I believe that we are in danger of being swamped by Asians. Between 1984 and 1995, 40 per cent of all migrants into this country were of Asian origin. They have their own culture and religion, form ghettos and do not assimilate. Of course, I will be called racist but if I can invite who I want into my home, then I should have the right to have a say in who comes into my country. A truly multicultural country can NEVER be strong or united and the world is full of failed and tragic examples, ranging from Ireland to Bosnia, to Africa and closer to home, Papua New Guinea. America and Great Britain are currently paying the price.

Mr Deputy Speaker, Arthur Calwell was a great Australian and Labor leader and it is a pity that there are not men of his stature sitting on the Opposition benches today. Arthur Calwell said, and I quote:

'Japan, India, Burma, Ceylon and every new African nation are fiercely anti-white and anti one another. Do we want or need any of these people here? I am one red-blooded Australian who says NO and who speaks for 90 per cent of Australians.'

I have no hesitation in echoing the words of Arthur Calwell.

Mr Deputy Speaker, there IS light at the end of the tunnel and there ARE solutions. If this government wants to be fair dinkum, then it must stop kowtowing to financial markets, international organisations, world bankers, investment companies and big business people. The Howard Government must become visionary and be prepared to act, even at the risk of making mistakes.

In this financial year, we will be spending at least $1.5 billion on foreign aid and we cannot be sure that this money will be properly spent, as corruption and mismanagement in many of the recipient countries are legend. Australia must review its membership and funding of the UN, as it is a little like ATSIC on a grander scale, with huge tax free American dollar salaries, duty free cars and diplomatic status. The World Health Organisation has a lot of its medical experts sitting in Geneva, while hospitals in Africa have no drugs and desperate patients are forced to seek medication on the black market. I am going to find out how many treaties we have signed with the UN, will have them exposed, then call for their repudiation.

THE GOVERNMENT SHOULD CEASE ALL FOREIGN AID IMMEDIATELY AND APPLY THE SAVINGS TO GENERATING EMPLOYMENT HERE AT HOME!

Mr Deputy Speaker, abolishing the policy of multiculturalism will save billions of dollars and allow those from ethnic backgrounds to join mainstream Australia, paving the way to a strong, united country.

Immigration must be halted in the short-term, so that our dole queues are not added to by, in many cases, unskilled migrants not fluent in the English language. This would be one positive step to rescue many young and older Australians from a predicament which has become a national disgrace and crisis.

I MUST STRESS AT THIS STAGE, THAT I DO NOT CONSIDER THOSE PEOPLE FROM ETHNIC BACKGROUNDS CURRENTLY LIVING IN AUSTRALIA, ANYTHING BUT FIRST CLASS CITIZENS, PROVIDED OF COURSE THAT THEY GIVE THIS COUNTRY THEIR FULL, UNDIVIDED LOYALTY.

Mr Deputy Speaker, the Government must be imaginative enough to become involved in the short-term at least, in job creating projects that will help establish the foundation for a resurgence of national development and enterprise. Such schemes would be the building of the Alice Springs to Darwin railway line, new roads and ports, water conservation, reafforestation and other sensible and practical environmental projects.

Therefore, I call for the introduction of National Service, compulsory for male and female, upon finishing year 12 or 18 years of age, for a period of 12 months. This could be a civil service with a touch of military training because I don't feel we can go on living in a dream world for ever and a day, believing that war will never touch our lives again.

The Government must do all it can to help reduce interest rates for business. How can we compete with Japan, Germany and Singapore who enjoy rates of 2, 5.5 and 3.5 per cent respectively? Reduced tariffs on foreign goods that compete with local products only seem to cost Australians their jobs. We must look after our own before lining the pockets of overseas countries and investors at the expense of our living standards and future.

Mr Deputy Speaker, time is running out. We may only have

10–15 years left to turn things around. Because of our resources and our position in the world, we won't have a say because neighbouring countries such as Japan with 125 million people, China (1.2 billion), India (846 million), Indonesia (178 million) and Malaysia (20 million), are well aware of our resources and potential.

WAKE UP AUSTRALIA BEFORE IT IS TOO LATE!

Australians need and want leaders who can inspire and give hope in difficult times. Now is the time for the Howard Government to accept the challenge.

Mr Deputy Speaker, everything I have said is relevant to my electorate of Oxley, which is typical of mainstream Australia. I do have concerns for my country and I am going to do my best to speak my mind and stand up for what I believe in. As an independent, I am confident that I can look after the needs of the people of Oxley and I will always be guided by their advice. It is refreshing to be able to express my views without having to toe a Party line. It has got me into trouble on the odd occasion but I am not going to stop saying what I think.

I consider myself just an ordinary Australian who wants to keep this great country strong and independent and my greatest desire is to see all Australians treat each other as equals, as we travel together towards the new century. I will fight hard to keep my Seat in this place but that will depend on the people who sent me here.

Mr Deputy Speaker, I thank you for your attention and trust that you will not think me presumptuous if I dedicate this speech to the people of Oxley and those other Australians who have supported me. I SALUTE THEM ALL!

It was over, over at last. Waves of relief washed over me and I really felt for Pauline after what she had been through. She had survived and that was the main thing. She had stumbled a little along the way and her voice had flattened here and there but that was nothing. She was the last of 'the new class of 1996' to deliver her maiden speech. The other speeches would never see the light of day again — Pauline Hanson's would become part of Australia's political history.

Graeme Campbell was the first person to congratulate Pauline and he kissed her. Alan Rocher who was in front of her, turned around and shook her hand. Joanna Gash the Liberal MP for the NSW Seat of Gilmore was next in line to offer Pauline congratulations, followed by De-Anne Kelly the National Party member for the North Queensland Seat of Dawson. Teresa Gambaro the Liberal MP for the Queensland Seat of Petrie offered her congratulations to the now Parliamentary-blooded red-head from Ipswich. Ross Cameron, the new Liberal MP for Parramatta, came with two friends to Pauline's office after the speech to shake her hand.

During the speech, the incorrect population figures for the Asian nations came arcing towards me out of the TV screen like anti-aircraft fire. Before we were blown completely out of the sky, I had the *Hansard* office on the telephone and immediately corrected the figures. A few friendly calls came in quickly, alerting me to the mistake. It took a while for Pauline's political and media enemies to wake up. When they did, some of them went 'off their brain' as if Pauline had totally destroyed herself and they would be the harbingers of this incredibly significant and momentous event. Admittedly, it was a stupid mistake. I made it. The mistake was corrected in *Hansard* before the speech was published — so what?

Morrie Marsden helped me to distribute copies of the speech to the press gallery boxes and I handed a few out personally to selected journalists. It would take a little while for the impact of the speech to properly sink in. I have come to learn that expecting most of the media to pick up quickly on a 'hot' story is like shooting big game with a high velocity, hard metal jacketed bullet. The projectile enters the target, severing a vital artery, and exits having caused little visible damage. The beast charges on, finally crashing down when its small, starved brain and other vital parts are no longer fuelled by precious blood.

Back in the office I congratulated a buoyant Pauline and told her that our disagreement just before the speech had obviously helped her 'fire up'. She agreed, giggling and confident. I felt happy for her and shared her jubilance — just like the trainer who gets a problem filly up to win her maiden race by 'streeting' the rest of the field. Pauline, Morrie, Barbara Hazelton and a female friend of Barbara's went off to have dinner and celebrate. In my bad old days I would have gone with them and got very drunk indeed, but my Ménière's Disease has taken the sting out of my tail. I went off with two out-of-town mates, ate Japanese and drank plenty of mineral water. I was among good company. Kim Beazley was sitting at the next table.

Morrie Marsden left Pauline's group after dinner and returned disconsolately to his motel, after having been ignored by Pauline. His trip to Canberra had not been all that successful. Pauline and the others went off to the La Grange bar in Manuka to party on. It was at La Grange, on this night of Pauline Hanson's triumph, that she met David Oldfield for the first time. I would not realise until May 1997 that David Oldfield had, at that chance meeting, taken the first steps down the road that would see him ending up in my job.

The waves of relief that had washed over me earlier in the evening would soon be replaced by ones of anger and turbulence. Who was it who said, 'Life isn't meant to be easy'?

NINETEEN

The Maiden Speech — Post Natal

Brett Heffernan had stayed behind at the Ipswich office, holding the fort with Heidi Lewis. After periods of frenetic activity interspersed with brief lulls, the office had been very quiet leading up to the maiden speech. Brett told me that, on the day of the speech, the office had received only six telephone calls and two visits by constituents. The day after the speech, all hell broke loose.

At Parliament House, the switchboard threatened to become gridlocked and, at one stage, there were moves to take on temporary relief staff. The three telephones in Pauline's Canberra office and the same number in her Ipswich office were continually jammed. The fax machines in both offices threatened to melt down and I am certain that I will be the first positively-diagnosed case of brain cancer to be caused by over-use of a mobile phone! For weeks after the maiden speech, I was receiving between forty and sixty calls daily on the mobile and, on a few occasions, hit the eighty mark. Calls came in from all around Australia, Europe, Canada, USA and Japan but the call to beat all calls came from a very switched-on political commentator in Iceland!

Dealing with the media became more than a full-time job and I was really trying to do the work of three or four people. It was made even more daunting knowing that I had no permanent, efficient and loyal back-up. Brett Heffernan was coming close to resigning and I would be on my own again. I was starting to feel the same way I had one day up on the Sepik River in PNG, when one of my very expensive twelve-passenger jetboats caught fire, nearly killing my most trusted and loyal native 'boss boi' and his infant son. I cut the boat's lines and watched it drift off down the river, blazing like a Viking funeral barge.

My media strategy needed to be simple. I would 'ration' Pauline out like bread on a Moscow food queue. There were four media people I could rely on to at least give Pauline a chance to have her say. Two of these would actively defend her from time to time. The rest of the 'chooks' could line up for the scraps.

On the Tuesday a week after her maiden speech, Pauline's father became gravely ill, so she and Barbara left Canberra to fly back to Ipswich. Pauline was to go on to the Gold Coast to be with her father. Earlier in the day, the prophet in me took over. I told Pauline that with all the fuss stirred up about the maiden speech, it was more than likely she would face the prospect of violence to herself. I asked her how she would feel, for example, if somebody spat on her. She recoiled and told me that even the thought of that happening was her worst nightmare. She said that someone had done that to her once before and she had never forgotten the incident. Later, just before Christmas 1996, Pauline was to be allegedly spat on by two Aboriginal children. The charges were later dropped.

On Wednesday, September 18, former Liberal Senator Noel Crichton-Browne from WA came to Pauline's office to renew acquaintances with me. I had first met Noel in WA when I was working on Graeme Campbell's election campaign. He met Pauline briefly, for the first time, on this visit when she was busy leaving the office on her way back to Brisbane. He congratulated her on her maiden speech and said he would catch up with her later on.

Parliament House has its own 'bush telegraph'. Paul Filing, the former Liberal, now independent, MP for the Western Australian Seat of Moore, and a mortal enemy of Crichton-Browne's, stopped me in the corridor later that day. He was rather strained and puffed up and asked me if Noel was working out of Pauline's office. I could have told the former Fraud Squad detective to mind his own business but, ever my polite self, told him Noel was a mate of mine who had dropped in for a cup of tea.

Noel would subsequently have two more meetings with Pauline in her Canberra office, over a cup of coffee. In addition, he took her out to dinner in Canberra once, at my suggestion, when I told him Pauline rarely received social invitations from other politicians. For his trouble and good-natured concern, and Pauline's acceptance of his friendship, Noel and she became victims of the vicious Canberra rumour mill which had them sleeping together. Tongue in cheek, I told Pauline she had finally made the big time. We all had a laugh and I got the impression that Pauline had lightened up a bit, having cast the pre-maiden-speech jitters aside.

Noel Crichton-Browne is an astute political operative and tactician — just ask John Howard and the WA Liberals. As a young man, he went out into the rough and tumble WA mining towns and organised Liberal Party branches, while the trendy and soft city-slicker Libs stayed close to their espresso bars and rarely strayed off the bitumen.

Noel Crichton-Browne was genuinely interested in Pauline's political progress and asked me if he should write her a letter offering advice on a take-it-or-leave-it basis. On October 26, 1996, he wrote to Pauline, also sending a copy to me. I don't think Pauline read Noel's letter. If she did, she never acknowledged it, but she gets a second chance in Appendix One at the back of this book.

The letter from the hardened, political warhorse to the raw, inexperienced novice is fascinating. It is interesting that the astute and adroit 'numbers man' assessed 'Hansonite' candidates as having a great chance of winning the balance of power in the WA upper house, in that State's December 1996 elections. His view reinforced my strategy of having Pauline concentrate on winning Senate Seats at the next Federal Election. As time rolls on, it will be interesting to see if any of Crichton-Browne's advice to Pauline assumes the status of prophecy.

On Tuesday, September 24, I returned to the Ipswich office to find it akin to a battlefield. There were boxes of faxes and mail everywhere, and the phones just didn't stop. Heidi Lewis was the only person in the office with the ability to establish a data base on the computer and she was now confronted with a huge workload. Barbara Hazelton, though having completed an Access data base course in Canberra at the end of June, gave me no indication at any time of helping Heidi in this area. I constantly made

Pauline aware of the continuing poor performance of the office, but the 'girls' club' maintained its solidarity.

From the day I started with Pauline, I stressed the great importance of storing, on computer, all the names and addresses of Pauline's supporters as they came into the office by way of personal visit, or from telephone, fax or mail. Up until the maiden speech we had about 3000 names on file. After the speech, the floodgates opened and, when I left Pauline, the database had grown by thousands. I told Heidi Lewis to make back-up tapes and to keep one set at her home while providing another set to me for lodgement in a bank safety deposit box. I thought this action would provide sufficient insurance against any combination of disasters.

The tidal wave of incoming calls to Pauline's Ipswich and Canberra offices made a normal daily office routine out of the question. The overwhelming majority of support was from all around Australia and made it impossible for Pauline to properly service her constituents. This problem was not confined to Pauline's office. The majority dared not admit it but she was having an effect on the offices of other State and Federal politicians. I was told by a few of my spies that irate constituents were contacting their MP's offices demanding they support Pauline. It would still take time for the penny to drop with the pundits and the commentators about the level of her support.

Pauline needed double the number of phones and treble the staff to even keep her head above water. In late November 1996, I had started to organise with the Department of Administrative Services to connect more phone lines to the Ipswich office and had begun the process of organising some volunteers to come and work in the office to help with processing mail, sending out copies of Pauline's maiden speech and other material, and answering the telephones. I had spoken about the need for using volunteers previously with Pauline, but she was never enthusiastic and, what worried me more, was unable to even start giving me a list of candidates. It seemed ridiculous but the Member for Oxley seemed to have no personal network of helpers at all. Earlier in the year I had stressed to Pauline and Morrie Marsden the urgency of compiling, from the computer data base, a comprehensive list of people to help on the polling booths come election time. Nothing was done. I received the same response when I asked for a list of people who would help send off 'Letters to the Editor' when the situation demanded it. I found it impossible to properly delegate those important tasks that needed to be carried out by local supporters.

It was the same story when I suggested that Pauline create a committee for her re-election. I was surprised that Morrie Marsden resisted this initiative, saying that Pauline was 'very suspicious about committees' as she did not want to be controlled by anyone.

I told Morrie that it was up to Pauline to make sure she ran her own committee and, besides, she had no Party to be responsible to anyway, so what was the point? At that stage I wrote on the office whiteboard, 'The committee for the re-election of Pauline Hanson' and 'The friends of Pauline Hanson'. Under this I wrote, 'President, Secretary and Treasurer'. I thought that, sooner or later, the message would spark some discussion. It stayed there for weeks, until I got sick and tired of looking at it and rubbed it off in mild disgust.

The next problem that confronted Pauline's office was how she could turn it into a printing and publishing house. The demand for her maiden speech and the Aboriginal research paper reached ridiculous proportions, and this increased further after Pauline delivered a speech to Ted Drane's Australia Reform Party in Melbourne on Saturday, October 12, 1996. The photocopier in the Ipswich office was running out of life and the technician who came to nurse it along said that it would be easier on everyone if he put his bed next to the machine.

Many people wanted copies of the speeches faxed to them, which was just ridiculous, totally impractical and clogged up our fax machine during normal office hours. Despite having told everyone in the office to bear this in mind, I would arrive to find the quite smart Xerox fax machine groaning in agony.

Every Parliamentarian is supplied with unlimited quantities of A4 paper, so that presented no problem, but our Ipswich photocopier was out of the race because it was expected to process normal office work as well. At Parliament House there is an in-house printing and photocopying office that caters for the needs of members. Backbenchers are entitled to a quota of 42 000 sheets of A4 for printing and photocopying, but it took no time at all for Pauline to exhaust her quota. I drove Andy Hall, the good-natured manager of Registry Stores and Printing, to near distraction with requests for more and more printing and, when he finally told me that there could be no more, he did so with considerable relief. Andy said that Pauline had broken all the records by exhausting her paper entitlement so quickly.

It was important to keep the speeches and research going out, since I was acutely aware that I was witnessing the first signs of what could become a revolution in Australian politics. I told Pauline that, short of resigning, she would have to allow herself to be pulled along by the massive undertow of support, while we worked out how to handle it and plotted the best course to follow. To reject or even partially shun such an outpouring would be sheer madness. It had to be all the way or nothing.

I began casting around for a 'fairy godmother' to do some free printing for Pauline — except, in this case the godmother turned out to be a god-father, and certainly no fairy! Joe Bryant was referred to me by a Hanson supporter, John McRae from Sydney. Bryant works out of premises in the industrial suburb of St Marys in Sydney's west. He is a bluff, straight-up-and-down man who lives in a well-worn body. He has been an earth mover, cattleman and sometimes publisher who has had his fair share of run-ins with the banks. He vehemently opposes what he sees as an uncaring and ruthless global economic and banking system that ignores small business, farmers and blue-collar workers.

I went out to St Marys and saw Joe Bryant in the first week of November 1996. His workshops and yard are reminiscent of a *Mad Max* set. Joe and I got on well and he said he would get his family to organise the printing for Pauline. When I got back to Ipswich, I sent Joe down disks containing the maiden speech, what I call 'The Melbourne Speech', and the Aboriginal research paper that had been compiled by Brett Heffernan. Joe incorporated the first two speeches in one booklet. He organised 16 000 copies and even paid to send them to Ipswich. It was an enormous boost, just when we needed it. Joe is a 'believer' and he welcomed Pauline's arrival into the political bullring. In June 1997, Joe told me that a network of his mates was still helping as best they could. Joe said that he was aware of Pauline's shortcomings but she had become the catalyst for ordinary Australians to have their say. There are plenty of Joe Bryants in Australia and many of them are biding their time until the next election.

Joe went out to the Qantas lounge at Mascot to meet Pauline and she thanked him for his help. This was just after I had been sacked. According to Joe, David Ettridge who was to become the National Director for One Nation was with Pauline, and he presented as being politically naïve — something he has admitted to in a media interview. Time will tell.

At a later date, Cheyenne MacLeod, one of the women from Pauline's Ipswich office, rang Joe Bryant and asked if he would do some more printing. Joe said he would, but that it would have to be charged out this time. Joe has had no further communication from Pauline's office since that time. This was her *modus operandi* and it constantly irritated me. Instead of contacting Joe herself, she had left it to one of her staff. Joe Bryant had done Pauline a big favour and she seemed almost dismissive of it. She had no idea of how to positively 'stroke' people, such an important tool in business and in politics. Really, it is mostly about manners and gratitude.

The weeks after the maiden speech were frantic and full of drama. Overflowing mail bags at the Ipswich and Parliamentary Post Offices, bundles and bundles of letters stacked in boxes stacked on top of other full boxes, miles of faxes, reams of telephone messages, enough flowers to start a florist shop, and people lined up in the office reception area like winners at a TAB window.

Pauline's response to her massive support was interesting. At her Canberra and Ipswich offices, the mail came in bag loads and I found that I had another problem with which to deal. As if hypnotised by her fan mail, Pauline would sit down at her desk and read through hundreds of letters, wasting hours of valuable time that should have been spent working on the job of being an effective politician. I tried to impress on her that reading the letters served no meaningful purpose — after going through the first hundred or so, the basic message of support was coming through loud and clear. Pauline ignored my advice and stuck to her task. My strategy was simple. When in Canberra I would gather up the mail as soon as it came in and redirect it to the Ipswich office. All I was doing was delaying the inevitable because, when Pauline returned to the electorate, she would take boxes of letters home with her. She was starting to like being a 'star'.

The invitations for Pauline to attend and speak at functions came in thick and fast from all over Australia. National Party branches in particular were keen to seek her out, and a few Liberal Party branches put in their bids. The Queensland Division of the Liberal Party issued dire warnings to its branches that no invitations to speak should be issued to Pauline Hanson. A Labor Party branch on the NSW south coast bravely put up its hand but had it quickly slapped down by the Party machine. Free speech does have its limits.

If the Canberra press gallery and the other politicians had been able to see at first hand the level of support for Pauline, it would have been interesting to observe their reactions — even more so if some of the politicians had been able to read what a lot of their own constituents were telling this political novice who had lit the fuse that was racing madly towards a magazine of political dynamite. Time may tell but, at the end of 1997, that fuse was still well and truly alight.

TWENTY

Watch your Back!

Peter Slipper is the Liberal Party Member for the Queensland Federal Seat of Fisher and has held the Seat since 1993. He held the Seat for the National Party from 1984 until it was wrested from him by Labor's Michael Lavarch in 1987. In between playing this political version of musical chairs, Michael Lavarch was Labor's Attorney-General. Given the incestuous currents ebbing and flowing in the turbulent and murky seas of politics, it comes as no surprise to learn that Barbara Hazelton once worked for Peter Slipper as one of his electorate officers in the term leading up to his defeat in the Federal Election of 1987. Coincidence explains the trivial fact that Peter Slipper went to school at Ipswich Grammar, at the same time as Morrie Marsden Pauline's ex-lover and campaign manager. After Slipper's defeat in 1987, Barbara Hazelton went to work for the then National Party Senator, John Stone. As it transpired, she had allegedly sought an alternative employer before going to Stone.

The electorate offices of MPs are the cradles of their political survival. Their next election campaign begins on the first day after their election to office. This is a never-ending cycle and so much depends on the staff who work in those offices. The electorate staff are in the front lines of the battle, along with their employer. They are face-to-face with constituents all the time and many of them become involved in the local Party branch structure. It goes without saying that unqualified and reciprocated loyalty is an essential ingredient in any successful political office.

I was, therefore, more than surprised when Barbara Hazelton 'paid out' in no uncertain terms on her former employer Peter Slipper on several occasions. Barbara attacked Slipper savagely in front of Pauline and I wondered what she thought of this behaviour. I was soon to find out.

Barbara's attacks on Slipper were particularly nasty and I wondered what the working environment must have been like in his electorate office. Barbara told a story that Slipper had allegedly asked her to stop wearing a particular red dress and she had obviously been incensed by this directive. Irrespective of what sort of person Peter Slipper was when Barbara Hazelton was employed by him, I wondered why she had not simply resigned if she had been so obviously unhappy in his employ.

When I was in Canberra in September 1996, I dined at a Chinese restaurant one evening with Noel Crichton-Browne. We were asked to join another table where Liberal Senators Bob Woods and Warwick Parer were sitting with Peter Slipper. During the course of the evening, I could not resist mentioning Barbara Hazelton to Peter Slipper. I took a rise out of him by remarking what a terrible boss he must have been to engender such abuse of him by her. Slipper was nonplussed and genuinely surprised, and then shocked when I told him what Hazelton had been saying about him. He then went on to tell me that, on the day of the declaration of the poll for the Seat of Fisher when he lost it to Labor's Michael Lavarch in 1987, Margaret Woodgate the then Electorate Officer for Lavarch had told him that Barbara Hazelton had approached Lavarch, asking for a job. Peter Slipper said that, on one of the blackest days of his life, his reaction had been a feeling of shock and disbelief, having been apparently betrayed by a person he had trusted.

I joined the ranks of the nonplussed when I passed on the story to Pauline on the basis that she should know for her own protection and at least have the story checked out. I was amazed when she stoutly defended Hazelton, saying that Barbara was forced to look after herself and find a job when Peter Slipper was defeated. For one of the rare occasions in my life I was speechless. Pauline just seemed to have no comprehension or understanding of what running a political office meant, and standards such as loyalty and integrity seemed to have no currency with her. I would be made painfully aware of this when Pauline sacked Jeff Babb and myself on December 9, 1996.

On December 16, 1996, the Brisbane *Courier-Mail* ran a story on its front page wherein it referred to what Peter Slipper had told me about Barbara Hazelton. According to the report, Michael Lavarch said: 'Before the poll was declared, she [Hazelton] telephoned me, at that stage an electorate officer for Slipper, and said she would like to work for me . . . Mrs Hazelton told me that despite working for a National Party Member she was "a Labor sympathiser".' According to the report, Barbara Hazelton had said Mr Lavarch's claims were, 'So laughable I am not even going to comment'. Laughable or not, the sorry tale was out in the open and only confirmed my worst fears.

On the day after the publication of the story, I telephoned Michael Lavarch and he confirmed the details of it to me. He said that he had told both his wife Linda and Margaret Woodgate about Hazelton's conversation with him and, despite the fact that the incident had occurred almost ten years ago, it was not something that he could easily forget, given that it was so extraordinary and unprecedented.

I spoke to Michael Lavarch again in July 1997, to advise him that I would be mentioning him in this book in relation to the Hazelton matter and he told me that he had no problems at all with that.

Barbara Hazelton stands condemned by her silence in this matter and did not take any legal action against Michael Lavarch, which is telling in itself. As I asked Pauline, had she discerned some special circumstance that would guarantee her immunity from the possibility of being betrayed in a similar way at some time in the future? I read the *Courier-Mail* article a second time and thought of all the tumult and stress that I had endured in order to further Pauline's cause. I felt as if I had been kicked in the guts. Now I know how Peter Slipper had felt.

TWENTY-ONE

Pauline for PM

'John, can an independent become Prime Minister?' I felt as if my inner being had just moved outside my physical body and I was looking down in a detached way at Pauline and myself sitting in her Ipswich office making small talk when she asked me that question. Like a faulty firearm cartridge that discharges milliseconds after it should, those words took longer than they should have to penetrate and enter my consciousness. At first I grinned stupidly, thinking that Pauline was having a joke at my expense but, when I looked hard at her, I could see that she was being deadly serious!

It was a couple of weeks after the maiden speech and the first tidal waves of support had started rolling into Pauline's office, flooding it with thousands of letters, faxes and telephone calls. At one stage the office looked like Interflora's clearing house, there were so many arrangements of flowers coming in by courier. Some wag, or maybe a deadly-serious person, had stuck a properly printed 'Pauline for PM' bumper-sticker on the glass front of the fish and chip shop and that had obviously been the catalyst for Pauline's question.

Pauline was still looking at me, waiting for an answer, and she started to giggle — obviously at me sitting there like a stunned mullet. Once I regained my composure, my first reaction was to scoff and ridicule Pauline for being so bloody ridiculous, and I think that would have been the general reaction — even from some Hanson supporters — but then I started to get my brain into gear.

I told Pauline that her question was not as silly as it first seemed and

140

that an independent could in fact become PM, but only after undergoing a transitional process. In Pauline's case she would have to rejoin the Liberal Party, thus becoming the Liberal Member for Oxley. Her supporters would then have to be sufficient in number to move, in the Party room, for a spill of leadership positions and then to vote her in as leader and PM. It could be done, but I suggested to Pauline that I thought the scenario very unlikely.

On one occasion, Barbara Hazelton told me that John Howard should make Pauline a minister. I also had to explain to her about the mechanics of politics. At another time, Barbara told Pauline and myself that Pauline would be able to 'do deals' over her vote in Parliament. When I asked Barbara how this would come about with John Howard's huge majority her answer was that, when a lot of government members left Parliament to go back to the electorate with Parliament still sitting, the government might find itself short of numbers. I found this proposition of Barbara's quite bizarre as she obviously did not understand the role of the Government Whip whose job it is to manage the members very strictly to ensure that there are always adequate numbers of them in the House of Representatives at any given time.

When sampling the messages of support for Pauline that steadily flowed into her office, a considerable number of them did make the 'Pauline for PM' call. These messages were telling me that a lot of Australians were well and truly fed up with all mainstream politicians. While no doubt a morale booster for Pauline, I felt that the 'Pauline for PM' stuff was going over the top and the end result would be Pauline with a swelled head, making my job just that little bit harder.

I saw Pauline being interviewed on TV in her Canberra office just after the launch of her One Nation Party in April 1997 and a reporter asked her if she had any ambition to be Prime Minister. Instead of Pauline laughing this off and asking for a sensible question, she looked suitably serious and said that it would indeed be a great honour to be PM. As I watched Pauline, I wondered if I was looking at a person who was beginning to take the first steps along that so familiar road to becoming just another politician.

TWENTY-TWO

Pauline in Peril

Prior to the maiden speech, Pauline received what I term low-level 'hate' mail. The worst example was a razor blade carefully attached to the inside flap of an envelope so that a person opening it by finger could suffer injury. There was a fair sprinkling of obscenities and crude cartoons and the majority of this interesting material was from people identifying themselves, perhaps spuriously, as Aborigines and their purported supporters.

After the maiden speech, the real 'nutters' started turning up and making their presence felt. I took one of the first death-threat calls in Pauline's Canberra office. The Parliamentary telephone system indicates the number of the caller on a digital screen if the call is made within the building. In this case, the call came from outside. The caller was a well-spoken man and obviously Australian. He said very coolly, 'If that woman is going to cause chaos in this country, she will be the first to die.' I asked him if he had anything more to say and he said, 'No, that's all,' and hung up. I immediately reported the call to the Federal Police, and to the Protective Services Unit which looks after politicians and other notables.

A steady trickle of death threats came in to both Pauline's Canberra and Ipswich offices, as well as a considerable amount of 'hate' mail with messages of increased intensity and obscenity — a lot of it incredibly vile and pornographic. There are some very sick and twisted people out there who look just like the rest of us, except that a certain part of their brains has blown its fuse box and gone into irreversible maniacal meltdown. Some of them actually even look a lot better and nicer than some of us. Some photos of the monster of Port Arthur have what has been described as an almost angelic quality about them. It's a scary world we now live in, far removed from the world I knew in the days when I caught redfin perch and flew model aeroplanes on the shores of Lake Colac in the Western District of Victoria.

Pauline's personal security problems renewed my acquaintance with Federal Agent Alistair Bain whom I had first met in PNG when I was younger and had hair. Alistair was based in Brisbane, so he was handy to Ipswich. The local Ipswich Police, under the command of Bill Padget, were a great help and I arranged a getting-to-know-you meeting for Pauline with Commander Padget and some of his senior personnel. In late September, 1996, one of Pauline's Aboriginal supporters warned me of possible anti-Hanson trouble erupting in Ipswich during an Aboriginal Football Carnival set down for October 26 and 27. I alerted the authorities and, thankfully, there were no problems. You always need to be on the lookout for the few ratbags who start the ball rolling.

During my guard duties at Pauline's fish and chip shop I didn't encounter any real problems. A couple of Aboriginal kids yelled out some abuse as they ran past the shop on one occasion but that was that. These days my bark is much worse than my bite — but that's pretty well the way it has always been.

As well as Pauline's security, that of her staff had also to be considered. I took steps to make sure Heidi Lewis and Barbara Hazelton were given parking spaces in the security car park under the W. G. Hayden building that houses Pauline's Ipswich office and I organised for stronger office doors to be installed, as well as bulletproof glass in the reception area.

'Pauline Hanson is the most heavily guarded politician in Australian history with the annual cost of protecting her running at more than twice her annual Parliamentary wages bill,' we were told by Gerard McManus of the Melbourne *Sunday Herald Sun*, on June 22, 1997. According to McManus, Pauline Hanson has received dozens of threatening letters from left-wing extremist groups opposed to her views, including organisations that have connections with overseas paramilitary groups. This has prompted ASIO to judge her the highest security risk of any Australian public figure, with her security arrangements exceeded only by those for visiting overseas leaders.

McManus went on to say that Hanson was embarrassed by the cost of her security and had not requested it. It had been imposed on her by ASIO, the police and the Australian Protective Services unit. Such heavy security has its costs, the more obvious one being borne by the taxpayers, but another is the heavy personal cost being shouldered by Pauline and her family. She has a female detective accompany her to the lavatory and she has 24-hour guards. As Pauline said on *Four Corners* on Monday, June 16, 1997, 'I am living in a goldfish bowl.' The strain on her private life with ever-present guards, irrespective of how discreet they try to be, must be a great burden.

The threat to Pauline Hanson's security from organised Asian drug syndicates has been given serious credence by the authorities, with the still unsolved murder of NSW State MP John Newman being a possible precedent for this.

I often talked to Pauline about the security aspect, before things really hotted up. She said that her main concern was the safety of her two young children who lived with her before they went to boarding school. I used to 'rev' Pauline up by telling her I would use her as a shield to protect myself in the event of an assassin's attack. She laughed, albeit a little weakly. Pauline became angry when the *Queensland Times* printed a front page article on her security and included a photo of her young son and daughter. She must have forgotten the time when she had been interviewed with her children on the Channel 7 *Today Tonight* show. I remember talking to the TV screen, telling Pauline how silly she was for allowing the identities of her children to be so publicly revealed.

The increasingly violent response to Pauline and her One Nation Party by an orchestrated minority is cause for grave concern and is foreign to 'the Australian way'. It is pretty clear from the TV coverage that the same old 'rent-a-rabble' faces are starting to crop up at venue after venue. The nutty Socialist Left and the wild-eyed, rabid Trotskyites are well to the fore with their clearly identifiable placards and banners. It would be interesting to know the source of their funding.

There are also large numbers of young Aborigines and Asians joining the violent protests. I doubt whether one of them has read Pauline Hanson's maiden speech, let alone the 'Melbourne speech' which is probably the more important of the two. Ordinary Australians look on and pay the police to keep the peace while radical ratbags, with nothing to offer but mindless violence, chip away at the democratic process by attempting to disrupt Pauline Hanson's legitimate public meetings.

Constant, concerted attacks on Hanson by the National Party Leader Tim Fischer, his Senate Leader Ron Boswell, National Party Senator Bill O'Chee, and other assorted Parliamentary flotsam and jetsam during the June 1997 sitting of Parliament, are likely to have had the very opposite effect of what they were hoping for. Indeed, these very people may well be responsible for 'egging on' the anti-Hanson rabble with the subliminal messages they are sending out. The headline of an article in the *Australian* on June 14, 1997, was 'Fischer threat to torch Oxley MP'. In the article, Fischer is reported as 'promising a slow torching of Ms Hanson'. Tim Fischer constantly calls Pauline Hanson 'dumb and divisive'. 'Dumb' is not a word Tim Fischer should use to abuse other people. Even the Prime Minister seems to be showing signs of being sucked into the vortex of anti-Hanson bile and diatribe being spewed out by her detractors, by linking her with the Ku Klux Klan.

If tragedy was to strike at Pauline Hanson, those who have bleated the loudest from their public pulpits will have to share responsibility. In the time I was with Pauline, I never heard her denigrate or abuse any ethnic group. The strongest language I heard her use was 'blasted' and the very occasional 'bloody.' She would get very angry with those who abused her viciously, whether in the Parliament or the media. After all, like you and me, she is only human.

Coalition supporters, defecting to Hanson in frustration, must wonder at the vehemence of the personal attacks against her. It, in fact, confirms their worst suspicions — that she is right about all politicians conspiring against the people on the major issues. Hanson wants to talk about issues like Native Title, the imbalance of immigration, unemployment, and economic theories that don't seem to be working all that well. All her political

145

opponents seem able to do is to vilify her in an hysterical and panic-stricken way. John Howard's promise of a higher standard of Parliamentary performance and behaviour has not been lived up to.

Pauline Hanson, her family and her staff should be able to go about their business and work and live confidently in a safe environment, but that is not the case at present. It is a sad indictment of our society that a determined and stubborn woman of no particular brilliance can be considered by the 'establishment' as such a threat that they will stoop as low as they can to destroy her. If all sides of politics are kicked hard in the backside at the next election, no tears will be shed except their own.

On Tuesday, November 25, 1997, Pauline Hanson stunned supporters and detractors alike when excerpts from her videoed political 'last will and testament' were presented on Channel 7's *Witness* programme. Over one million Australians saw Pauline deliver her now famous and parodied lines, 'Fellow Australians, if you are seeing me now, it means I have been murdered.' Her adviser, David Oldfield, defended the strategy, claiming it was not a stunt designed to arrest Pauline's dramatic slide in the polls. A rumour swept the Canberra press gallery that Oldfield had been inspired by the movie *The Pelican Brief* which features a 'video from the grave'. The Melbourne *Herald Sun* ran a phone call and, from 916 calls, received a 78.9 per cent 'yes' response to the question: 'Was Pauline Hanson right to make her "after death" video?'

Pauline was attacked in Parliament the day after this *Witness* appearance by politicians who acted like hyenas. Their posturing and pomposity was sickening, with Leo Macleay, the former Labor Speaker, calling on his colleagues to turn their backs 'on this disgraceful woman'. The florid, fleshy Macleay, described by *Age* journalist Geoffrey Barker as 'arguably one of the Australian Parliament's worst Speakers', had his own well-documented experience with allegations of disgraceful behaviour and derision when the details of his taxpayer-funded $65 000 pay-out for falling off a bicycle hit the headlines in 1993.

Ian Sinclair, elder National Party MP, attacked Pauline for drawing attention to death threats to herself in her appearance on *Witness*, saying that this impacted on the safety of all MPs. Sinclair was full of self-righteousness and indignation — a far cry from the gung-ho and colourful politician that he once was. Both sides of Parliament, eager in their condemnation of Hanson, had conveniently forgotten that Prime Minister John Howard, in early 1996, had stood in front of a crowd at Sale, Victoria, wearing a bullet-proof vest for all the world to see. On that occasion no words were needed — that act in itself was enough to tell the Prime Minister's fellow Australians that he didn't trust them and feared for his life. In certain ways, John Howard's appearance at Sale had parallels to the Hanson video.

A clever and very funny advertisement by a take-away cooked chicken distributor was out in the marketplace twenty-four hours after Pauline went to air on *Witness*. Ridicule is a powerful vote killer and can infect the electorate like a flu epidemic.

Pauline and her advisers, instead of taking Aboriginal activist Noel Pearson head-on over his crazy threats of civil war, had opted for flim-flam instead. Hanson should have led the Wik debate with a series of hard-hitting questions and statements in the last sitting of Parliament for 1997, but she failed to do so, only issuing two press releases at the last moment on the last day. It was vital for Hanson to finish 1997 on a high note, ready to re-ignite the fuse in 1998. Instead she fizzled, with many of her supporters starting to have second thoughts about her videoed 'will'. The Hanson camp will need to do a lot of rethinking about its strategy before Parliament sits again in March 1998. It must resist taking its political advice from Hollywood!

TWENTY-THREE

Greeks and 'Eyeties'

When I was attending school as a young teenager in Melbourne in the early 1950s, I remember being called a 'dago' and it was quite obvious to me that I was not being complimented. My father told me what the word meant and went on to explain that other kids at school would have to live with 'pom,' 'boong' and 'chink'.

He told me that it would be better if nobody was ever called those sort of names, but it was all part of growing up. If the name-calling persisted and caused me problems I was to let him know immediately.

With a name like 'Pasquarelli' I had to expect variants of it. When I was called 'pass the jelly', that offended me far more than being called 'dago' and I was too embarrassed to report that indignity to my very busy, medico father. As my teenage years sped by, I became far too busy to worry about becoming a 'victim'. Besides mundane things such as exams, there were new challenges awaiting me on the horizon, like smoking and drinking and, more importantly, girls!

'Eyetie' is a British slang word for 'Italian' and, as my dictionary says, is a jocular mispronunciation of 'Italian'. It travelled to Australia, no doubt, with British migrants. In 1997, I still hear people mispronounce 'Italian' — saying 'Eyetalian'. If I can be bothered, I politely correct them. When Pauline and I were discussing the now much-quoted statement of hers to the *Australian* newspaper on March 4, 1996, wherein she said she was fighting for: 'the white community, the immigrants, Italians, Greeks, whoever', Pauline in speaking to me said 'Eyeties' instead of 'Italians'. This made me sit up and take notice. It had been a long time since I had heard that word and, as far as I was concerned, I thought that it had died out about twenty or thirty years ago. I asked Pauline why she had used that particular slang word and she couldn't give me an answer. She didn't use the word in a nasty way and seemed to think that it was acceptable. I told her that I couldn't care less but that a lot of people of Italian background might. I told her in no uncertain manner that she should never use that word again. I envisaged Pauline standing up in front of the cameras and 'Eyeties' getting a run on the evening news.

I asked Morrie Marsden if he had ever heard Pauline use the word and he said that he couldn't recollect her saying it in his hearing. I told Barbara Hazelton about Pauline's gaffe and enlisted her help in making sure there was no repeat performance. It was likely that Pauline could have heard the word at home when she was a young girl, because her parents belonged to the post-World War II generation when 'Eyetie' would have had plenty of currency.

Simon Kelly, the young *Queensland Times* reporter who had been reporting Pauline since she won Liberal preselection, and doing it in a fairly objective way, had come to Pauline's Ipswich office to talk about her settling-in days as the local Member. I was sitting at the back of the room just to keep an eye on things when Pauline let go with 'Eyetie' in her conversation with him. I couldn't believe that she could be so stupid. Here was my predicted scenario happening right before my eyes. Of course I had nothing to worry about. Simon Kelly belonged to a generation that used a different slang dictionary and the word had gone over his head at 30 000 feet. After Simon Kelly had gone, I got stuck into Pauline again about using the word, but she just laughed it off. I was left in no doubt that she thought I was making a fuss about nothing. I made sure that I told Barbara Hazelton about the incident, hoping that she would impress on Pauline that I was being serious. My only concern was to protect Pauline from herself, but I couldn't seem to get that message through to her.

Paul Bongiorno is the chief newsman for Channel 10 in the Parliamentary press gallery. Like myself, he has an Italian background. He was born and bred in the Victorian provincial city of Ballarat. I attended boarding school at Ballarat Grammar. With my name I should have gone to St Patrick's

College, but that is another story. I used to visit the Channel 10 crew often when I was prowling the Canberra press gallery, to keep on top of things and 'take the mickey' out of the journos. Paul Bongiorno, who is 53, has a sense of humour and he and I would 'rev' each other up now and again. When I was rationing Pauline out to the media, Paul was always asking me to let him have an interview with her because he was concerned that I was letting Channel 9 get under his neck and he was copping flak from his boss. On one particular occasion after he had been nagging me to let him talk to Pauline, I called him 'a good Italian boy' and he responded by saying, 'Us wogs have got to stick together.' Everyone had a good laugh.

I finally relented and organised an interview with Pauline for Paul Bongiorno, to take place in her Parliamentary office. After having patiently put up with me, he was going to get what he wanted at last.

It was a busy day, and I had crews from Channels 7 and 9 waiting in Pauline's outer office. I took up my customary position at the back of the office where I had a good frontal view of Pauline, looking over the back of Paul Bongiorno's visibly balding head. During the interview, Paul asked Pauline the question about her allegedly saying that she would not represent Aborigines.

I tensed a little and started to feel uneasy because I knew this was taking Pauline into that territory where she was likely to talk about 'Greeks and Italians'. I had good reason to tense up. Like a bolt out of the blue, Pauline used 'Eyeties' again to describe 'Italians'. My mouth was starting to dry out as I leaned forward. My eyes were locked on to the back of Bongiorno's head, looking for tell-tale signs such as his hair standing on end or his ears glowing. I started to stand up ready for the worst. I was waiting for some sort of angry and indignant response from Bongiorno, but none came. A wave of temporary relief washed over me and I started to make saliva again. I just couldn't believe that he had not reacted to Pauline's use of the word. The interview concluded and Paul Bongiorno was still swapping small talk with Pauline while his crew started packing up. They were too young to have picked up on Pauline's gaffe. I was flabbergasted and immensely relieved all at the same time. I couldn't believe our luck. I was sure that a person of Paul Bongiorno's experience and age would have reacted to the word 'Eyetie'. Maybe he gets called that a lot and is used to it! Whatever the reason, he had just missed out on a sensational, headline news scoop that could have caused Pauline Hanson real political damage.

After the Channel 10 crew had left the office, I asked Barbara Hazelton to come and listen to what I had to say. I knew from the look on Pauline's face that she knew she had blundered. She tried her usual defence of trying to laugh off my admonishment of her, but I wasn't going to cop that. 'Pauline,' I said, 'I am going to take you to a neuro-surgeon and have him perform a frontal lobotomy on you to excise that word "Eyetie" forever from your senses.' I picked up my mobile phone and went off to have a cup of tea and calm down.

Later in the day, I couldn't help myself and, like a criminal who returns to the scene of his crime, I went back up to the Channel 10 studio in the press gallery to see if Paul Bongiorno had been 'foxing' me. I was unable to accept the fact that he had missed Pauline's use of 'Eyetie' and I was sure that he would triumphantly run the 'scoop' in the evening news. After swapping some small talk with Bongiorno I was convinced, despite all my doubts, that we were safe. If he had been acting he deserved an 'Oscar'. I held my breath as I watched that evening's Channel 10 news but nothing happened. Pauline's incredible luck had held up again.

TWENTY - FOUR

Massacre at *Midday*

The *Midday* show on Channel 9 has now become part of Australia's television history. It began in February 1973, coming from the studios of Channel 10 and being hosted by the Godfather of TV hosts, Mike Walsh. In February 1976, Walsh took the show to Channel 9 and was there until November 1984. Ray Martin took the reins of *Midday* from 1985 to 1993, claiming a mortgage on gold 'Logies'. With Martin's departure, *Midday* fell into a forgettable trough until it was rescued by Kerri-Anne Kennerley in February 1996. It is now back on the top of a ratings crest, bigger and better than ever.

Five days a week, during lunchtime, *Midday* is beamed all over Australia and beyond by the miracle of satellite and its ratings are the stuff that TV executives would sell their wives into slavery for. The show reaches out to an Australian audience of 800 000 in the capital cities and regional areas.

Kerri-Anne Kennerley has climbed the showbusiness ladder from the bottom — singing and 'hoofing it' on the cabaret circuit. As they say in the industry, Kerri-Anne has 'paid her dues'. *Midday* was in the middle of a ratings death-dive when the Kerry Packer–controlled Channel 9 took a gamble and gave the show to a person some in the industry thought an 'airhead'. Kerri-Anne had successfully co-hosted *Good Morning Australia* for the Ten Network and had the credentials. Channel 9 won the bet and the *Midday* show is well and truly back on top of the ratings tree. Kerri-Anne Kennerley is no 'airhead'.

Early on the Wednesday morning after her maiden speech, Lyndal Marks, *Midday's* producer, contacted me to arrange for Pauline to be on the show

152

that day. This was Pauline's first opportunity to appear live on a high rating show with an Australia-wide audience. It was an important follow-up to the maiden speech and I was hoping she would do well. The interview with Kerri-Anne Kennerley was conducted long distance, with Pauline in the Channel 9 studio in the Canberra Parliamentary press gallery. Pauline's appearance was a spectacular success with the obviously average Australian audience clapping and cheering her.

The high points were when Pauline said: 'I want all immigration stopped until we clean up our own backyard' and 'Let's look after our own before we start looking after others.' It was an easily digested populist message and one the people had not heard from other politicians.

The station ran a phone poll on Pauline's maiden speech and the results that came in the next day must have made senior government and opposition pollsters feel like a Bex and a good lie down. The poll question was: 'Are Pauline Hanson's views racist?' Thousands of calls poured in and the result was: 'Yes' 6 per cent, and 'No' 94 per cent. Something different and unexpected was happening.

Kerri-Anne and her producers must have sniffed ratings because Lyndal Marks was soon back for a second serve, with a twist. She wanted Pauline to appear live on *Midday*, in the Sydney Channel 9 studios with Charles Perkins, the Aboriginal activist. At this stage, I could see no harm coming to Pauline in such a confrontation. I knew from his past performances that Perkins had a short temper and I was pretty sure that the studio audience would lean Pauline's way. I told Barbara Hazelton to organise things with Lyndal Marks and told Pauline that there was no need for me to go to Sydney with her and hold her hand.

Charles Perkins has been around for a long time and has done very, very well out of a system that he claims disadvantages his people. He was for a time the Deputy Head of ATSIC, enjoying the salary and all the financial benefits of that position.

If Pauline Hanson is a racist then Charles Perkins is also a racist. On January 8, 1988, Charles Perkins, as the then head of the Federal Aboriginal Affairs Department, spoke to the National Lutheran Youth Assembly in Canberra. He spoke on what was expected of him on Aboriginal issues but, at the end of his prepared speech, he suddenly took the hard right-hand turn into new territory quoted in the following paragraph.

There is no doubt that our economic future relies heavily on trade with our Asian neighbours. While we need to bear these factors in mind we must be careful to carefully monitor immigration. While I accept that we should have an international obligation to accept some refugees we should ensure that such migrants are able to contribute to the development of this nation. I believe we should examine our current migration policy and practice and ask whether it is in balance. I would like to see more public debate on this matter.

His comments created a minor media flurry and, on January 11, 1988, he was interviewed by the ABC's radio programme, *A.M.* He was introduced on the show as having:

... attacked the Government's immigration policies, saying it allows too many Asians into Australia.

[In response to a question Perkins replied:]

It's just my general impression and as I've seen some of the facts, that I think that we ought to hold on South-East Asian immigration for a while until we find out where we're going, what we're doing and we're not getting enough of our immigrants from our normal sources, from Italy and from Greece. It's very difficult for Italians and Greeks to get over here and to be able to be accepted as immigrants into this country when it's very easy for South-East Asians to get in and I think that some of the quality of some of the people who are getting into this country is not very good at all.

[When Perkins was asked what his problem with South-East Asian migrants was he said:]

154

Some of them are getting into criminal activities, and you would have seen reports in the newspaper, of a very heavy kind and I think that these sorts of people, we don't want them in this country. We've got enough of our home-grown criminals.

[On more questioning on his anti-Asian immigration comments, Perkins said:]

The fact is that my point is that I think we ought to get more of a balance in our immigration policy than we've got at the present time.

[In answer to the predictable ABC question of whether he was a racist, Perkins had this to say:]

No, that's not the point. That, I think, is a wrong definition of a racist. The fact is I'm saying we ought to have a better balance and if that's racism, well I'm rather amazed.

Charles Perkins made his 1988 comments as a Commonwealth Public Service bureaucrat, albeit under the protective mantle of the Hawke, politically-correct Labor Government. It could very well have been Pauline Hanson speaking, calling for a debate on immigration, questioning the rate of Asian immigration and asking for a restoration of the balance of Australia's migrant intake towards drawing it from Anglo-European sources. We all have very short memories. For his trouble, Perkins was swiped at by the then (and politically-correct) president of the Human Rights and Equal Opportunity Commission, Justice Marcus Einfeld, who said of Perkins, 'As a prominent Aboriginal spokesman, Mr Perkins should know better than to attack the suitability of Asian or any other ethnically identified migrants whether on the grounds of supposed excessive criminality or for any other reasons.'

On December 1, 1996, Charles Perkins was revisited by the media when he was reported by journalist Greg Abbott in a story that said he still stood behind controversial statements he made in 1988 calling for a halt to Asian immigration. 'My view is exactly the same as it was at the time,' Perkins said.

Perkins was not alone in his partial support of Pauline Hanson. At an indigenous affairs conference in Toowoomba, Queensland, in November, 1996, Gary Foley one of Australia's more radical Aboriginal activists called for ATSIC to be abolished saying, 'There are a lot more people than just me nationally in the Aboriginal community who've been saying that, almost since the organisation's inception. Pauline Hanson has stolen the line from me.' Foley described the bureaucracy that had sprung up around the indigenous cause as an Aboriginal 'industry'.

Like a lot of Aboriginal activists, Charles Perkins would be able to pass as a local on a Greek island. In summer I am most probably darker than him. It is the definition of 'Aboriginality' and the confusion surrounding it that gets right up the noses of mainstream Australians when they are being hectored and harangued by the commissars of the Aboriginal 'industry'. If my father was Italian (which he was) and my mother had Aboriginal blood, the Italian community would regard me as being Italian but the Aboriginal community would see me as one of theirs.

It is technically possible for people with no Aboriginal blood at all to become Aborigines. This can happen through the marriage of a non-Aboriginal to an Aboriginal. The transition can also occur if a non-Aboriginal is accepted by Aboriginal elders as demonstrating an empathy for the Aboriginal race and its culture. The conversion of non-Aboriginals to Aboriginals by marriage or by cultural acceptance is formalised by respective initiation ceremonies. This system of all-too-easy racial classification is very confusing and is wide open to allegations of a kind of 'race-fixing' to facilitate the obtaining of benefits, ranging from DSS payments to eligibility for lodging possible multi-million dollar land claims. The cynicism of many mainstream white Australians is understandable.

On Monday, September 16, 1996, just six days after her maiden speech, Pauline Hanson flew from Canberra to Sydney with Barbara Hazelton to do battle with Charles Perkins on the *Midday* show. I sat in her Canberra office and watched the event on TV.

Pauline was dressed in a mauve frock and looked more confident than I had seen her. Kerri-Anne Kennerley played the role of honest broker and was a capable and professional adjudicator, given the circumstances. I knew Charles Perkins was going to lose it when I saw him bristle as he made eye contact with Pauline. He totally lost his composure, calling Pauline 'a racist person' and saying, 'She's telling a lot of bullshit.' Apparently hell-bent on self-destruction, he accused Pauline of '. . . using the privilege of Parliament to slam Asians, Aborigines and all good Australians.' He then committed the fatal sin of attacking the audience, referring to them as 'the blue rinse set' and Pauline's 'cheer squad'. He went into full kamikaze mode towards the end of the segment, throwing back at Pauline a copy of her Aboriginal research paper which I had told her to hand him. The audience reacted angrily towards him. Becoming increasingly flustered and angry, he kept turning on the studio audience when he couldn't land a blow on his enemy who was sitting just a couple of feet away. He tried to attack Pauline over her ownership of property and her divorce settlements, but this just dug his grave deeper. When Pauline said that she had worked hard for all she had, the audience applause drowned Perkins out. He became even more agitated when the angry audience continually jeered and booed him.

Charles Perkins' primary audience was not in the Channel 9 studio, it was out in Redfern, Fitzroy, Bourke and Kempsey — wherever there were Aboriginal settlements — and it was also in the ranks of the 'chattering classes' and the foot-soldiers of the Aboriginal 'industry'. He had desperately wanted to do well in the eyes of the people he thinks he represents. Instead he had seriously damaged the cause by stupidly expressing his obvious hatred for Pauline Hanson. The confrontation was a disaster for Perkins and the whole Aboriginal 'industry'. Decent Aboriginal Australians were badly let down and many of them are increasingly realising that they are not being served well by their mainly self-appointed spokesmen and spokeswomen.

As the Perkins–Hanson bout was winding up, Kerri-Anne Kennerley put a proposal to Pauline and Charles Perkins that made me sit up and take notice. She asked Pauline if she would be prepared to visit a remote, outback Aboriginal settlement in company with Charles Perkins, if *Midday* set the whole deal up. The question took Pauline by surprise. Perkins leant forward as if he sensed a chance to drag himself back into the fight. I was willing Pauline to say 'no' because it was far too risky an enterprise, and there was a real security risk involved. Pauline hesitated while she tried to make a decision and I almost felt as if she was looking at me through the camera asking for a 'yes' or a 'no'. Kerri-Anne became more and more insistent and kept putting the question. Pauline looked at Perkins and I saw her eyes harden and her jaw twitch. She had made up her mind. 'Well . . . I . . . Yes!'

Charles Perkins looked almost happy. He had just been granted the reprieve of a return bout.

Despite Pauline's obvious victory, I was kicking myself very hard. I had briefed Pauline on Perkins' 1988 comments on immigration but the copy of his speech and the transcript of his interview with the ABC were still sitting on my desk. I had meant to have her expose him in regard to this damaging material and hand him that paperwork together with the research paper. It could have been a full-on demolition job of Charles Perkins, but he had suffered enough damage anyway! Besides, Pauline had forgotten to even bring up the topic. She had been under a lot of pressure and had done exceptionally well under the circumstances.

Pauline Hanson came back to Canberra with Charles Perkins' scalp hanging from her belt. It had been an impressive victory and I was proud of the 'fish and chip shop lady' from Ipswich who had taken on an experienced 'hotshot' and had done him like a dinner!

TWENTY-FIVE

A Town Like Alice

Lyndal Marks, producer of the *Midday* show, wanted to start negotiating Pauline's proposed outback trip immediately after her appearance with Charles Perkins, but things were complicated because of Pauline's father suddenly taking ill. I told Lyndal that we would give things time to settle down and organise something when Pauline was ready. I was very non-committal because I was still working out how to cancel the whole deal — that is, if I could get Pauline to agree. I was concerned primarily about security and, of course, her 'mates' in the media.

I was back in the Ipswich office on Wednesday, September 25, 1996, tripping over boxes of faxes and mail with my mobile phone grafted to my right ear, when Dennis Passa of *Who Weekly* magazine arrived at the office to keep an appointment to interview Pauline. He and a photographer went off with Pauline to her fish and chip shop and then out to her out-of-town property which I called 'the farm'. I was surprised to be told by Passa that *Who Weekly* 'fact checked' with their interviewees before going to press. It sounded to me almost like responsible journalism.

Dennis Passa had not long left the office when Peter Wilkinson the experienced *60 Minutes* producer was ushered in. Peter had heard about the Kerri-Anne challenge to Pauline and had come to Ipswich to put in his bid. Wilkinson put a convincing case as to why his show should do the visit to an Aboriginal settlement rather than Kerri-Anne's *Midday* and he quickly persuaded me to lean his way. The best argument he had was the ratings. Despite *Midday's* outstanding ratings, *60 Minutes* can attract an Australia-wide audience of 2.5 million viewers as against *Midday's* 800 000. On the debit side, Wilkinson's interviewers had the potential to give Pauline a very hard time. I think the idea of appearing on *60 Minutes* had started to appeal to Pauline and I had resigned myself to going along with the idea. I had kept her briefed from the start and my major concern, that of security, had started to diminish somewhat the more I thought about it. After more discussions with Pauline I eventually told Peter Wilkinson that we would go with his organisation.

What happened next made me realise how cut-throat and competitive TV can be, even within the same network. The people at *Midday* went 'ballistic', as the kids say, and I was bombarded with calls from Lyndal Marks and her team, as well as with calls from Kerri-Anne herself. It all got very willing and there were lots of angry words and tears. I got back to Peter Wilkinson and told him that I didn't want to help cause civil war in the Channel 9 studios — it was all getting a little bit silly. It was obvious that he was copping his fair share too, so that made me feel a bit happier. *Midday* blamed me. I kept them from making contact with Pauline and that only made them more frustrated. It is said that TV people would kill for ratings and I have been convinced.

Peter Wilkinson's strategy was for me to accompany him to Alice Springs, visit some outback Aboriginal settlements and pick a suitable one for the visit by Pauline and Perkins. Peter had been in contact with Charles Perkins and it was suggested we go to Papunya and Yuendumu, both places about three hours drive from Alice Springs.

On Wednesday, October 2, 1996, Peter Wilkinson and I flew from Sydney to Alice Springs. Once we had cleared the limits of the barely-populated fringes of western New South Wales, the landscape below changed suddenly as if we had turned the page of a book. The desert had a soft, pinkish hue to it and would not start to look really harsh until the summer months arrived. It was a clear, fresh day and, looking down at the flattened and folded landscape racing away to the horizon, I thought of those intrepid, and often foolish and quite unprepared, explorers who had ventured out into the vast Australian outback seeking fame and fortune. Many of them had started their journeys in a picnic atmosphere with great bravado and style — and were never seen again.

I had first visited Alice Springs with John Bennett, when we had driven there from Coober Pedy in 1959. The purpose of the trip was to have a field break from the self-imposed, chain gang-like work on the opal fields. We drove there in the 1936 Chrysler sedan I had bought in Melbourne for 100 pounds from a deceased estate. The immaculate, low mileage vehicle wondered what it had struck when it hit the treacherous outback's car-eating tracks that passed for roads. Miles of bottomless potholes and trenches that must have been imported from World War I were hidden beneath tons of red talcum powder that is quaintly called 'bulldust'.

We spent a couple of weeks in Alice Springs and could not fail to notice the Aborigines camped out along the banks of the dried out Todd River. They were sad, derelict people living in decrepit squalor. A lot of them were obviously drunk, despite the law that at that time forbade them access to alcohol. 'Gin jockeys' traded the white fella's grog for brief, fumbling sexual favours that made a mockery of good honest passion and desire.

At Coober Pedy, Aborigines — mainly the women and kids — would 'noodle' the mullock heaps at the top of the mine shafts. This meant going through the discarded, crumbled sandstone, picking up chips of opal and, sometimes, quite large and valuable stones. Some of the men were always offering their women in return for grog — methylated spirits was the currency most in demand. Any takers took incredible risks, as the visiting medical team that used to come up from Port Augusta told vivid stories about the extremely high rate of venereal disease present in the Coober Pedy Aboriginal community. Images of granuloma eroded penises guaranteed celibacy!

The next time I saw 'The Alice' was in 1981 when back in Australia from PNG. I drove solo around most of Australia and made a nostalgic return to Coober Pedy. This time I was driving a Range Rover which I had purchased in Port Moresby in 1976. 'The Alice' had changed dramatically, but not the banks of the Todd River where time had frozen and the Aborigines were still there in the same state that they been back in 1959. Sadly, nothing had changed.

Now it was 1996 and, as the Boeing 737 banked on the final leg of its approach to the Alice Springs runway, I looked down at a sprawling metropolis that seemed strangely out of place in its rusty-brown, khaki-green surroundings.

As Peter Wilkinson and I drove to our hotel, we passed the Todd River. There, as if in a weird time warp, were the images of 1959 and 1981. Like figures in a diorama come to life, the Aborigines were still there. A man and a woman were fighting as if in slow motion — stumbling in a drunken, pawing embrace while two barking dogs scratching up puffs of dust, egged them on.

There was no rest for the wicked. After checking our bags into the Alice Springs Sheraton Plaza, Peter Wilkinson and I headed out to the Aboriginal settlement of Papunya. We flew in a chartered Cessna 402, climbing to 10 000 feet and then flying west for about an hour, buffeted up and down as we rode the thermals rising off the desert floor. The headlining of the cabin took skin off my bald skull on one savage bump. The flight brought back memories of flying over the hot kunai plains in PNG's Ramu Valley. I reminded myself not to tell Pauline about the rough flying conditions — she is a nervous flier!

As we taxied to the parking bay at the Papunya airstrip, a couple of vehicles came down the dusty track to pick us up. Papunya is wholly administered by Aborigines and we were greeted by Alice Anderson who I mentally nicknamed 'the boss lady'. I was pretty spot-on because she was the administrator of the settlement which is run by the Papunya Council. As we drove the short distance into the settlement, I started to notice things. Large clumps of plastic bags, and other plastic and paper debris, were scattered over the landscape like some sort of space-age tumbleweed. Interspersed were wrecked car bodies, rusting engine blocks, sheets of rusted roofing iron and bottles and cans, glinting like baubles in the bright orange sunlight.

We were taken to a basic office which was Alice's headquarters. Both Peter Wilkinson and I noticed Alice's wonderful fingernails — long plastic add-ons that featured miniature Aboriginal dot-painted designs. It was all wasted on Papunya.

A lot of the houses at Papunya have brothers and sisters in Beirut. Trashed, derelict houses with missing roofs, doors, architraves and window frames lined the streets of the settlement. On a vacant block, a crooked line of curved, corrugated-iron water tank halves looked like a grotesque silver caterpillar. When I asked who had vandalised and destroyed the houses, I was told that the culprits had been the occupants. When I asked why, I was told, 'Because they were drunk.' Papunya is supposed to be 'dry', but the grog is easily smuggled in. The water tank halves had become homes for those who had once lived in, but then destroyed, perfectly good houses. Does the desert make one mad?

The school at Papunya has a razor-wire topped, cyclone-wire fence that would do a maximum security prison proud. When I asked why again, I was told that the fence was there to stop the 'vandals'. I looked out at the shimmering desert horizon, squinting to see if I could see the enemy encampment from where the vandals would launch their raids on Papunya. Of course there was none. The vandals, I was told, were members of the Papunya community.

In reply to Peter Wilkinson's asking of some questions, Alice said that more police were needed at Papunya to help 'stop the kids sniffing petrol'. I was amazed at this total abrogation of parental and community responsibility in a closed settlement where it should be possible to maintain high levels of discipline over those who wish to behave anti-socially.

Papunya is supposed to cater for 1500 residents but 'men's business', as distinct from 'women's business', causes that figure to fluctuate. I was told that 'men's business' often degenerated into bouts of uncontrolled drinking during the time the men stayed away from their home settlement. At the time of our visit, the population had dropped to 350–400. A three-man police station looks after law and order — but, in June 1997, it was a two man, one woman station — with Glenys Green, a Kiwi, being the Officer in Charge. She has a hard job in a harsh environment and I wish her and her crew well. Many of the damaged houses I saw at Papunya have since been repaired but that will certainly only prove to be a band-aid solution.

Peter Wilkinson and I flew on to Yuendumu and a white Australian manager was waiting for us. Yuendumu seemed better organised than Papunya, but the scattered debris and litter was the common denominator and I noticed several houses in a very poor state of repair. We were taken to a rather neat council house and had a general discussion. A politically-correct white, female media adviser sternly took issue with me when I used the words 'truancy' and 'wagging school' to describe absenteeism at the local school. I was told, rather icily, that absences were due to 'cultural responsibilities' when there was a 'sorry time'. Translated, this meant that the children would stay away from school at times of mourning. I am not being smart when I say that no particular race has a mortgage on the grieving process. Like the Aborigines at Papunya, the people complained about there being no jobs and about the poor standard of services. One man put his case in a very aggrieved way about the underground asbestos water pipes. I needed to remind him that in many suburbs of Melbourne that was also the case. The sun was setting so we took our leave and returned to Alice Springs. The return flight was smooth because the thermal activity had disappeared with the cooling of the earth. It was too noisy to speak to Peter Wilkinson but I had plenty to think about.

I had started to feel a bit off-colour back at Yuendumu and, while I was having a shower, I started getting symptoms of a Ménière's attack. They are nowhere as severe as they once were but they still have the capacity to make my life uncomfortable.

That night at dinner, Peter Wilkinson said that the two settlements we had visited would be ideal venues for the visit by Pauline and Charles Perkins. The locals had stipulated, however, that no other media were to accompany *60 Minutes* and Peter would need to clear all this with Perkins. I was quite comfortable with the whole deal and was more than confident that Pauline would come out on top of things, as long as she just stuck to her guns. During the meal I tried to solve the problems of the world, starting with our experiences that day at Papunya and Yuendumu.

The people on those settlements are living on their own tribal land, more than three hours drive from Alice Springs. They are the masters of their own destiny and they have chosen to be where they are. Every fortnight, the welfare cheques come in by plane and are cashed in at the local store. Practically everyone is on benefits. The settlements are supposed to be 'dry' areas but 'sly grog' is par for the course.

The people have become so mendicant that they cannot control petrol sniffing in a very closed community. They cannot control vandalism of their own houses and their own school, in a situation where everyone knows everyone else through blood ties and family association, and where strangers would stand out like snowmen in a desert. We do live in a crazy world!

The people in the settlements say that they want jobs but have isolated themselves so far from the marketplace that it is a joke. One hopeful soul said that companies should bring their factories to the settlements. I am sure that Ford or General Motors Holden will send their executives scurrying out to the desert immediately!

How many taxpayers know that, in these Aboriginal settlements, English is taught as a second language to those pupils that do attend school? The misguided motive behind this retrograde step is apparently based on cultural considerations. I think Peter Wilkinson was in basic agreement with me at that dinner table, but he now thinks that Pauline Hanson is a racist. Maybe he thinks the same of me.

During 1996, I listened to and read what thousands of ordinary Australians had to say about Pauline Hanson and her policies, and I spoke directly to many of them. These people do not have cloven hooves and horns on their foreheads. They do not wear white sheets and illuminate their backyards with flaming crosses. They are the family that run the local corner store. They are the neighbours next door, the husband working at the Ford factory while his wife has a part-time cleaning job. They are the man who comes to mow the lawn, the building worker on a concrete pour, the mother dropping her daughter off at kindergarten, or the local postmaster. They are the police settling a domestic dispute, the dentist drilling his patient's tooth, the young woman working on the supermarket checkout. They are the crowd at the football watching their team lose yet another game. They are John Howard's battlers. They are mainstream Australia who have to pay the mortgage, the rent, the school fees, the council rates, the wages, the levy for this and the levy for that and, worst of all, the taxes. These Australians have had it up to their back teeth with the agenda being run by the Aboriginal 'industry' and its mouthpieces in the Parliament and in academia.

It is no longer acceptable for taxpayers to see perfectly good housing

reduced to pigsties by its drunken occupants. Uninformed TV viewers overseas see images of settlements like Papunya in the desert and the inner
Sydney suburb of Redfern and think that white Australia has purposely, as
a matter of government policy, consigned its indigenous peoples to live in
these hovels.

It is no longer acceptable for Aboriginal communities to negligently shirk
their responsibilities over controlling their youth, particularly on abhorrent
social behaviour such as petrol sniffing and vandalism. This applies more
than anywhere else to such self-administered communities as Papunya,
Yuendumu and Palm Island.

Australians have become thoroughly sick and tired of hearing about how
Aboriginal people have some mystical and ethereal connection with the
land, and how they are so concerned about its conservation. Why then,
wherever Aborigines congregate in communities, whether in rural or urban
surroundings, do they show such contempt for their environment by littering the landscape with such a bewildering variety of rubbish — or do
they have some contrived 'cultural' excuse for this anti-social behaviour?

On Thursday, October 3, Peter Wilkinson and I flew back to Sydney and
I was back in Ipswich that evening. The following evening, I was back in
Canberra, preparing for Pauline's visit to Melbourne to speak to Ted
Drane's people and getting ready for the *60 Minutes* visit to Papunya and
Yuendumu with Charles Perkins. I had spoken to Pauline and briefed her
on the outback trip telling her that as long as she performed well she would
reinforce her position on the Aboriginal issue. The script and set would
change a bit, but I would be proved right and Charles Perkins would hit
the canvas again.

TWENTY-SIX

The Melbourne Speech

Ted Drane was very impressed with Pauline and told me that, after her maiden speech, she was attracting a lot of support in Victoria — particularly in the bush. When I first started working for Pauline, I thought that an alliance between her, Graeme Campbell and Ted Drane would maximise the pro-gun, small business, farming and anti-Canberra support in the bush, and to me this made good political common sense. It was never to be. For some reason, Graeme could not flick off the League of Rights people clinging to his coat tails. Ted Drane wanted nothing to do with them and Graeme's insistence at having some of these people present at proposed meetings between Drane and himself finally drove Ted Drane away.

At one stage, very briefly, an Australian First Reform Party almost came into being with Graeme Campbell as President and Ted Drane holding a senior position. Graeme had heavy financial commitments as the result of losing a defamation action brought against him by the WA Director of Public Prosecutions. Ted Drane's organisation, the Sporting Shooters Association of Australia, was pretty flush with funds. Ted Drane thought that Graeme's political experience would be an asset to the proposed party and announced to his National Executive that he was considering offering Campbell money to help form a new political party. It would have been a straightforward, legally-cleared commercial arrangement for services rendered, but Graeme seemed to want everything to happen at once. He ended up saying that Drane was 'bullshitting' and didn't have the money. It seemed to be sour grapes on Graeme's part. From time to time, I tried to patch things up but I had no luck. I told Graeme to stand in the middle of the Melbourne Cricket Ground alone with Ted Drane and have a talk but, in the end, I gave up. After all, Graeme Campbell is a pom!

Ted Drane had organised a conference for his Australian Reform Party to be held at, of all places, Melbourne University on Saturday, October 12. The choice of venue seemed a strange one and had a certain 'red rag to a bull' quality to it. As an act of good will, Ted invited Graeme Campbell and he was very keen for Pauline to appear and speak. Pauline seemed to be getting along well with Ted and I told her that this would help reinforce their relationship as well as spread her influence to another State.

I had always told Pauline that she would never be able to stand alone even if she were possessed of a lot more political savvy and experience. I was feeling that I was getting somewhere by organising some political alliances for her, but my optimism would be short-lived.

I welcomed the chance for Pauline to speak publicly so soon after her maiden speech, because I wanted to expand and qualify some parts of it. I started to write this 'follow-up' speech in the Canberra office on Saturday, October 5, 1996. Parliament was not sitting the following week and I had stayed in Canberra to work, away from the disorganised chaos that was the Ipswich office. I gave Pauline the speech on the morning of the day she presented it and told her to deliver it in the same manner as she had the maiden speech. That speech went from the laser printer to the public without a single alteration.

On Friday, October 11, I heard on the news that demonstrators were preparing to appear in their thousands at my old *alma mater*, Melbourne University. This was not in the least surprising. I had wondered why on earth Ted Drane had chosen that venue, but I had not wanted to raise the matter with him because, after all, it was his show. I was pretty impressed however when, at the very last moment, Ted switched venues to the other side of Melbourne. He managed to move almost three hundred people in the process, totally eluding the media and the protesters. The journalists finally woke up late in the afternoon when all the action was over. A couple of TV crews were given exclusive coverage. Ironically, the new venue was the Italian Veneto Club in Bulleen Road,

Bulleen, where I had listened to Professor Geoffrey Blainey speak in 1987. Ted Drane was to tell me later that the Veneto Club official who had hired out the auditorium to him was sacked for his action, but was eventually reinstated.

Pauline was wearing a striking red dress, though I have been told that redheads shouldn't wear red. She received what can only be described as a rousing welcome and the interaction between her and the audience was very evident. After a brief introduction, Pauline stood up and started to speak:

Ted Drane, Diane Worrall, members of the Australian Reform Party, ladies and gentlemen.

I thank Ted Drane for inviting me here today, as it gives me the opportunity to expand and define what I said about immigration and multiculturalism in my maiden speech.

Mainstream Australia is firmly based on its Anglo-Celtic European heritage, Judaeo-Christian beliefs, English law and the Westminster Parliamentary system.

It is the blending of these elements with the unique Australian environment that has produced a nation of people who are tolerant and prepared to give others a 'fair go'.

Arthur Calwell was the last great Immigration Minister and he was firmly tuned in to what ordinary Australians wanted. He listened to the people and then tried to give the majority what they desired, while still respecting the views of the minority. What a difference from the politicians from both sides of the political fence we have all come to know!

With Gough Whitlam and Malcolm Fraser came a completely different style of politics and Australians started to see the emergence of political bipartisanship in relation to many issues. Multiculturalism became a policy and Malcolm Fraser created an Institute of Multicultural Affairs, with its head Petro Georgiou, the present Liberal MP for the blue ribbon seat of Kooyong. In his maiden speech, Mr Georgiou referred to assimilation as 'discredited', while Andrew Theophanous the Labor MP described it as 'mean spirited'.

These sorts of comments from both sides of the political fence were 'correct' and designed to send a message to any critics that it was pointless to argue any differently.

During the period I am talking about, political correctness started to rear its ugly head and political bipartisanship meant that ordinary Australians were kept out of the debate on so-called sensitive issues like immigration and multiculturalism. Street smart minority lobby groups realised that they could peddle their votes to gutless politicians in return for dollars paid out by ordinary, long suffering Australian taxpayers. Those who dared to break the 'rules' were subjected to vicious attacks by most politicians and the media. Personal vilification and insults became the order of the day and the word 'racist' became so overused that it has become completely devalued.

Ladies and gentlemen, I wish to pay tribute to those people who were prepared to take on the priests of political correctness and their political lackeys long before I came on the scene. In 1984, Professor Geoffrey Blainey delivered a speech to a Rotary Club in country Victoria, in which he made a reasoned call for a debate on the levels of Asian immigration. For his trouble, Professor Blainey was attacked in a most cowardly way and suffered a great deal of personal abuse and stress. He was betrayed by his academic peers and the thing that annoys me most is that he was not stoutly defended in Parliament by the Coalition. Australia's greatest historian had to fight his battle largely with the help of friends from outside those places where democracy and free speech are supposed to be defended.

Others who manned the barricades on the immigration and multiculturalism issues were Bruce Ruxton, Peter Walsh, John Stone and, of course, Graeme Campbell. I hope you will not be too offended, if I say that it took a woman to come along and let the genie out of the bottle!

Since my maiden speech I have received thousands upon thousands of letters, faxes and telephone calls. As you all know, the debate that has been denied mainstream Australia for so long is now well and truly on and I call on all Australians to keep the debate alive so that politicians have no doubt about the message being sent them.

I wish to briefly talk about the Australian culture, as it is the backdrop to our performance as a nation.

There is a clearly definable Australian culture that has many components. It is based on the early settlers and the outback, and I wish to state quite clearly here that Aboriginal culture is part of the Australian whole. Our diverse environment and history helped to create a rich mix of writers, artists and poets and the tradition has been carried on through the years. Our unique humour is reflected in the theatre, film and electronic media, and Australian ballet and opera have a worldwide reputation. Woven through our culture is the Anzac Spirit and the Australian reputation for toughness and fairness, seen in the sporting prowess of our young people. I call on all Australians to be fiercely proud of our culture and to keep the spirit alive. Like anything worthwhile, it must be defended.

Ladies and gentlemen, there are those who wish to denigrate the Australian culture. Some of these people are the leaders of ethnic groups, some are what I call academic snobs, some are in Parliament and some come from the media.

They say that there is no Australian culture, that mainstream Australians are basically 'yobbos' and that the only good things are those which are imported. Well, these people can live in their ivory towers and say what they want but the annoying thing is that many of them feed off ordinary Australian taxpayers by way of the job they have or the grant they receive. Most of them would not be able to get a job in the 'real' world!

I have no hesitation at all, in acknowledging that our Australian culture has been greatly enriched by the wonderful contributions from those who have migrated here but the overwhelming majority of these people have wholeheartedly embraced the Australian way of life — to use that 'terrible' word, they have assimilated!

Let me now turn to the question of immigration. The most important issue in this country is that of unemployment and it is an absolute tragedy that 1.5 to 1.9 million young and older Australians are unemployed. There is every reason to believe that the current rate of unemployment is really 12 to 13 per cent taking into account the 'creative' criteria used to define 'employed'. A person who works at least one hour per week is considered to be 'employed'.

JOBS MUST BE FOUND FOR AUSTRALIANS BEFORE ANY FURTHER IMMIGRATION!

It is simply crazy to keep on bringing people into this country, especially when so many of them are unskilled and have no fluency in English. This does not stimulate the economy at all. All it does is make our welfare bill larger and results in huge amounts being spent on the teaching of English, not to mention the resultant loss of productivity in the workplace.

All immigration must cease immediately so that we can clean up our own backyard and reduce those depressing dole queues. Charity begins at home!

If this strategy was successful, we would then completely review our immigration policy.

The first step would be to redefine the sources of migration to Australia.

I must make one important point. I made it in my maiden speech and it has been conveniently forgotten by the media and my critics. I will repeat it again exactly as I said it.

'I must stress at this stage, that I do not consider those people from [other] ethnic backgrounds currently living in Australia, anything but first class citizens, provided of course that they give this country their full, undivided loyalty.'

From 1985 to 1995, 40 per cent of all migrants were from Asian regions and that is simply too high and must be corrected. As I have said, I can invite who I like into my home, but I have no say in who comes into my country. This situation must change.

Mainstream Australia must be allowed to have a say in how this country will look in a hundred years time! We owe this to future generations and now is the time to tell your politicians to start listening or you will throw them out at the next election!

Ladies and gentlemen, I want my critics to listen carefully, I want them to read my lips! I am not saying that I want all Asian immigration to cease. There has always been an Asian presence in Australia and all I want is the balance restored. I will now outline how I would view a redefined immigration policy.

When immigration was recommenced after our unemployment situation was resolved, it would be on a zero nett basis, that is, we only replace those who leave Australia permanently.

Prospective citizens would have to wait five years before applying for citizenship.

Prospective citizens committing serious crimes would be deported and any property held by them would be seized to defray the costs of deportation.

Health quarantine requirements for migrants must be tightened up immediately.

Migrants must have skills and basic fluency in English.

Spouse and family reunion migration would have to meet stringent criteria.

Our new immigration policy must be selective and restrictive — just like Japan's!

Any increase in immigration beyond zero nett would have to be balanced against employment and economic trends.

The powerful Asian nations would have to be encouraged to accept their responsibilities in respect of Asian refugees.

Ladies and gentlemen, I think our politicians and the 'chattering classes' are starting to get the message that we are not Asians and not part of Asia. I respect the right of Asian nations to run their countries as they see fit and I just want them to let Australians do the same!

Our men and women have spilt blood defending this homeland

of ours and it is up to us now to make sure their sacrifice was not in vain!

Before moving on to the topic of multiculturalism, I would like to comment on what has been said about me by the National Party Leader, Tim Fischer. Mr Fischer has said that my comments could affect some of the business Australia does with some Asian countries. I find this attack a little strange. Mr Fischer was being politically correct and trying to intimidate me which is stranger still coming from the leader of a so-called conservative party. Many National Party members have contacted me about this, telling me to ignore Mr Fischer and that they are not happy with his leadership.

Now it looks as if Mr Fischer has recruited the assistance of Ian McFarlane of the Queensland Graingrowers Association, who has also said that my comments on Asian immigration could cause the loss of business from the region.

It seems strange that in 1985 our share of the East Asian market was 4 per cent but it is now less than 3 per cent. Our share of the Japanese import market has fallen by 25 per cent since 1991 and this was all before anyone heard of Pauline Hanson!

About the only thing that I haven't been blamed for, is the Sydney Swans losing the Grand Final!

Ladies and gentlemen, our exports will continue to sell as long as the price is right — it is simple as that. If what Mr Fischer and Mr McFarlane are predicting really happened, it would mean that Australia and Australians were being held to ransom by external powers and that the free speech of ordinary Australians was under grave threat from foreigners. I hope this will not prove to be the case and that our overseas trading partners have the good sense not to meddle in our internal and domestic affairs.

In my maiden speech I called for the policy of multiculturalism to be abolished and this must be done as soon as possible.

A truly multicultural country can never be strong or united, as continual friction and conflict is created by rivalry between people with ethnic and religious differences.

In Australia, multiculturalism has come to mean minority ethnic groups, funded by ordinary taxpayers, playing games with gutless politicians at the expense of the greater majority. It is a divisive policy that puts people in compartments and prevents them joining the mainstream community.

Australians are tolerant but their patience is being sorely tested by their politicians who have never allowed a full and open debate on immigration and multiculturalism.

Multiculturalism or the 'melting pot' has been a dismal failure all over the world and the record of disasters fill the alphabet. As I speak, men, women and children are being butchered because they are different in some way from their murderers, their only crime being that of living in a multicultural society imposed historically by politicians, colonisers or other external forces. The African continent is in constant turmoil and the horrors of Rwanda, Somalia and Ethiopa are still fresh in our minds. The atrocities in Ireland and Bosnia appal us all but the really terrifying thing is, that we see people who look like each other, raping, murdering and blowing each other up.

Closer to home, we have multicultural Papua New Guinea, where there are 720 different language groups in a population of just four million. To us, the people look the same but tribalism, combined with massive corruption, is ripping the country apart.

Britain and America are currently paying the price for their experiments with multiculturalism. America's policy has been that a society can absorb people from every ethnic group and background but just look at the problems confronting that country. Racial tension and inequality have created a growing underclass where unemployment, drug problems and crime flourishes, feeding off the rest of society. Australia still has the chance to learn from the mistakes of others before it is too late.

There are figures available that indicate multiculturalism is costing Australia at least $1 billion a year. A leaked Tax Office study which was published in the *Australian* in 1995, stated that the

Vietnamese community could be evading $343 million in income tax annually and wrongfully claiming a further $211 million annually in unemployment benefits and Austudy. New settlers to this country should be encouraged to embrace mainstream Australia without abandoning their cultural heritage but they must realise that the celebration of their culture must be at their expense and not at that of the ordinary taxpayer. Fluency in English is essential if they are really to take their place in the general community at the least cost to their new homeland.

I must stress, especially for my critics, that I am totally aware of the great contributions made to this country by migrants, especially during the last 100 years. Many of the stories are inspiring and should be provided as examples for new settlers to follow. Men and women have come to this country with nothing but hope and the ability to work hard. They could see the wonderful opportunities and carved out careers and, in many cases, fortunes for themselves and their families.

Most of these people had one thing in common. They joined in. They did not stand back on the fringe of the Australian community, expecting special privileges. These people became Australians, body and soul and many of them died for their new homeland. Their memories will live on forever.

Ladies and gentlemen, I came here today to reinforce the message in my maiden speech. I also came because of the support given me by Ted Drane and Graeme Campbell. My brief stint to date in politics has taught me that it is important to have support and friends.

I have learnt one lesson very quickly and that is to listen to the people out there. This is a lesson sadly not learnt by most of our politicians and a lot of them will have to learn the hard way at the next election. At the next election I will be prepared to endorse candidates whose views I share. These people may belong to minor parties or they may be independents. The time has come for ordinary Australians to be heard on the big issues before it is too late.

It will be a long, hard slog to the next election and there are a lot of bridges to be crossed. My only wish is to justify the faith that so many Australians have placed in me. I thank you all from the bottom of my heart for your patience and attention.

Pauline sat down to another burst of rousing applause and cheers. She had been a big hit with the audience, most of it drawn from country Victoria, and I guessed that a lot of its members were disaffected National Party people with a sprinkling of Liberals. I was also able to identify some Labor people. In the speech I used the words 'let the genie out of the bottle'. I must ask Graeme Campbell to stop using them.

Ted Drane's people in Melbourne warmed to Pauline and were very hospitable to her during her short, overnight stay. When Pauline launched her One Nation Party in April 1997, she sent an invitation to a couple with whom she had got on well, but Ted Drane missed out. All my grand plans for an alliance had come unstuck and this became very clear later in 1996.

As 1996 rolled on, Pauline was very busy and she never met Ted Drane again, nor spoke to him. I spoke to Ted on a reasonably regular basis and would relay his best wishes to Pauline in an effort to keep him in the game. All my efforts proved futile.

TWENTY-SEVEN

Palm Island is No Paradise

We stayed in Melbourne on the Sunday after Pauline's Melbourne speech, getting ready for the trip on Monday to Alice Springs and the Aboriginal settlements. Pauline was staying at the Como Hotel in South Yarra and was being looked after by some of Ted Drane's people.

It was mid-morning when Peter Wilkinson from *60 Minutes* rang to tell me there had been last minute complications. The media was in full cry and a contingent of journalists had arrived in Alice Springs determined to follow Pauline out to the settlements. This would have contravened the agreement between *60 Minutes* and the people of the settlements that the visit would not be allowed to degenerate into a media circus. The intervention of a Northern Territory part-Aboriginal Labor politician, John Ah Kit MLA, was also threatening to torpedo the venture. Because the settlements were in the Northern Territory, John Ah Kit was staking his claim to join the media caravan that was fast building up. Wilkinson told me he had heard that the media were already waiting for us at the Alice Springs airport. My mobile phone had been running hot with media calls about Pauline's movements and I was throwing plenty of red herrings around. At the last moment, and after consulting with Charles Perkins, Peter Wilkinson switched plans and we were off to the Palm Island Aboriginal settlement on the North Queensland coast, just a few miles from Townsville.

Pauline and I left Melbourne at 8:00 am on Monday, October 14, 1996, and arrived in Townsville in the early afternoon. There was to be no rest for the wicked, with Peter Wilkinson organising charter planes to take us out to Palm Island there and then. Charles Perkins had made his own way from Sydney and was already on the island waiting for us.

A twenty-minute plane flight and we were on Palm Island. Similar to the mainland around Townsville, to which it was once attached, Palm Island lacks the lushness of the jungle green seen in typical rainforest country further to the north. The colour scheme of Palm Island is based on drab browns and khaki-green, highlighted by the rusty dark blue-green of rocky outcrops, dulled by the winds and rains of thousands of years. Some scrawny, past their use-by-date, coconut palms fringe part of the island.

A small media scrum had somehow managed to tag along with us but it was puny compared to what could have been. I smiled to myself as I thought of all those media maggots squirming and wriggling in the hot desert sun at Alice Springs.

The agenda was that Pauline would have a getting-to-know-you meeting with Charles Perkins and members of the local Council, including prominent local female leaders. After that, Pauline would be taken on a drive around the island and would then sit down with Perkins and the others in a closed meeting and talk about what she had seen. She would then return the following day to visit the school.

We used one of the local Council's residential houses as the 'set' for the filmed discussion. While Pauline and Perkins and the others were talking, the small media crew that had followed us were standing in the backyard of the premises — the cameramen among them trying to take shots through the windows of the house. There were about eight reporters in all. At their insistence, I went out to speak to them. As I started speaking to the group, I noticed a girl stupidly sporting ABC identification. That was all I needed. 'You're from the ABC,' I said to her. 'We don't speak to the ABC.' In reply the reporter said, 'I'll just stand here with the microphone then.' I then made a production of rolling my eyes and simultaneously raising my eyebrows and said to the members of the commercial press, 'No, now you've poisoned the chalice, I'm going.' As I walked back to the house I could hear the ABC reporter copping plenty of flak from her disgruntled colleagues from other media outlets.

We were taken on a tour of Palm Island and it was a rerun of what I had seen on the settlements outside Alice Springs — the same decrepit, vandalised housing and the rubbish and litter. The rubbish was all pervading. It was on the streets, around the houses, in the open areas along the foreshore, and in front of the small commercial strip. It was as if Palm Island was in the grip of a permanent garbage collectors' strike. Before we returned to the house for the general discussion, I was able to take Pauline aside and reinforce what I had already told her about the other settlements. I advised her to hit Charles Perkins hard on the obvious lack of civic pride on the island, bring up the drink problem and attack his evident lack of leadership skills.

The meeting was closed to all media apart from the *60 Minutes* crew and was more orderly than I thought possible. While Charles Perkins had the 'home ground' advantage and was playing to an Aboriginal audience, he was not as 'gung-ho' as he could have been. I detected more than a hint from the response of the Palm Island people to him, that Perkins was not the all-powerful, charismatic leader he thought he was in that neck of the woods.

During the meeting, one woman in particular tried to take Pauline on but was not very effective. A very kind and motherly woman with peroxided hair told Pauline in a matter-of-fact way that she needed 'to be educated'. Pauline gained confidence when the women in particular supported her criticism of ATSIC and its spending habits. I noticed Perkins looking a bit uncomfortable during this part of the discussion. As a past ATSIC commissioner, he was vulnerable and seemed relieved when the discussion moved on to other topics.

Perkins came to life when Pauline challenged the claim constantly made by Aboriginal leaders about their spiritual relationship with the land. 'If this was the case,' she said, 'how could the people live surrounded by litter and garbage?' Charles Perkins fired up and said all the wrong things. He was obviously flustered and had no answer. His defence was to retreat to a position of stupidity and illogicality. 'It's a minor thing — it's a cultural thing,' he said. Pauline had discovered his glass jaw. Perkins tried to rationalise his position with me later saying that, when the Aborigines were

180

nomads, they would just move on and leave their camp sites for nature to reclaim. I felt sorry for him being forced to fall back on such a transparent and ridiculous premise.

While Perkins was still off balance, Pauline got on to the problem of alcohol abuse by Aborigines. A Palm Island Councillor, frankly and without any attempt at deceit, acknowledged in a rather matter of fact way that 'seventy' per cent of the islanders had problems with alcohol. In that instant I knew what it could be like to cop a Mike Tyson uppercut that came from nowhere. I was amazed by the figure, never thinking that it could be so high. Because of my hearing problem, I thought that the Councillor must have said 'seven' or 'seventeen', but 'seventy' it was. Perkins could not handle that statistic either. All he could do was bluster and protest as he panicked and went on the attack. 'The greatest drunks in the world are white Australians,' he said. That outburst had no impact on his audience as the people on Palm Island obviously knew that they had a very real problem. The kindly woman shut Perkins up in a flash. 'We live here Charles, you don't,' she said.

Pauline went for the jugular on the trashed houses. The only explanation given in response was 'overcrowding'. In the end it all seemed so depressing and pathetic. We packed up and headed back to the airstrip. It was dark and the twinkling lights of Townsville reminded me that it had been a long day and I needed a nice hot shower. I had been quickly convinced of one thing — Palm Island is no paradise!

Pauline and I were up early and had breakfast in the dining room of the Sheraton Breakwater Hotel which houses the Townsville casino. The waitresses lined up to have Pauline autograph menus for them. It was amazing stuff. Pauline was scheduled to go back to Palm Island to visit the school and then to come back for a final interview with Tracey Curro. After Peter Wilkinson took Pauline away, I went into town to see an old PNG mate who was now working for the local electricity supplier. He took me for a quick tour of Townsville and told me that Pauline was very much the 'flavour of the month' up there. He dropped me off at the local taxi rank where the drivers reinforced what he had told me. There was no doubt in my mind — a phenomenon was in the making.

The final interview session for *60 Minutes* took place in a suite at the Sheraton. Tracey Curro went head-to-head with Pauline and I was sitting just out of camera range. Tracey Curro was putting the heat on. I could see a reaction coming with the tell-tale flattening of Pauline's eyes. Out of the blue, Tracey Curro asked Pauline, 'Are you xenophobic?' I held my breath, groaned inwardly and tried to look nowhere in particular. It seemed like an eternity before Pauline responded. Tracey Curro was learning forward, ready to go in for the kill.

Pauline glared at Curro and, after a few seconds deliberation, spoke those now famous words, 'Please explain!' From out of nowhere she had delivered a haymaker. It was now Tracey Curro's turn to be on the ropes. Regaining her composure she gave a lengthy definition of 'xenophobic' and, after a brief pause, Pauline said, 'No, I don't think I am.' She thought for an instant more and then said quite forcefully, 'No, I'm not.' At that stage I didn't think Pauline had suffered all that much damage but only the viewing of the completed *60 Minutes* would tell the story.

When Pauline and I boarded the Qantas aircraft at Townsville Airport on Tuesday, October 15, she was cheered and clapped on board by the ground crew. During the flight, well-wishers came up to speak to her. I was amazed. It was real celebrity stuff and was one of the factors in the public response to Pauline that was telling me how low the public estimation of other politicians had become.

We arrived in Canberra late that afternoon and I walked out of Pauline's Canberra office that night at 8:30 pm, starting to feel a bit tired and drained and wondering how everything was going to end up.

60 Minutes went to air on Sunday, October 20, 1996. Pauline's mother took credit for her daughter's stand on National Service saying, 'Pauline was too young to know about National Service, that's one of my ideas.' Mrs Seccombe then went on to really raise eyebrows when she told Tracey Curro at a Hanson clan barbecue, 'The yellow race will rule the world!'

During the screened programme, Tracey Curro asked me how a person with my surname came to subscribe to anti-migrant policies. My Italian grandparents had settled in Ingham and I knew that Tracey was an Ingham girl herself, so my, 'I've been dewogged', reply was meant to stir her up as much as anything. The politically correct among us are often boring and humourless. My 'Eyetie' background has not left me wandering around with a chip on my shoulder bleating about my problems and the cross I must bear. A good sense of humour is a wonderful asset and makes life much more bearable and enjoyable. (Have you heard that World War II joke about Italian tanks?)

Tracey Curro's 'xenophobic' question went to air in its original form and I think that *60 Minutes* thought that it would be a 'king hit' against Pauline. Not so. It backfired terribly, like an air-to-air missile returning to destroy the aircraft that launched it. Channel 9's switchboard glowed in the dark, and Sydney's night-time talkback shows went 'ballistic' with callers overwhelmingly attacking *60 Minutes*, and particularly Tracey Curro who was viewed as just another 'smart-arsed, academic journo'. Viewers related to Pauline's honest and simple response — it was the anti-politician at work again. I was surprised at the number of people who didn't know what 'xenophobic' meant. A couple of days after the *60 Minutes* show, a friend of mine (who is a millionaire and went to Melbourne Grammar) telephoned me to tell me that he hadn't known either. The *60 Minutes* office mailbags overflowed with pro-Hanson mail and the show rated its socks off, with the best results for the year. That programme went out to an incredible 2.6 million viewers, Australia-wide. I had watched the show in Melbourne and, within minutes of it finishing, I was receiving favourable feedback from my media contacts. That hectic and mostly frantic week had been well worth the effort. I don't think Charles Perkins will ever want to step into the ring with Pauline Hanson again.

Sitting alone in my darkened Canberra motel room, I thought about the settlements and the Aboriginal people I had seen at Papunya, Yuendumu and Palm Island. I must assume that the majority of settlements throughout Australia suffer from the same problems — whether they be in the outback, country towns or the cities. My own experience has indicated this, it has been supported by other qualified people, and was confirmed by Charles Perkins when I was talking to him on Palm Island. There do exist some exceptions but only a depressing few. To find a solution, there is no point camouflaging the cause, but that is what has been happening for countless decades in the case of the basic problems that confront Aboriginal Australians. A huge smokescreen has been created by white apologists and their fellow travellers. They have been aided and abetted by the functionaries of the Aboriginal 'industry', judges and academics. The simple, basic, unpalatable truth has been hidden in a blatant, dishonest way.

The majority of Aboriginal communities teeter precariously on the brink of anarchy — pure and simple. On their own tribal land, older generations, unable to control themselves, cannot control their young people. Vandalism and destruction of one's own home is an expression of anarchy — as is the defiant, brain-pickling act of petrol sniffing. The destruction of one's own school buildings is anarchy. The wanton and indifferent littering of one's own land, in particular, is environmental anarchy.

This anarchy affects all classes of Aboriginal society and flows from one fountainhead alone — it flows from a bottle. The cause is alcohol and it has been flowing ever since the white man came ashore. For me, the scales dropped from my eyes and I experienced my Damascan conversion when that councillor on Palm Island honestly and openly said that his people had a 70 per cent rate of alcoholism. All Charles Perkins could do in response was to rant and say that white Australians were the world's greatest drunks. Hundreds of thousands of Australians saw and heard this on the *60 Minutes* programme, but it simply did not impact. White Australians have become accustomed to images of their drunken black brothers and have become so over-exposed to the problem through the media that they don't wish to become involved at any level. White Australians have enough of their own demons to conquer.

It is the grog that causes the fighting and the vandalism. It triggers the domestic and sexual abuse and other crimes of violence. It is the catalyst that leads to the malnutrition of babies and children. It sets its victims on the road to other drugs of dependency and, along the way, they can meet the grimmest of all reapers — AIDS. Alcohol can strip dignity and pride from the poor and rich alike — it does not discriminate.

The solution for this 'sickness' does not rest with white Australia, it rests squarely on the shoulders of Aboriginal Australia. Blaming white Australia is simply a convenient 'cop-out' and has never been credible — all it has done is create a very strident and unfavourable reaction.

The alcohol scourge in Aboriginal communities is a black problem. It must be solved by black people, or the curse will continue unabated as it has since that day the first inhabitants of this land hesitantly took their first searing sips of rum from the first white settlers in the fledgling colony.

The history of the Aboriginal people reveals a total lack of cultural experience with alcohol. Dare I ask, whether, through the processes of evolution, some part of their genetic chain leaves them collectively vulnerable to a substance that other societies have been, as a group, able to cope with? This outrageously politically incorrect question needs to be asked of a geneticist.

Aboriginals have comrades in adversity. Russia, with its long history of experience with the demon drink, finds itself gripped by an alcohol-related crisis that is threatening the life expectancy and growth of its male population as sperm counts diminish. The Russian government is trying to plan a strategy to stop its citizens from becoming Vodka freaks.

Solutions require strong leadership. The present crop of Aboriginal leaders, generally speaking, have let their people down. It is impossible to lead from the comfort of the major cities when so much of the problem lies in remote areas — not so remote, of course, that vast quantities of alcohol can't be easily smuggled in. When leaders go out into the communities and lead from the trenches, a solution may start to be within reach. Can those leaders come from ATSIC, the core Aboriginal body that Pauline Hanson wants abolished? The answer must be a categorical 'no'. That organisation was crippled from within when, from its inception under a Labor Government, its criteria for the appointment of commissioners was amended to allow people with serious criminal records to be eligible. The Howard Government has done nothing to rectify this situation.

I may never revisit Alice Springs, but I wonder whether visitors there in the year 2050 will drive past the Todd River and wonder at the bizarre and tragic dramas still being played out on its dried-out banks? Will my ghosts of 1959, 1981 and 1996 still be there playing out their tragic parts? I fear so.

TWENTY-EIGHT

The Cowards' Castle

The Queensland Federal Seat of Moreton was made famous by Sir James Killen who held it for twenty-eight years from 1955. In 1961 the Menzies Government won the Federal Election in a cliff-hanger by one Seat — that of Moreton. At the time, Jim Killen, speaking to a journalist, scripted the alleged accolade to him by Robert Menzies: 'Killen, you are magnificent.' Menzies of course never said this, but he should have.

I came to know Jim Killen when I was an MP in Papua New Guinea. I first met him in 1966 when I led a Parliamentary delegation to Canberra. I would sometimes drop in to see Jim in his Brisbane office when I was passing through on my way south. I had the greatest admiration for him and, to me, he was the sort of Liberal that I expected other Liberals to be. Jim Killen was a straight-shooter and had spent more than his fair share of time in the 'real' world, including swimming 'bare-arsed in the Condamine with Aborigines!' In recent years I have had chance meetings with Sir James Killen at Melbourne racetracks. He reminds me of kinder times.

Jim Killen, throughout his Parliamentary career, was a great champion of Parliament and its conduct. During a recent telephone conversation he told me that, 'I would never say anything in Parliament that I wouldn't say outside it.'

In 1996, the seat of Moreton was won from the Labor Party by a Liberal first-timer, Gary Hardgrave. I had met Hardgrave very briefly when I was with Pauline Hanson at a Department of Administrative Services 'getting-to-know-you' function in Brisbane just after the election. His Electorate Officer was Tania Roberts who I had worked with when I was with John

Stone in 1989–1990. She in turn had known Barbara Hazelton in Stone's Sunshine Coast senatorial office before I arrived on the scene. As I have said, politics is an incestuous business.

Gary Hardgrave's electorate of Moreton borders Pauline Hanson's electorate of Oxley, south of Brisbane. Soon after Pauline's maiden speech, Hardgrave launched into her in the Parliament. He was one of those many 'soft' Liberals who aligned themselves with members of the Labor Party in attacking her. Hardgrave clearly attacked Pauline in the house in early October, calling on Prime Minister John Howard to stand up to her (in his opinion) anti-Asian views. Not once however in his speech, did Hardgrave actually name Pauline. The member for Moreton seemed to have a distinct aversion to naming people he attacked, even with the cowardly protection of Parliamentary privilege. In a joint Party meeting, Hardgrave told the Prime Minister that Asian people in his electorate had been spat on because of community tensions sparked by Pauline Hanson's comments. I was wondering what Hardgrave was up to. My intelligence was that he had been getting plenty of calls from his constituents asking him to stand up and support Pauline.

My relationship with Tania Roberts during the nine months I worked with her had been forgettable. There had been moments of nothing-out-of-the-ordinary friction, that are expected, especially in a political office. I did not regard Tania as a 'political' person and guessed that she was the sort who would most probably vote Democrat. After John Stone was defeated in the 1990 Federal Election, we all went our separate ways until I had a chance meeting with Tania in Double Bay, Sydney, when she was working for John Hewson. The next time I met her was in Brisbane at the Department of Administrative Services' function. When Parliament was sitting, I would often see her in the staff cafeteria and exchange basic pleasantries with her.

On Thursday, October 17, 1996, I went into Aussie's café in Parliament House to buy the Melbourne *Herald Sun* and the Sydney *Telegraph*, because both papers had photos of Pauline on the front page. I noticed Tania Roberts standing outside the Westpac Bank, obviously waiting for it to open. At the time I was about three metres away from her. Taking into account her employer's quite nasty and snide attacks on Pauline, I decided to stir her up, saying, 'Tania, tell your boss that Pauline will run a candidate against him at the next election and stitch him up.' It was purely and simply a political comment and I certainly didn't think I was on hallowed ground when I said it.

That afternoon, the Member for Moreton, Gary Hardgrave rose to his feet and asked a question of the Speaker:

Mr Speaker, you would be aware of provisions within Standing Order No. 75 regarding the use of offensive words and in particular, Standing Order No. 76. A female member of my staff has been subject to intimidation and threat, also aimed at me through her, by a certain male member of the staff of the honourable member for Oxley. I have attempted to advise the member for Oxley directly but I understand she is not here this afternoon — she is in the air.

Mr Speaker, I ask you to advise whether these or any other standing orders restrict such behaviour? Is sexual harassment a matter covered within the standing orders? Will you ensure that matters which could lead to disrepute of Parliament itself are expressly prohibited both within the chamber and also the Parliament House precinct?

[The Speaker replied:]

I thank the Member for Moreton for his question. You raise a very serious issue. I will reflect on the matter and report to you and the Parliament separately.

I was in Pauline's Parliamentary office at the time Hardgrave launched this gutless attack on me. It didn't take long for my mobile phone to start ringing. I went to the press gallery to have a look at the videotape of the member for Moreton's heroic efforts. He had obviously decided to declare full-scale war on Pauline and her staff.

I didn't beat about the bush like Hardgrave. He had mentioned a male member of Pauline's staff — I was the only male member! The female member of his staff had to be Tania Roberts because she was the only member of his staff that I had spoken to that morning. I sailed right into Hardgrave and Roberts through the media, asking them both to immediately repeat their allegations outside Parliament. I called specifically for Hardgrave to do that and for Tania Roberts to report my alleged sexual harassment to the appropriate authorities, whether that be the police, the Speaker's office or the Parliamentary security controller. There was absolute, damning silence coming from the Hardgrave office. Nothing happened.

I was all over Australia on the TV news the night of Hardgrave's attack, and next day's national papers gave the story plenty of exposure. I had calls from my two nieces and nephew wanting to know what their uncle had been up to. I was furious at having been attacked and smeared by Hardgrave under Parliamentary privilege. Members of Parliament can defame anyone without risk of legal action if they use a Parliamentary speech as the weapon — as Hardgrave had done.

On October 28, the Speaker, Bob Halvorsen, replied to Gary Hardgrave's question, by saying:

On 17 October, 1996, the honourable Member for Moreton directed a question to me in which he alleged that there had been harassment of a female member of his staff and sought advice about the application of standing orders 75 and 76.

Standing orders 75 and 76 concerning the use of offensive words or personal reflection relate to proceedings within the Chamber. Those standing orders do not have a more general application and do not apply outside the Chamber or the Main Committee.

Having said that, I would be very concerned if the matters alleged to have occurred did occur in this building or anywhere else for that matter. However, on the assumption that the allegations do not involve the possibility of the laying of any charges, this is an issue which needs to be settled between the individuals involved and I would see the two Members as the respective employers of those staff having a role in resolving the matter.

I had spoken to the Speaker's office immediately after the incident and had put my side of the story. The Speaker's careful reply to Hardgrave told me that he was not taking the matter all that seriously but this did not help me much. My family and I had been greatly damaged out in the community as a result of the media running such headlines as: 'Hanson aide subject of sex claim', 'Hanson staffer denies sex harassment claim', 'Hanson staffer in harass claim' and 'Hanson aide in harassment row'. The Speaker's response also told me that Hardgrave, having made his stupid, baseless attack, was now certainly 'hoist with his own petard' and stranded in 'no man's land'. Every day he and Tania Roberts remained silent on the issue, the deeper and quicker they dug graves for their own political and personal credibility. He was showing how green and naïve he was. Tania Roberts failed to prosecute her allegations against me. At no time had she any reason to fear attracting my attention for anything other than a professional working relationship. A woman in her late thirties with sallowish skin and stooped shoulders, she indulged far too much in a habit that is one of my pet aversions — she smokes.

I had been a member of the Liberal Party since joining in Sydney in 1979, when I had arrived there from PNG. At the time, I was living in Sydney and had been approached to stand for preselection for a NSW State Seat. The Fraser Liberal Government was in power but the earth was not moving. Before I could commit myself politically in NSW, I moved to Melbourne in 1982, to live with Ann Knappett whom I married in 1984. In 1987 I won Liberal preselection for the Federal Seat of Jagajaga and started to lose my marriage. Ann wouldn't let me bring Bruce Ruxton home for dinner and I lowered the boom on her friend, communist John Halfpenny. The 1987 campaign was a disaster and losing to the Socialist Left Labor incumbent Peter Staples was a bitter pill for me to swallow.

When I stood for preselection, I had indicated my strong opposition to the taxpayer-funded policy of multiculturalism and, despite it being very much part of Liberal Party policy, I didn't cop much flak over my stand.

Jagajaga was a safe Labor Seat so I posed no threat to the Victorian Liberal Party 'establishment'. I was preselected early and spent six months door-knocking thousands of houses. I wore a pedometer and clocked up about 1300 kilometres, which gave my Rossi bushwalking boots something to think about.

At the time, I told some of my colleagues that, if Bruce Ruxton had stood as an independent on an anti-Asian immigration platform for the Seat, he may have won it. Jagajaga had high unemployment levels and there were a lot of blue-collar workers in the electorate. It was fertile ground for the candidate who could touch the right buttons. I was getting clear messages of dissatisfaction about multiculturalism and the imbalance of the migrant intake. The seeds of Hansonism were already out there, waiting to be germinated.

At the Victorian State Liberal Party conference held in Geelong after the 1987 election loss, I attempted to circulate a letter strongly criticising the party at all levels. In the letter I stated, among other things, that:

> ... one of the hard issues that is going to affect future generations of Australians is the question of coloured immigration.

That was more than enough to send State Director John Ridley and his helpers into a frenzy. They confiscated the document. I was told that it could have disrupted the conference, but I have never been able to understand what all the fuss had been about. I used the words 'coloured immigration' to be controversial and to put the case for a balanced immigration programme based on the successful post-World War II years. If Bill Hayden and many others wanted to argue for a future 'coloured' Australia, I could argue the opposite — or could I?

My piece was run in Des Keegan's national affairs column in the *Australian* on July 28, 1987, but no-one else in the media picked up on it. I was a nobody anyway, and a defeated candidate to boot.

After the conference I posted the letter to all Victorian branch members at my own expense, and received a fair bit of response. I was disenchanted with the whole political scene and could see that the Liberals would be out in the cold for quite a few years. In early 1988 my marriage ended and I went to country Victoria to run a pub for a while.

With this background, it is little wonder that the snide, covert and very open attacks on Pauline by many gormless Liberal members, coupled with Hardgrave's attack on me, finally snapped the barely-visible thread connecting me to the Liberal Party and most of its Parliamentarians and administration people.

On Monday, October 28, 1996, I issued the following press release.

At the last sitting of the House of Representatives, the Liberal Member for Moreton made references to a male staffer in the employ of Pauline Hanson and that person could only be me. I consider the references a vicious personal attack, conducted in such a way as to constitute an abuse of Parliamentary privilege. The Seat of Moreton was once held by, the now Sir, James Killen who was a tough but fair politician who held in great respect, the Parliament and Parliamentary conduct.

I have been a member of the Liberal Party since 1979 and have worked on several campaigns as well as fundraising for conservative candidates. I have good reason to believe that my standing as a Federal Liberal candidate in Victoria in 1987 cost me my then business which was based on working for government departments during the Cain Labor Government. My father and cousin between them, served in four different theatres of war and were respected members of the medical and engineering professions during peace time. I strongly resent the clumsy and baseless attempts to smear me by a member of the Party I belong to.

Pauline Hanson has been treated in a most disgraceful way by the Queensland division of the Liberal Party who have, by using the letter of the law, exploited a loophole in the Electoral Act, thus depriving her of substantial electoral funding, which by any normal standards of decency would have been due to her. All Australia knows that Pauline Hanson won the Seat of Oxley as an independent. Well before polling day, Pauline Hanson told the voters that if she was successful, she would return this funding to the electorate (by way of purchase of a sorely needed Police car), after deducting her legitimate expenses. The Queensland Liberal Party is not only ripping off Pauline Hanson, it is also ripping off the voters of Oxley, many of whom are John Howard's 'battlers'.

On a recent Channel 9 *Sunday* show, Federal Liberal Director Andrew Robb and Labor National Secretary Gary Gray, agreed to swap preferences in Pauline Hanson's Seat of Oxley at the next election. This 'conspiracy' between the two major parties to politically destroy a brave woman has astounded and shocked the rank and file members of both Parties. Andrew Robb, in essence, agreed to attempt to ensure a Labor win in Oxley, which most Liberals totally fail to understand. This despicable 'strategy' is not directed against Pauline Hanson alone but also against the ordinary Australian voters who have so massively supported her in recent weeks.

In view of the treatment of Pauline Hanson and myself by the Liberal Party, I can no longer remain a member of the Party and will resign this day. I call on the overwhelming majority of fair and honest Liberal Party members to repudiate the actions of some of their politicians and administrators.

I mailed my press release and a formal, one-sentence letter of resignation to Ted Baillieu the Victorian Liberal Party President. It was such a non-event that it was never acknowledged.

Gary Hardgrave was still yapping like a Jack Russell terrier. On October 28, he wrote to Pauline in a very precious way telling her that, if he had wanted to, he could have had me hauled before the Privileges Committee but, fair man that he was, he would take the lesser course of seeking the Speaker's advice in resolving the matter. Obviously having not succeeded even in that arena, Hardgrave was forced to resort to trying to get Pauline to discipline me in some way for my alleged crimes by appealing to her as a fellow Parliamentarian, but his patronising and condescending manner made absolutely no impression on the woman that he had attacked in Parliament only a couple of weeks earlier.

On the following day, Pauline replied to Hardgrave, saying:

Dear Mr Hardgrave

As you did in Parliament, you seem to be unable to name the member of my staff and describe the allegations against him.

You should have the courage to do this and then I will be able to assess the situation. Until such time, I intend taking no action in relation to this matter.

Hardgrave's letter to Pauline only served to dig himself in deeper. Again he had the opportunity to name me but failed to do so. On the afternoon of Tuesday, October 29, Gary Hardgrave asked another question of the Speaker, whom I suspect by this time had started to lose a degree of patience with the honourable Member for Moreton. Hardgrave was desperately trying to save something from the wreckage of his despicable attempt to smear me. The shortish Hardgrave with a doughy face looking at the world through spectacles like blow-fly eyes was now trying to have me nailed for contempt of Parliament. He looked smug as he spoke:

Mr Speaker, I refer you to your answer given yesterday to a question which I asked you on 17 October regarding the conduct of a certain male member of the staff of the honourable Member for Oxley. Mr Speaker, I thank you for your advice which I have followed in the form of a letter to the Member for Oxley sent yesterday afternoon.

Mr Speaker, I seek further clarification and advice from you, as an article printed in today's Brisbane *Courier-Mail* newspaper reports Mr John Pasquarelli, a staff member of the Member for Oxley, as saying he believed Mrs Hanson would treat the call — your call, Mr Speaker — for talks with the contempt it deserved.

Does this statement constitute a breach of any standing order because it reflects upon your conduct as Speaker and does it represent a form of contempt of this Parliament?

194

[For the first time, Hardgrave had actually mentioned my name after all his pathetic pussyfooting. The Speaker was very much to the point saying:]

I thank the honourable Member for Moreton for his question. My attention has indeed been drawn to the reported statements of the employee of the honourable Member for Oxley. In my response to the original complaint I made it clear that the rules of the House did not extend to the particular matter complained of. I did make the practical suggestion that the two members could have a role in resolving the issue.

I note the reported comments. I did not call for talks but I did refer to a possible way in which the dispute could be resolved. Even if the latest report of comments were accurate, there is no question of contempt. I gave no directive on the subject. Neither my feelings nor my authority are likely to be affected by such comments which do not merit the attention of this House.

It was now clearly obvious to everyone except the member for Moreton that the Speaker had endured enough. Hardgrave had isolated himself well and truly, and he and Tania Roberts had failed dismally to put up or shut up. A few journalists called Hardgrave's office in an attempt to contact him and Roberts about the matter but their calls were never returned and, months later, they received the same response.

My undiminished anger is not directed at Hardgrave alone. He was never obviously brought to heel in the Coalition Party room over his behaviour. He should have been. He should have been told to instruct Tania Roberts to make good her allegation against me and to clearly define how I had intimidated him, and such action should have been taken within twenty-four hours. If he had not been able to do this, he should have been instructed to get up in the House, withdraw and apologise. In this way he would have partially redeemed himself and mitigated to some extent the serious damage he had caused me. As it was, he smeared me and my family name wantonly and with impunity, using the cloak of Parliamentary privilege to do so. The *cowards' castle* is well named. It may just be that, in the months ahead, the preselectors of Moreton may grant me the vindication their Member's peers, in their ignorance, failed to accord me — but I won't be holding my breath.

What were these senior members of the Coalition doing who should have known better and have taken steps to discipline this new and very junior member of their team? Where were John Howard and Peter Reith the Leader of the House? I now have nothing but contempt for those Parliamentarians who prattle on about raising Parliamentary standards, who burble on about values, and who question the morality of others. The Lyons forum within the Liberal Party is a perfect example of the hypocrisy of politicians and I took issue with Kevin Andrews of anti-euthanasia fame about this very point when I was in Canberra in June 1997. He could offer me no solution. I asked Kevin why he did not think to pull Hardgrave into line himself, but he had no answer. As a person who goes out of his way to give the impression of standing up for what is right, even Kevin Andrews had failed to notice the gross abuse of Parliament committed by Gary Hardgrave. There was obviously not a skerrick of political merit to be gained in defending a person like myself. Maybe it suited a lot of Pauline's political opponents to see her office knocked out of action, whatever it took. The unctuousness and piety of many MPs of all political persuasions, when it suits them, is totally lost on us — mere mortals who must live in the 'real' world.

On June 10, 1997, the *Bulletin* magazine carried a poll on how occupations rate for ethics and honesty. In 1976, Federal MPs rated 19 on a scale of 1–100. In 1997 they had dropped to 9, just ahead of journalists on a rating of 7 — and this was prior to the travel rorts scandal. I remind all honourable members they are not too far off the absolute bottom of the dung pile, wherein crawl paedophiles and drug dealers.

The Hardgrave affair should have been a warning to me that I needed to be protecting my rear. On Monday, November 18, 1996, I was in the Parliament House staff cafeteria with Jeff Babb, Pauline's new (but to be short-lived) research officer, when we came across Barbara Hazelton beaming smiles and brightness at Tania Roberts, the woman who Hardgrave said I had sexually harassed. I was furious and gave Hazelton a good blast. She knew very well how angry I was about the matter and, besides, Hardgrave had also attacked her boss. As far as I was concerned, war had been declared between the two offices and there was absolutely no room for people to safely stand on the sidelines.

To be objective about the whole Hardgrave mess, Pauline had defended me but I prepared all the material, and she never gave me the impression that she really understood how badly I felt about the whole affair. My decision to resign from the Liberal Party (which, to be fair, was overdue) and my constant and ceaseless defence of Pauline against all her enemies should have left her in no doubt as to where my loyalties lay but, in the end, it was a one-sided arrangement. When the big test finally came, Pauline Hanson was found sadly wanting in the loyalty department.

To Market We Will Go

As the polls started reacting positively to Pauline in the wake of her maiden speech, the major Parties began to realise that they could have a real problem on their hands. Backbenchers from both sides of the political fence were getting strong feedback from their constituents and it was not what they were wanting to hear. They were being told by significant numbers of voters that they should be getting up in Parliament and supporting Pauline Hanson. Shackled by Party politics, they were forced to hear what they were being told but couldn't respond positively for fear of being disciplined by the Party machine. I was told 'off the record' about this by several backbenchers and staffers. Some MPs told Pauline directly that they supported much of what she said but couldn't do anything about it publicly.

Pauline was starting to make inroads into National Party territory, particularly in Queensland and NSW, and she was gaining support from small business Liberals and blue-collar Labor people. The Labor and Liberal Parties were desperately trying to outmanoeuvre each other to gain the high ground on what was stupidly starting to be called a 'race debate'.

John Howard was being strongly criticised by the Labor Party, its media mates, and the 'pointy-heads' in academia for not taking on Pauline 'head-on'. To be fair, he was just as strongly resisting these calls and from my present position, outside the Hanson camp, I still think his strategy has been basically correct. National Party Senators Ron Boswell and Bill O'Chee and National Party Leader Tim Fischer may yet learn the hard way at the next election — attacking Pauline Hanson on such a vicious and personal basis only increases her support from their Party's traditional base. It was also noticeable that despite odd puffs of bluster, Kim Beazley, the Labor leader, never really got stuck into Pauline (certainly nowhere near as hard as the Nationals did) and there was hardly a 'peep' from the right wing of the trade union movement.

As some sort of compromise, both Liberal and Labor Parties decided to share the high ground by running a motion on racial tolerance in the House of Representatives. This had been organised by Liberal Peter Reith, the Leader of the House, and Labor's Gareth Evans, the Deputy Opposition Leader. I had heard on the grapevine that John Howard would move the motion during the afternoon of Wednesday, October 30, 1996.

A week earlier I had been in Melbourne and had gone to the Melbourne Wholesale Fruit and Vegetable Markets in Footscray to see some mates. I had polled the markets comprehensively on the GST during late 1992 and 1993, when I was battling my Ménière's Disease. My research conducted on Sydney Harbour ferries and shopping strips in Melbourne, such as Puckle Street in Moonee Ponds and Glenferrie Road in Hawthorn, clearly predicted John Hewson's defeat. When I alerted Liberal Party headquarters I was called a 'nervous Nellie' and a 'dissident' for my trouble.

I had plenty of contacts among the Australian Greeks and Italians at the markets and I was curious to know their reaction to Pauline Hanson. I was interested to know whether they regarded her comments on immigration levels as being anti-all migrants. Their response astounded me.

The support for Pauline was quite remarkable, unlike anything I have ever seen expressed in the political arena. The dealers and spruikers at the markets are mainly of Anglo-European migrant stock and they seemed to easily identify with Pauline. Her well publicised occupation as a fish and chip shop owner reinforced the empathy they had for her. The anti-politician factor was coming to the fore again. Pauline was somehow trans-mitting a message through the TV screens and the general media that said, 'Look, things out there are not going well at all. You and I look the same and have a lot in common. The politicians, the academics, the media and big business interests are plotting our economic and social future but won't let us in on the secret. Let's give them all a big kick in the backside.'

I also detected an anti-Vietnamese sentiment at the markets, that seemed to be based on perceptions of 'shonky' trading practices combined with the tendency of the Vietnamese traders to keep to themselves. One Australian-born Chinese dealer said that he was very wary of the Vietnamese and feared violence if he went public with his concerns — which he would not reveal. I found no 'hard' evidence to substantiate any of the allegations.

What was evident, however, was strong criticism of the policy of multiculturalism, but that didn't surprise me all that much. The majority of migrants from Europe have assimilated well and have become proud and loyal Australians, but I cannot say the same for those Australian-Chinese who, on Australian TV, wildly applauded the return of Hong Kong to Communist China.

I was told by some traders of Greek and Italian background that they didn't want to be 'put in boxes' or categorised by the powers that be. They saw themselves as distinctly and fiercely Australian, even when relaxing at home with their ouzo or grappa. They acknowledged that the celebration of one's own culture should be at one's own expense. As a throwaway line, I asked whether I should bring Pauline to the markets to hear for herself what was being said. A chorus of 'yes' told me I was digging in fertile soil.

I decided to put the Melbourne Fruit and Vegetable Markets on top of the list of places for Pauline to visit outside of her electorate. I realised that such a visit would be reduced to a shambles if it degenerated into a general media event, so I took a calculated risk.

I had first met Charles Slade, Channel 9's Melbourne newsman, at Graeme Campbell's Australia Day meeting in Melbourne at the Heidelberg Town Hall in 1996. I contacted Slade and he came to my Melbourne home to hear what I had in mind. I told him that, if Pauline's visit to the markets eventuated, he could have exclusivity on the basis that if other media turned up Pauline would cancel the whole deal. I thought I could trust Charles Slade, but considered my chances of keeping the visit secret very slim indeed. Anyway, this was all part and parcel of my job and I expected no dream-run from the media. The next thing to do was to organise the best time for Pauline to visit the markets. I would shortly have my mind made up for me. I did not need to be Einstein to work out that the bipartisan motion on racial tolerance would have Pauline strapped in the political stocks with every so-righteous Tom, Dick and Harriet MP throwing his or her eggs and tomatoes at her. It would be a very difficult and stressful time for Pauline, sitting in the chamber copping it all without being able to effectively fight back.

The most important consideration was a vital procedural problem. Under the rules of debate, only one of the five independent Members would be allowed to speak, and I could see no chance of Pauline being given the call. As it was, Graeme Campbell ended up being the only independent Member in the House of Representatives during the debate, and I am sure that he would not have deferred to Pauline. She would have been behind the eight ball anyway if she had stayed in the Parliament. Pauline needed to take the risks attached to her being absent from Parliament during the debate, and I knew exactly where she would be going.

I explained the plan to visit the Melbourne markets to Pauline, telling her that she would be able to stay overnight in Yarraville with the friends of mine she had stayed with previously. In this way, there would be no chance of a leak from a media-friendly employee at a hotel or motel. I always allowed for every possible contingency.

Pauline said that she didn't want to inconvenience my friends or cause them problems. She got on well with them during her previous stay. She also knew I was right about security, so I went ahead with the preparations for the visit.

Wednesday, October 30, began on a positive note for Pauline. John Elliott, the former Federal President of the Liberal Party, Carlton football team head-honcho, unrepentant smoker and the man whose satirised signature catch-cry is 'pig's arse!', was on Neil Mitchell's 3AW talkback radio show in Melbourne and basically supported Pauline's stand on immigration. Elliott was echoing what he said back in 1988 when John Howard called for a controlled slowdown in the rate of Asian immigration. On that occasion John Elliott had said: 'This multiculturalism idea is a load of nonsense. Really, our immigration policy has to be beneficial for all Australians.'

That afternoon, at about 2:30 pm, Pauline and myself did our best to slip out of Canberra unnoticed, and flew to Melbourne. We were on descent to Melbourne Airport when John Howard rose to his feet in the House of Representatives to move the bipartisan motion on racial tolerance.

That this House —

(1) reaffirms its commitment to the right of all Australians to enjoy equal rights and be treated with equal respect regardless of race, colour, creed or origin;

(2) reaffirms its commitment to maintaining an immigration policy wholly non-discriminatory on grounds of race, colour, creed or origin;

(3) reaffirms its commitment to the process of reconciliation with Aboriginal and Torres Strait Islander people, in the context of redressing their profound social and economic disadvantage;

(4) reaffirms its commitment to maintaining Australia as a culturally diverse, tolerant and open society, united by an overriding commitment to our nation and its democratic institutions and values and

(5) denounces racial intolerance in any form as incompatible with the kind of society we are and want to be.

I wonder how comfortable John Howard was with some of the wording of this motion given his albeit moderate call for a reduction in Asian immigration in 1988? With their words so well recorded, politicians are always haunted by their pasts.

As Pauline and I walked up the airbridge into Melbourne's Tullamarine Airport terminal, I was holding my breath hoping that there would be no media to welcome us. How false were my hopes. As soon as we entered the gate lounge area, a media pack was upon us like slavering hounds. Tom Worland who usually reports crime for Channel 9 was in the front line grinning — teeth bared like a nervous greyhound, undecided whether to lick or to bite! I decided to change the species of our tormentors by saying: 'You're all a lot of crocodiles.' To which Worland replied with obvious relish: 'Yes, John, yes we are!' I used my trusty and battered Samsonite briefcase to fend off the baying reporters as I shepherded Pauline to the safety of the Qantas Manager's Lounge. As we entered the lounge, a group of passengers in the cafeteria next door stood up from their tables and cheered and clapped Pauline. When I went to collect our bags, the media made another run, this time bowling over a middle-aged woman. They were being their usual polite selves.

With the help of the very helpful Qantas ground manager, Pauline and I were driven to the Travelodge carpark where a Commonwealth car was waiting. We took off along the new Western Ring Road and safely reached our destination in Yarraville after a lot of anxious monitoring of the rear vision mirror. We had given the media maggots the slip, but I was very pessimistic about our prospects for the following morning. I couldn't see how they could fail to track us down to the markets. My friends hosted a barbecue for Pauline and a small group attended, including some disgruntled local Labor people. It was at this small, informal function that Pauline met with and offered the job of researcher to Jeff Babb, who would be sacked by her after only twenty-two days in the job.

In Canberra, true to form, Senator Ron Boswell attacked Pauline for being gutless in leaving the Parliament. The evening news had Pauline and myself battling with the TV cameras at Tullamarine. That night at least, I had the last laugh on the media. One of my journalist contacts had carefully leaked the story in the Canberra press gallery that Pauline was absent because she was speaking at the Springvale Town Hall in Melbourne. This would have really excited the media, because Springvale has a large Vietnamese population. This red herring caused some hapless TV interviewers and camera crews to make the long drive, in heavy traffic, out to the decoy address. Sorry boys and girls.

Before I called it a day, I contacted Charles Slade of Channel 9 and arranged for him to come and pick us up at 5:30 am next morning. We had survived day one. Would our luck last?

Charles Slade and his crew turned up, on time, in the quiet Yarraville Street. The weather was cool and clear. My friend's wife had organised an early breakfast and Pauline was keen to get on with her market visit. Her pre-dawn visits to the Brisbane Fish Markets had trained her well for early morning starts. Pauline was dressed in blue jeans, denim shirt and white runners. As it was still pretty cool, she was wearing a dark blue top coat. She was dressed perfectly for the part.

My friends had organised some informal security including a senior ex-policeman. I was concerned that the Socialist-left protestors who had been thwarted when Ted Drane had switched venues on Pauline's last Melbourne visit, may have worked out where we were going. In my par-anoid state I had reasoned that a 'leak' to protestors would ensure some sensational TV footage. The only people with a good motive to give the game away would be from Channel 9. I was wondering if I had put too much trust in Charles Slade.

It was still dark as our small convoy drove to the markets, only about five minutes away. As we pulled up at the security office at the entry to the main carpark we hit our first hurdle. On Pauline being recognised, we were asked if we had sought permission from the Minister's office to make the visit. That would have meant approaching Pat McNamara, the Victorian Deputy Premier and National Party Leader. I had never even contemplated such an approach, as it would have blown our cover completely. Given the number of ordinary citizens I saw wandering unchallenged at will into the market, I knew that bureaucracy had caught up with us. As luck would have it, the ex-policeman with us knew the security controller and common sense prevailed. As we parked, I was scanning the path ahead for tell-tale signs of a media and protestor ambush, but the coast looked clear. I couldn't believe our luck, but I wasn't going into self-congratulation mode until we had completed the exercise. I had taken a big punt on a lot of factors and the finishing line was still a long way off.

I walked ahead of Pauline, looking for the people I had been talking to a week earlier. They soon acknowledged me and I introduced Pauline. Walking around the markets at its busiest time is a very risky business. Fork lifts and motorised carts whiz around like dodgem cars. It is a marvel that there are not spectacular accidents. I wondered how many of the drivers' alcohol levels would be over .05 per cent. Most of the men in the mostly male population of the markets are at the end of their working day, and it is quite normal for cans and stubbies of beer to be 'popped' at 6:00 in the morning when the rest of us are still in bed or eating cornflakes.

Pauline's market walk was a spectacular success. The warmth of the response given her by the 'hardheads' who have worked and played hard all their lives was amazing. One Australian Greek told Pauline not to worry about the other male MPs: 'They are just a lot of shirtlifters!' They don't mince words at the Melbourne markets.

One man, obviously of European extraction, objected to Pauline's stance on Asian immigration. He was not rude but quite matter of fact and told Pauline, 'You're about to wreck the country the way you're going.' Pauline took his criticism in her stride, telling him that the country was already in a mess. That exchange was the only one of dissent during her visit to the markets. Pauline spoke privately to the Australian-Chinese man I had met previously and they had a lengthy conversation — but he would not appear on camera. We passed quite a few Asian traders working at their stalls, but I felt it prudent not to have Pauline engage with them. Language problems and the way Pauline had been taken out of context would make any dialogue very tense and difficult. That was a swinging ball that we let go through to the keeper.

I was genuinely amazed at the reaction we received to the policy of multiculturalism. The men we spoke to stated very clearly that, putting their roots to one side, they were Australians first and foremost and resented being tagged with ethnic labels. What a pity John Howard and some of his colleagues don't take the time to break free of their 'minders' to visit places like the Melbourne markets.

At the end of Pauline's walk, we stopped at the cafeteria for a coffee break. Pauline was fascinated by a female clerk who was sitting at a table processing orders on a calculator. Her fingers flew over the keys in a blur, beating a frantic tattoo without missing a beat. I am sure we were watching a world champion at work.

While Pauline sat and chatted with the people in the café, Charles Slade and I swapped notes. He said that, when I had first suggested the visit, he thought I was mad as he expected that the large numbers of people at the markets with European migrant backgrounds would regard Pauline as being anti-all-migrants. He said that he found the response to Pauline 'simply amazing'. I told Charles Slade that the message Pauline Hanson had managed to get through was that Australia was founded very firmly on Anglo-European roots and that those Australians who subscribed to this premise had the right to challenge and fight against what was seen to be an orchestrated and deliberate attempt to Asianise Australia. It was this message that had struck such a chord with ordinary, mainstream Australians.

During the previous day's Parliamentary debate on the racial tolerance motion, Graeme Campbell, the Independent Member for Kalgoorlie and the man who sits next to Pauline in the House of Representatives, had been given his chance to speak. During his speech he offered the following quotes:

I don't think it is wrong, racist, immoral or anything else for a country to say we will decide what the cultural identity and the cultural destiny of this country will be and nobody else.

Just about every self-respecting country does, and I find the most extraordinary argument the one that says by talking about these issues we are offending our friends in Asia. That is bunkum.

Those countries will make judgments based on their own hard-headed interests. Has anybody asked an Australian coal exporter about the rights of an Australian to immigrate to Japan before we sign a coal deal with the Japanese? What absurd nonsense.

Campbell then told the Parliament that these words (that could have come from the lips of Pauline Hanson) were in fact spoken by John Howard in 1988! They are words calling for ordinary Australians to be allowed a say in how their great-grandchildren's country will look. How John Howard must wish he could erase 1988 from the record books.

As we were preparing to leave the markets, a man came up and presented Pauline with a punnet of magnificent strawberries. She was forced to decline other gifts of fruit and vegetables because we were in a hurry and travelling light. On the way to Melbourne Airport, I could at last afford myself the luxury of self-congratulation. I told Pauline how well she had performed. She had been in her element, scoring huge public relations points, and was genuinely pleased. At that moment, some of the doubts that I had been harbouring about her started to fade.

By 8:30 am we were in the air on our way back to Canberra. I was mentally taking myself to task for having doubted Charles Slade's integrity. He had kept his end of the bargain and the whole operation had remained watertight. A photographer took a shot of Pauline walking into the baggage collection area at Canberra Airport, still proudly holding her prize strawberries. Pauline went back to her motel to freshen up, while I returned to Parliament House. We had beaten the news back to Canberra. As I walked at a brisk pace into the House of Representatives entrance, I was 'door-stopped' by a TV crew. 'Where have you and Pauline Hanson been?' was the question. As I swept by I turned back and said, 'We went to Melbourne to meet some real Australians!'

How Ray Martin wins Gold Logies

R ay Martin is one of Australia's most successful TV personalities. From 1965 to 1978, he worked with the ABC as a journalist and then took the plunge into commercial TV as a member of the very successful *60 Minutes* team on Channel 9 until 1985. From 1985 to 1993, Ray Martin took the ratings for Channel 9's *Midday* show to new heights. He is currently the anchor for the evergreen *A Current Affair* on Channel 9. He has won five Gold Logies during his star-studded career. Ray Martin has also been suggested as the inspiration behind the creation of the central, shallow and insincere Mike Moore character in the outstandingly successful current affairs spoof *Frontline*.

Ray Martin is also possessed of a social conscience that is demonstrated by his membership of the Council for Aboriginal Reconciliation. This is a taxpayer-funded, government-organised body having as its main charter reconciliation between Aboriginal Australians and the rest of the community. Its members travel business class, receive tax free travelling allowance (the same as for ATSIC commissioners but more than that paid to ordinary politicians) and sitting fees when the Council is doing its business. For those of us who must pay our own way, it is interesting to know the actual figures. Travel allowance is paid at the rate of $320 per day tax free in the capital cities and $165 in country areas. Sitting fees are $310 per day, irrespective of where the meetings are held.

When Pauline attracted considerable media and political attention during Reconciliation Week in May 1996, the producer of *A Current Affair* was very keen to have her interviewed by Martin on the show. I strongly opposed any such confrontation and impressed upon Pauline that Ray Martin's position on the Council for Aboriginal Reconciliation must lead her to question his objectivity. For several years it had been rumoured that Martin had some Aboriginality in his family. If these rumours were true it would only make me more certain that to allow Pauline to go on Ray Martin's show would be to cast her to the wolves. I had visions of Ray Martin using everything at his disposal to 'do over' Pauline and then being hailed by the Aboriginal 'industry' as one of its heroes.

My paranoia was fuelled when sitting in a doctor's surgery in Canberra in June 1996. As I thumbed through some old women's magazines, I came across a copy of the *New Idea* magazine dated February 12, 1994. It was as if some mysterious hand of fate had guided me to that magazine. Page 19 featured a general article on Ray Martin, with a headline proclaiming 'Ray's Aboriginal Roots?' Below this was the subheading 'The Best Of Both Worlds'. The subsequent patients of that surgery now know who stole that missing page.

In this *New Idea* article, Ray Martin was quoted as saying he believed there was Aboriginal blood on his maternal grandmother's side of the family. He went on to say, 'But I would love to find out and I would be quite pleased if there was.'

Maybe the 'rumours' were right. I was now more determined than ever to keep Ray Martin at bay. He telephoned me twice seeking interviews with Pauline. Both times my impression was of a transparent eagerness that I believed gave him away.

I had previously voiced concerns with one of Martin's female staff regarding doubts as to his ability to remain objective, considering his position on the Council for Aboriginal Reconciliation, coupled with the fact that he was taking the taxpayer-funded benefits of that position on top of his lucrative Channel 9 contract. The person I spoke to corrected me on this latter point and was adamant that Ray Martin did not gain any financial benefit at all from his position on the Council.

In one of my telephone conversations with Martin I raised this point, congratulating him for not allowing himself to be perceived as 'double-dipping'. But, to my surprise, he corrected me, saying that he did in fact accept the airfares and the travel allowance but not the daily sitting fee. I made the point that he should advise his staff member to stop telling the wrong story — at the very best it was bad public relations.

For the rest of that year I heard nothing more from Ray Martin's people at *A Current Affair* and believed that they had got the message and dropped off. How wrong I was. They were merely biding their time.

On Wednesday, November 27, 1996, I received a telephone call from Lisa Ryan, the Brisbane producer of *A Current Affair*. She told me that *A Current Affair* was intending to run a national phone poll on Pauline and that Ray Martin wanted to launch the polling by interviewing Pauline on Thursday, November 28. I was not happy. A very attractive bait had been cast, but the dangerous barbs on the hooks were easily visible. I told Lisa Ryan I would get back to her later that day. I explained the situation to Pauline and told her that there was plenty of 'downside' and not much 'upside' in the situation.

Pauline was feeling a lot more confident. She was running strongly on the support that was still coming in from all around the country, and she had survived Tracey Curro's attack on *60 Minutes*. She was showing signs of getting a little 'cocky' (which was not such a bad thing as long as it didn't make her too big-headed). I made it clear to Pauline that Ray Martin was not Tracey Curro and that he would have his team of researchers working flat out on her. I was on the horns of a dilemma. For Pauline not to appear at the launch of a national poll testing her support would be bad public relations and a slap in the face for her supporters. If she appeared and Martin badly wounded her, it would be just as disastrous. I was very confident that such a poll would be positive for Pauline as it would be running hot on the heels of the *Bulletin*-Morgan poll of November 5, which floated the startling possibility of Hanson candidates winning up to seven Senate Seats! That poll seemed more than optimistic but, coming from Morgan, it had to be taken on board.

I sought reassurance from a couple of experienced friends whom it was my custom to consult on tricky situations like this. Yes, the Martin interview would certainly be a very risky venture, but it had to be done to fly the flag for Pauline's supporters. She could not afford to be seen as 'chickening out'. As long as she played a straight bat, she would more than likely survive. I went back to Pauline and she did not hesitate about going head-to-head with Ray Martin. I got back to Lisa Ryan and told her the interview would be on. I asked her about its duration and she said, 'Enough for a four-minute clip.' A time was set, for 11:00 am the next day, and the interview would take place in Pauline's Ipswich office. I was still not feeling confident, but I really wanted Pauline to do well since it would finish off her year on a high note.

I sat down with Pauline and tried to brief her, telling her how important the interview with Martin would be and impressing on her how I wanted her to put on a good show, but she didn't pay much attention. I told her that Martin would surely hit hard on the Aboriginal issue and the best line to run was to highlight the enormous, crippling effect alcohol has had on the Aboriginal community plus the squandering of billions of dollars by ATSIC. We discussed some responses on multicultural and immigration issues but Pauline became impatient and told me she had to leave the office. She gave me the impression that she had a non-political social engagement that evening. Then she dropped the bombshell that she intended going down to the Brisbane Fish Markets very early next morning. I tried to persuade her to cancel the trip but she wouldn't hear of it. I told her that she was just being irresponsible considering the importance of the next day's events, but she brushed my concerns aside. In retrospect, I think Pauline was, by then, already travelling on a different road.

I was in the Ipswich office next morning at 7:15 am ready for the fray. Time drifted by. The camera and sound crew arrived and started setting up. It was getting close to starting time and Pauline had still not arrived, which was making me decidedly edgy. Jeff Babb, the new research officer, was in the office along with Barbara Hazelton, Heidi Lewis and Cheyenne McLeod. It was a full house and I was starting to get cranky. I immediately got crankier when Pauline finally arrived in the office.

My heart sank. Pauline looked as if she had been up all night. She looked tired and frazzled, and all over the place. But worse still, she was not her usually well-groomed, well-presented self. She was wearing a mini skirt that appeared to me to be a size too small, which seemed totally uncharacteristic to those of us accustomed to her conventional and stylish mid-leg length skirts. I couldn't comprehend this last minute fashion change into what seemed inappropriate dress for an interview that would go to air after the evening news. Lisa Ryan then arrived with Ray Martin who already had his make-up on.

It was the first time I had met Martin and we exchanged pleasantries while his crew was sorting out the final details. Looking at Martin at close quarters, I couldn't resist thinking this could be the set of *Frontline*. I looked at him closely to see if the stories about him wearing a hairpiece were true. I stopped the mental wandering and returned to reality.

Pauline was to be sitting next to the large, wall-width bookshelves in her office with an assortment of books as a backdrop. I was idly glancing along the rows of books that would be in camera view, when I saw it! I felt as if someone had jabbed me in a very sensitive part of my anatomy with a cattle prod. There, in full view, with its title clearly displayed on the spine was a copy of *The Protocols of the Elders of Zion*. *The Protocols* is a viciously anti-Jewish propaganda work that has been circulating since about 1905. It is a total hoax, but still manages to do the rounds. I had visions of the camera zooming in on the title during the interview and then having the phones melt down next morning as every Rabbi and Jewish leader in Australia rang up to attack Pauline — not to mention every journalist from Canberra to Carnarvon. Pauline and I had already been defamed and attacked for no good reason by the left-wing *Australia/Israeli Review* magazine, so I could just imagine the righteous and vindicated outcry if *The Protocols* had hit the screen.

While all the pre-interview activity was proceeding, I managed to get myself between the bookshelves and the camera and with quick sleight of hand managed to turn the book around and hide its title.

After her maiden speech, Pauline's office had been constantly deluged by a never-ending stream of books and publications which she and Barbara Hazelton would put on the shelves without knowing what most of the titles were about. From time to time, when I was in the Ipswich office, I would cull any rubbish or silly material from the shelves and trash it. Pauline and Barbara would simply not have known what *The Protocols* was about. Another disaster had been averted, but the prognosis for a successful interview seemed remote as I looked at Pauline who was seated and kept tugging down the errant hem on her far too short skirt.

The interview started and I noticed that Ray Martin, as I had predicted, had a thick wad of reference notes. Right from the first exchange, Pauline was on her back foot. Instead of the straight bat, she made wild swings that left her open to further attack. She couldn't get any figures correct and forgot altogether to mention the effects of alcohol on the Aboriginal community. She quoted polling figures, saying that she was still getting strong support for her policies, but on intense probing by Martin she was unable to nominate the specific polls, all simply because she hadn't done her homework.

I froze as Pauline mentioned those by now dreaded words, 'Greeks' and 'Italians'. The mention of 'Eyeties' to Martin would have surely meant all would have been lost. The moment passed and we were safe for the time being. Ray Martin looked smug and he had good reason. The long wait to get to Pauline had been worth it. He was bowling her middle stump every time.

I started to look at my watch and realised that time was marching on. Fifteen minutes had passed and I started to look at Lisa Ryan who was standing above at the end of the room. I pointed to my watch but she pointedly avoided eye contact with me. I began to smell a very big rat. I looked hard at Pauline and then at Ray Martin and I started to move, cutting my throat with my hand in the conventional signal to stop the interview. The interview had run over the twenty-minute mark and something was dreadfully wrong.

Sensing something was terribly amiss, Pauline suddenly snapped out of her reverie. She and I said, almost in unison, to Ray Martin, 'What about the poll?'

I was trying to watch Martin and Lisa Ryan simultaneously in those brief, racing split seconds of time. Ryan was looking everywhere except at me and had that 'trapped' look. To be fair, Ray Martin looked a bit puzzled. It was all coming together for me.

I sailed into Lisa Ryan and accused her of setting Pauline up, in between telling her and the camera crew to get their bits and pieces together and get out of the office quick-smart before the whole lot ended up on the busy road outside! I was furious and in full cry. Lisa Ryan tried to defend herself by saying that she had got back to me at the last moment and told me that the poll was going to be postponed, but it would be definitely run in early 1997. I had been badly burnt and wasn't prepared to listen to any lame excuses.

I managed to explain to Martin, while cameras and cables were being packed up, about Lisa Ryan's first call to me about the supposed 'poll'. If Ray Martin knew about the 'sting' then he deserved another Gold Logie for acting. All this time, Pauline was trying very unsuccessfully to calm me down. The *A Current Affair* crew had gone, led by a scampering Lisa Ryan. Ray Martin had moved out into the main office and was holding his ground, determined to make a dignified departure.

'I always thought you were a straight shooter, Ray,' I said to Martin as he was talking to Pauline. That did it. He glowed with incandescent indignation under his make-up and without realising it, slipped automatically into the persona of his alter ego, 'Mike Moore'. His pompous attempt to be righteously angry almost made me forget how very angry I still was. For just one mad, crazy moment, I almost rushed at Martin intending to grab his hair to see if he was wearing a wig! However, with hindsight, if we were conned, I doubt Ray Martin knew anything about it.

While I battled to control myself, Pauline continued her role as peacemaker and, after we had all finally cooled down a bit, Ray Martin took his leave. He had finally got what he wanted but it had taken six months to get it. Lisa Ryan had certainly raced her way to the top of the *A Current Affair* production kudos ladder. She had managed to do what others in the Sydney head office had failed to do — she had got her boss into the ring with Pauline Hanson. She had pulled off quite a coup at my expense, and I didn't like it one little bit.

I kept kicking myself for being so stupid and told Pauline that the whole disaster had been my fault. I should have stuck to my guns and kept Ray Martin stranded out in that media no-man's-land along with his old boss, the ABC.

The rest of the day was a total disaster, with Pauline and I having a stupid and wasteful argument over Barbara Hazelton and petty office politics, totally unrelated to the serious political issues that surrounded us on all fronts. The events of that afternoon, after the Ray Martin interview, set in motion the beginning of the chain reaction that would lead to my dismissal twelve days later.

The evening of that hectic day ended in anticlimax. From a purely critical and objective viewpoint, Ray Martin exposed Pauline's weaknesses over a broad front during that evening's showing of *A Current Affair*, and he was clearly the winner of the contest. Pauline looked badly rattled and stumbled many times, forgetting all the points on which I had primed her. Her enemies must have been gloating as they viewed the show. Politically, however, it was a very different matter — with public response very much in favour of Pauline as the viewers bombarded the Channel 9 switchboard with anti-Ray Martin calls. It was almost a re-run of the response to Tracey Curro and the *60 Minutes* show. Same station, different show, same audience, same result! The audiences of Channel 9's three top-rating shows — *60 Minutes*, *Midday* and *A Current Affair* — were, time-after-time, clearly identifying themselves as Hansonites. Again, all my fears and concerns had been groundless — a waste of nervous energy and squandered adrenalin. Pauline had survived yet again and she was giving me the distinct impression that she had become 'bulletproof'.

A Current Affair did not run a poll on Pauline in 1997, only confirming beyond doubt my suspicions about the way Pauline and I had been treated. As it turned out, Pauline had gained the last laugh at the expense of yet another media hotshot.

Ray Martin, in a radio interview with Neil Mitchell of Melbourne's radio station 3AW in 1997, referred to me as a 'Rottweiler'. If I am a Rottweiler, then Ray Martin is a Chihuahua!

THIRTY-ONE

Not a 'Good Weekend'

The *Good Weekend* is an insert magazine in the Melbourne *Age* and its Sydney sister paper the *Sydney Morning Herald*. It comes out every Saturday, often carrying important cover stories that 'grow legs' and are then picked up by other journalists. The magazine has a weekly circulation of 760 000 and the actual readership is assessed by market research at being close to 2.5 million. It usually ends its life in medical and dental waiting rooms and hairdressing salons.

David Leser is a contributing journalist to the *Good Weekend* and is based in Sydney. He was the author of a very forgettable book about Bronwyn Bishop's disastrous campaign for the Parliamentary leadership of the Federal Liberal Party. Leser's father is Bernard Leser who, until his recent retirement, was the driving force behind the Australian *Vogue* women's magazine.

My advice to Pauline, which was endorsed by her and relayed to the rest of her staff, was that all media outlets seeking interviews with Pauline should be channelled through me, for obvious reasons. I personally knew or knew about most of the leading media and TV journalists, and was in a position to assess those who were likely to give her a fair go — that being hardly any of them, picking the 'enemy' was fairly easy.

Pauline had featured in a *Who Weekly* magazine article in the October 14, 1996 issue and had not been all that unfairly treated. I knew that there were several journalists out there just chomping at the bit for a chance to do her over. It was one of my jobs to make sure that she was protected from the more fanatical and nasty members of the fourth estate. I was aware of a more or less unofficial competition among journalists to see who would be the first to have Pauline's scalp hanging from his or her belt.

Pauline's confidence had been growing throughout the year, helped to a certain extent by some of the almost miraculous escapes she had experienced in many of her media confrontations. Another factor was the constant flattery and praise heaped on Pauline by Barbara Hazelton, providing no help at all in keeping her feet firmly on the ground. When Pauline started making quite defensive 'I am the Member for Oxley' statements, indicating an obvious sense of insecurity, I could see Barbara's influence at work. I was constantly forced to combat what Morrie Marsden had dubbed, 'The girls' club'. It had nothing to do with real politics.

On Tuesday, October 22, 1996, while I was in Melbourne laying the groundwork for Pauline's visit to the Melbourne markets, David Leser of the *Good Weekend* magazine was flying from Sydney to Brisbane, en route to Ipswich, to try and corner Pauline Hanson for an interview. He intended backgrounding his piece by speaking to people who had been involved with Pauline over the years, including her two ex-husbands. As it was, he only spoke to her first husband, Walter Zagorski, because Pauline had silenced her second husband, Mark Hanson, by hitting him with a Supreme Court writ.

On the following Wednesday afternoon, David Leser managed to gain an interview with Pauline Hanson. He must have found it hard to believe his luck. He has since told me that he clinched things when he told Barbara Hazelton about the advantages of Pauline reaching out to an audience of 2.5 million readers. It was seductive stuff and that did it. Instead of checking things out with me, as she should have, Barbara Hazelton ushered David Leser into Pauline's office, his scalping knife at the ready.

David Leser's interview with Pauline Hanson moved from her Ipswich office to her out-of-town country property, where it was continued over the dinner table. Leser's luck was running wild.

The first I knew about the interview was when I telephoned Pauline's farm early that evening and spoke to her thirteen-year-old daughter, Lee. She told me that Pauline was talking to a journalist named 'David' but she didn't know his surname, so I asked her to call her mother to the phone.

I became quickly irritated by Pauline's flippant responses to my questions, accompanied by a burst of giggling. Leser described his evening with Pauline as 'Bundy-soaked' so maybe that explains it. 'Bundy', short for Bundaberg Rum, is Pauline's favourite drink, mixed with dry ginger ale. In response to my persistent questioning, she said that the journalist that was sitting at her kitchen table was known to her only as 'David' and he had told her that he worked for 'some sort of weekend magazine'. At least she had part of the story right.

Dripping with sarcasm, I told Pauline that 'David' might turn out to be a hired assassin still recovering from his amazement as to how easily he had cornered his prey. This was greeted by more giggles from Pauline, which only increased my anger. I often wondered if Pauline took the job seriously because she kept on giving me plenty of reasons for doubting that she did. After what seemed like a day later, Pauline's voice came back on the phone and she told me she was entertaining David *Leser*. I told her it would be far better to terminate the interview, there and then — but I was much too late. David Leser had found an easy vein and was drawing off blood.

I was still in Melbourne the next day, installing a computer at my home which I was going to use as a subsidiary to the Ipswich office, when my contact in the Fairfax organisation (which publishes the *Good Weekend* magazine) called me on my mobile. The message was loud and clear — David Leser was 'bad news' for Pauline. I called Pauline on her mobile and told her not to have anything more to do with David Leser, and definitely not to have any photographs taken. 'He is going to do you over Pauline,' I said. I may as well have been talking to that proverbial brick wall.

The day didn't get any better. The October 21 issue of the *Australia/ Israel Review* was out and about, peddling a scurrilous and defamatory story about Pauline and myself, entitled 'Pauline's Puppeteer'. I was depicted as the evil genius manipulating this simple woman from Ipswich. It was yet another brushfire that threatened to blaze out of control. The article would only strengthen the argument of those who were whispering in Pauline's ear telling her how she was the 'Member for Oxley' and that I was out there stealing her thunder. Pauline's rapidly blooming ego would provide very fertile ground for the peddling of such meddlesome and fanciful stuff.

David Leser struck again, this time in Pauline's Canberra office the day after our trip to the Melbourne markets. I had been flat out up at the Parliamentary press gallery and his presence in Pauline's office had escaped my notice until Barbara Hazelton told me he was there. I couldn't believe it. I couldn't believe that Pauline could be so stupid, and I was almost going to ask Leser to leave immediately but thought better of it. Any damage that had been done had surely occurred when he had interviewed Pauline at her property outside Ipswich. He had noted my obvious agitation, commenting in his article, 'Pasquarelli pokes his big, bald head through her door for what must be the fourth time during our interview.' In the end, Pauline lost her temper and asked Leser to leave her office. His profile on her concludes, 'But then Pauline Hanson has had enough. She stands up and, in a white heat, walks me to the door.'

I couldn't resist telling Pauline that she would regret cooperating with Leser when she read the final product. A couple of Saturdays ticked by and no Davis Leser profile on Pauline — then another Saturday. I started to think that maybe there had been a stuff-up. Maybe the editor had thought that the public had read enough about Pauline Hanson. I had almost convinced myself that the David Leser article had gone to reject heaven. No such luck.

I came to almost believe far-fetched conspiracy theories involving the media being out 'to get' Pauline Hanson. I started to fantasise. The evidence was everywhere. Somewhere out there, was a secret, soundproofed room set up like the operations centre in the *Dr Strangelove* movie. Of course, all the ABC notables were there, along with Ray Martin, Laurie Oakes, Philip Adams, Tracey Curro and all the other 'heavies', too numerous to name. From time to time, Kim Beazley, Tim Fischer, Ron Boswell and, only now and again, John Howard would put their heads around the door. What set me off on this wild flight of fantasy? Simply my mobile phone gloatingly proclaiming that the David Leser *Good Weekend* article had finally appeared — just over twenty-four hours after the Ray Martin interview. What a double whammy!

It was Saturday, November 30, 1996, and I was stranded at Gladstone Airport in Queensland, waiting for an unserviceable aircraft to be declared airworthy again. No southern newspapers had arrived. I would have to wait until I got to Cairns to see the article.

On the Sunday morning, in Cairns, I finally managed to get my hands on a *Sydney Morning Herald*. I shook out the insert magazine and there was a full-frontal of Pauline's face filling the whole cover, from border to border. She looked just like one of the principal players in *Cats*! Her blue-green eyes bored into mine and her jaw had that familiar hard-set look. Her nose looked spread and flattened on top of her lop-sided, left upper lip. She looked so grim and hard it was scary. It was the worst photo of Pauline I have ever seen. I wandered off to find a place to sit down, have breakfast and read David Leser's hatchet job.

Leser had written a very savage, but very clever and very smart, profile of Pauline entitled 'Pauline Hanson's Bitter Harvest' (see Appendix Two in this book). As I read on, I cursed Pauline and Barbara for their combined stupidity in allowing David Leser on board. Woven through the piece were naked references to Hitler and Nazism — the unusually named Goebels Road near Pauline's property, her first mother-in-law's fear that Pauline will deport her, and the allegation that Pauline directed preferences to an alleged neo-Nazi candidate at her election. It was all pretty nasty stuff, and made some similar points to those made in the *Australia/Israel Review* article but, in the eyes of a lot of readers, the story was raising some serious doubts about a woman who was presenting herself as just another 'Aussie battler'. Leser's snide reference to 'Goebels Road' was totally unwarranted and unnecessary. Yes, Goebbels (with the extra 'b') was Hitler's propaganda minister, whereas the 'Goebels' family after whom the local road was named, were well-known and popular local residents in the area near Pauline's property.

What David Leser's article did was expose, for the first time, the most questionable and unpleasant aspects of Pauline's character in a straightforward and very telling way. Take for example his question to Pauline about who her best friend was. She replied that Barbara Hazelton or Cheyenne McLeod was. At the time of the interview, Pauline had known Hazelton for just on eight months and Cheyenne McLeod had reappeared in her life after a break of ten years. It was an interesting response, and leaves Hazelton and McLeod wondering who the winner is! I am left wondering at Pauline's capacity to assess people, which is a most important tool in the political process.

A journalist in the Canberra press gallery, who is a devout Catholic and a good family man, told me later that the Leser story had made him change his previously ambivalent view about Pauline and, for him, the most telling and damaging point was Pauline's response to a question about the best thing that had ever happened to her. Pauline had replied that getting divorced had been the best thing that had happened and two divorces had meant, 'That's two good things.' Leser noticed the 'unmistakeable look of forlornness' that came over the face of Pauline's thirteen-year-old daughter Lee, as she listened to her mother. Pauline's second husband, Mark Hanson, is of course Lee's father with whom she still stays from time to time. It was a heartless and very inconsiderate thing for Pauline to say, but I was not surprised. Pauline's professed concern regarding family values does not sit at all well with her own experience in this area though, on my advice, she did acknowledge quite openly her two failed marriages. During my time with her, she made comments about her two older sons that confirmed what appeared in the *Good Weekend* article regarding them.

By the time I had read through the article a couple of times and highlighted Leser's verbal hand grenades, I was feeling very depressed. The article would never have seen the light of day if Pauline and Barbara Hazelton had let me do my job. It was frustrating and annoying being forced to do battle on unnecessary fronts. It was a little like being bombed by 'friendly' aircraft.

I was sure that, this time, Pauline would sustain some fairly substantial damage. Unlike TV shows that are here today and gone tomorrow, the Leser article would live on, handed around by the journos in the Parliamentary press gallery, sitting on tables in doctors' waiting rooms and waiting to be picked up by coffee drinkers at their local cafés. The magazine would still be circulating in a couple of years' time in all those places where human beings find themselves sitting down and waiting.

I arrived back in Canberra that Sunday night and worked in Pauline's Parliamentary office until 10:00 pm to burn off some energy, as I was still fuming about the article and found it hard to relax. I hardly drink these days, so I was unable to drown my sorrows. I made a few calls to some of my contacts, and those who had already read the article immediately asked me why I had let David Leser interview Pauline. After repeating the sorry story four times in the way I have here, I stopped ringing around. I was sick and tired of being a masochist, so I called it a day.

The next day, my worst fears were confirmed by the feedback I received in the press gallery. The Leser article had not dealt Pauline a mortal blow but it had established a bench mark — identifying areas of her vulnerability. It was there as a reference point for future stories by other writers, and it had the potential to come back and haunt her time and time again. It had not been a good weekend!

When Pauline arrived in the office on Monday, December 2, she still had not read David Leser's article, so I made her sit down and read it. When I came back into her office, I could tell that she was not happy with what she was reading and I let her know how angry and frustrated I was. I was not able to pay out on Barbara Hazelton because she had stayed behind to look after the Ipswich office.

A few days later I was collecting my bag from the carousel at Melbourne's Tullamarine Airport when a young man who was obviously not one of Pauline's fans walked past me and said, 'That bitch has eyes like a dingo!' He was referring to Pauline's full-face photo on the front cover of the *Good Weekend* magazine. 'Have you got anything else nice to say?' I shouted after him as he disappeared into the crowd. His right arm was flung back defiantly giving me the single-finger salute.

How Pauline Hanson Almost Blew It

On Tuesday, December 3, 1996, Pauline Hanson got to within an ace of getting up in Parliament and totally and utterly destroying her credibility and her political career. The media would have had a field day with her, and her supporters would have deserted her in droves. She would have become a laughing stock and would have retreated to her electorate of Oxley to be hardly heard of again. David Oldfield and David Ettridge, her current adviser and fundraiser respectively, would never have been able to get her One Nation Party off the ground. The panic stricken Queensland Nationals, particularly Senators Ron Boswell and Bill O'Chee, would have enjoyed a happy Christmas, and Kim Beazley and John Howard would have been able to concentrate on other matters. The Aboriginal 'industry' could have organised a very fine corroboree, and the Human Rights and Equal Opportunity Commission would have been able to celebrate the return of political correctness to its 'correct' place in our political vocabulary. The multiculturalists could have instructed their lobbies to come up with more preposterous and divisive proposals to be funded by ordinary, long-suffering Australian taxpayers — and I would not have been able to find a publisher for this book.

The *Migration Legislation Amendment Bill (No. 3) 1996* and its related bills, the *Migration (Visa Application) Charge Bill 1996* and the *Immigration (Education) Charge Amendment Bill 1996* were to be debated in Parliament, and I thought that this would provide a good opportunity for Pauline to make further comment on the issues of immigration and multi-culturalism. It was important to keep the pot bubbling away after the impact of her maiden and Melbourne speeches. On Monday, December 2, in Pauline's Canberra office, I asked Jeff Babb who had been hired by Pauline as a researcher and speechwriter just two weeks earlier, to draft a speech that I would review and then pass on to Pauline.

The previous day in Parliament, Pauline had hit back at her enemies in the Human Rights and Equal Opportunity Commission during the grievance debate. I had written the speech with the assistance of a well-known civil libertarian QC who had offered his services to Pauline on a no-fee basis. While not endorsing what she stood for, he thought the orchestrated campaign against her by various groups and organisations a disgraceful attack on free speech, and he was prepared to help her as much as he could. I was particularly grateful for his help, contacting him on quite a few occasions and visiting him in Sydney twice. I briefed Pauline on who he was, but she never met him while I was with her.

Pauline was starting to feel the pressure as the flak from the *Good Weekend* article started to burst all around us. On the Tuesday when Pauline nearly went up in self-ignited flames, Piers Akerman had written an article supporting her in the Sydney *Daily Telegraph*, and former WA Labor Senator Peter Walsh had done the same thing in his *Financial Review* column, so the holes in the dyke wall had been temporarily plugged.

Jeff Babb had come back to me with a fairly pithy speech of about 2000 words, which Pauline would be able to handle in her allotted time of twenty minutes for a debate on the second reading of a Bill. The speech read well, but I gave it my treatment, which meant making sure it was translated into the plain, simple language that I had used with Pauline from the first time I wrote for her. I had developed a certain rhythm that was easy to maintain and it seemed to help Pauline strike the right notes out there among her supporters.

I also wanted Pauline to quote Ted Seng in this particular speech. Ted Seng was the Deputy Mayor of the NSW Randwick City Council in 1996 (and he was until September 30, 1997). Ted Seng is a Malaysian-born Chinese who arrived in Australia in 1984 and who, quite courageously and out of the blue, made public comments that were very supportive of Pauline's stand on immigration and multiculturalism. He was reported in the

Sydney Morning Herald on Saturday, November 16, 1996, as saying he did not want Australia to be 'Asianised, Americanised or Africanised' and warning that Australia should not continue to be the 'Mother Teresa of the world' by providing a sanctuary for economic refugees.

Seng went on to say, 'I do not want to see a situation in Australia where values are dramatically changed to Asian values — that's what I'd define as Asianised . . . I'm saying if Asian migrants want to come to Australia and live as they do in Asia, then why do they come here in the first place?' Ted Seng was further reported as saying that he condemned racism, but said migrants had to make 'sacrifices' and accept that Australia was predominantly 'Anglo-Saxon and Christian'. He went on to say that a three-year moratorium on immigration should be introduced until issues, including Australia's trade and cultural relationship with its Asian neighbours, were 'thrashed out'. This last comment of Ted Seng's, in particular, should have made national headlines but it fizzled.

Ted Seng's statements were pure gold from Pauline's point of view, and they came at a most opportune time. I contacted and spoke to Seng but he was obviously already under enormous pressure to shut up, particularly from influential members of the Asian community. Free speech is a very precious commodity these days. I introduced Ted to Pauline on the telephone and they later met in the Qantas Chairman's Lounge at Sydney Airport. Ted Seng's comments in the *Sydney Morning Herald* were run again in the Sydney suburban newspaper, the *Southern Courier*. I was amazed that he had not been given more media exposure because, if he had, I think that the initial anti-Hanson fury would have certainly been defused to a great extent and there may have been some sensible debate on the issue rather than the hysteria about Pauline's views that still exists in and outside our Parliaments.

I started to think again about media conspiracies. It would not have suited Pauline's many media enemies to publicise support for her from a high profile Asian-Australian. That would have meant the media being objective — and that is against the rules! On Friday, November 22, I had gone to the Parliamentary press gallery, trying to resuscitate the Ted Seng story and to get it up and running again, but I had no luck. At least I could assist Pauline to get some more mileage out of it by giving it another run in her speech.

I cleaned up Jeff Babb's draft, wrote in the Ted Seng material and then gave the speech to Pauline to read and amend as she saw fit. I was trying to get her into the habit of becoming involved in the development and writing of speeches, on the basis that I would provide the framework and the language and she could help develop themes after discussing the issues. Now that all the drama and crisis of the maiden speech was behind us, I felt that I should try and stabilise the political output of Pauline's office but, right up until the end, I was never able to get her cooperation to the extent that she sat down with pen and paper and had a proper political discussion from start to finish. On more than one occasion, Pauline complained, 'John, you live and breathe politics, but I'll never be like you.' I didn't want her to become some sort of Pasquarelli clone, I just wanted her to take an active interest in the job she had endured so much to acquire.

Jeff Babb and I arrived in the office at 7:15 am on the Tuesday morning and got ready for another day — but it was to be one that I will not forget in a hurry. When Pauline arrived mid-morning, I saw her hand Jeff Babb the draft speech and heard her tell him that she had written in some changes. I told Jeff to have the speech amended and ready for me when I returned from one of my forays to the press gallery.

When I returned to the office Jeff Babb told me the speech was in my computer and that he had made the changes requested by Pauline. He said that I might want to discuss the changes further with her. I sat down and started scrolling through the speech until I got to the paragraphs dealing with Asian immigration and refugees.

I was scrolling line by line when, suddenly, some words caught my eye. Like a scud missile, seconds before obliterating its target, the words leapt out of the computer screen and my eyes were riveted on them. I couldn't believe what I was seeing. I sat bolt upright staring at the changes Pauline had made to the speech in her reference to Asians. I will never forget the sentence that screamed out at me:

I wouldn't mind if there were more Asians in Australia than Anglo-European Australians as long as they [the Asians] spoke English.

In one simple sentence Pauline Hanson was poised to commit political *hari-kari*. In one sentence she had just become a fervent preacher for the Asianisation of Australia. In one sentence she had jettisoned overboard her policies on multiculturalism and immigration. In one fell sentence, she had totally and utterly repudiated her 'swamped by Asians' statement, converting Asianisation into a desirable goal and embracing Bill Hayden, the man who had said in 1983 that the Asianisation of Australia was 'inevitable and desirable'. One sentence would carry the message out there to maybe millions of Hanson supporters. As I sat there in front of the computer screen, frozen as if in a state of suspended animation, images of newspaper banner headlines suddenly appeared, marching before my eyes like a giant ticker-tape parade:

'HANSON BACKFLIPS ON ASIA!'

'HANSON DUMPS SUPPORTERS!'

'HANSON SURRENDERS!'

'HANSON SELLS-OUT!'

I shook my head like a boxer who has just been on the receiving end of an uppercut, and the headlines disappeared. It was only a minute or two, but it felt like years before I came to life again. I walked over to Jeff Babb's desk and found the amended speech that had Pauline's longhand changes to it clearly indicated in blue biro. I winced as I read the kamikaze sentence again, and took the speech back to my computer terminal. Babb had changed exactly what Pauline had told him to. He had said that I may want to discuss these changes further with her. That was putting it mildly. I went into Pauline's office and asked her to come and have a look at the speech. I asked Jeff Babb to join us.

With Pauline and Jeff Babb standing behind me, I brought up the doomsday sentence and read it aloud slowly. I half-turned to look at Pauline to gauge her reaction, but there was none. So I read the sentence again, and then again. Pauline was not registering. She was just standing there looking blankly at the computer screen. She didn't seem to comprehend how, in one short sentence, she would have surely destroyed the major thrust of her maiden speech, made a foolish spectacle of herself, and brought her office and all those close to her crashing down to earth in a spectacular and fiery political tailspin.

I think Pauline was experiencing some sort of mental block all this time, and I just couldn't get through to her. I was wound up and talking pretty fast and loud, trying to provoke reaction from her — but it never came. I spelt out clearly how careful she needed to be when changing speeches. I told her that if I had been away from the office, and unable to check the changes, there is no doubt that she would have been in a lot of trouble. I told Pauline I would fix the speech, and she walked back to her office as if nothing had happened. Jeff Babb had only been on the job for fifteen hectic days, without the chance to settle in properly, and had certainly been thrown in at the deep end. He had already experienced plenty of drama in that short time. I was desperately hoping and praying he would last the distance.

I wondered if Pauline had experienced some sort of mental fatigue that had caused her to make that inexplicable blunder. The year had been tumultuous and had swept us all up in a maelstrom of crazy media publicity and brutal political attacks that had left their mark. Had Pauline's twenty-two word political suicide note been a Freudian slip that exposed what she really thought? Was I really the sinister puppeteer depicted by the media who, in the end, had pulled the strings just too hard? We will never really know.

On Tuesday, December 10, 1996, at 2:40 pm, Pauline Hanson stood up in Parliament and delivered the repaired speech that, seven days earlier, had contained the seed of her destruction. Despite points of order being called against her for allegedly not speaking specifically to the spirit of the bill, Pauline managed to see out the distance. As she sat down after giving the speech, I wonder if Pauline realised just how close she had come to destroying herself. Whatever the answer to that question, she was back on the rails again, setting sail for 1997 and all the political drama and intrigue that lay ahead.

THIRTY-THREE

The Dismissal — the Prelude

I worked for Pauline Hanson from Thursday, March 7, 1996, to Monday, December 9, 1996, and will take the memories of that turbulent and crisis-filled year to my grave. At my age, that may not be all that far away.

In my late twenties I was in the political spotlight in PNG and received plenty of coverage in the Australian press. In my late fifties I was back in the spotlight and, in 1996, was the most publicly sacked man in Australia.

From the first day I started to work with Pauline Hanson, one of my main objectives was to establish a professionally operated and politically effective office for her. One that would provide a first-class service to her constituents and ensure her re-election. I was never able to achieve those goals and was continually frustrated by what I call 'petticoat office politics'. Having recommended to Pauline that she employ Barbara Hazelton, I quickly realised that I had made a serious mistake but, when I tried to correct it by advising Pauline to sack her and find a replacement, my advice fell on deaf ears. Pauline would tell me many times during the year, 'I will never sack Barbara', and later in her damaging interview with the *Good Weekend* magazine, accorded Barbara 'best friend' status after only knowing her for eight months. What began as my reasonable demand for a professional and politically intelligent chain of command, degenerated into a clash of personalities and a tacky and petty struggle for supremacy in Pauline's office. On reflection, I am not proud of my involvement in the whole sorry mess but it must be reported, as the fall-out from it contributed to the wrongful dismissal of myself and Jeff Babb and created the circumstances that have allowed me to write this book.

Barbara Hazelton was supposed to be Pauline's Ipswich office manager but, since she always travelled to Canberra when Pauline was attending Parliament, the electorate office — the most crucially important office — was left undermanned. One of the reasons Barbara was chosen for the position was the understanding that she was experienced in handling constituent matters but, by spending all that precious time in Canberra, the heavy Ipswich workload fell squarely on the shoulders of the very willing but politically inexperienced Heidi Lewis. I told Pauline that she and I could easily handle things in Canberra but, for some reason, she gave me the impression that she didn't want to be on her own after working hours. It was a great waste of resources and I couldn't reconcile the hard-working 'fish and chip shop lady' with the politician who was reluctant to 'pitch in' on her own and who seemed to want a professional companion to hold her hand.

When Brett Heffernan, our research officer, resigned on Friday, September 20, 1996, he had become completely disillusioned with the working environment in Pauline's office after only four months on the job. With his departure, I lost a valuable and reliable backstop and, like an aircraft forced to abort its take-off, the office lost all its momentum. I was left trying to fight a number of battles on different fronts. Any job is made much harder when there is no back-up but, when there is constant white-anting from within one's own ranks as well, then things can become impossible.

I advised Pauline that we needed to quickly fill the vacancy created by Brett Heffernan's departure, even if it was just on a temporary basis, until we could sit down and search out a competent and qualified researcher. There were quite a few applications on file in the office as a result of the original advertisement, so I drew up a short list for Pauline. As a result, Pauline appointed Kirsten Jackson who lived in Brisbane and had a degree in politics but no political experience to speak of. I undertook to give her some basic schooling in preparing press releases and other related media matters. Pauline agreed to give Kirsten time to prove herself, after which a decision would be made about a permanent appointment. I was becoming very edgy. The media pressure on Pauline was escalating and the need for a hard-nosed, experienced researcher was becoming more urgent —

so much so that Pauline agreed I should start putting out the necessary feelers. I told Pauline that it would be futile to advertise, because we would just get bogged down in the time-wasting job of processing applications. Pauline conceded to me on a further point. I suggested that, if possible, we look to appointing a male researcher, with the aspect of office security in mind.

I spoke to a few of my contacts and told them I was looking for an experienced researcher-cum-political-operative who could jump into the job without any running-in period. The person needed to be a good writer and be computer literate. I was not feeling too optimistic about the chances of finding the right person in a hurry. As the mounting opposition to Pauline grew in the Parliament and the media, I thought it unlikely that anyone with a conventional view about working in politics would consider Pauline's office a step in the right direction. Rather they would see her office as a time-bomb ready to explode, destroying all within. I decided not to hold my breath waiting for Mr Right to turn up.

As 1996 marched on, my problems continued with an office that drifted this way and that, like a rudderless ship. A few weeks after Pauline's maiden speech, I received a telephone call from a Department of Administrative Services official advising me that their computer had rejected payment of a $900 Qantas account for Morrie Marsden's return Brisbane–Canberra airfare when he had accompanied Pauline to Canberra for her maiden speech.

Federal Parliamentarians receive travel entitlements for a certain number of flights for their spouses and immediate family. 'Immediate family' is self explanatory, but a 'spouse' can be married or de facto. Under special circumstances, the Minister for DAS can approve travel for other persons after receiving an official request from the MP concerned. Entitled spouses and relatives are nominated on official forms that must be signed by the member.

Morrie Marsden, at the time he travelled with Pauline, was not her spouse nor was he an immediate relative. When Pauline had invited Morrie to go with her to Canberra to hear her deliver her maiden speech, he had been told that his fare would be paid for. Barbara Hazelton had filled in a travel warrant for Qantas but, when it was presented for payment, it was rejected by the computer.

I referred the matter to Barbara, and she told me that Barry Murray, a DAS officer, had given her approval for charging out Morrie's fare to the department. But, when I cross-checked with Murray, he denied any such thing. It was hard to imagine Murray compromising himself on such an issue, particularly as he gave the clear impression he was a do-it-by-the-book man. I tried to sort things out retrospectively with the Minister's office but the ministerial adviser, quite correctly, sent me packing. I told Barbara that it would be necessary for Pauline to pay the ticket out of her own pocket or out of her electoral allowance. I considered that taking the money from the allowance could be justified because Morrie, after all, had been Pauline's campaign manager. The upshot of this exercise was that I became embroiled in yet another time-wasting exercise that would never have occurred if Barbara Hazelton had known the correct procedures. There was nothing I could do, however, but grit my teeth and push on to deal with the next problem when it presented itself. I did not have long to wait.

Graeme Campbell's telephone accounts will show that he spoke to me for about forty-five minutes on Sunday, July 14, 1996. The conversation was spirited — Graeme accusing me of intending to stand for the Senate in Queensland at the next election, as well as becoming the National Director for Ted Drane's Australian Reform Party. There was no doubt that Pauline's spectacular appearance on the political centre stage was aggravating Graeme. In late August, Brett Heffernan had told me that, according to Barbara Hazelton, Graeme Campbell had said to Pauline, 'It's a wonder you haven't sacked Pasquarelli by now.' I let that information 'go through to the keeper', on the basis that it could have been Graeme being Graeme, or Barbara just trying to be Barbara.

It was during October 1996, that I sensed that my relationship with Graeme Campbell had really changed. It seemed to be common knowledge in the press gallery that Graeme was concerned about Pauline's massive surge of publicity and her support from the same voters to which he was appealing. Let's face it — Pauline Hanson is admittedly more attractive than Graeme Campbell! I thought Graeme had a thicker skin, but he was apparently not amused when a journalist ribbed him by saying that he might need to be endorsed by Pauline in order to hold his seat of Kalgoorlie.

A court of disputed returns had declared a by-election in the NSW Federal Seat of Lindsay which, in the March 1996 Federal Election, had been taken from the Labor incumbent Ross Free by the Liberal Jackie Kelly. The Seat of Lindsay is in Sydney's outer west and has Penrith as its centre. It was held by Labor since its proclamation as a Seat in 1984. The election had been set down for Caulfield Cup Day, Saturday, October 19, and Graeme Campbell the independent Member for Kalgoorlie was backing his old Labor mate, Ross Free.

Graeme had spoken to me several times about convincing Pauline to go to Lindsay with him and campaign for Ross Free on the immigration and multicultural issues, but I strongly rejected his overtures, as did Pauline. I think that Graeme blamed me for her resistance. Free had stated that he was inflexible on Labor's stand on the issues, whereas the Coalition appeared to be starting to take steps in the right direction by making it harder for new migrants to go straight on to DSS benefits the moment they arrived in Australia.

Two weeks away from the by-election, I visited Graeme in his Parliamentary office with some polling results that showed Ross Free was about to get beaten. I repeated the dose four days before election day, with further conclusive proof indicating a clear Liberal win — but Graeme didn't want to listen. On the eve of the election, Channel 9 ran a news clip featuring Laurie Oakes saying, 'The Liberals are angry at the decision of The Australians Against Further Immigration Party (AAFI) to direct preferences to Labor. Anti-Immigration MP Pauline Hanson today bought into the argument on the Liberals' side.' Pauline then appeared, saying, 'The people out there are going to be duped out of their vote, where they really want it to go.' It was a slap in the face for AAFI and Graeme Campbell.

The next day, Jackie Kelly, the New Zealand-born ex-RAAF lawyer, won the seat easily for the second time in just over seven months. After her first win in March, she held the seat by 1.3 per cent. After her second win, she increased her margin to 6 per cent — which was a great blow to Labor and to Graeme. Graeme had a repeat performance when he again backed the wrong candidates in the WA State elections later in the year. Fifteen years in Parliament had done little to hone his political skills and judgment.

In the immediate weeks before my dismissal I became aware that Graeme was strongly promoting Denis McCormack to Pauline. McCormack is Graeme's sometime adviser on immigration and multiculturalism issues and, when cleaning up Pauline's desk in her Parliamentary office, I found a substantial file of McCormack's writings plus some audio-tapes buried under other papers. I smiled wryly as I knew there was no danger of Pauline suddenly swotting up on material Graeme Campbell had given her. She had never done that for me, so why should she have suddenly mended her ways and done it for him?

I was in Melbourne the weekend after Gary Hardgrave's despicable attack on me, and was discussing all my problems with a person whose experience and advice I respect, when Jeffry Babb's name was mentioned. I was told that, as chance would have it, Jeff Babb was 'on the loose', having recently parted company as a researcher with the Institute of Public Affairs after that organisation had undergone restructuring. I was told that he was a competent writer and had worked in a political office before. What I was hearing sounded very encouraging, but I wasn't about to get my hopes up too high.

On Thursday, October 24, 1996, Jeff Babb came to see me at my Melbourne home. A shortish, bookish person with thick-lensed spectacles, Jeff Babb had done many things during his forty-two years. He was a graduate of the University of Western Australia and had a post-graduate qualification from the Royal Melbourne Institute of Technology. He had worked for WA Liberal Senator Peter Sim, and had been Senior Research Officer in the Victorian Parliamentary Library. He had travelled extensively in Asia, Europe and the Middle East, spending time in Japan, Hong Kong, Singapore, Malaysia, Indonesia, Israel, Egypt and Turkey. To complement his academic qualifications Babb had been a truck driver, handyman, trades assistant and gardener. When Babb told me he could speak Mandarin and

Bahasa Indonesian I was more than impressed. It was all too good to be true, but there was more to come. Jeff Babb was married to a Taiwanese woman who apparently was not averse to having that fact publicised. It would be great public relations for Pauline. She already had a minder with a 'spaghetti' name and now she would have a researcher married to an Asian. I was already mentally writing the press releases to 'bore it up' all her mealy-mouthed critics. I was in high spirits as I picked up my mobile to tell Pauline the good news. I told her that, at the first opportunity, she would need to come to Melbourne and meet Jeff Babb.

Pauline met Jeff sooner than expected, when I brought her to Melbourne for her visit to the Melbourne Wholesale Fruit and Vegetable Markets. It had been only six days since I had first met Babb when he came to meet Pauline where she was staying overnight in Yarraville. Pauline offered Jeff Babb the position of researcher while talking to him in the front bedroom of my friend's house where she was staying. I was elated and looking forward to arriving back in Canberra and Ipswich and getting stuck into things. I now had my best chance ever to get the office up and running again, if only I could make Pauline listen to reason about the way the office should be structured — but I was kidding myself. It was never going to be.

By rights, Jeff Babb should have been given the highest paid of the three positions in Pauline's office, but Barbara Hazelton was holding that spot down and Pauline would not drop her back to the middle position. Jeff had the necessary experience and he had the qualifications. As a compromise, Pauline agreed to let Jeff Babb work the maximum number of weekly overtime hours allowed by DAS in order to make up the difference in salary between the middle and top positions. That would present no problem, since the only way to keep up with the workload in Pauline's office was to work a lot of overtime. Overtime didn't concern me because I received a yearly allowance of $11 200 in lieu, irrespective of the hours I worked. Some electorate staff have been known to claim $20 000 or more in overtime per year, so I had the short end of the stick. My diary tells me I was working 100-hour-plus weeks.

The deluge of Australia-wide support that continued to rain down on Pauline gave me plenty to think about. It was support that either needed to be constructively employed or to be acknowledged but then let lie fallow. I had discussed this particular point with Pauline in general terms on other occasions. On Monday, November 4, in her Parliamentary office, I was much more specific.

A *Bulletin*-Morgan poll due to be on the news-stands on Melbourne Cup Day (the following day), had been heavily promoted in the media and was predicting at least seven Senate Seats for Hanson candidates at the next Federal Election. It sounded heady stuff.

I told Pauline that she had only two options. One was to acknowledge and thank her supporters all around Australia, but tell them that she intended to limit her political activities only to her electorate of Oxley. The second option was to embrace the support and convert it into a political organisation, with the main objective being to win Seats in the Senate at the expense of the Democrats and the Greens. I stressed to Pauline that the second option was the most obvious one. Not since Don Chipp had formed the Democrats had a similar opportunity presented itself to any Federal politician.

Pauline was standing with her arms folded, half-sitting on the front of her desk while I paced up and down. I was very aware of the immense potential of the situation and thought that, despite all that Pauline and I had been through, it could still end up being well worth all the pain.

It would be patently obvious, even to the most casual political observer, that for Pauline to retreat to Oxley would simply result in her political death by a thousand cuts. Ted Mack had learnt his lesson the hard way. To be a force in Australian politics she had to try to win the balance of power in the Senate. It was the most effective strategy to adopt and I told Pauline that, in the end, she might need to opt for a Queensland Senate spot herself if the chances of her re-election in the lower house Seat of Oxley became doubtful. It could also become a very difficult and unwieldy situation if Pauline was sitting in the lower house while a couple of her people were in the Senate. 'Always leave the back door open,' I told her. 'Pauline, you'll never have another chance like this in your lifetime and nor will anyone else,' I said. 'It's like the wave every surfer dreams about. Once you're on it you have to stay on your feet and ride it right through to the beach. If you drop off, you'll never get back on it.' I stopped speaking and looked inquiringly at her.

She stood there, staring at a point on the floor in front of her. She looked almost wistful as she started to speak, 'Well, I suppose I could just go back home and be the little old Member for Oxley and do the best job I can, or . . .' She paused and looked straight at me. 'Or I can try and do something to get this country out of the blasted mess it's in.' She was starting to fire up.

'Well, Pauline,' I said, 'It's your decision and your decision alone and, whatever you decide, don't have any regrets. You can look back on all this one day and have a good laugh. Don't ever get too serious.' I then saw Pauline's jaw give that tell-tale, almost imperceptible twitch. 'Go for it!' she said.

Next morning I 'wagged' it from work and flew from Canberra, at my own expense, to Melbourne for the Melbourne Cup — but, even there, I couldn't leave Pauline Hanson behind. I was greeted by Hanson well-wishers everywhere I went — including the Members' enclosure and the carpark where all the marquees and the festivities were. Cries of, 'Go Hanson go', 'Tell her to keep going', and just plain, 'Pauline Hanson', followed me around the track. John Elliott's wife Amanda told me Pauline 'was the best thing since sliced bread'. All this diversion affected my tipping skills and instead of backing Saintly (the horse I had backed to victory in the Cox Plate) I transferred my allegiance to Nothin' Leica Dane.

John Brown the Australian Tourist Board chief, ex-Labor Minister for Tourism and self-confessed former desk-jockey had launched a savage attack on Pauline the previous week, blaming her for the tourist industry's imagined woes and going so far as to lend his name to a shameless request to the Federal government for a $25 million 'rescue' package. Brown was also at the Melbourne Cup and, after being told that I had also been there, he was reported in the Melbourne *Herald Sun* newspaper as saying that he would have liked to have kicked me in the balls! For John Brown's benefit I wore my best steel-capped boots to the 1997 Melbourne Cup. I saw Brown there but he sensibly kept his distance.

Back in Canberra the following day, I went to the Australian Electoral

Commission (AEC) and obtained the relevant forms for registering a political Party. Registering a political Party that does not already have one of its members in Parliament, requires supplying a list of the names and addresses of five hundred members. This involves a lot of valuable time, and copious paperwork. With Pauline already an MP, the registration process would be almost a formality. I even had a ready-made name for her Party. The Morgan organisation's press release for its poll, published in the *Bulletin*, referred to the 'Pauline Hanson Movement'. There it was, plain and simple — just Pauline's name and no mention of that dreaded word 'Party'.

I established a 'Pauline Hanson Movement' file and briefed Pauline on the registration procedures. She asked me whether I thought that having her name involved was being 'too egotistical' but I told her that her name was the beacon that would attract voters to her Senate candidates. I must have convinced Pauline because on April 11, 1997, she launched her 'Pauline Hanson's One Nation Party'. My intended version, the PHM, would have had membership at large and no formal branch structure. I told Pauline that, with the little time left to us to get an organisation up and running, the creation of branches would lead to factions and then, in turn, to chaos. I was also confident that I would be able to have either 'Pauline' or 'Hanson' registered as her Party's abbreviated name, which would mean that her Senate candidates would have either of her names under their own on the ballot paper. To this end, I had discussions with Mr Song Woon Kon of the Canberra AEC office, a man with whom I had previously had dealings when I was working for Graeme Campbell. If either of the abbreviations were to be approved, it would be a vote-winning masterstroke that would save hundreds of thousands of dollars in advertising. All her candidates would simply have 'Pauline' or 'Hanson' under their names on the ballot paper.

I advised Pauline that she would need to set up a 'Pauline Hanson Movement Trust Fund', to be operated by a firm of accountants in conjunction with a signatory to be nominated by her but not involved with her office. I stressed to her how important it was to have the financial affairs of her organisation properly distanced from her electorate and Parliamentary offices and, as the first step in this direction, I asked Barbara Hazelton to apply for a separate post box at the Ipswich Post Office. Things were starting to hot up. I told Pauline that the sooner we had her organisation up and running the better.

We agreed that the launch would be a 'controlled' affair from her Ipswich office on Australia Day, 1997. I was on the brink of helping bring about a major change in the way the political game is played in Australia. I could almost reach out and touch the prize, so tantalisingly close — but that would be as far as I got.

THIRTY-FOUR

The Dismissal — the Real Thing

In late 1996, Alan Brown the Victorian Transport Minister had accepted a Victorian Government posting to London and his blue ribbon Liberal Seat of Wonthaggi was up for grabs. A by-election was set down for February 1, 1997 and it was assumed that the Liberals would bolt in.

Ted Drane contacted me, saying that his Australian Reform Party would be fielding a candidate and he was very keen to have Pauline come to Wonthaggi and endorse his candidate. I agreed with him and said that I would do my best to convince Pauline, even though she was very busy. It would give her a taste of electioneering from a different perspective and I was sure that she would be well received in that part of Victoria.

I made the suggestion to Pauline in her Ipswich office and I was astounded by her response. She was not in the best of moods at the time and became even sourer. In fact, she was very dismissive of the whole idea once I had outlined it to her. Her face hardened and her eyes flattened to look decidedly unattractive. I thought she was being very ungrateful in the extreme given the open, no-strings-attached offer of friendship Ted Drane had extended to her. Pauline said that she didn't owe Ted anything and she wasn't going to be used by anyone. I wondered if Graeme Campbell had said anything to Pauline that may have influenced her, because his relationship with Ted Drane had deteriorated rapidly almost as soon as it had begun.

I had one last throw of the dice in early December, 1996, to try to convince Pauline that she should go to Wonthaggi to help Ted Drane during the Victorian by-election. This was after speaking to Charles Slade, the

Channel 9 news reporter in Melbourne. I spoke to him on Sunday, December 8, and he told me that a 'vox pop' or street survey in Wonthaggi had shown an 80 per cent response in favour of a Pauline Hanson endorsed candidate. This was very good news, so I rang Pauline to tell her that she should seriously reconsider her decision not to assist Ted Drane, but my advice fell on deaf ears. At the time I did not realise how deaf. I flew from Melbourne to Canberra on December 9, 1996 and, at about 3:30 that afternoon, in her Parliamentary office, Pauline Hanson sacked me without any explanation.

November 1996 had been a month of developing intrigue, an escalating media offensive against Pauline and myself, and just plain madness. In between keeping Pauline on track and getting the 'Pauline Hanson Movement' ready for formal registration with the Australian Electoral Commission, I made lightning trips to Adelaide, Perth and North Queensland in response to requests from supporters in those places for Pauline to come and discuss their political concerns with them.

I knew that Pauline was coming under increasing pressure from a number of sources about my alleged personal political motives and the criticism that I was trying to steal her media thunder. Very early in the piece I had told Pauline that, sooner or later, the media would catch up with me and my 'colourful' past and we would both be forced to live with what turned up in the papers. I told her that if she could let all the nonsense pass overhead and ignore it, everything would be fine. 'Take it seriously and react accordingly,' I told her 'and a wedge will be very quickly driven between us.' It was.

The rumour mills were running hot with the story that I was manipulating Pauline to further my political ambition to run for the Senate in Queensland. I felt like the boss of a wild west wagon train that was being circled by whooping Red Indians. The stories were given added impetus by a sixty-three year old New Zealand painter and decorator living on Queensland's Gold Coast.

Bruce Whiteside received some media attention a number of years ago when he held protest meetings on the Gold Coast about the increasing purchases of local real estate, particularly by the Japanese. Out of the blue, and not long after Pauline's maiden speech, Whiteside formed a 'Pauline Hanson Support Movement' on the Gold Coast. This was one of the things I had feared most — the sudden appearance of groups, created no doubt with all the best intentions in the world, that could act as vehicles for all sorts of people wishing to promote their own agendas. Monitoring and controlling these groups was out of the question because we didn't have the manpower or the resources. As if I didn't have enough to do.

I was told about Bruce Whiteside on my return to the Ipswich office from one of my many rushed trips. He had spoken to Pauline and Barbara Hazelton and, at the time, there were other pressing matters requiring my attention, so I didn't get involved. I eventually spoke to Bruce Whiteside myself when I asked him if any of his contacts could help with the printing of Pauline's maiden speech for further distribution to the people requesting it from all around Australia. I found out far too late that Bruce Whiteside had what amounted to a compulsion to seek out and then speak to any journalists he could find who were looking for a story. To make matters much worse, the two journalists he fed most were avowed enemies of Pauline Hanson.

On Thursday, November 7, 1996, I heard on my 'grapevine' that Whiteside had 'dumped' on me to Greg Roberts of the *Sydney Morning Herald*. Later on, Whiteside would accuse Jeff Babb of being an economic rationalist — implying that Babb was part of some sort of sinister, economic ultra-right-wing infiltration of Pauline's office. I had not even met the man and here he was, doing as much damage to Pauline as he was to me. Sure enough, the following Saturday's *Sydney Morning Herald* ran an article by Greg Roberts blazing away at Pauline and myself. In the article, Whiteside voiced his concerns about me, saying, 'I would prefer to see someone in the office who is more moderate in their views . . . There is a perception out there that Mr Pasquarelli is pulling the strings.' Greg Roberts linked me with the League of Rights, quoting its leader Eric Butler as saying he knew Pasquarelli 'well'. I have met Eric Butler and his wife together on one occasion only, and his wife on her own on another occasion when I visited her bookshop to check out reports that the League of Rights was selling the maiden speech. I phoned Whiteside immediately after reading the *Sydney Morning Herald* article and, managing to stay calm, urged him to stop running off to the press with such fanciful ideas and theories formulated at what I considered to be extremely long range. I had wasted my breath.

On December 8, the day before my dismissal, Bruce Whiteside was stricken by another bout of 'media madness' and, in the Melbourne *Sunday Herald Sun*, this time described me as a 'mind-bender instead of a minder'. He attacked Pauline for losing touch and said that she had fallen under my spell. He then gave Noel Crichton-Browne a swipe, saying that I was using Pauline's appeal to organise Crichton-Browne's return to the Senate as a 'pay back' against John Howard. It was stupid, groundless and damaging stuff but obviously had an impact on Pauline. In September, 1997, David Ettridge, the National Director of One Nation told me that it was this particular scenario that was the primary cause for Pauline becoming involved in a plan to dump me.

The media must have rejoiced in having Bruce Whiteside around as their compliant and eager informant. I could sense that Pauline was definitely being affected by all the scuttlebutt surging around us. She told me more than once, in a concerned way, not to speak to the media about myself — but all I could say, again and again, was that I had no control over journalists digging up my PNG and other pasts. It was hopeless trying to get her to understand my predicament. I was starting to feel like a man in a badly leaking lifeboat being encircled by sharks sensing that their next meal was not too far away.

On Monday, November 18, 1996, I was granted a temporary stay of execution when Jeff Babb arrived in the Canberra office to start work. I had briefed him on the state of play in the office. He was quickly 'blooded' when he came with me to the Parliament House cafeteria and stood by, a little taken aback, as he watched me take issue in no uncertain terms with Barbara Hazelton being too friendly with Tania Roberts, the woman who Gary Hardgrave alleged that I had sexually harassed.

President Clinton's visit to Canberra in November, 1996, provided a little welcome relief by taking the media heat off Pauline for a while, but it was only a temporary respite.

Jeff Babb had a brief taste of what I was contending with on the home front when he put an addressed, but unstamped, letter on Barbara Hazelton's desk thinking that it would be put with the day's 'out' mail. Barbara opened the letter, obviously without looking at it, then embarrassedly announced her mistake. Babb looked at me quizzically over Barbara's shoulder. I responded by shrugging my shoulders. I had become accustomed to having my mail opened in error.

While we were still in Canberra, Jeff Babb was at work drafting a couple of speeches for Pauline to use in Parliament — I was already starting to feel a little relaxed and was able to concentrate on more pressing matters. I just kept hoping Pauline would see the light and let me reorganise the office before it was all too late.

On Saturday, November 23, 1996, Jeff Babb and I were in Pauline's Ipswich office, working and organising a strategy for the final weeks of the year. I told Babb that apart from the basic Christmas holidays, he and I would be required to hold the fort. I was encouraging Pauline to disappear for a couple of weeks, and Barbara Hazelton was talking about going to Hong Kong to be with her husband. That day in Ipswich there was an anti-racial-discrimination protest so I spent some time at Pauline's fish and chip shop where she was working for the day, just to see that there were no problems and to be of some support to her.

On the Sunday, I drove down to the Gold Coast to meet with Bruce Whiteside for the first time. I was carrying a letter drafted by me and signed by Pauline, asking Whiteside to consult with her instead of constantly feeding the media. I was with him for about one strained hour and gained the impression that Bruce Whiteside had become involved in something that, like a runaway horse, left him with no option but to cling grimly to the saddle. My visit had been utterly in vain. That very night, Bruce Whiteside was back in action feeding his media 'chooks'. Whiteside would later be sacked by David Ettridge, the National Director for One Nation and his last media splash earned him the sad headline of 'Pauline Hanson Sent Me Mad' in the June 1997 issue of *Woman's Day* magazine.

I left the Gold Coast after visiting Bruce Whiteside and drove to Cooroy and Nambour on the Sunshine Coast to meet with a group of Pauline's supporters who wanted her to also come and meet with them. I wasn't really all that surprised to see a couple of prominent National Party people I knew. The feedback I was receiving indicated that Pauline was making large inroads into the National Party's grass roots throughout Queensland. As I drove back to Ipswich late that evening with a tropical storm buffeting the car, I started wondering if all my efforts during the year to keep Pauline's ship afloat had been worth it. Her persistent refusals to do her 'homework' had disappointed and discouraged me. I continually found myself trying to equate the intellectually indolent Pauline with the energetic and tireless 'fish and chip shop lady'. As I drove into the outskirts of Ipswich I shook my head to clear it. The prospect of serving it up to those stuck-up pretenders in Canberra temporarily swept away my doubts.

On Monday, November 25, 1996, I went to the offices of Ipswich accountants, Harding & Martin and spoke to Neil Harding about his firm accepting a brief to manage the 'Pauline Hanson Movement trust account'. Harding said he would be only too happy to operate the account and I told him I would bring Pauline back to his office the following day to confirm all the arrangements. Pauline had taken the day off, so it had given me the chance to organise a few things with Jeff Babb who was working flat-out acquainting himself with the Ipswich office and handling some constituent matters.

The next day I had another discussion with Pauline about my views regarding what I considered to be the continuing unsatisfactory operation of her Ipswich office. I tried to impress on her that, if I was to get her political movement up and running, it was essential to have the home office running smoothly and efficiently. I was sounding like a broken record, but nothing had improved and Jeff Babb had remarked in a polite and quite matter-of-fact way, after only a few days there, that the office was a shambles. I told Pauline that I was confident of raising at least one million dollars to fund her movement, which would allow me to set up a separate secretariat to start organising people to man polling booths around the country in readiness for her run on the Senate. Just as importantly, the secretariat could deal with all the non-constituent material coming into the Ipswich office, thereby taking a lot of pressure away from it — at least allowing it to get out of its wheelchair and on to crutches for a start.

I had known 'the man in the white suit' at Melbourne University and, though we had gone our separate ways, we had remained in contact over the years and met from time to time when he was on business trips to PNG. We shared a fondness for the racetrack, Australian art and colonial furniture. Another thing we shared was a deep-seated contempt for the modern-day professional politicians and the Party machines that controlled them. Apart from that we never socialised. He was the head of a closely knit family and had a high profile in the business community. He ran his race, I ran mine.

When polling started to show Pauline's support in the electorate, 'the man in the white suit' told me that he thought she had a real chance of getting some people up in the Senate, including herself, and I realised that he was being more than serious when he volunteered to help with raising money for the venture. His strategy was to raise money from his contacts in the mining industry in WA and Queensland, as well as contributing himself. The middle-level and smaller miners were very apprehensive about Wik and Native Title — many of them considered it was only a matter of time before their businesses were wiped out. Desperate men, they acknowledged the real possibility of an eleventh-hour rescue at the hands of Hansonites in the Senate and they were prepared to put their hands in their pockets.

I was hurrying into the Qantas terminal at Sydney Airport when my mobile broke into its grating muzak mode. 'I'll have $500 000 ready when you want it,' the voice of 'white suit' said. For the first time since I had started working for Pauline Hanson, I suddenly realised that I was playing first grade.

To make up the million dollar budget I had targetted, the remaining balance of $500 000 would need to be raised from the rank and file of Pauline's supporters but, with her huge data base of names and addresses, I could see no problems in that. I had told Pauline about my contact's role, but never told her his name, nor the names of the companies involved. I just couldn't afford any leaks until everything was finalised. The arrangement was that, once the movement was registered at the Australian Electoral Commission, sufficient funds to get it up and running would be advanced. The bulk of the money would be reserved for the election campaign. There was nothing sinister about the arrangement because, ultimately, the funds and their sources would be revealed to the AEC under the provisions of the Electoral Act. There was only one proviso governing the whole deal — Pauline needed to give an undertaking that I would remain her adviser assuming that she was re-elected.

It was appropriate that on Friday, December 13, four days after Pauline sacked me, my mobile phone came alive. The message was short and simple: 'You know why I'm calling — all bets are off — good luck.'

On Tuesday afternoon, November 26, I took Pauline along to meet Neil Harding, the Ipswich accountant I had seen the previous day about operating the Pauline Hanson Movement trust account. Pauline confirmed my brief to him. He was to establish the account and was to be a signatory for it. It was arranged that monies already in the office 'Pauline Hanson Account' would be transferred across — all funds to be deposited in an interest bearing account with the local First Provincial Building Society. All that was left for Pauline to do was to appoint a second signatory. Back at her office, she decided to ask Trevor Nardi to accept the role. Nardi, a respected Ipswich small businessman was a Liberal Party backer at the last election. He had been very publicly supportive of Pauline and had no hesitation in taking up her offer. I spoke to Trevor Nardi in July 1997 and he said that, since the day Pauline had appointed him, he had never been called on to countersign a single cheque because none had ever been issued.

The next day I took the initiative on an issue I had been talking about for months. I started to recruit volunteers to work in the Ipswich office and help with answering the telephones and carrying out simple clerical tasks. It was something I had been urging Pauline to do, because I wanted her to use people with whom she felt comfortable — but she never came to the party. I was starting to be possessed of a real sense of urgency as the year started to rapidly slip away. The three office phones were simply not enough to cope with the traffic, so I contacted Telstra and the Department of Administrative Services in Brisbane to give us some extra lines. One of the first people I recruited was Phyllis Knox, whose father was part-Aboriginal. Phyllis Knox was a regular contributor to 'Letters to the Editor' in the *Queensland Times*, and she was not on her own. A lot of Aborigines supported Pauline, particularly on her stand to abolish ATSIC but some of them, understandably, were nervous about declaring themselves publicly for her. Democracy and free speech, where art thou?

The day of the taping of the Ray Martin interview with Pauline for *A Current Affair* was a milestone in the chain of events that led to the sacking of Jeff Babb and myself. After Ray Martin had departed, I left the office to go and have a cup of tea and cool down. I was hoping that the rest of the day would proceed smoothly after the crazy way that it had started. On my return to the office, Pauline's office door was closed. Jeff Babb told me that Pauline was having a meeting with Barbara Hazelton, Heidi Lewis and Cheyenne MacLeod. It looked as if 'the girls' club' was in session again.

Some time later Pauline asked me to come into her office. She was still obviously recovering from her early morning start at the Brisbane Fish Markets and her savaging at the hands of Ray Martin, but I was not prepared for what came next. 'Jeff Babb has been eavesdropping at my door, and what's all this business about him ringing up about overtime?' she said, looking very grim. My first reaction was to fall to the ground, assume the foetal position and start sobbing but I managed to control myself and be serious. 'Pauline, just say all that again — slowly,' I said. Pauline's repeat performance was no better than her first. It took me only a few moments to find out that Barbara Hazelton had carried these incredible tales to Pauline. Pauline admitted this, but said that Heidi and Cheyenne had also been witnesses to the 'eavesdropping' allegation. I deduced that the behind-closed-doors meeting of the 'girls' club' had produced this latest farce. The outer office at Ipswich was a large 'open plan' space with three workplaces spaced equally down one side. There were no partitions to separate people from each other. In such an environment it is impossible for anyone to act in a clandestine manner.

It was all simple stuff. I, myself, had seen Jeff Babb walk up to Pauline's closed door, put his ear to the door to see whether Pauline was free or had someone with her or was on the phone. If he discerned either of the latter, he would walk away. I had done the same thing myself on occasions. Jeff must have had good hearing, because the close-fitting door was fairly soundproof. As for the nonsense about overtime, I had instructed Jeff that, because of his agreement with Pauline on this subject, he was to contact DAS and be briefed on all the details. He was then to prepare a short briefing note to give to the other staff members because this enquiry was something that I should have taken care of. He had made his enquiries on a telephone only a couple of metres away from Barbara Hazelton's desk.

'This is crazy Pauline,' I said. 'It's all mad stuff and is the reason why this office will never, never work.' I reminded Pauline about her agreement with Babb on the overtime question, but she brushed this aside. Not to be denied, Pauline (who was obviously working up into one of her bad moods) took off on another tack.

She told an incredible story about me being responsible for reducing Heidi Lewis to tears when I was in Canberra and Heidi was in Ipswich. I had allegedly telephoned Heidi close to knock-off time on one occasion and had asked her to fax some information to me. Heidi had an appointment to keep with her parents and I had delayed her — hence the tears.

This was an event that possibly had occurred but, if it had happened, Heidi had never made me aware of it. By now I could scarcely contain my anger and, again, it was Barbara who had carried the story to Pauline — not Heidi. As in the TV sales advertisement — 'Wait, there's more!' Pauline seemed to be dredging all these mad stories out of a bottomless barrel.

She looked at me almost slyly. 'What did you mean when you said that you had Graeme Campbell and myself in your pocket?' This revelation had me well and truly on the ropes. I was almost ready for a TKO count.

Kirsten Jackson, who had temporarily worked in the office before Jeff Babb came on board, had travelled to Canberra with Pauline and myself for one sitting of Parliament and had allegedly overheard me saying the words in question during one of my telephone conversations. She told Barbara who, in turn, had taken the story to Pauline.

Kirsten had spent most of her time at the reception desk in the outer office and, unless I had someone with me or was making a confidential telephone call, I always left the connecting door to the outer office open. I speak loudly because of my deafness problem, so Kirsten certainly could have overheard me speaking on the telephone when the door was open — whether she could hear me clearly was a matter of contention. I just couldn't be bothered trying to argue with Pauline about all this bizarre nonsense. I was bitterly disappointed that Kirsten had chosen to carry tales back to Ipswich.

I told Pauline to ring Kirsten there and then and to put the phone on speaker. Pauline rang and started speaking to Kirsten about the matter but, as soon as Kirsten knew I was in the room, there was silence. When I pressed her for a repetition of what she had alleged I said, she responded that she could not be specific about what I had said but the 'gist' of my conversation was what she had relayed to Barbara.

Kirsten was obviously keen to end the call. My patience had evaporated. I told Pauline that Kirsten's credibility was nil and that I had more important things to do. She looked sulky. I was sure that she was still spoiling for a fight. I wish that she had applied herself as vigorously to all the briefing notes and other information I had wanted her to study on past occasions.

Later in the day, when Heidi came to my office, I told her how disappointed I was about the story of me reducing her to tears. Heidi registered surprise and said that she didn't know what I was talking about. As she was speaking, her eyes started sparkling and my first response was to feel guilty, but then I thought that I should be the one crying with all the crazy nonsense that was going on.

Shortly after my exchange with Heidi, I had reason to see Pauline, so went to her office. The door was closed, so I knocked and entered. Heidi was sitting down with Pauline and was crying. By now, I desperately wanted the day to come to an end and for everyone to go away and leave me alone.

I spoke to Heidi, telling her that all I wanted was for the office to work properly so that Pauline would be re-elected. I had always encouraged Heidi in her job and had been concerned that her workload was too much for her. Heidi had always stoically maintained that she was coping, but I knew that Barbara's trips to Canberra meant that Heidi was constantly saddled with all the computer work on top of constituent enquiries.

I told Heidi that I was totally confounded by the story of me having brought her to tears and asked her to clear the whole matter up once and for all. Heidi then told Pauline and myself that no such thing had ever happened and went on to say that Barbara had been giving her too much work at times. On the brink of exploding, I sat back and closed my eyes, just wishing that I was somewhere else. I sat up, locked eyes with Pauline and asked her to apologise to me for all the nonsense to which I had been subjected. To her credit, she did so immediately, without any qualification. Pauline asked me if we should call Barbara in, but I said that I was in no frame of mind for any further inanity and we could discuss the matter at a later date. A whole day had been wasted in a welter of stupidity and trivia. It had all been about personal issues and power-plays — it had not had anything to do with politics. I just wanted everyone to get out of the office and go home, so that I could get myself back on track.

Jeff Babb and I left the office at 7:00 pm that evening and went to one of the local pubs for dinner. I was feeling despondent, and sick and tired of all the moronic and childish stop-start, on-again, off-again stuff. Jeff Babb had been in the job for only eleven days and was visibly shell-shocked after the events of the day that had just, mercifully, finished. He told me that he had never experienced that sort of behaviour before in a political office and he quoted his five years experience in a Senatorial office. It was a terrible start for him and I felt responsible. It was a re-run of what had happened to Brett Heffernan, only this time things were happening faster.

The following day I made ready to fly to Gladstone and Cairns. I told Pauline that we would again make an effort to sort out her office problems when we met in Canberra the following Monday. To me, all the aborted efforts were now sounding just like a broken record — the same song getting stuck suddenly at the same spot, with no possibility of playing to its end.

That weekend saw the publication of the disastrous David Leser *Good Weekend* article. This made sure that the coming week would start with plenty of negative media. During the afternoon of Monday, December 2, 1996, I had a telephone conversation with Morrie Marsden who was in Ipswich. Morrie was excited and almost ecstatic when he told me that Pauline had asked him to be her campaign manager again, but I couldn't help thinking that all Morrie was doing was setting himself up for yet another fall. I had seen and heard enough during the year to know that Pauline would not be renewing any sort of deeper relationship with him. With all the problems I was forced to deal with, all I could do was feel sorry for him.

Next day was another gut-wrenching, downhill run on the Pauline Hanson rollercoaster. Sadly, my prediction about Morrie Marsden was all too correct, too soon. From what I could work out from his angry and agitated phone calls, he had gone into Pauline's Ipswich office the previous day and announced to Barbara Hazelton that he 'was back in business' as Pauline's campaign manager. Pauline had been told by her office staff that, during this triumphal visit, Morrie had looked at some files and at Pauline's desk diary. One thing had led to another and, during a phone call with an angry Pauline, Morrie Marsden had been 'barred' from the Ipswich office. His return to grace had been very brief indeed. Morrie told me that he had only looked at some opened and filed support letters, and that the diary had been the 1997 one — as yet, unused.

The rest of the day dragged on, with crisis levels at their peak because this was the day that Pauline Hanson almost blew it (as I have described earlier). To top things off, I took a phone call late that afternoon from a very angry Mr Brian Broadhead, who alleged that Pauline owed him $1280 for fees incurred in setting up an Internet presentation for her. It didn't rain, it just continued to pour. After I wrote in my diary, 'What a f . . . ing shambles!', Jeff Babb and I left the office that night at 10:30 pm, both wondering when we would step on the next land mine. Little did we know that the 'Daddy' of them all was not that far away.

My diary tells me that the next day, Wednesday, December 4, 1996, was 'another crazy day'. For some reason Pauline had started getting stuck into Jeff Babb about the overtime he had worked, effectively breaking the agreement she had made with him, in my presence, when she had taken him on. Jeff had been with Pauline for sixteen days and had worked long and hard for most of that time. I had worked with him for most of those sixteen days and, as Pauline's nominee, I had signed out his overtime claims. Everything was above board as far as I was concerned. Pauline's main gripe seemed to be that she simply didn't think that he should be paid as much as he had legitimately claimed for. It was almost as if she was jealous of him getting the extra money. On several occasions, before Jeff Babb had even arrived on the scene, when I had discussed the subject of overtime in relation to her staff, she had triumphantly made the point that Barbara Hazelton rarely claimed for overtime. That rationale only served to unfairly compromise anyone that worked long hours and expected to be fairly paid. It was a selfish and unreasonable attitude for an employer to have.

During a saner moment that afternoon, Pauline asked me whether she could make an ISD call on her mobile phone and my answer was, 'Yes.' The office phones in Canberra are ISD barred but those back at the electorate offices are not, nor are the mobile phones. I had told Pauline to 'disappear' for a couple of weeks during the holiday period so that she would be fresh and ready for the launch of her Party on Australia Day. Earlier in the day, I had accompanied Pauline to the Qantas office in Parliament House where she paid for a ticket to Magnetic Island in Queensland, but she had later changed her mind and cancelled it. Later that day she took me unawares when she told me she would be leaving for America on December 22.

It was during the course of this day that Pauline made the only concession she ever had in respect of Barbara Hazelton. 'Well, what if I got rid of Barbara — what would you do?' she said. My reply was that we would put on a highly competent office manager with top computer skills until such time as we recruited an Ipswich person for the job. It was as simple as that, but Pauline made no comment.

Earlier in the day, Pauline had surprised me by asking me if it was true that I was going to resign. She had obviously heard the rumours that had been sweeping the press gallery for the past week that I was going to resign or that she was going to sack me. 'You wouldn't do that to me would you, John?' she said. Fighting back the urge to tell Pauline that her erratic and unreasonable behaviour often tempted me, I laughed her question off and told her that there were bigger issues at stake than both our egos. As she was leaving the office at the end of the day, I decided to reassure her. Taking her by the arm and facing her I said, 'Pauline, I just want you to know that I'm here for the long haul, however long that will be. If the ship sinks, you and I will go down with it.' I leant forward and kissed her on the cheek.

That evening, Noel Crichton-Browne took Pauline out for dinner at my behest. The only result of that innocent social event was some smutty reports in the newspaper gossip columns. Next morning, the moment Pauline arrived in the office, she started carping again about Jeff Babb's overtime. She was like a fox let loose in a fowl house and I could see that her attacks were starting to unsettle Jeff. When Pauline left the office, he blew up and I thought he was going to walk off the job right there and then. I wouldn't have blamed him. The damage had been done, of course, and Jeff Babb's morale had sunk out of sight. Despite my encouragement, Pauline had made absolutely no attempt to establish any sort of rapport with Jeff Babb. It was a great shame and, if I had been a sensitive New Age guy, I would have sat in the corner and howled my eyes out. Being myself, if Pauline had been 'Paul', I would have asked 'him' to come down to the Parliamentary gym and put the boxing gloves on.

During that day Pauline had been taking telephone calls from someone who was feeding her information and, suddenly, quite out of the blue, she accused me of planning to organise my own Senate team. I was so disgusted and tired that I didn't even feel like defending myself against such lunatic stuff. I made a prophetic entry in my diary: 'Pauline talking to the "wankers" now — the beginning of the end.' Pauline was going back to Ipswich late that afternoon and I told her to think about everything over the weekend. That night I was back in Melbourne, safe in my own bed.

On Friday, December 6, 1996, I was in Melbourne meeting with some small business contacts who were disappointed with John Howard's policies in that area and wanted to know what Pauline's views were. Later in the day, I managed to have a quiet drink with 'the man in the white suit'. I was flat and listless and not much in the mood for anything, so I paid a visit to my doctor. I was disappointed when she told me that my blood pressure was normal.

All weekend the media were chasing me for comment about Bruce

Whiteside's call for Pauline to be rescued from me and my alleged efforts to turn her into my puppet. My friendly 'voice' in the Canberra press gallery told me that Whiteside had been talking a lot to Barbara Hazelton, which didn't help my paranoia. I knew that Pauline was going to the Gold Coast to celebrate Hazelton's fiftieth birthday and I wondered if Whiteside was on the guest list. Jeff Babb rang me to tell me how disillusioned he was with his new job. I couldn't say anything positive to him other than that we would go back to Canberra on Monday and tough things out.

On Sunday, I put on a hat in an attempt to disguise my give-away head and went into the Melbourne CBD where an anti-racism rally was being held. The event had been publicised as a 60 000 person turn-out, but the evening news estimated it at 20 000. There was the usual roll-call of 'true-believers': ranging from the loony and hysterical Socialist Left; through Aboriginal 'gravy-trainers'; to the frowning and earnest, taut-faced technocrats and 'pointyheads' from academia and the public service. Sprinkled throughout this potpourri of citizenry were those people of undoubted goodwill who genuinely believe in the brotherhood of man and of a world where happy, laughing people of different hues skip, hand-in-hand through fields of swaying flowers towards a brilliant rainbow on the horizon. I was reminded of one of Pauline's very own one-liners which she delivered on the pay-TV show *Beauty and the Beast*: 'I'm a realist, not a racist.'

That evening I called Pauline on the Gold Coast and spoke to her daughter who told me that Pauline was still recovering from the previous night's party. Pauline finally came to the phone and I briefed her on the Melbourne anti-racism meeting, but she wasn't that interested. I told her to take it easy and I would see her in Canberra. I had a feeling that she wouldn't be all sweetness and light on Monday morning. I didn't mention Jeff Babb or the office.

Back in the Canberra office at 8:30 am on Monday, December 9, 1996, I sat down at the computer and typed a memo to Pauline.

Pauline

Bruce Whiteside has become extremely damaging and is causing many of your silent and influential supporters to have serious concerns.

With this memo are some clippings and two faxes from George Wakelin from Gympie. Wakelin is the member of the Labor Party who Whiteside 'dobbed in' to Greg Roberts.

The clipping from the [*Sydney Morning Herald*], entitled 'Tensions in Hanson office', was given directly by Whiteside to the journo Millett. The journos love Whiteside as he contacts them and gives them their stories . . .

. . . Bob Bottom, who has spoken briefly to you and runs a paper on Bribie, has told John Samuel and Whiteside to stop using his name as a referee and he has told Whiteside not to call him [Bottom] anymore.

Bonita Brutnall, a Sister at Allamanda Hospital on the Gold Coast, contacted me yesterday and told me that she rang Whiteside to support you and ended up talking to Mrs Whiteside who asked all sorts of 'strange' questions about me. Bonita said she wants to talk to you about this. [A person whose experience and advice I respect] is of the opinion that Whiteside is out of control and that you should issue an injunction to stop him using your name any more. A decision needs to be made quickly.

Your office has now become 'public property' and that is totally unacceptable.

The memo was signed by me and dated Monday, December 9, 1996.

It was easy to see Pauline was in one of her bad moods when she arrived in her Canberra office just before midday. Heidi Lewis had come to Canberra with Pauline, leaving Barbara Hazelton looking after the Ipswich office, for a change. I gave Pauline the memo to read, telling her to think about it and that we could discuss it later in the day. Jeff Babb was working in the staff office and I took off for the press gallery.

I came back to the office a couple of times but Pauline was not there. I assumed that she was sitting in the House of Representatives chamber. Jeff Babb was working on some research about the major Asian nations. We had decided to do some reverse comparisons — how foreigners fared if they wanted to apply for citizenship in, migrate to, or buy a domestic residence or a small business or big business in those countries. The research, even in its early stages looked like giving Pauline plenty of opportunities for further headlines.

Pauline returned to the office at about 3:30 pm after question time. I couldn't put my finger on it, but I sensed that there was something wrong. I was standing in her office and she was standing to the side of her desk near her telephone.

'Is Jeff there?' Pauline asked. 'Yes,' I replied. 'He's working in the next office.' As I looked at Pauline she was starting to get that flat-eyed look that characteristically signalled something was on.

'Could you tell Jeff to come here,' she said, without a 'please'. I went into the other office and told Jeff that Pauline wanted to see him. We both walked back into Pauline's office and stood in the centre of the room.

'I am dismissing you both,' Pauline said. 'I want you to clear your stuff out of the office and leave immediately.' Pauline was still standing near her phone and her jaw was hard-set. She was starting to look like the Pauline Hanson on the front cover of the *Good Weekend* magazine.

Time stood still. I glanced across at Jeff Babb who looked inquiringly at Pauline as if he hadn't heard her properly. Then I saw realisation marching across his frowning brow. I heard myself laugh quite loudly in a disbelieving way, but then the messages that had been on some sort of shock-induced time-delay surged through my nerves into my frontal lobes and I was back in control. 'Why are you sacking us, Pauline?' I asked. 'I'm not telling you,' she said.

I looked at Jeff Babb, but he looked as if he had tuned out. 'You have to tell us Pauline,' I retorted as I started to fully realise the implications of what was happening. 'We had better sit down and talk about this before you go any further,' I said but, before I could continue, the outer office door opened and two ominously suited men walked in. (Why do policemen always look like policemen?)

Superintendent Graham Taylor of the Federal Police and Tony Murney, Deputy Security Controller of Parliament House's Security Office, had arrived in response to Pauline's call. I can only surmise that she made the call during the time I walked out of her office into mine to get Jeff. After identifying themselves, the two men told Jeff Babb and myself to obey Pauline's instructions and leave her office. They asked for our office keys and our Parliamentary security passes. At that moment I felt just a little sad. I had a lot of hardcopy files in the office as well as those stored in the computer. While many of them belonged to the office, some were mine. I also kept a change of clothes in the office. I was told that I could return the following day to collect what was left of my property. All the rest of my personal gear was in Ipswich.

I was starting to feel foolish as I gathered up a few belongings under the scrutiny of the two policemen. I wondered when the last time may have been that they had been required to perform a similar eviction. I managed to walk back into Pauline's office and retrieve the memo I had given her that morning. She tried to take it back from me, but I told her firmly it was my property. As Jeff and I were being ushered out of the office, I called back to Pauline as she stood in front of her desk. 'You don't know the meaning of gratitude, Pauline.' We started walking to the lift.

I was struggling to carry my briefcase, a travel bag and a large sheepskin jacket. While going from the second floor to the ground floor in the lift, a bewildered Jeff Babb said, 'John, I've never been sacked before.'

I was searching for an appropriate answer. 'Jeff, you've just been sacked,' I said, 'and don't you f . . . ing-well forget it!'

The walk from the lift to the House of Representatives entrance seemed to take forever and, for me, it was like running the gauntlet in slow motion. We had to walk past Opposition Leader Kim Beazley's office and the body language of our little group was unmistakeable. Jeff Babb and I were being shepherded along, obviously by two plain-clothed policemen, and the only things missing were the handcuffs. Simon Crean walked past us from the opposite direction and, as I made eye contact with him, he wrinkled his forehead with curiosity.

That walk was the most humiliating time of my life and I will never forget it, nor will I ever forgive Pauline Hanson for causing it. Jeff and I were escorted by Taylor and Murney out of the House of Representatives through the heavy entrance and left there like two stray dogs who had been chased away after somehow managing to invade a very fine home.

I was familiar with the 'bush telegraph' in PNG but was surprised to find that one existed in Parliament House, Canberra. A couple of TV crews suddenly materialised from nowhere, and it was on.

'Mr Pasquarelli, why did Pauline Hanson sack you? She has said she fears for her life.' I rounded on the interviewer and went for her. 'What did you say? . . . Did she say she feared for her *life*, or for her *safety*? . . . You had better correct that.'

The interviewer backed off, having obviously received that defamatory information second-hand from other journos. Not to be denied, however, she tried to savage me again. 'Have you made threats against her?' she said. It was all becoming very silly.

'That's a stupid question. Have you heard those allegations directly from her?' I said. Taking the silence as a 'no', I went on. 'You should direct all those sort of questions to Pauline.'

The TV crews followed Babb and myself over to the footpath opposite the entrance to the House of Representatives where we dumped our gear. John Stone, who had been in Canberra on official business, had contacted me on my mobile and I had asked him to come outside the House and see me. As he and I walked away to discuss my predicament, I looked back at Jeff Babb. He was standing with one foot nonchalantly resting on his brief-case, leaning against the parapet alongside the footpath. He was looking out over the panoramic view of Canberra city from that vantage point and, for some crazy reason, with everything crashing down around me, I found myself thinking that he looked for all the world like a European tourist casting his eyes over Bondi Beach. John Stone walked back into Parliament House and, as I returned to where Babb was standing, my mobile started its bleating which would continue unabated for the rest of the day.

In the confusion surrounding my removal from Parliament House, I realised that I had left my mobile phone charger, motel room key and my reading glasses back in Pauline's office. As a former parliamentarian from my days in PNG, I was a member of the Commonwealth Parliamentary Association (CPA) and, as such, was entitled to certain privileges — including unaccompanied entry to Parliament Houses anywhere in the Commonwealth. About an hour had elapsed since Babb and I had been thrown out and, by now, most of the population of Parliament House had heard the news of our dismissal. I returned to the security desk and attempted to regain entry through my CPA membership, but was denied. Back outside the Parliament, I decided on another course of action. I telephoned Kim Sweetman, a reporter with News Limited, in the press gallery. She came outside and met with me. Together we went back inside and, for some inexplicable reason, I was able to be signed in by Kim Sweetman on an escorted visitor's pass. It was an amazing contradiction of security, only confirming to me the grossly inadequate system operating at Parliament House. Something of which I had become aware since I had started working there.

Kim Sweetman and I walked up to the press gallery, where I met Gerard McManus and told him what had happened. The gallery was just starting to get its teeth into the story and I was trying to work out how I would handle things. Escorted back to the main security office by Kim Sweetman, I met Tony Murney one of the security men who had all but arrested me earlier in the afternoon. I told him about the things I had left behind in Pauline's office. He then escorted me back up to the second floor, telling me to stand at a point where I was out of sight of her office door. Murney then went into the office, reappearing a short time later with my possessions. At no time did I see Pauline.

That evening, I dined with a few friends at the Italo-Australian Club in Forrest, then returned to my motel where I switched off my mobile phone for the first time in a long time and went to bed. I lay there for ages, trying to come to grips with all that had happened. Different emotions swept over me — anger, frustration, disappointment and humiliation all hacked at me. Like Jeff Babb I had never been sacked before, and now I had been, by a woman whom I had fiercely protected in more ways than one, despite all the disincentives that she had given me along the way. I had always given my loyalty to Pauline but, when the crunch came, she had been unable to reciprocate. Stone cold sober, I managed to fall asleep.

THIRTY-FIVE

The Dismissal — the Aftermath

T he next morning, I was the most publicly sacked man in Australia, with newsagents' posters proclaiming 'Sacked — The Man Behind Hanson' and 'Banished — Hanson Sacks Minder.' Stories were being run that said Pauline feared for her safety but, as I angrily told TV interviewers at the time, I found those reports 'sad and bizarre'. Australians ate their breakfasts, confronted by me on Channel 9's *Today* show. Not the best way to start the day!

That day flashed by at breakneck speed. In a day interspersed with the full gamut of media interviews, I managed to try and organise myself. Jeff Babb and I spent some time at the Department of Administrative Services' office in central Canberra trying to sort out the economics of our dismissal. At 10:45 am, we were handed formal dismissal notices by Barry Murray advising us to be in Ipswich that day at 2:00 pm to clean out our offices. It was an absurd timeframe but, when I looked at the date and time at the top of the faxed documents, they indicated the date of faxing as being '09.12.96' and the time of faxing as '19:19', which translates as nineteen minutes past seven in the evening. This had been the previous day and, with daylight saving operating in all the eastern States except Queensland, those faxes would have reached Pauline's Canberra office at 8:20 pm Canberra time, or thereabouts. I also noticed that Pauline's signature was obviously not that of her hand but that of her signature stamp which I had bought for her from a Canberra rubber stamp supplier. It was obvious that those notices had been prepared by Barbara Hazelton who had remained in Ipswich to look after the office. Pauline was to say later that she had given me that dismissal notice at the time she sacked me. That was obviously impossible and untrue. The Member for Oxley was quickly learning to be just another politician.

'You have an excellent case for unfair dismissal and you should do something about it right away,' said the voice on my mobile phone. It was the same person who had advised me when I first started with Pauline that all her staff should sign ninety-day probationary employment agreements.

To that moment I had been far too busy involved in personal crisis management to start thinking about litigation — but now I certainly was. Pauline was not going to treat me the way she had and get away with it. Jeff Babb needed no prompting, so we took ourselves off to the Canberra office of the Commonwealth Public Sector Union where we took steps to join the union as a preliminary move to taking action against Pauline.

Later in the day I returned to Parliament House and was escorted back to Pauline's office to pick up the rest of my belongings. Pauline was there and her only acknowledgement of me was a grin that could have been nervous. Lyn Barlin the Clerk of the House of Representatives told me as I was leaving Parliament House that I could no longer enter the House until my position was reviewed in a week's time. Getting sacked by Pauline Hanson was proving to be no ordinary affair.

Late that afternoon, Jeff Babb flew out of Canberra bound for Melbourne and home. He had worked for Pauline for just twenty-two tumultuous days and had been treated in a most shabby and unwarranted way. Five people had now been in and out of Pauline's office in nine months — six if Morrie Marsden was included.

On the afternoon of Wednesday, December 11, 1996, I arrived back at my Melbourne home and flopped into my favourite chair. I was as flat as a tack and drained of all energy. I had left Melbourne on December 20, 1995, to go and work on Graeme Campbell's election campaign in Kalgoorlie. By a mix of chance and design I had clambered on board a political juggernaut that had rushed across the Australian political landscape at a frightening speed. I had never been able to fully control it and had been flung off as it careered on its way.

After just short of twelve months I was back where I had started from.

I had burnt a lot of political bridges in a very short time and had been told that, as far as jobs in the political arena went, I was 'too hot to handle'. I was well-and-truly unemployed again and all I had to show for my time was an extensive video and newspaper clipping library and a lot more political and media enemies. All my efforts to drink from the Holy Grail of politics which, for me, meant Pauline gaining control of the Senate, had become a failed and shattered venture. The next election will decide whether Pauline Hanson gets the chance to raise that bowl to her lips.

That afternoon I featured on a talkback programme with Bob Byrne of Radio Station 5DN Adelaide. He told me that, on the previous day, Pauline Hanson had told him that she had given me no reason when she had sacked me. She was demonstrating that she knew nothing about the unfair dismissal laws.

Jeff Babb and I quickly realised we were not about to become the darlings of the industrial relations legal clique in Melbourne. For starters, the Commonwealth Public Sector Union denied us membership. This was highly discriminatory and worthy of a writ in itself — which we may still issue, but we had neither the money nor the time to become pro-fessional litigants. The gung-ho, civil-libertarian, crusading Labor lawyers, Slater & Gordon, refused our brief while a couple of conservative indus-trial relations advocates did the same thing because they supported Pau-line's views.

Tanya Cirkovic is a prominent Melbourne industrial relations lawyer and workplace consultant who usually acts for employers. She was once in partnership with Michael Kroger, the former State President of the Victorian Liberal Party, touted future Prime Minister and now successful merchant banker. Tanya Cirkovic was recommended to me by a senior mining company executive who spoke very highly of her negotiating and court-room performances. She had also been mentioned very favourably in dis-patches by other industrial relations lawyers.

Tanya is a striking, blonde woman in her middle thirties. The prospect of this very 'full on', down-to-earth, obviously very intelligent woman ques-tioning Pauline Hanson in the witness box provided an attractive scenario. After some consideration she took Babb and myself on as clients, despite our impecunity and the very real possibility of attracting unfavourable publicity to herself. I was determined not to let Pauline Hanson escape her responsibilities as an employer. I issued the following press release after Tanya Cirkovic accepted our brief.

I gave Pauline Hanson my undivided loyalty at all times and her personal safety was one of my greatest priorities. I worked long, unrelenting hours under great pressure and copped a lot of personal flak. I am extremely disappointed at the results of the last week but, as the pundits say, 'A week is a long time in politics!' . . . My personal view on industrial relations is that, at the end of the day, employers and employees should treat each other fairly and equitably.

Pauline had treated Jeff Babb and myself very badly. She had caused us to be publicly humiliated and I had been defamed by media reports that Pauline had feared for her life and her safety. Putting myself to one side, she had seriously jeopardised Jeff Babb's future employment prospects. He had been a professional, hired to do a professional job and he had done his best from day one, but Pauline had virtually ignored him. Married with three children, he was still unemployed at the end of 1997. Pauline Hanson had said that she wanted a 'fair go' for all Australians. I just wanted to be part of the deal.

On Thursday, December 19, 1996, Pauline Hanson was allegedly spat on by some Aboriginal children in Ipswich. The following day I telephoned Heidi Lewis to see if Pauline was all right. I was still in 'minder' mode. The charges were later dismissed.

For me, the end of 1996 was an anti-climax. My tongue-in-cheek diary entry said, 'End of an eventful year!'

For me, 1996 ended with a 'bang' but 1997 started with a 'whimper'. I didn't want to admit it but I was feeling very burnt out. All that medical tests revealed was a 'fatty' liver. I was also having low-grade, sporadic attacks of Ménière's Disease which I couldn't do anything about. A low-fat diet and increased exercise were the only concessions my doctor could make to my hypochondria. Twelve years of listening to my self-diagnoses had well and truly immunised her.

Thursday, January 30, 1997, was the day set down for Jeff Babb and myself to attend at the Australian Industrial Relations Commission for a conciliation hearing in relation to our action against Pauline Hanson for unfair dismissal. Pauline was not appearing and would be represented by a Department of Administrative Services official and a solicitor from the Federal Attorney-General's office. As Tanya Cirkovic, her assistant Chris Muir, Jeff Babb and myself walked out of 101 Collins Street on to the footpath, the media ambush was upon us. As we walked, we faced a phalanx of reporters bristling with TV cameras, still cameras, microphones and tape-recorders which then moved backwards in front of us as we crossed Collins Street, stopping the traffic. Inside the Commission located in Nauru House, the proceedings ended in stalemate. Seven weeks after our sacking, we were still unable to be given reasons for it. It was obvious that Pauline's only resort would be to reconstruct the circumstances surrounding our dismissal. With conciliation now out of the question, the matter was adjourned to the Federal Court in Melbourne for a four-day hearing commencing on Monday, June 16. As Tanya and I jostled with the media on our way back to her office, she told me that she had never seen a larger media circus at the Commission. 'Wait until Pauline turns up,' I said.

The June 16 Federal Court hearing was adjourned at the request of the Commonwealth until Monday, September 8. It was starting to become a long, drawn-out affair. Both Jeff Babb and myself were still unemployed. The day finally arrived and what had promised to be a huge media event ended up more like a flute of flat champagne. The media backwash following the death of Princess Diana and the Commonwealth settling with me out of court, defused the whole deal. In what I consider to have been an unfair decision, Jeff Babb lost his case because the court judged him to have been on probation at the time of his dismissal. I now know how other employees in my position feel. Justice is hard to obtain and is very expensive. Pauline had legal advice worth several thousands of dollars a day, all at the taxpayer's expense, which included her travelling and accommodation expenses.

With the court case behind me, it was a case of getting on with my life.

As the year ground on I made several media appearances as a 'Hanson watcher' which helped me keep my oar in the water. I had maintained my contacts in Ipswich and in the Canberra press gallery and sometimes I felt as if I was still working for Pauline. Old habits die hard.

On Wednesday, February 5, 1997, Pauline Hanson gave my former job to David Thomas whom I had introduced her to earlier in 1996. Thomas had worked for the free-wheeling Queensland National Party maverick Bob Katter and North Queensland crocodile-farming Liberal MP Warren Entsch. I wondered how he would fit into the 'mantrap' that Pauline's office had become. I didn't need to wait long to find out.

As the new year progressed, Pauline started to lose media momentum and the media attributed this to my absence from her side. Gail Jennings of the Melbourne radio station 3LO said of Pauline, on February 17, 1997, 'She has just disappeared from view since her adviser was sacked.' This line was repeated by other radio talkback hosts and the print media. During this period, the weekly media surveys such as Rehame and Media Monitors clearly showed that the wind had dropped from Pauline Hanson's sails and she was lying becalmed in the political doldrums. But there were signs that a fresh wind was starting to blow from a different direction that would soon have her racing away under full-sail again.

During February and March 1997, Pauline was remarkably silent on all the major issues that were parading across the nation's headlines: the potentially explosive issue of Wik; the troubles in PNG and Bougainville; Malaysian PM Mahathir's attacks on the tardiness of Chinese migrants to assimilate; the ever-present problems of unemployment; and the failure of the Howard Government to deliver on small business. These had all obviously escaped her notice. She was heading very quickly into a media 'black hole' from which she would find it very difficult to escape. Those in the media and academia who had predicted that Pauline Hanson would 'fizzle' like Bronwyn Bishop were starting to look like prophets in their own time.

The first whiff of a fresh wind for the Hanson flagship began in mid-March 1997, when 'the voice' appeared on my mobile phone that had been enjoying a holiday from those mad days in 1996. He told me that there were very strong rumours Pauline would be launching her own political Party in Sydney on April 11. Right date, wrong place.

The 'voice' was vindicated on Wednesday, March 26, 1997, when a news flash on Sydney radio station 2UE announced that Pauline would be launching her One Nation Party on April 11 in her home town of Ipswich. The breeze was starting to build up into a full-blown gale.

On Tuesday, April 1, 1997, Morrie Marsden telephoned me from Ipswich to tell me he had received an invitation via Barbara Hazelton to attend the launch of Pauline's One Nation Party. It had been the first communication he had received from Pauline's office since early December 1996, when he had been effectively banned. I told Morrie that I hoped it being April Fool's Day had no significance. Morrie Marsden did not attend the launch of One Nation.

April Fool's Day, 1997, was a significant day for another man who had previously been a slavish Hanson supporter. Bruce Whiteside, the man from the Gold Coast who had caused me so much trouble in the weeks leading up to my dismissal, received his marching orders from One Nation's National Director David Ettridge on that day. In a letter with 'April Fools Day 1997' clearly indicated in the area usually reserved for the formal date, Whiteside was told by Ettridge, 'If you have any dignity, you will now withdraw and have nothing more to do with our organisation and we will have nothing more to do with you.'

On Friday, April 11, 1997, Pauline Hanson's One Nation Party was launched at the Ipswich Civic Hall and she was up under full-sail again. The media pack was back in business after a lull of three months and the Hanson phenomenon had entered a new phase, proving all the prophets of her downfall terribly wrong. The cartoonists and the gossip peddlers were back in business and would remain so until the next election. At the One Nation launch, but unnoticed by the media and other observers, was a bespectacled dark-haired man in his late thirties. He had 'slick southerner' stamped all over him and somehow he didn't fit in with the local crowd. He was still in the employ of Federal Liberal MP and ministerial hopeful, Tony Abbott, who had no idea that his employee was attending the launch of a rival political Party nor that he was doing this apparently on the travel entitlements of his office. The stranger's parents, Bill and June, lived in Manly on Sydney's North Shore and were active members of the local branch of the Liberal Party. They had high hopes for their son's political future and shared the quiet, strong confidence that parents have, that their son could climb all the way to the top of the political tree of the Liberal Party. David Ernest Oldfield, however, had other ideas.

On Wednesday, May 14, 1997, David Thomas was dismissed by Pauline Hanson after his resignation was prematurely announced some two weeks earlier. He had lasted a mere three-and-a-half months and, on the face of it, had burnt all his political bridges — having come to Pauline Hanson from National Party MP Bob Katter and Liberal MP Warren Entsch. Very soon after his departure from the Hanson camp, David Thomas told the media that the One Nation Party was, 'A Party founded on deceit.' By the following Monday, David Oldfield had resigned from Tony Abbott's office, amid much controversy and speculation, and was installed as the third senior adviser Pauline Hanson had employed in twelve months. According to reports, Oldfield had told Abbott that he was going to a 'job in marketing'. Standing behind Oldfield and Pauline Hanson was another David. David Ettridge, a political virgin and sometime fundraiser for World Vision, had popped up from nowhere to be the National Director for One Nation. Pauline Hanson had left a trail of male advisers and political-employee corpses in her wake that would have done an Agatha Christie whodunit novel proud. Morrie Marsden, John Pasquarelli, Brett Heffernan, Jeff Babb and now David Thomas had been cast aside. Two of her staunchest Queensland support group organisers, Bruce Whiteside and Victor Piccone had been sacked. Most of us had tried to do our best for Pauline but conceit, blind ignorance and ingratitude had combined to make her retreat behind a barricade of mistrust and suspicion. She had become a captive of those most practised in the art of pandering to her rapidly growing egoism. These people were the real puppeteers and Pauline Hanson, who had once been a battling 'fish and chip shop lady' from Ipswich, had truly become their puppet.

With the arrival of One Nation on the Australian political scene, the Pauline Hanson phenomenon took on a new dimension. Pauline Hanson and her One Nation roadshow gave Australians an unpleasant, front-row view of the new political landscape. Television images of young thugs, wearing balaclavas beating up on Hanson supporters and throwing urine-filled condoms, contrasted dramatically with candle-lit vigils conducted by community groups proclaiming the virtues of multiculturalism. The violent and well-organised opposition to Pauline Hanson and her Party was tacitly encouraged by the comments of many politicians, academics and community leaders.

Those who, when it suited them, self-righteously proclaimed the sanctity and enshrinement of free speech from their various pulpits, were now calling stridently for its denial to those Australians who wanted to do no more than exercise their democratic rights and peacefully attend One Nation meetings. If Pauline Hanson and One Nation can get to the next election with sufficient money, manpower and basic, simple policies, the conventional political order that has become so entrenched in Australian politics may well still be turned on its head. One thing is certain — 1998 will be a very interesting year.

THIRTY-SIX

The Dismissal — the Truth?

In the immediate aftermath of my dismissal, and during the early weeks of 1997, I had thought that Pauline's sacking of myself and Jeff Babb had simply been a 'knee-jerk' reaction in response to me giving her an ultimatum about the operation of her office. This was, in turn, linked to my constant criticism of the performance, or more correctly the lack of it, of Barbara Hazelton. Pauline had told me that she would 'never sack Barbara Hazelton' so I thought that, in a 'rush of blood to the head' situation, I had simply been a victim of 'the girls' club' and that Jeff Babb had suffered the same fate simply because I had brought him on board. I thought that I had sufficient evidence to support my theory that Pauline had, in fact, acted in impetuous haste. Her apparently genuine concern at the groundless rumours I was going to resign, her comments to various people that I was very good at my job (which were reported back to me), her approval of my plans to register the 'Pauline Hanson Movement', and the signing on of Jeff Babb, were all very positive indications that my position was secure. On the eve of my sacking, Pauline was interviewed on the telephone by journalist Amanda Blair, who asked her what she didn't leave home without and Pauline's answer was, 'My mobile phone and John Pasquarelli.' It all looked to have been pretty well the way it appeared to have happened but, like gas in a stagnant swamp, new evidence was about to bubble to the surface that would turn my sacking into an almost farcical political whodunit.

After the launch of Pauline's One Nation Party on April 11, some interesting information started to come my way that made me begin to think differently about the motive behind my sacking. Like the missing pieces of an unfinished jigsaw that have been found under a lounge chair cushion, three convincing reasons came to light that changed my mind about why I had been sacked.

On Saturday, May 31, 1997, Brian Woodley of the *Weekend Australian* wrote an article entitled 'Fellow Travellers' which was all about the two 'Davids' who had apparently arrived suddenly in Pauline's increasingly interesting life. David Oldfield was the thirty-eight year old second-string adviser to Federal Liberal MP and monarchist Tony Abbott who had resigned from Abbott's office on April 20 to become Pauline Hanson's third senior adviser (after myself and David Thomas). Oldfield has been accused of gross disloyalty to Abbott and the Liberal Party, in that he was allegedly working on the creation and organisation of the One Nation Party while he was still ostensibly working for Abbott and being paid to do so. He has also been accused of using taxpayer-funded travel on One Nation business while still in Abbott's employ. In the *Australian* article, Helen Sham-Ho, a Liberal MP in the NSW upper house accused Oldfield of being 'two-faced' and a 'cheat'.

The other David was David Ettridge who describes himself as 'a salesman for hire'. His last major activity was fundraising for World Vision. David Ettridge the political neophyte has admitted that he is 'politically naive', but such an admission is attractive in these days of 'shonky' politicians and slick image-makers. He confirmed his naivety, however, by stating during a radio interview in June 1997, on Melbourne Radio Station 3AW, that he had an 'unblemished background'. He immediately threw down the gauntlet to every journalist in the land to prove otherwise. The *Australia/Israel Review* was quick to pick up Ettridge's glove. Sending one of its men winging off to Port Vila, the result was a headline story alleging in the August–September 1997 issue that Ettridge has 'secret' companies and bank accounts in the tax haven of Vanuatu. Perceptions such as these, in an election year could be fatal for the National Director and fundraiser of One Nation, not to mention the Party itself.

In various statements to the media concerning the establishment of One Nation, David Ettridge has gone out of his way to create the impression that he was not involved with the organisation until well into 1997, but Brian Woodley's article bluntly contradicts this, as does other evidence.

For me, the nub of Woodley's *Weekend Australian* story is when, unbeknown to me, Pauline Hanson first met David Oldfield. Woodley recounts how this meeting took place at a Canberra bar after Pauline had delivered the most famous maiden speech in Australian political history. Writing how Oldfield had once helped Ettridge out of difficulties while the pair were scuba diving, Woodley describes the meeting. A meeting that would prove to have great significance for me:

> Last September, at the Canberra restaurant where Hanson and her personal secretary, Barbara Hazelton, went after Hanson's maiden speech to Parliament, Oldfield struck up a friendship with the pair after they, too, got into difficulties. He was in the restaurant when a man approached Hanson's table and abused her with epithets such as 'white trash'. Oldfield intervened, got talking with the women and soon became involved in plotting the launch of One Nation. On his recommendation Hanson met Ettridge in Sydney last November and enlisted him. On April 1, Ettridge told World Vision he was resigning to join Hanson the following day. On April 11, Hanson launched One Nation in Ipswich. On April 20, Oldfield told Abbott he was quitting.

My first real knowledge of the 'two Davids' would come only with all the media publicity after the launch of One Nation. What became obvious was the fact that the relationship between Hanson, Oldfield and Ettridge had not been 'sudden'. It had existed well before the public launch of One Nation, and well before my political execution.

The second piece of evidence would come from the third 'David' involved with Pauline. David Thomas, the former staffer of Bob Katter had taken my job early in 1997 and had lasted just a tad over three months, severing ties with the Hanson office on Wednesday, May 14. The actual terms of his departure are something of a mystery. There is some confusion over whether he was sacked or whether he resigned. He has told me that he did not encounter the same problems I had with the 'office from hell', mainly because he had a role different from mine. His description of Pauline Hanson as being 'dead from the neck up' says a little bit more. A bitterly disappointed and disillusioned Thomas prepared a statement and released it on Friday, May 23, to Tony Abbott, David Oldfield's ex-employer. It makes interesting reading:

1. I was appointed to the position of Senior Adviser to Pauline Hanson MP on 6 February, 1997.

2. The terms of my appointment were that I would occupy this position until about the end of April, 1997 when I would be ter-minated from this position, another person would take my position and I would have the option of taking a lower position as an Elec-torate Officer Grade B.

3. It was made perfectly clear to me that negotiations with this (to me) unknown person were already complete at the time of my negotiations with Ms Hanson.

4. Despite repeated enquiries by me, the name of my successor was withheld from me. All I knew him by was the codename 'David O'.

5. I was informed that 'David O' was a senior official with the Liberal Party from Sydney and that he was widely experienced in politics. In my attempts to discover the identity of 'David O', Ms Hanson's private secretary Barbara Hazelton (who was experienc-ing the same doubts as me as to the bona fides of this person) told me that their first contact had come on the night of Ms Hanson's maiden speech to the House when Ms Hanson was subject to an abusive attack from a staff member of NSW Opposition Leader Mr Collins in the Grange Hotel, Manuka. 'David O' has apparently intervened and had sympathised with Ms Hanson's comments in her maiden speech.

6. I was told that his role would be to establish Ms Hanson's new political Party and, following his appointment, he would be responsible for developing the national role of Ms Hanson and

that my revised role (if I took it) would be dealing with the electorate of Oxley and working on Ms Hanson's re-election campaign.

7. From the time of my appointment on February 6, 1997, virtually everything that I did for Ms Hanson as regards media was first checked by her by phone with 'David O'. There were regular daily telephone conversations with him by Ms Hanson and there was no doubt in my mind that she rarely made a single move without first checking it with him.

8. Either late in February or early in March, David Ettridge came to Canberra to meet with Ms Hanson, at which time I was introduced to him as the fundraiser for the new party.

9. In a meeting in Ms Hanson's office at that time, the formation of the new party was discussed. Present at that meeting were Ms Hanson, David Ettridge, Barbara Hazelton, myself and Paul Filing MP who was invited by Ms Hanson to offer advice regarding the decision to go ahead with One Nation.

10. At that time, both Paul Filing and myself warned Ms Hanson that she endangered her position if she was to use the services of 'David O' in a Party political manner. Mr Filing even warned her that by establishing her own Party, she was in danger of losing the ministerial entitlements to which independent MPs are entitled (i.e. the extra Senior Adviser staff member).

11. As the process of setting up One Nation proceeded, there was never any doubt in my mind that all moves were orchestrated by 'David O' using David Ettridge as the front man for the party.

12. From time to time I had contact with 'David O' by telephone when he would ring me with instructions or comments. Following the launch of the One Nation party in Ipswich on April 11, I spoke with him a couple of days later and we discussed the launch. During that conversation he informed me that he had been present in Ipswich at the launch.

13. On the night of the launch, as I was making copies of Ms Hanson's speech for distribution to the media, David Ettridge asked

19.

20. Don't shoot! Prime Minister John Howard dons a flak jacket to address an open-air meeting in Sale, Victoria.

21. *Left:* High noon on *Midday with Kerri-Anne.* Charles Perkins and Pauline Hanson lock horns on Kerri-Anne Kennerley's high rating show.

22. *Below:* Flying high. After registering the One Nation Party.

23. *Opposite:* One Nation takes off. The launch of the Party on April 11, 1997.

24. *Above:* Reconciliation? Meeting with Aboriginal Jawoyn leader Robert Lee and Phyllis Wiynjorrotj at Katherine Gorge, 1997.

25. *Left:* Friends in the west. Pauline with independent Western Australian MP Paul Filing and a security guard on a visit to Challenge Stadium, WA, in May 1997.

26. *Opposite:* Striding through the portals of power at Parliament House, Canberra.

27. Bruce Whiteside, sacked by David Ettridge on April Fools' Day, 1997.

28. Who's the boss? Pauline Hanson and David Oldfield.

29. From political virgin to One Nation bagman. David Ettridge, National Director of One Nation.

30. The girls' club. Pauline Hanson and Barbara Hazelton.

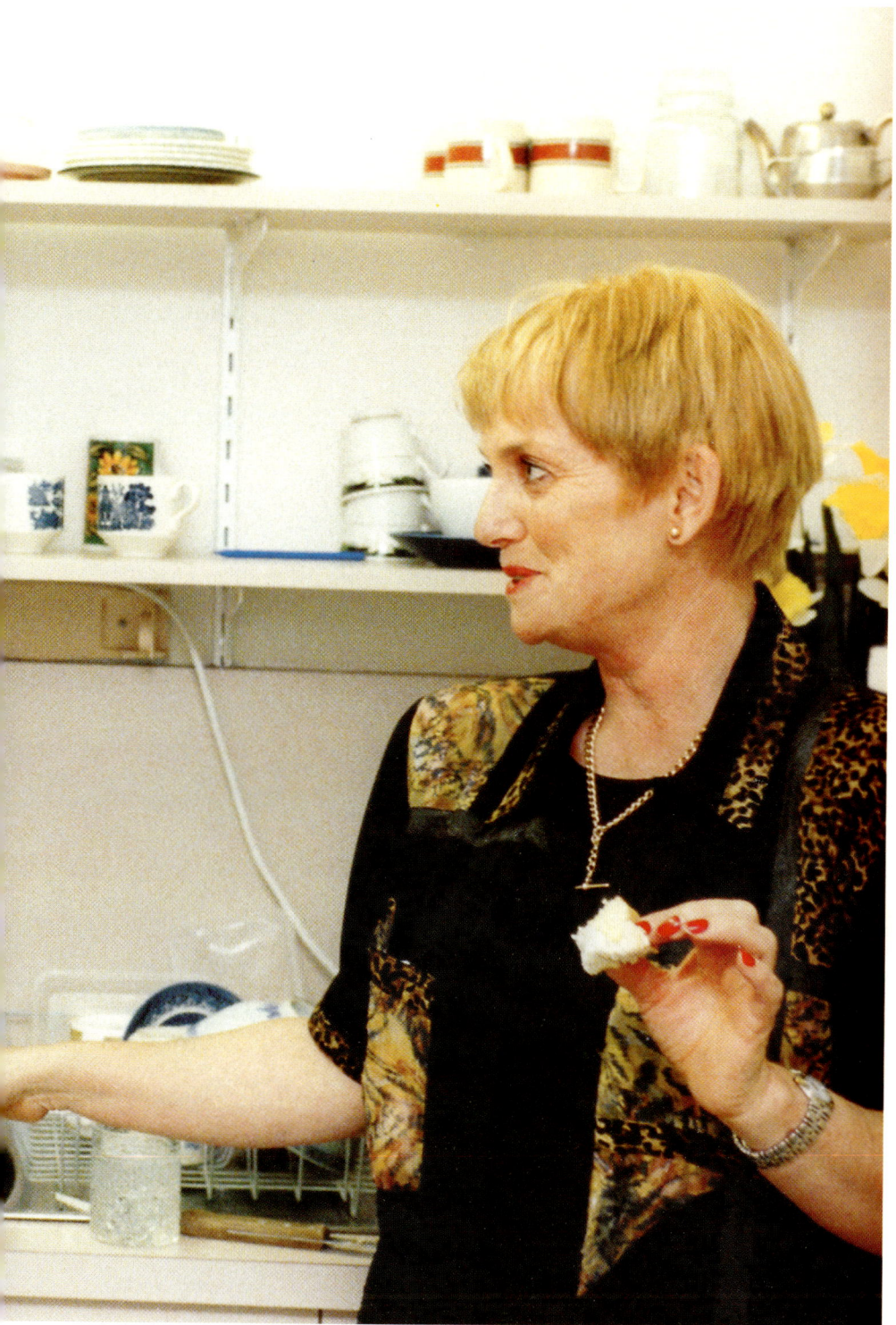

31. *Above:* It goes with the job. A political supporter receives a birthday kiss at a One Nation rally in Geelong, Victoria.

32. *Right:* Oh, lonesome me! Peter Andren's new seat, away from Pauline Hanson.

33. *Opposite:* Our taxes at work? The Pauline Hanson float in Sydney's Gay and Lesbian Mardi Gras.

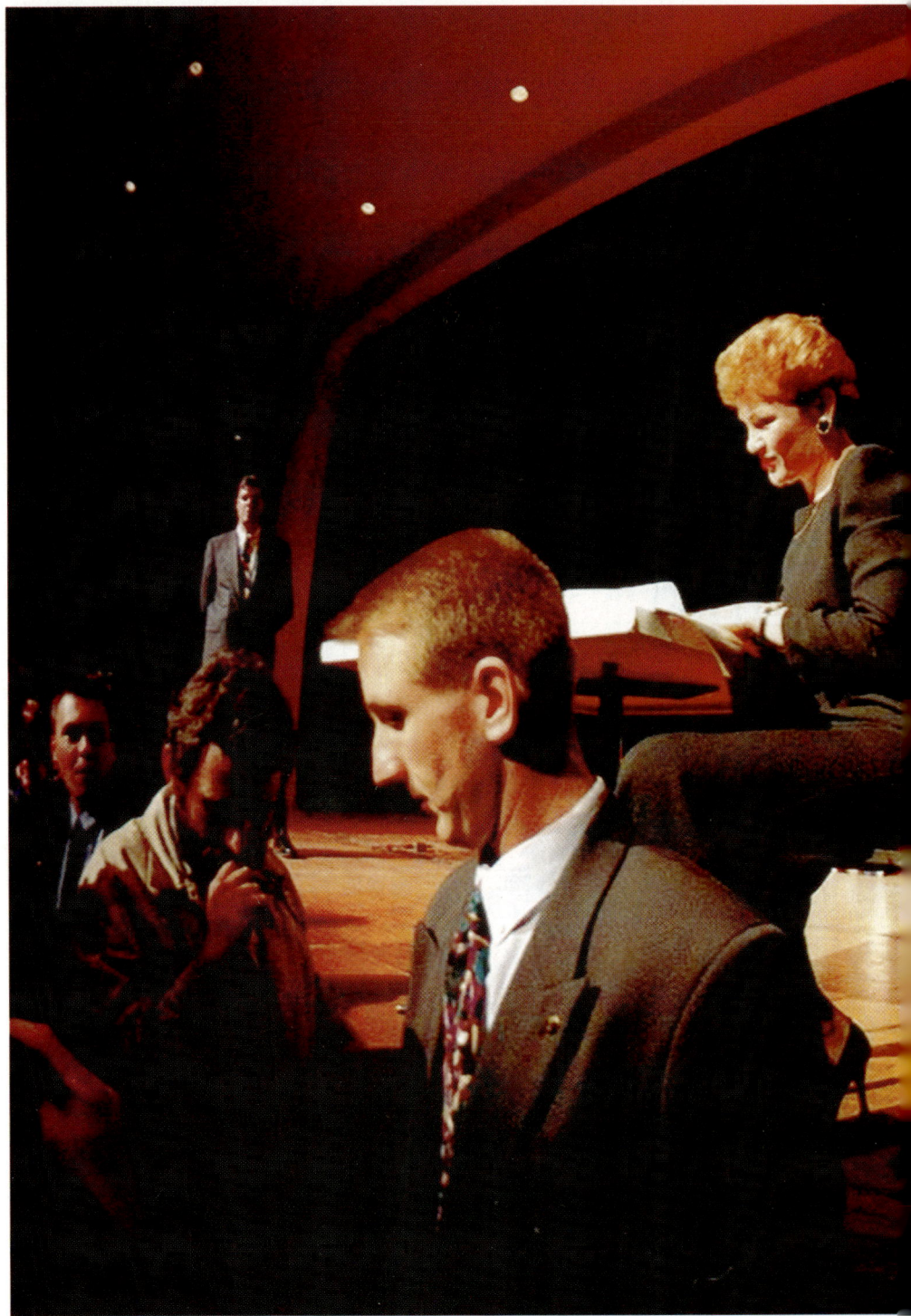

34. Australian politics in 1997. Pauline Hanson surrounded by five Federal Police at a One Nation meeting in Bathurst, NSW.

35. *Above:* A voice from the grave. Excerpts from Pauline Hanson's 'living will' appeared on Channel 7's *Witness* programme.

36. *Left:* Will it come to this?

37. *Above:* Departing after my unfair dismissal case had been settled out of court.

me what I thought of it and informed me that it had been totally written by 'David O'.

14. By this time I was becoming quite disenchanted with the direction in which Ms Hanson and One Nation were heading and I was contemplating not taking up the offer of the lower position . . . after my dismissal to make way for 'David O'. This was exacerbated by the release of the book, *Pauline Hanson — The Truth* to which I strongly objected as to its content, advising Ms Hanson not to become involved with it.

15. When, on Sunday, 11 May, 1997, I read in the *Sun-Herald* the identity of David Oldfield and the fact that he had been working for and on the payroll of Hon. Tony Abbott right up until the previous Friday, I immediately decided in disgust that I would definitely not be continuing my relationship with Ms Hanson. I found it totally abhorrent that a staff member of an MP would abuse his situation by not only working for another MP but be totally instrumental in the setting up of another political Party while on that MP's payroll.

16. My employment with Ms Hanson [was] terminated by her on Wednesday, May 14, 1997.

17. After much soul searching as to whether I would 'kiss and tell' what I knew of David Oldfield's treachery to his previous employer, I contacted and advised Hon. Tony Abbott of what I knew on Thursday, May 15, 1997.

18. There is no doubt in my mind that Pauline Hanson's One Nation Party is the total creation of David Oldfield; that he was intimately involved in all aspects of its setting up; that he has deceived his previous employer for at least the past three months and most likely longer; and that it is the intention of Ms Hanson and Mr Oldfield that he be used to continue the development of One Nation while on the Commonwealth payroll.

19. One of the last tasks asked of me by Mr Oldfield was to draw up a list of those who I knew were Party apparatchiks who were employed full-time by Federal MPs but who were primarily involved with Party business. It is my belief that he wanted this

information so as to use it as a defence when his abuse of his role as a Party operative on the public payroll became known. I did not supply such a list.

David Thomas's statement is a potent precis of deception and treachery, reinforcing his comment to a journalist that, 'The One Nation Party is a Party founded on deceit.' All the signposts were there, pointing to an orchestrated plot that resulted in humiliation caused to me by my very public sacking for no good reason and without the slightest regard for the personal damage it did me. The third source of evidence provided to me is the most damning and compelling. It represents the next best thing to having an eye witness turning up on one's front doorstep — or in this case, in one's letterbox.

Mobile telephone accounts are just like fingerprints which have been carelessly left at the scene of a crime. They give, in meticulous detail, the date and the time of the call, the origin of the call (the geographical location of the nearest repeater station), the destination of the call (the geographical location of the recipient), the telephone number of the recipient and, finally, the duration and cost of the call. Many criminals have been 'fingered' by their mobile telephone accounts and are caught because they are just plain stupid.

Under the terms of his employment with Tony Abbott MP, David Oldfield was provided with a mobile phone and the Commonwealth paid for his calls. People working in the political arena wonder now how they ever survived before the burbling mini-communicators arrived on the scene.

David Oldfield's mobile phone started talking to Pauline Hanson's mobile phone and her office phone well before she sacked me. On November 8, his mobile phone made three calls to Pauline's mobile for a total of eighteen minutes. When these calls were made, I was in Melbourne. On November 12, communication was made again from Oldfield's mobile to Pauline's Ipswich office on two occasions for a total of forty-three minutes, twenty-one seconds. This time I was in Adelaide. On December 1, Pauline's mobile was again contacted for two calls totalling three minutes and, this time, I was in Cairns.

It seems to be no coincidence that whenever communications were made between David Oldfield's mobile phone and Pauline Hanson's mobile phone, I was always somewhere else.

On December 9, the day of my dismissal, David Oldfield's mobile phone suffered a severe dose of verbal diarrhoea. During the day, his phone made thirty-two calls, thirteen of them to numbers related to Pauline Hanson. The first of these took place shortly after midday, for a duration of just under seven minutes, to a number advertised as being One Nation's at the time of its launch on April 11, 1997. Calls to this number are often diverted to David Ettridge, One Nation's National Director, who answers personally. At 12:33 pm, Oldfield's mobile engaged Pauline's mobile for a marathon twenty-one minutes, twenty-three seconds. Just three hours after this call, I was sacked and escorted out of Parliament House. Shortly after I left Pauline's office, there was a brief thirty-three second call to her mobile, followed by a five minute, forty-seven second call to her Ipswich office. During the day, other calls were made to Pauline's mobile and a total of just under eighteen minutes was spent on calls to her Ipswich office. During that day, Pauline and I were in Canberra and Barbara Hazelton was in the Ipswich office.

In the days after I was sacked, David Oldfield's mobile phone kept up its noisy chatter to Pauline's, as well as to her Ipswich office. All during November and December 1996, Oldfield's phone was also burbling merrily away to the One Nation number of (02) 9975 6767.

The mobile phone allocated to David Oldfield was part of his employment package with Tony Abbott — other components of that package being such intangibles as loyalty, trust and integrity.

Pauline Hanson launched her One Nation party on April 11, 1997. On the same date she launched her counter-attack against my unfair dismissal action against her. A thirty-five point 'reason-for-sacking Pasquarelli' document was dated that day by the Commonwealth solicitor who was acting for Pauline. It was the first time Pauline had given any reasons for the action she had taken seventeen weeks and four days earlier. Apart from being an obvious reconstruction of an event over four months old, the document in part reflects Pauline Hanson's almost obsessional concern about her role as the Member for Oxley, making the absurd allegations that I was trying to undermine her position and was setting up a political organisation without her knowledge.

Speaking at the launch of her Party, Pauline Hanson said, 'Lies are so deeply-rooted in the Australian political culture that even the politicians cannot tell the difference any more.' She went on to say, 'It is the truth that will save Australia, not the lies.' According to her, One Nation was, 'The Party of truth, fairness and equality for all Australians.' This last statement is somewhat at odds with what Pauline was reported as saying by her local paper, the *Queensland Times*, on March 29, 1997. 'I am the Party,' said an autocratic Pauline Hanson who then slipped into confused mode by saying, 'Of course I'll still consider myself an independent after I join the Party.'

Bruce Whiteside heard alarm bells when Pauline told him, 'I'll do it my way or not at all.' To a concerned Alf Dennis, a retired Liberal MP in the NSW Askin Government, who accused Pauline of abandoning principles of public participation and accountability she had this to say: 'Please trust me and believe in me. That is all I ask.'

Both David Ettridge and David Oldfield have often pontificated to supporters of One Nation about the need for loyalty to their leader and their Party. Is their brand of 'loyalty' a selective commodity? David Oldfield's former employer Tony Abbott certainly appeared to think so in a bitter speech to Parliament on Thursday, June 19, 1997. Tony Abbott, the Rugby University Blue, ran straight at his man, accusing his ex-employee of treachery, disloyalty and betrayal. Abbott named Pauline Hanson and David Ettridge as recipients of calls from David Oldfield's mobile phone during Oldfield's employment with him. Abbott's charges have never been challenged and Oldfield, Ettridge and Pauline Hanson stand condemned by their silence.

While I was busily making a fool of myself getting the 'Pauline Hanson Movement' organised and ready for launching on Australia Day 1997, the available evidence would make it seem that Pauline Hanson, David Oldfield and David Ettridge were busily working away on their separate agenda behind my back. Another person also knew what was going on. I am now on speaking terms with Bruce Whiteside, who caused me so much trouble back in November 1996 and who was 'sacked' himself on April

Fool's Day, 1997, by David Ettridge. Whiteside has told me that he was talking to Barbara Hazelton in mid-November 1996, asking her when Pauline was going to take action and dismiss me. According to Whiteside, Barbara Hazelton said, 'Don't worry about it Bruce — things are going to happen.' They certainly did.

I gave Pauline Hanson my undivided loyalty and trusted her in return. But she was unable to accord me the same respect. There are questions I would like to ask her one day. Why did she pretend not to know I was setting up a Party structure for her, despite coming with me to an Ipswich accountant to establish the bank account for that Party — an account that has never had a cheque drawn on it? Did the verging-on-pompous David Ettridge, the man with an 'unblemished background', not have qualms about becoming involved in an organisation that was, without doubt, 'founded on deceit?' The calculated deception of Tony Abbott and the Liberal Party by David Oldfield is clear for all to see. Pauline Hanson and David Ettridge were knowing witnesses to it. When David Oldfield finally resigned from Tony Abbott's office to go to Pauline Hanson, he did so on the spineless pretext of taking up a job in marketing.

'Hanson aide rorted Liberals, MPs told' was a headline in the *Australian* on August 19, 1997. The accompanying article described the request for David Oldfield to reimburse the Commonwealth for $873.40 in unauthorised tax-payer-funded mobile telephone calls. Pauline Hanson has stridently and con-tinually called for accountability at all levels of government and public administration. She has said that her, 'One Nation Party is the Party of truth, fairness and equality for all Australians.' After David Oldfield's performance, how can Pauline Hanson allow him to stay in her employ? What of David Ettridge, her National Director, who cannot continue to plead his innocence any longer, given his now revealed involvement? What of Pauline herself? Is there one set of rules for One Nation and another set for the rest of us?

The fools and troublemakers who played on Pauline's paranoia, suspicious nature and insecurity, by whispering into her ear that I was running my own political agenda and using her as a puppet, must wonder at the role now assumed by David Oldfield. David Ettridge boasted to David Thomas that Pauline Hanson's One Nation launch speech had been totally written by

David Oldfield. David Oldfield has been caught by TV cameras, sitting at the feet of Pauline Hanson during radio talkback shows, handing hastily-written slips of paper to her. He has appeared on several TV panel shows, when one would have expected the appearance of his employer. More often than not, David Oldfield makes public pronouncements instead of Pauline Hanson to an extent that commentators were confused when it was Oldfield and not Hanson who commented on the death of Princess Diana.

Offerings to 'Letters to the Editor' now describe Oldfield as 'the new Member for Oxley', and the Canberra press gallery call him 'the proxy for Oxley'. What exactly does Pauline Hanson see now when she looks into that mirror?

THIRTY-SEVEN

Will the Real Pauline Hanson Please Stand Up!

'**M**en robbed me of my teenage years,' Pauline Hanson told one of her former menfriends as if, in some way, she felt compelled to give a reason for the procession of shattered relationships with husbands and lovers that began with her first marriage in 1971. Added to this list are other men whose only involvement with her has been in the workplace.

The known men in Pauline's life make an interesting list. First husband Walter Zagorski was followed by her second, Mark Hanson, then came her de facto relationship with mentor Morrie Marsden. After Pauline cast Marsden aside, she briefly had a rekindled relationship with former first husband Zagorski. Next came a four-year on-again, off-again, de facto relationship with Rick Gluyas, an Ipswich City Councillor. Gluyas has consistently refused to open up on Pauline apart from saying that he thought, 'Pauline is totally out of her depth.' Gluyas says that his split with Pauline was the final paragraph of a chapter of his life — end of story. Interspersed with these male milestones in Pauline's life there have also been a procession of suitors who came and went.

Pauline Hanson's sex appeal became very evident in the weeks after her maiden speech. Those men seeking dates with Pauline sent her gifts of chocolates and flowers, together with letters couched in polite but amorous language. Practically all were accompanied by photographs, some showing her admirers standing proudly next to their carefully restored cars — Ford Customlines and FJ Holdens being the popular marques. A few dispensed with the preliminaries altogether and made proposals of marriage! These Sir Galahads saw Pauline as a classical damsel in distress — feisty and tough, yet vulnerable and almost girlish as she stood alone against her assorted foes.

In the hothouse climate of Parliament House, Canberra, where inhibitions are shed like Mintie wrappers, Pauline quickly became the target of the gossip columnists. She was linked to several well-known alleged admirers and, on Friday, June 20, 1997, John Laws declared that she and David Oldfield were 'an item' — but this was hotly denied by both parties. One senior married Liberal Senator who is always prattling on about the virtue of 'family values' made a fool of himself. His day of reckoning is yet to come.

Another queue of men in Pauline's recent life, who also came and went, jettisoned overboard, were those who had worked in her office — not least of these, myself. Brett Heffernan's research helped fuel Pauline's rocket-like launch across the Australian political landscape, before she frightened him away after only four months. Jeff Babb wanted to do his best for Pauline and worked assiduously for twenty-two mad days, before he was thrown out of Parliament House with me. David Thomas battled on for just over three months, before walking the plank amid considerable confusion over the terms of his departure. The Hanson ship is not a happy vessel.

Pauline's first and second marriages, to Walter Zagorski and Mark Hanson, have been well documented in popular magazines and the gossip columns. When I was in her employ, Pauline served a writ on Mark Hanson after he had made allegations about her having had an affair during her time with him. Both marriages had deteriorated into venomous, acrimonious affairs laced with allegations on one side of infidelity and questioned paternity, and counter allegations of alcoholism on the other.

All these men, each cast off by Pauline Hanson, could not bear sole guilt — but this is Pauline's charge. After speaking to some of the men in her private life I now know how they felt. One of them told me that her method of ending a relationship was short but not sweet. On waking up one morning, following an uneventful evening, he was told that the relationship was over and he was called on to collect his belongings and depart. I had much in common with him considering Pauline sacked me in pretty much the same way — 'I'm dismissing you and I want you to get your things and leave the office immediately.'

The sadder aspect of Pauline's first marriage is the well-documented estrangement between herself and her two sons from that union. I have never met Tony, the eldest son, but met Steven in Ipswich when, for a short period of time, he was helping his mother in the fish and chip shop at weekends. Pauline brought Steven to Canberra in mid-June, 1996, during this brief period of rapprochement. I found Steven to be a pleasant young man who handled himself confidently, and he seemed to be genuinely interested in his mother's political progress. In 1997, it was reported that a more durable reconciliation had been effected between Pauline and her two eldest sons.

Early in my relationship with Pauline I had innocently asked her about her two oldest children, but was not prepared for her waspish response — confirmed by David Leser's wounding profile of her in the *Good Weekend* magazine. Claiming that she had been metaphorically 'kicked' by her two sons, Pauline laid all blame at the feet of her first husband, saying that his genes were responsible for her sons' behaviour. I found this almost flippant surrender of her parental responsibility bewildering, but Pauline had other surprises in store for me.

In the last week of November, 1996, we were back at the Ipswich office. The pace was quickening as the year started to disappear. On Wednesday, November 27, I started organising some local volunteers to work in the office to relieve some of the pressure on the permanent staff. It was a long-overdue course of action. I should have done something along these lines a lot sooner, but better late than never. I returned to the office about midday and advised Pauline of what I had been doing. Knocking on her closed office door, I entered to find a young man in his early thirties sitting directly and very closely opposite Pauline at her desk. They were busily eating hamburgers, using the daily headlines as a tablecloth. The scene seemed so casual and intimate that for an instant I felt like a peeping Tom caught in the act. Pauline looked at me and I looked back at her. For a moment no one spoke. Flicking back into work mode I broke the silence. 'Pauline, can I have a word to you, on your own please?' I said, putting on my public relations mask for the benefit of Pauline's friend who, quite good-naturedly, picked up the remnants of his lunch and went out into the main office.

I had not been introduced to the stranger, so I decided to take the ball up to Pauline. 'Who's the young bloke Pauline?' I said in a straightforward manner. Pauline was in a good mood, coming straight back at me with a knowing, almost conspiratorial half-smile on her face. 'Never you mind, John,' she said, and that was that.

I met the young man a couple more times before I was sacked. Once I met him at Pauline's fish and chip shop and, on another occasion, spoke to him when he was driving Pauline's two youngest children in the Commonwealth car allocated to her. I was looking after her interests when I told her that any person driving that car should have been listed as a nominated driver for legal and insurance purposes — as she and I both were. That was the last time I saw the boyfriend, but my contacts in Ipswich kept me up to date. Pauline set local tongues wagging when she took her new friend to the local Coalition end-of-year party.

According to all reports, the young man was allegedly ordered off Pauline's farm by her late one night, sometime in March 1997. The boyfriend had travelled a long way in a very short time. He had first met Pauline at the Search and Rescue Club on the Gold Coast, sometime in October 1996 — incredibly not knowing who she was at the time. He had come to the coast on a football club trip and, purely by chance, had dropped in at the club for a drink. Returning to Newcastle, he sold his prized motorbike before packing up and moving to Ipswich to start what he thought was going to be an exciting new chapter in his life. Like so many before him, his heady emotions of optimism and expectation were swept away by bitterness and recrimination.

Is Pauline Hanson a ruthless, man-eating, closet-feminist or is she a simple, battling single mum who simply has appalling taste in men? Pauline would often call me a 'male chauvinist' and I am sure that she was being serious. But I also wondered if she really knew what she meant. She also insisted on being called 'Ms' despite me 'taking the mickey' out of her by telling her that it was a feminist tag and asking her if she had burned her bra. I think she thought that 'Mrs' was a title with an innuendo of age to it. For someone trying to recover her teenage years, that would never do. Pauline would react fiercely to my mock allegations of her feminism but would then 'pay out' on men in general. Changing course again, she would then vent her spleen on female journos, saying that they were much worse than the men. It was almost as if she had a Jekyll and Hyde view on the issue. Pauline has no longstanding female friends to speak of, apart from her recent association with a couple of staffers. I laugh when I think of those ball-breaking, hairy-legged feminists who find themselves on the horns of a dilemma. On the one hand they would dearly love to embrace Pauline Hanson the Amazon, who wears a belt strung with dripping male scalps, but they also find themselves totally repulsed by their perception of her policies.

Despite her savage and ferocious encounters with men, Pauline Hanson has always walked away the victor — emotionally and financially. Giving one of her young, female fish and chip shop employees some advice on love and marriage, Pauline said, 'Use men for their bodies — get what you can out of them, then give them the flick.' Pauline Hanson has been a great survivor and there is no doubt that she worked very hard, physically, in her business to get where she is — but her lack of both gratitude and generosity of spirit makes her a lesser person.

What of Pauline Hanson the employer? Jodi Blaine first started working in Pauline's fish and chip shop when she was fifteen and continued working there after Pauline sold the shop in early 1997. Now twenty, Jodi finally left the shop and started a new job in August, 1997. When Pauline was getting ready for the handover of her shop to its new owners in March, she asked Jodi Blaine to spend four hours cleaning the premises. For some reason, Jodi was not paid immediately on completing her task, and what started as a very minor molehill became an industrial relations mountain for the Member for Oxley.

On several occasions over a period of one month, Jodi Blaine asked Pauline for her four-hours pay, but she was continually fobbed off. According to Jodi Blaine, she received a telephone call from Pauline asking her to come to Pauline's electorate office. She assumed that this summons would be for her to pick up her long-overdue money. In her stead, she sent her fiancé who, on his arrival at the office, found he was to deal not with Pauline Hanson but with Barbara Hazelton. Barbara gave him some telephone accounts from Pauline's fish and chip shop and told him to ask Jodi to identify any calls she had made on the shop telephone. A slanging match, initiated by the fiancé, resulted in Barbara Hazelton threatening to call security.

Finally, in desperation and determined to stand up for her rights, Jodi Blaine lodged a complaint against Pauline Hanson with the District Industrial Inspector at the local Ipswich Courthouse. As her claim proceeded, Blaine revealed more allegations of Pauline Hanson's poor performance as an employer, which led to a decision being handed down in her favour. As a consequence, Pauline's niggardly attitude over a casual wages payment of about $40 resulted in her being ordered to pay Jodi Blaine the rather more substantial sum of $1462.67.

In a letter to Blaine, the Acting District Industrial Inspector said:

> With reference to your complaint against P. L. Hanson, I wish to advise that the matter has been investigated by an Industrial Inspector. The investigation resulted in an amount of $1462.67 being paid to an Industrial Inspector on your behalf. This amount represents $1462.67 arrears of wages from which nil tax was deducted. This payment is the full claim assessed to you. Attached please find Department cheque No. 000587 for $1462.67. The Awards Management Branch is pleased to have been of assistance.

Jodi Blaine said that Pauline's attempt to confuse the issue with some telephone calls allegedly made by herself was a case of Pauline 'just being nasty because she had been caught out' over the late payment of wages. The telephone account in question reveals calls made to Pauline's mobile number, and some calls made to a Maryland number in the USA. Pauline had departed Australia for the USA late in December 1996 and the number called was related to that trip. One call was made on the Queensland Australia Day holiday, Monday, January 27, 1997, and lasted for a duration of thirty-two minutes and nine seconds. Nobody but Pauline would have dared to make such a call from her shop for that length of time. Jodi Blaine said that she did use the phone at the fish and chip shop on several occasions to contact

Pauline on her mobile number in relation to business matters at the shop — but what was wrong with that?

When the most famous fish and chip shop in Australia was sold, documents provided by Pauline Hanson to prospective purchasers showed a total wages bill of $32 333 for up to five full-time and casual employees for the 1995–1996 financial year, plus $5454 in Federal Government employment subsidies. During this period the business turned over $317 837. One accountant said the wages bill appeared to be 'pathetically low' while another described it as 'abnormal'.

From all accounts, relations between Pauline Hanson and her staff at the shop had been gradually deteriorating ever since she had become a local Councillor, in 1994. On Christmas Eve, 1996, Pauline worked back late at her shop with her staff, but left without wishing anyone a happy Christmas — confirming what I had been told about Christmases past. Pauline had worked in her shop on some Christmas Days, when closing it would have been a perfectly acceptable alternative. There is hardly any evidence of Pauline celebrating Christmas in a traditional way and, on some occasions, she spent the day virtually on her own.

Not long after she sold her business, Pauline visited her hairdresser, which is next door to the fish and chip shop. Her former employees were bewildered when Pauline did not pop in to say 'hello' while she was there, but that is how Pauline Hanson operates.

On the other side of the 'Pauline the employer' ledger is the story of 'Laotian Lilly'. Lilly Vichitthavong was a Laotian refugee who worked in Pauline's shop for three months in 1995, on a Federal Government Jobstart programme. In an interview with a reporter from the *Australian*, Lilly said, 'I don't want to get myself into the hot seat but Pauline Hanson's no racist. If I saw her in the street tomorrow, I'd want to give her a big hug, though I probably wouldn't because she's so famous now.' It was simple, open praise from a young Asian woman with no political or racist axe to grind.

Some of Pauline Hanson's detractors in Ipswich have given her the nickname 'Lady Di' in response to the spate of One Nation meetings at which an always smartly-dressed Pauline has been given the Princess Diana treatment with adoring crowds, bodyguards, presentations of flowers, and lots of hugging and kissing. The use of the word 'Lady' is a little unkind because it implies that Pauline is beyond the age of a 'Princess'.

The global outpouring of grief at the death of Diana carries a message for all political, religious and community leaders. Politicians all over the world are on the nose. President Clinton is facing a tacky and sordid court case, and the bizarre sexual antics of many British MPs have been well documented. Australian politicians have been rating at an all-time low in the eyes of their voters and dipped even further in the wake of the crippling travel rorts scandal. Members of the clergy being prosecuted and convicted for paedophilia and other sexual crimes has become commonplace. Ordinary citizens, feeling betrayed and frustrated, are casting around for new champions.

Princess Diana and Pauline Hanson have many basics in common. Diana was a classic beauty and Pauline is attractive to many people. Both women failed in marriage and their relationships with men have been less than perfect. A lot of men and women can relate to these examples of life's knocks in today's world. Both women have given the two-finger salute to their respective 'establishments', to the applause of ordinary citizens, and they also shared a common enemy — the media. Many Hansonites grieved over Diana. Let's hope that there is no further comparison in this area.

Most of 1998 will see all Federal MPs in election mode. The indications are that the political environment will be favourable to Pauline Hanson. A lot will depend on the performance of those close to her.

Pauline Hanson, the phenomenon, now stands in the spotlight beaming down on the Australian political stage. Pauline Hanson, the battling fish and chip shop lady, was entitled to her domestic and business privacy but now, completely overshadowed by her alter ego, must endure the most searching scrutiny of any political figure in recent times. She cannot change her mind and run for cover. She has issued the challenge and her many enemies have accepted it.

By virtue of her leadership of her One Nation Party and her intention to stand candidates in all Seats at the next Federal Election, Pauline Hanson is now a contender for the highest job in the land — the Prime Ministership. There can be no equivocation about that. She has attacked in response to attack, and has strongly criticised the way the major political Parties are run. She has passed judgment on single mothers and has called for the preservation of traditional values. She has made a virtue out of calling for truth, honesty and accountability regarding the way in which the taxpayer's monies are expended. Her own behaviour and that of her Party must reflect those high principles, but serious questions have already been raised in this area.

Pauline Hanson has now become a prisoner of her own inadequacies and will need to continue to defend her position from now until election day. She has surrounded herself with people that she knows have been accused of disloyalty, deceit and treachery and yet she persists in having them close to her. Her party is enduring internal conflict as many disappointed members struggle with an autocracy based in Manly, Sydney. Intending office holders have been offended and angered by being asked to sign undated letters of resignation.

National Director David Ettridge and others receive salaries from One Nation membership. As a demonstration of accountability from a Party that preaches it, will all these details be revealed to its members?

The last word on Pauline comes from her twenty-two year old son, Steven. In an interview in June, 1997, Steven was very bitter about his mother. 'I don't really deal with my mother at all,' he said. 'If she can't manage her own family, how can she expect to manage bigger issues?' Another question that could be asked is, 'If she can't run her own office how can she run a Party?' Will the real Pauline Hanson please stand up!

THIRTY-EIGHT

Media Maggots

The slowly decaying carcass that is Australian politics provides a host for media maggots to feed off. Some of the stronger and more adventurous maggots manage to flourish and go on to become very busy and energetic blowflies. How can one write about Pauline Hanson without writing about the media?

When Pauline Hanson took her One Nation roadshow on tour in 1997, I noticed that a few assorted journalists kept popping up at her meetings without filing much in the way of stories. I telephoned one of them and asked him what was going on, but I was not prepared for his off-hand and almost flippant reply. According to him, he and other journalists had been instructed by their bosses to follow Pauline Hanson around the country so that, if she was assassinated, they would be there on the spot for the scoop. Now, that is forward planning!

The final stretch of the road that lead me to Pauline Hanson started with Graeme Campbell in Kalgoorlie during his 1996 election campaign to hold his seat as an independent. Compared to Pauline Hanson, Campbell enjoyed a relatively good relationship with the media and even had some supporters within the ranks. There was great excitement in the Campbell office during the early days of the 1996 election campaign when one of Australia's most senior and respected TV interviewers donated $1000 to Graeme's cause. Campbell had been vilified and pilloried by many of his Labor Party colleagues, well before Keating did the bidding of his Party's Left and hit the ejector-seat lever that expelled the maverick from Kalgoorlie. Bob Hawke, puffed up to his most pompous and outraged best, called Campbell a racist. The $1000 donation told me that, despite the verbal shrapnel directed at him, Campbell still had friends in strange and interesting places.

When I started working for Pauline, I realised that dealing with the media was going to be one of my hardest jobs. Even before the maiden speech, the pressure was on. With a near-record Coalition majority almost certainly guaranteeing numbing news boredom, the media needed a diversion — and Pauline provided it. Other diversions were briefly provided by Senators Colston and Woods, and the travelling allowance gill net that entangled Coalition Ministers David Jull, John Sharp and Peter McGauran, and National Party MP Michael Cobb — culminating in the botched 'suicide by press release' attempt by Senator Nick Sherry. Pauline Hanson proved to be no such flash in the pan. From the newsworthy angle, she was obviously anything but a dreary political hack and, if nothing else, she would provide a few laughs. To add some spice there was the bonus of more than a suggestion of the element of controlled, implicit sex-appeal. A straight-laced and single senior Liberal Party operative told me that he found Pauline 'quite spunky'.

Pauline's often almost flirtatious manner has been the subject of media comment. There is one young photographer in the Canberra press gallery whose new, very switched-on girlfriend, is happy at the prospect of his transfer to Sydney. Further up the media ladder is a senior writer who, late in 1996, was seriously concerned about his career prospects being damaged by innuendo concerning himself and Pauline.

Until the maiden speech opened up a mother lode of rich story veins, the media were forced to make do with Pauline's supposed proclamation that she would not represent Aborigines or Torres Strait Islanders. The starting point for all this was the telephone interview of Pauline by Chris Dore of the *Australian* newspaper, on the Monday after election day 1996. A host of journalists, including Chris Dore and his boss David Armstrong, still continue to selectively quote from the transcript, notwithstanding being briefed by me, chapter and verse, about the actual content of it. Piers Akerman of the Sydney *Daily Telegraph*, to my knowledge, is the only writer in Australia to faithfully quote the entire passage. It is time that this particular matter was referred by the Hanson camp to the Press Council but, on second thoughts, what would that achieve? The full transcript in large bold type should certainly be faxed to every media outlet in the land.

With all the journalistic hysteria and outrage that followed the maiden speech, it would be assumed that the speech had been well read and researched but this was not the case. Many who wrote about the speech had not read it. They simply fed off each other, so that what Pauline Hanson said bore hardly any resemblance to what was read. Her 'Melbourne speech' seems to have been lost in space. A few energetic maggots researched the maiden speech in a most thorough way. Bill Birnbauer, David Elias and Duncan Graham writing for the Fairfax press, linked passages in Pauline Hanson's maiden speech with my early 1960s' speeches in the PNG Parliament.

The Purga Mission affair and the 'white trash' insult were a godsend because they gave me a legitimate reason to ban the ABC. It was also an incident that would fuel support from most of Pauline's supporters and those sympathetic onlookers in the general community. In one fell swoop we had done something that no other political office had dared attempt and, in the process, had 'Morteined' some very aggressive blowflies indeed. Over a period of months, the response from various ABC identities, ranging from management to on-screen and on-air personalities, was intriguing to say the least. It varied, from pompous aggression and dire threats of Pauline being consigned to that media no-man's land where she would never be heard of again, to wheedling entreaties laced with sugary promises to be fair and objective during interviews.

On my return to the Canberra press gallery after attending the Melbourne Cup, I came upon two young ABC ladies who had obviously not backed the winner. Legless drunk, and finding it difficult to even speak coherently, they vented all their obviously pent up frustration on Pauline and myself. I got off reasonably lightly but Pauline copped such a violent barrage of 'f . . . s' and 'c . . . s' that even I was wincing. I made sure to return next morning and gloat at their very obvious and painful hangovers. In early 1997, I was very disappointed to hear that Pauline had let the ABC off the hook and had started talking to its media representatives. As I had explained to Pauline originally, 'Why speak to an organisation that is dedicated to destroying you?'

Having sent the ABC off to Coventry, I decided that the most effective media strategy for Pauline was to ration her out very carefully, being extremely cautious about the choice of interviewers. There was no shortage of takers. Pauline was so much in demand for media interviews that there was a queue, and that queue was required to line up in front of me for its members to gain an audience with her. It was an effective strategy, and one that added to my list of enemies, but it worked. On some days I would take more than fifty calls on my mobile phone from eager journalists all over Australia and from abroad. I had great fun 'sticking it up' a lot of them. Most of them just didn't share my sense of humour.

When working in Canberra, I would often take Pauline's media releases up to the press gallery and try to 'sell' them to journalists. On one occasion, a young member of News Limited's much vaunted 'super bureau' treated my salesmanship of a press release with utter disdain. 'What's this piece of shit?' he said, hardly looking at the single page. 'The last press release you'll ever get from Pauline Hanson,' I replied, as I grabbed the sheet of paper out of his hand, shredded it to confetti and threw it over him, amid sniggers from some of his colleagues.

The press release and the *Bulletin* article I wrote for Pauline on 'Reconciliation' fired the media up again and had the 'pointyheads' and the 'chattering classes' absolutely besides themselves with self-righteous indignation. Their deadly-serious howling and caterwauling was deafening, and the larger media blowflies buzzed furiously. It was during this furore that Pauline copped the 'lumpenproletarian hag' insult from Malcolm McGregor writing for the *Financial Review*.

Insulting Pauline Hanson, in often the most vicious and nasty way, quickly became a media art form and what the media didn't create itself, it was quick to replicate. 'Oxley moron' was one slogan that was gleefully seized upon. Placards at so-called 'peaceful' anti-racism rallies proclaiming 'Racism in Australia is an Oxley moron' and 'Pauline Hanson — wanted dead' were published at every opportunity.

Quick off the mark after the maiden speech was a very nasty, full-scale attack on myself and Pauline in the October 1996 issue of the *Australia/Israel Review*. The article was entitled 'Pauline's Puppeteer' and was written by a very excitable Adam Indikt. Conveniently unnamed sources quoted me as calling PNG Nationals 'coons' and Indikt presented me as failing to obtain Liberal Party preselection in 1978 when, in fact, I was successful in being preselected as the Liberal candidate for the Victorian Federal Seat of Jagajaga in 1987. Indikt quoted me saying, on *60 Minutes*, that 'The Jewish lobby in Melbourne stood outside mainstream Australia', when the true and accurate quote was 'Part of the Jewish lobby.' The *Australia/Israel Review* seems to be adept at creating enemies where none originally existed, and the Indikt article was typical.

Following in this vein was my brief encounter in Pauline's Canberra office with Jewish personality Lisbeth Gorr, also more widely known as ABC presenter Elle McFeast. The pushy Gorr arrived, unannounced and uninvited, in the office — accompanied by an aura of stale tobacco smoke and wearing what could have been some sort of nightdress or toga, adorned with cigarette burns. Gorr wanted Pauline to deliver a New Year's message on her show but I was forced to remind her about the ABC being off-limits. She then tried to get me to deputise for Pauline and, when I refused to cooperate, she left in a fit of pique, firing an angry shot at me for the benefit of her camera crew skulking outside in the corridor. 'I suppose you don't like Jews either,' she said.

Some of the insults directed at Pauline by Robert Hughes, the absentee Australian art critic attacked her pronouncements as, 'The burps and farts from the deep gut of Australian racism.' Every so often, Hughes deems it necessary to rush back to Australia from the salons of New York to berate his Prime Minister and his fellow citizens for being so dull and cloddish. Where would Australians be without the likes of Robert Hughes and Germaine Greer to keep them on the politically, intellectually and culturally correct roads?

Imre Salusinszky of the *Financial Review* continued the nasty treatment by referring to Pauline as 'that Pious'n Anal Hen from Oxley' — not the sort of comment he would like made about female members of his family.

Other media report attacks on Pauline Hanson have been in a more dramatic and vengeful vein. Geoffrey Cousins, the former chief executive officer of Optus, became almost hysterical when he attacked Hanson, in November 1996, under the *Sydney Morning Herald* headline, 'Optus chief in attack on "evil" Hanson.' He said that Hanson's views on Asian immigrants and the Aboriginal community mirrored attacks on Jews in Nazi Germany. Warming up, he went on to call her a 'noted racist and bigot' and reaching fever pitch, said, 'The anti-Hanson forces need a clear political strategy to surgically remove this evil growth from the Parliament before it grafts itself on permanently.'

Six months later, in May 1997, Tony Barta, a research fellow in history at LaTrobe University in Melbourne, reviewed four books on Nazi Germany for the Melbourne *Age*. Mr Barta used his well-presented and sizeable book review to buy into the Hanson debate, using a much more chilling argument than that employed by Mr Cousins. Woven throughout his critique are obvious and barely cloaked analogies and references to Pauline Hanson whom he cleverly refuses to name. The review entitled 'Why Hitler is always with us' presents the idea that 'When Hitler was merely the leader of a big-noting One Nation Party, it seemed excessive to plot his removal.' The analogy drawn between Hitler and Hanson's One Nation Party could not be described as subtle. The theme of Barta's review is that, 'Killing Hitler is a project that has to be kept up by each generation,' and one is easily led to the conclusion that he equates Pauline Hanson with Hitler. Barta's barely concealed agenda prompted editorial comment from the *Bulletin* on May 27 when the question was posed; 'Was the Melbourne *Age* advocating the assassination of Pauline Hanson?'

The Canberra press gallery helped to create the Hanson phenomenon and now it must live with her. Nikki Savva of the *Age* is forced to write stories about Hanson but does so saying, through clenched teeth, 'I wish she would just go away.' Laura Tingle of the Melbourne *Age* performed a line-by-line post mortem on the maiden speech, that filled up columns of space and looked good but ended up going nowhere. Glenn Milne of the *Australian* originally attacked Pauline in set pieces but, after I managed to convince him that she did have enormous support out in the electorate, he started to veer towards a degree of objectivity — now he calls her 'a dill'. Milne ran off the straight and narrow again in his column on September 8, 1997. Quoting the 'powerful' speech of the mostly-silent Member for Kooyong, Petro Georgiou, Milne had Georgiou quoting Pauline Hanson as saying that, 'The yellow race would rule the world.' Pauline Hanson never said this, but her mother did, on *60 Minutes*.

Gerard McManus of the *Sunday Herald Sun* consistently ran balanced pieces, from the first day Pauline entered Parliament, but he too now seems to have changed course. Piers Akerman of the *Sydney Telegraph* told it as it was during 1996, but seems to have lost close contact with the Hanson office. Frank Devine, writing for the *Australian* in Sydney, has delivered both brickbats and bouquets to Hanson with balance and, thankfully, a sense of humour — a quality sadly lacking in many of the mainstream commentators. Other press gallery journos who managed to keep their 'cool' and reported Hanson in a matter-of-fact way were Tony Barrass of the *West Australian* and Michael Harvey of the *Herald Sun*. There has been plenty of lofty 'thundering' by those two 'ugly sisters' of the opinion pages, Gerard Henderson and Philip Adams, but that is expected from the duo who obediently serve and play to their respective audiences.

I have a tenuous link with that implacable Buddha of Australian political commentators, and receiver of stolen political goods, Channel 9's Laurie Oakes, in that his deceased father-in-law was Tom Cole, an old New Guinea mate of mine who kept the Johnnie Walker whisky company solvent while remaining stone cold sober. Oakes had a half-hearted try for an interview with Pauline, but I fobbed him off by tapping my head and saying in PNG pidgin, 'Mi save long yu, Laurie,' which meant, 'I'm a wake-up to you, Laurie.'

Laurie Oakes doesn't need to be reminded that there is plenty of evidence to suggest attacking Pauline Hanson only increases her support but, despite this, he soldiers on — unable to stop because he really hates her and all that she stands for. He was at it again in his *Bulletin* column of September 1997, referring to 'the Hanson poison'.

The media moguls have treated the Pauline Hanson phenomenon with some degree of ambivalence. On Sunday, October 13, 1996, the day after Pauline delivered her 'Melbourne speech', the Murdoch controlled News

Limited organisation gave a full report on it and ran excerpts from it in that day's *Sunday Herald Sun*. On page 78 of the same paper, her maiden speech was published in full. I considered this to be a coup. The paper's circulation of 600 000 plus represented significant progress in spreading Pauline's message, particularly in Victoria. On December 2, 1996, in a sudden change of direction, Mr Ken Cowley the then Executive Chairman of News Limited said that John Howard should have taken a stronger stand against Pauline Hanson. In 1997, the News Limited papers seemed to be out in full cry after Hanson.

The Fairfax organisation had declared war on Pauline Hanson, on all fronts, from day one, with one interesting exception. Michelle Grattan, an experienced and senior political commentator, who now writes for the Fairfax owned *Financial Review* out of the Canberra press gallery, put in a belated bid for an interview with Pauline about a month after the maiden speech. My first reaction was to run away and pretend that Michelle had never spoken to me. I had visions of Michelle Grattan, the clever and probing wordsmith, consolidating her position at the top of the press gallery tree at the expense of Pauline by doing her over unmercifully, showing the other scribes how it was all done. Over a cup of tea in the staff cafeteria, I indulged in some logic. A reasonably balanced article by Grattan, even if it contained some harsh criticism, would not do Pauline any great harm — as long as she didn't drop one of her clangers, such as the dreaded 'Eyeties'. On the other hand, I could also see Michelle Grattan not wanting to go overboard at the first opportunity. Far better for her to get a foot in the door with the first story and then see what eventuated. My final assessment of Michelle Grattan was that, while she was almost certainly a 'soft' Labor voter, she was not the sort of person who would devalue her professional standards by attacking Pauline in an hysterical and abusive way that could have been expected of many of her press gallery colleagues. Unlike so many of her peers, I knew that Grattan had properly read the maiden speech. On those bases, I took a calculated risk and set up the interview. I left the two women alone in Pauline's office and went down to the newspaper reading room.

Turning the pages of the October 10, 1996, issue of the *Financial Review*, ever so slowly, like revealing the cards in a poker hand with a certain degree of dread, I arrived at Michelle Grattan's piece on Pauline. A quick skim, a rush of adrenalin, and I knew that we had survived. I was so relieved that I went up to the press gallery and congratulated her for being fair and doing what I considered to be a good story. To put her right in the picture, I also told her that as long as I was around she would never get a second bite at the cherry. I was convinced that I had used up all my luck with her.

One of the Canberra press gallery's clear leaders in the anti-Hanson print-media stakes uses a slime-covered poison pen to create his maggoty pieces of invective. Lazy, sloppy, and a total stranger to objectivity and the facts, he is stoned out of his mind during most of his working days.

Having said all this, my most uncomfortable time in the Canberra press gallery would have to be when I was trapped in a lift with the frightful Fairfax assassin Margo Kingston.

The facts got lost again with the appearance, early in 1997, of the photograph of Pauline Hanson draped in the Australian flag. This has become a silent visual slogan for her One Nation Party. The image sent maggots and blowflies alike into a frenzy of speculation as to whether the event had been orchestrated by some sinister neo-Nazi group. Pauline had visited the USA during December and January 1996, and the rumours had her sitting at the feet of the Ku Klux Klann's David Duke and other luminaries.

The explanation for the photo is simple, ironic, and humourous. Some photographers were in Pauline's Canberra office looking for photo opportunities when Ray Strange of the *Australian* suggested she do something with the Australian flag. At that time, David Thomas was her adviser and, unable to find a flag in the office, he went and borrowed a flag from Tony Abbott's office where David Oldfield was working at the time. Ray Strange told Pauline to hold the flag out behind her with her arms outstretched and the resulting butterfly-like pose was snapped. Strange then asked Pauline to wrap the flag around herself and, at the moment she did, the lens of Dean McNicoll from the *Canberra Times* came over Strange's shoulder — the rest is history.

While journalists write the stories, sub-editors write the headlines meaning, all too often, for the sake of impact, truth is the casualty. On the Sunday after Pauline's 'Melbourne speech', the Sydney *Sun Herald* ran a story by Fia Cumming, with a screaming headline quoting Pauline as using the word 'Bloodbath' to describe the ultimate result of multiculturalism. She had actually said nothing of the sort.

On Monday, October 14, 1996, I was interviewed on Melbourne Radio Station 3AW's breakfast show along with Fia Cumming, the journalist involved. Cumming gave an interesting insight into the so-called profession of journalism.

When questioned about the word 'Bloodbath' headlining her story, Cumming blamed her sub-editor, without missing a beat. 'That is something that a sub-editor made up and it shouldn't have been as a quote,' she said. 'It's what subbies do — they sort of take the most alarmist line in the headline.' Cumming delivered the *coup de grace* when she said, 'The word "bloodbath" doesn't appear in my copy . . . Pauline certainly never said "bloodbath".' So that was that.

'There are three certainties in this world — the rising and setting of the sun and Pauline Hanson on the six o'clock news,' was one of my throw-away lines to a TV journalist. The TV screens are every politician's oasis in a media desert. Getting more than a 'grab' makes a backbencher imme-diately start thinking 'Ministry'. Becoming, more or less, a 'regular' makes that oasis waterhole become filled with champagne and visions of a retire-ment landmarked by a diplomatic posting become that much less than fantasy. Pauline Hanson has enjoyed huge TV coverage and, when I was with her, I enjoyed the naked chagrin and petty jealousy that was simply dripping off many of the non-entities who filled the leather benches in Parliament House, pretending to be their people's elected representatives. Many of these people and their offices became incensed and even more rattled when I, a mere staffer, began to be 'door stopped' by the media and had the audacity to issue a press release when I announced my res-ignation from the Liberal Party. I had a great deal of fun 'sticking it up' the po-faced establishment.

Pauline lost her major TV show virginity when she appeared on Channel 7's *Witness* in May 1996. Her performance, as the raw political newcomer who had put her hand up for the job, gave her the first taste of what lay ahead. I thought that Tracy Bowden, the interviewer, had been reasonably even-handed but Pauline didn't think so, saying Bowden was 'a smart-arse' — giving a hint of what would become her increasing antipathy towards female journos.

As time passed, the females more than equalled their male colleagues in the venom stakes when it came to abusing Pauline. According to Virginia Trioli of the *Age*, Hanson's previously described 'thin querulous voice' has now become a 'strident resentful whine' and 'mean spirited squalling.' Other female commentators have made incredibly bitchy comments about Pauline's dress, hairstyle and her sex appeal.

Underlying much of the abuse of Hanson has been a new wave of politically correct elitism and snobbishness. A letter to the *Age* described her as an 'uneducated, ill-informed fish fryer' and in November 1997, Janet Holmes à Court followed in the same snide vein, refusing to utter Hanson's name by referring to her only as 'that woman from a Queensland fish and chip shop.' Australia's richest woman who inherited her wealth and has highly paid advisers to keep her in that position is obviously of the view that many Australians need to be kept firmly in their place.

I gave Kerry Packer's Channel 9 favoured treatment, mainly because of the good relationship I think I had with Peter Wilkinson, the producer of *60 Minutes*, plus the high ratings enjoyed by the channel with most of its headline news and current affairs shows. Huge exposure and high ratings meant that equally high risks were to be taken but, as history has shown me, all my worries and concerns about Pauline suffering terminal media damage proved to be groundless.

On her first and now famous appearance on *60 Minutes*, Pauline Hanson was the victor and interviewer Tracey Curro the vanquished, in a clash that saw Channel 9's Sydney switchboard light up — with the overflow running into the evening radio talkback shows. The support was overwhelmingly in favour of Pauline, and this mini-phenomenon would be repeated in the aftermath of other TV appearances by her.

Pauline's *60 Minutes* appearance had whetted the appetites of other

Channel 9 'big guns'. On my return from Palm Island with Peter Wilkinson, we were met in the Sydney Qantas Club Lounge by Richard Carleton, the personable and charismatic senior interviewer from *60 Minutes*. Carleton was there to convince me that it would be to Pauline's advantage to appear on one of his forums — with racism in Australia being the subject for debate. His charm barely concealed the taipan ready to strike and I politely declined his offer.

The Ray Martin interview of Pauline in late 1996 was another example of the star inquisitor winning the battle but not the war. Ray Martin clearly had a decisive technical victory over a jaded and disconnected Pauline, but he suffered the same viewer-response fate as Tracey Curro. *Midday* host Kerri-Anne Kennerley has vowed not to have Pauline Hanson back on her show. According to Kennerley, the Hanson presence boosts the ratings but, 'I get badly burnt by audience reaction — the studio audience and viewers at home attacking me if I am perceived as having given Pauline a hard time.'

The Hanson camp now appears to have declared Channel 9, and *60 Minutes* in particular, off limits and I know that will not please the network's 'heavies'. Like it or not, the presence of Pauline Hanson increases their station's ratings which means all-important egos are massaged and the advertisers keep rolling the dollars in.

Since making her peace with the ABC, Pauline has appeared on *Lateline* and *Four Corners* in 1997. Maxine McKew, *Lateline's* moderator, was another TV luminary who bit the dust taking on Pauline. Confronted by an infuriatingly vacuous Hanson, McKew in desperation lost control and hectored and talked Pauline down in a most aggressive and patronising way. It was a terrible performance and McKew became well aware of her humiliation after the show and in the days that followed when the audience response started flowing in. My 'mole' in the ABC told me that McKew and her producers didn't want to hear the name 'Hanson' ever again and wished that the interview had never taken place.

When the ABC featured Pauline on *Four Corners* on June 16, 1997, I was expecting the worst, but was wrong again. The show ended up being a demolition job on John Howard and, to a lesser extent, the Queensland

Nationals, with Pauline coming away smelling of roses. It was the ABC at its devious best.

Riding the radio talkback airwaves, Pauline Hanson has many champions on the interviewers' side of the microphone — her most notable one on the east coast of Australia being Alan Jones of Sydney Radio 2UE. Jones, from time to time, has heavily promoted Pauline and she has appeared live in his studio. Three weeks after the maiden speech Jones said that, of the many thousands of calls to his talkback show, 98 per cent of them were in basic support of Pauline. In the west, Howard Sattler who runs Western Australia's top rating talkback show from Perth Radio Station 6PR, gives Pauline plenty of airtime with very positive response. During 1996, Pauline also got a fair go from Bob Byrne of Adelaide Radio Station 5DN.

I lowered the boom on Melbourne's 3AW morning talkback supremo Neil Mitchell because he called Pauline a 'twit' before he had ever spoken to her properly. I have spoken on the Mitchell show since my sacking, and Pauline took him off her 'blacklist' when she was interviewed by him on Tuesday, September 3, 1997. Prior to that time, she had favoured the station's drivetime host, Steve Price.

Back in Pauline's home territory, commentator John Miller and talkback host Greg Carey, both of Brisbane Radio Station 4BC, seem to be reasonably supportive of her and their criticism of her from time to time could not be described as aggressive or nasty.

John Laws, the high priest of Australian talkback, on Sydney's top-rating Radio 2UE, which is also home to Alan Jones, has approached the Hanson phenomenon differently. He opposes her on most issues, probably at the risk of offending a lot of his listeners. Laws has one thing in common with Pauline Hanson in that, over recent years, he has a history of firing off some very damaging shots at the Aboriginal 'industry'. Indeed, he has on occasions been much more derogatory than Hanson about ATSIC and Aboriginal 'fat cats'.

Terry Laidler of Melbourne's ABC Radio Station 3LO acknowledges that his audience is 'split 50–50 in support of Hanson' and he says, 'If I was to ask her a series of tough questions from the word go, I'd be perceived by those listeners as being a bastard.'

The print media is the messenger that carries the all important poll results into the political arena. Pauline burst into the political punting spotlight in November 1996 in a *Bulletin*-Morgan poll that gave a Pauline Hanson-led Party the possibility of winning up to seven Senate Seats. The results of the poll spilled over into the general media, confirming the worst fears of some of the major Parties' private pollsters. The first shock waves rolled over the National and Labor Parties and, for the first time since their creation, the smug complacency of the Democrats was jolted. The important question raised by the *Bulletin* article about the poll was 'Will she [Hanson] actually get that far?'

Since the creation of One Nation in April 1997, the polls have tended to trend downwards, from a peak of 12 per cent posted in the heady weeks after the Party's launch. The August 1997 Reuters Poll trend had One Nation stabilised at between seven and eight percentage points which again must be no source of joy, particularly to the Democrats. Most polls show that One Nation has its greatest strength in Queensland, with results as high as 14 per cent, no doubt due to the 'hometown' support for its leader.

Rehame Australia Monitoring Services publish their findings each week in Melbourne's Saturday *Herald Sun*. The statistics are based on the number of times an issue was raised across all media. Pauline Hanson and her One Nation Party have consistently starred, with Pauline often finishing ahead of John Howard and other major news events. During the Thredbo landslide disaster she was the person most talked about in Australia, rating 1228 mentions to John Howard's 1055. On some occasions she has polled a hat trick, her One Nation Party receiving the most mentions nationally and in Victoria, and herself scoring over John Howard and others in the 'people most talked about' category. Out of nine polls in this latter category, Pauline Hanson finished on top of the poll in front of John Howard five times — no wonder that many people in Asia think Pauline Hanson is Australia's Prime Minister. Rehame's end of 1997 scorecard for TV and radio stories had Hanson in second place behind Native Title, but ahead of the death of Princess Diana. For the second year, Pauline had rated highest in the land for mentions on radio talkback.

The Melbourne *Herald Sun* conducted an interesting telephone poll in

June 1997, posing the question, 'Is Pauline Hanson a racist?' The paper provided twenty-one Hanson quotes to help readers make up their minds. Eight thousand readers responded, an overwhelming 81 per cent answering 'no'. While the *Herald Sun* headlined the announcement of the poll, it did not headline the positive result for Pauline Hanson, burying it instead in an article proclaiming 'Hanson games fear'. The story said that the Hanson 'race debate' could jeopardise the awarding of the 2006 Commonwealth Games to Melbourne.

The media and Pauline Hanson are like two unwilling, brawling participants in a shotgun wedding. The next Federal Election will be the altar which they will approach in a blaze of local and international publicity. If Hanson and One Nation survive with any degree of success, a whole new chapter of Australian politics will be opened, contributing to one of the best selling stories of all times. If defeat claims Hanson, she and her media bridegroom-to-be will part company amid a cacophony of gloating and bitter recrimination. The withdrawal symptoms on both sides will be monumental, with the media suddenly finding itself deprived of the larger part of its accustomed diet, angrily scattering the picked-over bones of the cadaver to one side. For Pauline Hanson, the withdrawal will be just as excruciatingly painful. Just as she arrived on the political landscape, garishly illuminated like some sort of alien spacecraft, so will she disappear, rocketing out of sight over the horizon — possibly never to be sighted again until light years later when some TV host immersed in nostalgia brings her briefly back to life on a 'Where are they now?' show.

THIRTY-NINE

How I'd Destroy Pauline Hanson

I told Pauline Hanson on many occasions to stand in front of a mirror if she wanted to see who would ultimately destroy her. She has the capacity to self-destruct and, if she does, it will grant a desperately needed reprieve to many of her craven Parliamentary colleagues. They are terrified of being perceived by their constituents to be opposing her, for fear of retribution at the polls — such is the widespread feedback coming back from their electorates.

Can the Hanson/One Nation juggernaut be derailed? During 1997 the political novice successfully fended off such a concerted barrage of attacks from PM John Howard, some of his more limp ministers and a motley assortment of media assassins, that she gave the distinct impression she is bulletproof. People come up to me at the races and tell me that they know Pauline is a 'bit of a dill' but they are going to stick with her because, unlike other politicians, she has the guts to say what a lot of ordinary Australians are thinking.

Despite this, there is still that self-destructive time bomb ticking away and there are ways to encourage it to detonate sooner than later. As the man who is credited with creating Pauline Hanson, I know what I would be doing if I were John Howard.

My gratuitous advice to John Howard — and he certainly looks like he could use some as he wallows mid-term bogged down by 'Travelgate' — is qualified by my support for most of what Pauline Hanson stands for. The point I must stress here is that 'the cause' is far more important than the individual, more so when that person is so raw and unpredictable.

Now that the electoral boundaries have been redrawn in Queensland, it would be sensible for Pauline not to show her hand until the day nominations close. She has the choice of staying to fight for Oxley, standing in the new, nearby Lower House Seat of Blair, or making a run on the Senate. Wayne Goss must now be a very doubtful starter after the removal of a malignant brain tumour. He would have been a formidable opponent in Oxley and would have brought to it all his old personal, hard and fast Labor supporters as well as large numbers of anti-Hanson Asian voters.

Pauline did not perform well in Oxley in 1997. From day one I told her that it was vital she maintain a high level of exposure in her political back-yard. Fortnightly visits to the local shopping malls were organised and proved highly successful. Equally successful was 'Speaking Out', a weekly column with a logo and photograph we arranged in the high-circulation local free paper, the *Ipswich Advertiser*.

As far as I know, the regular mall visits ceased last year, while the column has failed to appear on several occasions and, when it does appear, is minus Pauline's photograph. This is suicidal behaviour for any politician, let alone a first-time independent and political novice. Support won, then lost, is almost impossible to regain.

The first ominous sign came on May 10, 1997, in a letter to the *Queensland Times*, Oxley's major newspaper. A small-businessman posed the damning question, 'Has Hanson deserted us?' He went on to ask what she had done for the electorate and who paid her salary when she was travelling around Australia on One Nation business. This letter is bound to spark more of the same and a flicker of flame could become a bushfire. Irrespective of what seat she stands for, 'What has Pauline Hanson done for Oxley?' should be her opponents' battle cry leading up to the next election.

The offensive against Hanson should be launched from a highly visible campaign office, fully resourced and professionally run right up until election night. This office should be established as soon as possible. The present Hanson electorate office is no match for an organised opponent. Its computer facilities have never been fully utilised and the staff reflect a 'jobs for the girls' mentality, irregardless of the need for expertise and political nous. It has always been in a state of disarray due to Pauline's inability to establish a clear chain of command uncluttered by personal relationships. For her, personal issues have always taken precedence over important political ones.

Pauline has dropped her guard in a most critical area, that concerning her relationships with Australians of European origin — especially Italians, Greeks, Yugoslavs and those from the Baltic States. When I took her to the Melbourne Wholesale Fruit and Vegetable Markets last year, her support from these groups was overwhelming, yet she has chosen not to build on it. After I was sacked, a person of Italian background asked me, 'Does she hate Italians now?' Other people of obviously European descent ask a similar question, 'Why does she hate migrants?' I had arranged with Pauline to send out her 'Melbourne speech' in early 1997, with a covering letter from her, to the presidents and committees of all the major ethnic community clubs in Australia but, as far as I know, this has not been done, despite me bringing the matter to David Ettridge's attention on several occasions. On the other hand former Prime Minister Malcolm Fraser, Victorian Premier Jeff Kennett, and others, are cleverly driving a wedge between Hanson and this particular audience by saying that the Hansonites are only sponsoring the interests of Anglo-Celts. If the Liberals develop and refine this tactic, it will help cripple One Nation.

John Howard should have realised by now that attacking Hanson using conventional weapons only strengthens, and indeed increases, her support. The stupid and grossly insulting personal attacks on her only demean the people making them. This includes the PM's clumsy attempt to link Pauline Hanson with the Ku Klux Klan. John Howard must understand that even if she disappears her support will not, and he will still need to deal with legions of Hansonites who are angry, disappointed, frustrated and just waiting for another Pauline (or maybe a Paul) to turn up. He must reconcile himself to the fact that what is called for here is not full frontal assault but a political pincer movement, probing for ways to defuse her support while stepping up the pressure on her to make her own mistakes.

One of Pauline's most serious flaws is a lack of intellectual discipline that prevents her reading and absorbing information on a regular basis. I tried to make the process simple and straightforward, but she would let me down time and time again by not reading the simplest of briefing notes. I would tell her that she was not pulling her weight, and the only feedback I received when I asked her if she liked the job was silence. The more Pauline is exposed to public and media scrutiny, the more her intellectual shortcomings are revealed, making it difficult for even her most ardent supporters to feel really confident about her leadership potential. After all, Pauline Hanson is now a contender for the top job in the land. When the election campaign begins in earnest, she will be found wanting. Debating on her feet without the luxury of prepared notes or continual prompting, and being required to prepare the specific policies and arguments she will need to present in the countdown to polling day will be a hurdle too high for her to clear.

John Howard has the ability and the machinery of office to make sensible decisions that will placate the Hansonites. Far better for him to choose the hard options now, rather than see a botched-up mess if One Nation controls the Senate. To do this he will need to straddle a high fence topped with razor wire, the angry Hansonites on one side and those jelly-backed members of the Coalition and the 'chattering classes' on the other. He is too smart not to realise that much more must be done to answer widespread concerns about migration. The debate on Asian migration will ebb and flow but Howard will ignore, at his peril, the deep-seated fears of mainstream Australia.

For a start, he should not merely reduce but should abolish the family reunion concessionary element. As it stands, such reunions allow the 20 000 Chinese 'student' refugee places granted by former Prime Minister Bob Hawke after the Tiananmen Square massacre to blow out up to 300 000. This would cause the so-called 'race debate' to assume new dimensions. Major Asian nations should be called on to take responsibility for Asian refugees instead of cynically and ruthlessly pushing them on to Australia.

Apart from migration, there are other crucial areas in which Howard can win back Hanson's followers while still keeping faith with traditional Liberal principles. He must be prepared to act decisively if the Wik legislation is rejected by the Senate. That would mean immediately calling a double dissolution without being fazed by those who would bleat to the heavens about holding an election on a racial issue.

He must, with urgency, bring to an end the shameless rorting associated with the taxpayer-funded policy of multiculturalism. Home-grown Australians freely acknowledge the contribution of new settlers but bitterly resent what has been going on in terms of the cynical exploitation by politicians and leaders of minority ethnic groups of the 'dollars for votes' syndrome. The PM will be pleasantly surprised at the applause he receives from ordinary Australians of all ethnic backgrounds if he takes action in this regard.

It seems impossible for Howard to remedy the disaster that is the Aboriginal and Torres Strait Islander Commission, one of Hanson's prime targets. The taunting and aggressive TV images of black and not-so-black 'fatcats' threatening sabotage of the 2000 Olympics and calling for United Nations endorsed trade sanctions against Australia only drive ordinary Australians farther into the Hanson bunker.

After early spectacular polling results, the signs are starting to appear that the Hanson/One Nation bandwagon has more than one of its wheels wobbling. Polls have shown a growing reduction of support with the *Bulletin*–Morgan poll indicating One Nation at 5 per cent in December 1997, down from a high of 13 per cent. The Party's Sydney headquarters is at very public loggerheads with some of its own people in Queensland, Victoria and South Australia, which does not augur well as a Federal Election draws closer. Things can change of course, depending on the political climate and the state of the economy come polling day, and on statistics such as the unemployment figures. The economic health of small business and the farmers will also play a big part in Pauline Hanson's political survival.

Decades of political gutlessness distilled into bipartisan policies on the Aboriginal issue, migration, multiculturalism and the economy have created the Hanson phenomenon. Mainstream Australians with Anglo-European roots are at the forefront of the Hanson onslaught and they have a burning desire to exact revenge at the first opportunity. They are sick and tired of being harangued by pointy-head academics and jumped-up minority groups.

We are seeing a revolution in Australian politics because of Pauline

Hanson's stubborn and courageous determination to grind on in an arena where she will never feel truly comfortable. If she is still on her feet at the next election, many of her political colleagues will have good reason to stumble in dread to the poll.

Epilogue

The stage has been set for the most dramatic shoot-out ever in the Australian political wild west. All the signs are starting to indicate that John Howard will call a Federal Election sometime in 1998, with October or November being the preferred months. A double dissolution could not reasonably be held earlier than July and, despite a degree of Government tub-thumping, this option is not likely to be exercised unless the Wik legislation is hopelessly log-jammed.

Pauline Hanson's maiden speech struck a responsive chord with mainstream Australians, encouraging them to come out for the first time ever and rebel against the big party bipartisanship that had frustrated and deceived them for decades. Freed of party shackles, Pauline Hanson was able to say in a simple, basic and powerful way, in the most public of forums, what the great majority of Australians had been thinking for years but had never had the chance to say. This Hanson-led 'mutiny' expressed itself in Letters to the Editor columns and was at its most vocal on radio talkback shows around the nation. Like a raging plague, it infected the offices of every politician in Australia with varying degrees of reaction. Some of those politicians steadfastly chose to ignore her, while others attacked her with invective and snide insults. Others, too timid to be seen openly supporting her, did so 'undercover' in telephone calls or almost whispered 'asides' out of range of any observers.

In 1998, the majority of ordinary Australians look back on decades of false promises made by politicians during the supercharged atmosphere of election campaigns. The cleverly crafted visions of economic prosperity

311

and low unemployment have proved to be nothing but cruel mirages that have left voters feeling disillusioned and cheated. They see a sudden rash of local manufacturing shutdowns that will consign more and more Australians to the dole queues while their jobs are sent to Asia. Will their children ever get steady work? Gone are the days of employment security when jobs could be handed down from father to son. Big, once flourishing regional cities, such as Newcastle and Geelong, suddenly have the real potential to become human scrap heaps.

Farmers face competition from cooked chicken meat, imported from Thailand and protected at its source by a 60 per cent tariff but attracting no tariff coming into Australia. Australian orange growers face the same type of problem with Brazilian concentrated juice, coming into Australia on a 5 per cent tariff compared to a 15 per cent tariff going back the other way. In 1996–1997, Australia imported $25 million worth of orange juice from Brazil, as well as $12.7 million worth of fresh oranges from other sources. 'The level playing field' is a joke and has always run uphill.

Thousands of workers in the clothing and footwear industries face the sack as the government prepares to wind back tariffs again. Small business believes that it has been 'conned' by the Howard Government from day one, with its totally ineffective window-dressing policy of cutting red tape and its sleight of hand changes to the Capital Gains Tax that has steadily shrivelled up entrepreneurial incentive since its inception in 1985. Small business now faces another GST onslaught, sponsored by big business that expects greatly reduced company taxes as a trade-off. Small business will be the unpaid tax collector, coping with all the paper work and lost unproductive time. With all the recent earnest and almost anguished cries for taxation reform, not one politician or big business person has called for cuts in government spending as an essential prerequisite. In September, 1997, Australia's foreign debt passed the $200 billion mark, mortgaging off more of the next generation's future.

With Pauline Hanson having stripped away their politically-correct gags, Australians have become suddenly more vocal about the things that, for years, have been niggling at them, like nagging burrs under a saddle. They know that they have never had a say on the crucial issues of multiculturalism and immigration and that those of them from Anglo-European backgrounds have been forced to endure their culture and heritage being constantly denigrated by multicultural spruikers in and outside Parliament. That great slogan of the multiculturalists — 'cultural diversity' — only means one thing to ordinary Australians — division. At election time the politicians finally come, grovelling for votes but they don't trust the people. The feeling is mutually palpable.

Wildly extravagant and blatantly greedy ambit claims made by black and not-so-black Aboriginal 'pretenders' have well and truly 'got up the noses' of mainstream Australia. Most Australians are now 'turned off' by images of 'stolen children' and the squalor of Aboriginal settlements, whether they be in the city or the bush — simply refusing to wear the 'black armbands' offered to them by the pedlars of guilt. The fruits of 'Reconciliation' will never ripen because they will never help to pay the mortgage, send children to university or provide for retirement. A separate flag and the loony demands for a separate Aboriginal State and reserved Seats in our Parliaments only harden the resolve of the Hansonites not to bow down. The repercussions of Wik have created a strong and bitter anti-black backlash which continues to grow. Highly provocative and stupidly nasty comments, such as those made by West Australian Aboriginal activist Ken Colbung about the death of Princess Diana, merely served to reinforce the hardening anti-Aboriginal sentiments of the general population. 'Because the Poms did the wrong thing they now have to suffer,' he said. 'They have to learn too, to live with it as we did and that is how nature goes.' With these few words, the former Korean War veteran obliterated his own credibility and damaged that of the general Aboriginal community.

The grand plan for the 'Asianisation' of Australia was the final straw for those Australians who had become thoroughly fed up with politicians of all hues. Over the years they had survived odd bursts of reverse racism, such as the global campaign of a few years ago that proclaimed 'black is beautiful'. Imagine the eruption of reaction if there had been a 'white is wonderful' slogan. White Australians rankled at being told that their descendants were destined to become Eurasian by former Governor-

General Bill Hayden. Lee Kuan Yew, when he was PM of Singapore, added insult to injury when he described Australians as potentially 'the white trash of Asia'. For years Paul Keating berated Australians about how their salvation lay in Asia. The best laid plans can always go astray. In 1997, with Asian economic tigers threatening to become castrated tomcats, 'the white trash' of Australia was forced to come to the rescue and prop up the Thai currency to the tune of $1.3 billion, with the real possiblity of having to do the same thing for the Malaysian ringgit. A sum of $1.3 billion could provide a lot of jobs for homegrown Australians. The possibility that the major Asian economies will collapse in a falling domino-like scenario is starting to be predicted. The fallout for Australia would be disastrous, with stalled exports and surging unemployment creating the environment for an economic nightmare. All the dire predictions that Australia has no future unless it embraces Asia are now starting to look very shaky indeed.

Pauline Hanson and her One Nation Party have attracted defectors from all sides of the political fence. This has been confirmed by the private polling of the major parties. But the big question is, 'Will her support be maintained at a high enough level to achieve electoral success?'

There are other intending defectors closer to home. A National Party backbencher in Queensland and two Liberal backbenchers in NSW are planning to switch to One Nation close to polling day. The three first-timers intend resigning from their respective parties and joining One Nation after nominations have closed. Their tactics will imitate the scenario that led to Pauline Hanson's election, but may not necessarily have the same result.

The big Parties are obviously concerned about the chances of One Nation's electoral success. The Labor Party and its junior acolyte, the Democrats, have pledged to put Hanson last on their how-to-vote cards and there has been tremendous pressure placed on John Howard by many of his own people, including Victorian Liberal State Premier Jeff Kennett, powerbroker Michael Kroger and Federal Liberal Party President Tony Staley, as well as the media, to take the Liberals down the same track. Howard continued to stubbornly resist.

In 1996, during a Channel 9 *Sunday* show interview, the then Federal

Liberal Party Director Andrew Robb (a recently self-outed republican), fool-ishly allowed himself to be dragooned into agreeing with Gary Gray, his Labor Party opposite number, to put Hanson last on the Liberal's how-to-vote card. Incensed grass roots Liberals drew a hasty retraction from a much chastened Robb. It was a terrible performance from the usually pro-fessional and politically savvy veteran.

Pauline Hanson and One Nation need the right political environment come election time. They need high unemployment, coupled with continued discontent from the farmers and small business. A few more big drug busts with Asian connections will do no harm at all. The fallout from Wik and other Aboriginal issues will be bonuses that will only help intend-ing Hansonites make up their minds.

Any concerted attempt by the major parties to swap preferences against Hanson will backfire against them badly. It will starkly contradict the Aus-tralian ethos of giving someone 'a fair go'. It will be seen by the electorate as the 'big boys' ganging up on an inexperienced woman who was thrust unceremoniously into the political bullring but who was then prepared to stand up and say things that all the other politicians were too frightened to talk about.

The travel rorts scandal that embroiled Federal Parliament in September and October 1997 will guarantee that all MPs will continue to be on the nose with the voters at the next election. The most inept political adviser could not fail but make the 'bullyboy' tactics of the major parties, and the perception of all politicians with their snouts in the trough, into a huge vote-winning issue for Pauline Hanson and One Nation.

Revenge is one of the most powerful human emotions. At the end of this first, perceived to be lacklustre and near-disastrous, Howard term, it could be revenge that will drive voters to savage many of the current crop of Parliamentarians. In such a situation, logic and commonsense will take a backseat.

Only an assassin's bullet or a monumental act of self-destruction can stop Pauline Hanson getting to the ballot box. On election night, all eyes in Australia, and certainly many eyes in Asia and further abroad, will be watching the count in whatever Seat she contests. The media and public concentration on Pauline Hanson will infuriate all those other candidates seeking their brief moments of glory. Only after her fate has been decided will attention swing back to the rest of the election.

Her political survival could see a revolution in Australian politics, in which the hitherto comfortable balance between the major Parties is rudely disrupted. The Hansonites have stood up and been counted and now they want their say. They have not yet tasted blood!

Letter from Noel Crichton-Browne

Letter to Pauline Hanson from Noel Crichton-Browne, October 26, 1996.

Dear Pauline

. . . The first question which you must address is what you wish to achieve from politics. You currently have a great ground swell of support which obviously extends beyond Oxley into many parts of Australia. However it is the type of support which will dissipate over time. When the public understand that their support is not materialising into change, they tire of the emotional energy which that support demands. In other words the voters will only support you as long as they think that support will make a difference. That of course is why Independents who do not hold that balance of power in a parliament have difficulty maintaining their profile over a long period.

The two options which are open to you are, either to seek to capitalise on your support by diverting it into votes for your re-election in Oxley, or to mobilise it into Australian wide support through candidates in the Senate and in strategic seats in the various State elections.

If you are not to maximise the national vote through supporting candidates outside Oxley, the very real risk is that as the nationwide publicity diminishes, so will the media coverage which reaches the people of your own electorate. Correspondingly voter support in Oxley will dwindle as voters drift back to their traditional parties. In other words the voter support in Oxley in the long term will very much equate to the national media coverage you are able to attract. This in turn will depend upon the national voter support you continue to receive which also in turn will, as I said earlier depend upon what incentive you give for people to continue to support you. Hence the necessity of having candidates in other parts of Australia whom the voters can support in a ballot box.

What I am saying in essence is that to maintain your support in Oxley you will need to maintain national coverage. That national support can only come from voters outside Oxley voting to support you through other candidates. Citizens can only vote for candidates, not ideas.

. . . [It] is not desirable for you to have a branch structure. The danger is that you will attract people into office bearing positions in the branches who may be thoroughly undesirable and over whom you will have no control. You most certainly will not have the resources to vet and monitor them.

A much more desirable system is to have a national membership controlled directly by you. Candidates who run under your banner should be vetted and checked by people whose judgement you can completely rely upon. One or two people with political nous are required in each State.

In my view your immediate challenge is to process the names of all those who have expressed support to you, through facsimiles, phone calls and letters. However in saying that, it is equally important that voters are able to communicate with you. I understand that the phones are presently permanently engaged.

I suggest that you have at least another six lines connected on a temporary basis and manned by volunteers. Their sole task should be to do no more than politely accept the calls of support and take down with great care, the names and addresses of the callers. They should also identify their marital status so that you know whether you are dealing with one or two potential voters. You should have John P. prepare a number of form letters which respond directly to the sentiments expressed in the voter's communication. It may be that one voter supports your view on immigration and gun controls, while another supports your position on Aborigines. Each voter should receive a letter which reflects the voter's expressed views. I would also send each correspondent a petition which again also does that. When the petition is returned, those who have signed it should also receive an appropriate form letter and a further petition.

Given the limited resources that are provided to Independents, fund raising should be an immediate priority. Each letter that is sent from your office acknowledging an expression of support should also contain a fund raising paragraph. I have enclosed a sample letter for your consideration. I think you will be very surprised at the response.

For every person who writes to you, there are ten others who intend to but do not do so. The appeal letter should be sent for the very same reason that the petition is important. Voters who express a point of view through a communication are looking for a way to manifest that expression of opinion. Inviting the voter to sign a petition or to send a donation, is providing [him or her] with an opportunity to support that cause in a material way.

The occasions upon which you will be able to offer voters an opportunity to vote for your views between now and the next Federal election are particularly limited. There will only be general State elections in Western Australia and South Australia. The prospects of Federal by-elections that will suit your purpose, are few and perilous.

. . . Given the construction of the ballot paper, for candidates to be in a favourable position in the draw for positioning on the ballot paper, they must be members of a registered party. In Western Australia at least, registering a political party is quite a simple matter. The Electoral Commission requires a Constitution, evidence of sixty financial members and an authorised officer. Membership should be seen as no more than a data base for finance and volunteers. If people are prepared to join a political party, they are invariably prepared to make a donation and to assist at election time. Often they are an excellent conduit to other people for campaign finance and election workers. It is desirable to make the membership cost as low as possible to ensure that no one is disqualified from joining. A special concession should be offered for pensioners.

At a personal level you will be very wise to begin to think of your attendance at functions and at speaking engagements in terms of effort and benefit. In other words each engagement should be accepted in accordance with this criteria: how will this appointment assist my determined strategy of attracting votes in the seats and electorates where I would wish my presence to reflect in the ballot box. This requires considerable discipline because some invitations are inevitably more attractive than others.

On the occasions that you travel inter-State, your campaign fund will accommodate your costs . . .

I should perhaps conclude on the note that time is of the absolute essence. I think you understand that the level and degree of your present public exposure is greater now than it is ever likely to be again unless there is evidence of your continuing influence and support. To that extent it is crucial that you exploit the window of opportunity which is presently available to you. The degree to which you pursue this opportunity will of course dictate the level of success that you will achieve in the future.

The amount of fund raising that is done now will of course control what you are able to do in the future. The success you have in gathering support in elections other than your own will also dictate the level of momentum you are able to generate in the period ahead. It will be very important in the degree to which the media take you seriously or more importantly the extent to which they are forced to acknowledge your public support . . .

Noel Crichton-Browne

Pauline Hanson's Bitter Harvest

Story by David Leser, *Good Weekend* magazine, November 30, 1996:

It's not just the nation that has been divided by this woman: upheavals and acrimony have characterised her family life as well. How has she inspired such loyalty and such loathing?

Pauline Hanson may be breaching the Racial Discrimination Act when she speaks, but she's definitely breaking the law when she drives. There was no catching her at 115 km per hour on the Cunningham Highway in Queensland one evening recently as we hurtled towards her farm at dusk, under a bank of clouds and a mob of black crows, past (no kidding) Goebels (sic) Road, and into the void of the bush.

Pauline Hanson thought it was a hoot, and her staffer-cum-domestic helper-cum-friend and fellow-traveller, Cheyenne MacLeod, said it was, for Hanson, a slow drive. 'You should see her when she's really travelling,' MacLeod said, laughing.

Pauline Hanson loves the rush of adrenaline. Her voice might quake in Federal Parliament, but in her heart there pumps the blood of a thrill-seeker. She lives close to the edge, in this case an hysterical environment which has spawned one of the most noisome racial debates this country has ever witnessed.

The stench has been all too well described. A politician refusing to represent her black constituents; adults and children of non-Caucasian background physically attacked, spat at, verbally abused or just simply made to feel like strangers in their own land; relations with our Asian-Pacific neighbours undermined; tourism and trade threatened; our reputation as an open, tolerant society defamed; and, perhaps most importantly, our sense of ourselves impoverished.

All blandishments and pleas to Hanson for commonsense or compassion have fallen on deaf ears. Her continual refrain has been that racism and bigotry are as old as the First Fleet; and that it is multiculturalism and generations of Aboriginal privilege which have created the divisions, not her. Far from being a racist, she says she is merely speaking for the silenced majority. Look at the polls and the flood of letters! What she ignores is that it is not just what she has said — although that, too, seems to have been based largely on fish-shop gossip and background briefings from her political Rasputin, John Pasquarelli — but the inflammatory way in which she has said it that has caused such a furore.

I have come, therefore, to Ipswich to try to understand the woman who has fired these muskets; a woman who has been both pilloried and lionised for her views, particularly on Aborigines and Asian immigration.

I have come to a working-class town that bears little resemblance to the cosmopolitan centres of Australia, a railway town of God and Rugby League worshippers that has been the butt of countless Brisbane jokes but which has thrown up over the years its local heroes such as Bill Hayden, Sir Llew Edwards, footballers Allan Langer and the Walters brothers and now, if you believe the same headlines, Pauline Hanson. A town where, unless you are talking about massive economic upheaval and unemployment, a lost generation of youth, fear of violence — yes, the fraying of an entire community — you are talking a foreign language.

To understand the formation of what has become a phenomenon is no easy task because while Pauline Hanson is a flamethrower on sensitive and complex issues of public policy, setting the country alight with her political credo, she is highly secretive about her private life. Broach it and you can virtually feel the daggers drawn.

'My private life is my private life,' she says indignantly as we sit at her dining table.

'It's no-one else's business but my own. I am not having a public discussion on my private life. And that's it. End of story.'

There are a couple of risks in doing this story. First, there will be those who will argue that it further boosts the profile of a woman who should never have been given a forum in the first place; that, now when the dust is perhaps settling, we are continuing to turn, in the words of one commentator, a 'misfit into a megastar'.

The second risk is that in trying to examine Pauline Hanson's life, we end up on an excursion through the ugly, primal landscape of the Australian character where bigotry and racism have always played their part, but which a noble bipartisanship in recent decades has attempted to obviate. By re-visiting such tribal prejudices we're in danger of causing further offence at home and abroad.

And yet the dark phenomenology of 'Hansonism' is here. She has not vaporised politically as some forecasters hoped. Media-driven though much of it might have been, she has been discussed passionately on trams, buses, in cafes, pubs, around dining tables, in local and State governments and, of course, in the national Parliament. An examination of her character and the issues she has raised, as well as a chronicling of how she ever got to this point, therefore demand our attention.

321

For those who wish this sordid saga had never been aired, spare a thought for the people in Hanson's private life, particularly her four children.

Her 13-year-old daughter from her second marriage has been subjected to kidnap threats and is now escorted to and from school. She is monitored closely by security officials. Hanson's eldest son, from her first marriage, with whom she hasn't spoken in nearly six years, lives literally in fear of his life. He works in a dangerous industry alongside Aborigines and people from mixed ethnic backgrounds. He waits for someone to learn who his mother is. Her second son refuses to speak to his mother.

There's also her eldest son's grandmother, Hanson's former mother-in-law, who almost single-handedly raised this son. She is an elderly woman who survived Dachau concentration camp and arrived in Australia with her three-year-old child (Hanson's first husband) after the war. She is petrified that Hanson wants to have her deported. You can see it in her trembling hands. When asked about this, Hanson declines to comment.

Then there's Hanson's second husband, Mark. He has been served with a Supreme Court writ by his former wife for having spoken to Brisbane's the *Courier-Mail* about their marriage. Understandably, he has declined to talk to *Good Weekend*.

Hanson, herself the subject of death threats, inspires fear (and adulation) not just in the wider community, but closer to home as well. The result is a grim sketch of domestic upheaval and unalloyed bitterness.

Ipswich, about 45 km south-west of Brisbane and the heart of Pauline Hanson's electorate, is an easy town to malign if you find stereotypes comforting. It's easy to concentrate on the grime and the earth removers and the roaring lorries instead of the palms and flowering jacarandas and level homes that sit on a rim overlooking the Bremer River. It's easy to focus on the racism and bigotry instead of the goodwill and moral rectitude which permeates the churches and charities. It's easy to see this as a town that turned on Labor instead of one that has always displayed mercurial voting habits. It's easy to see this as a provincial hub that has nothing to do with the sprawling metropolises, rather than everything to do with them.

In another incarnation the city might have become the capital of Queensland. Today it is the dumping ground for Brisbane's prisons and mental institutions, but also where a nationally recognised, multi-million dollar computerised library service called Global Info Links is situated and where a third Queensland University campus will soon go.

Still, the smart city concept is lost on many proud railway families who have watched with increasing dismay over the past decade and a half as the central pillars of economic life have toppled. Seventy per cent of the mines have closed, along with steel fabrication factories, wool scouring mills and railway workshops. Thousands of jobs have vanished.

In 1987 Reids, the biggest department store in town, burnt to the ground. Mark Hinchliffe, editor of Ipswich's local paper, the *Queensland Times*, describes it as a devastating blow to the city. 'It was 120 years old,' he said, 'and it was the heart of the city. They were desperate times.'

The 1980s were also times of significant social and demographic change with white Anglo-Saxon families being thrown into poverty and an increasing number of Aboriginal and migrant groups from countries like Vietnam, Taiwan and Tonga moving into the old housing commission areas that form part of Brisbane's western suburbs, the eastern extremity of Hanson's electorate.

Pauline Hanson, 42, is a third-generation Australian. Her father Jack Seccombe's parents were English migrants. Her mother Hannorah Webster's people came from Ireland. For 25 years Jack Seccombe was something of a local identity. He worked 106 hours a week running Jack's cafe, an all-purpose milk bar in Brisbane, which local legend would assert made the best hamburgers not just in Australia 'but in the whole world'. All seven children were raised with a strong work ethic — they were expected to iron their uniforms, peel the onions, haul the potatoes, hang the gherkins and pickled onions in the windows . . . Jack was the reserved, emotional one; Hannorah, the obdurate one who pulled her children into line.

Indeed, she is not a woman you'd want to cross. Hard-boiled and feisty, she displays the same angry defiance as her daughter, especially when it comes to defending her now-famous daughter or expounding on the virtues of old-fashioned discipline and child-rearing. 'Now, Pauline brought up national service [in her maiden speech],' she says. 'That came from me because Pauline was too young to know anything about national service.'

Pauline Seccombe left school in Brisbane at the age of 15. Two years later she was married — to a European migrant, Graham Powkowski. Powkowski is not his real name. Although recently identified in a newspaper article, he has asked that his name not be used so that his mother and, particularly, his son can remain anonymous. He says now that his life became a nightmare from the moment he met Hanson. He claims she became pregnant and that her family applied enormous pressure on him to marry her. 'I didn't want to marry her. She wasn't a person I was in love with. The only reason I got married was I thought it was the right thing to do, but I went through living hell because of that woman.'

Shortly after the birth of their son, Simon (not his real name), the couple separated, just when she had become pregnant again with her second son, Steven. Graham Powkowski has never accepted that Steven is his son. Hanson has always insisted the opposite and urged him to have a DNA test to prove paternity. Powkowski declined, saying it would have still been inconclusive. 'I believe I know who the father is,' he told me. 'When Steven was conceived she was seeing him. I have no doubts in the depth of my soul he is not my son.'

Hanson has not spoken with Simon for nearly six years. He was effectively raised by his paternal grandmother, Ruby Powkowski, and to this day feels devastated by his sense of abandonment by his mother. He refuses to discuss her. She and Steven are also not on speaking terms, although their estrangement is more recent.

In her electoral office in Ipswich, where we met for the first time, Hanson rebuffed all questions on her two marriages but was prepared to castigate both these sons for not showing her sufficient respect. 'Now, I've gone out of my way to look after the children ... because they are my responsibility and nobody else's,' she said. 'And when your children turn around and give you a kick ... you sort of think, what for? I've done nothing wrong.' 'Why did they give you a kick?' 'Because they don't like what I have apparently told them [about not showing me enough respect]. I am not going to be used by anyone, even my own children, and expect to cop it.' Hanson sees similarities between these two sons and Graham Powkowski. 'Same sort of arrogant attitude,' she has explained. 'He's a very irresponsible person. And they're sort of. It's in the genes.'

Hanson has been outspoken in support of family values and has criticised those who exploit the welfare system. Asked whether it was true — as, *Good Weekend* has been told — that when she was receiving child endowments for all four children she declined to pass on the allocation for her first child, Hanson snaps: 'I'm not going to answer that.'

Hanson's second marriage in 1980 to Mark Hanson, a plumber on the Gold Coast, was no less acrimonious when it ended seven years after it began. He has told the *Courier-Mail* that he, too, had felt pressured into marrying her because she was pregnant. 'I feel I was blackmailed into it,' he said.

Hanson has rejected this. She believes he is motivated by a vendetta because of her decision to leave him over what she says was his drinking problem.

Early in their marriage, life was more joyous. The wedding was followed by a honeymoon swing through South-east Asia. She hated it. 'I have no intention of going there again,' she has said.

Mark Hanson can plead special insight into his former wife's views on race. They were once partners in his plumbing business and included among their clients an Aboriginal organisation. She always referred to Aborigines as 'black bastards', he has said. Hanson has denied this, saying: 'Surely the fact that we did business with them demonstrates I am not a racist.'

I flew to Brisbane in late October to try to meet Pauline Hanson on a day of typical pandemonium. Her name was on every news bulletin in the country and she could barely move without colliding with the media. On one front, the major political parties had just declared war (temporarily) against her and a bipartisan resolution condemning intolerance and racism was in the air. Indignation and outrage had gathered at home and, within a week, was to spill out of Asia.

On another front, Hanson was considering a move to the Senate or forming a separate political party. The polls were buoying her. Ultra-right-wing groups such as the League of Rights were singing her praises and an avalanche of congratulatory faxes, letters and phone calls were continuing to pour in. Four thousand copies of her incendiary maiden speech were on order.

She was impossible to get to. I'd left three messages seeking an interview. No response. I'd tried her switchboard dozens of times. The three lines going in were jammed from morning till night. The only option seemed to be to get to Ipswich.

When I finally arrived, it was to the sound of music. A song written by a local crooner was blaring from a tape deck in Hanson's office. It sounded like Slim Dusty gone up-tempo: *Pauline, Pauline . . . Ipswich worker's hero; Pauline, Pauline, Oxley's number one . . . She's got little Johnny Howard and Beazley on the run, our fish and chip shop hero, to us she's number one . . .*

Hanson appeared cordial but wary. (She knows only too well now how journalists can twist things.) We shook hands. She was wearing a plum-coloured cotton suit and pink earrings. She looked composed but the quaver in her voice was a give-away. We began by talking about religion ('I'd call myself agnostic'); her parents and six siblings ('We're a close family. Do anything for each other but not in each other's pockets'); and her childhood. ('It's a part of your life that's finished with, gone . . . but I sometimes feel I'd love to step back in time and go back to those days again.')

She seemed artless and vulnerable. She smiled rarely but said that was because when talking to the media she was terrified of being quoted out of context. She

325

was astounded by the attention she'd received. 'How many have songs written for them and flowers dropped off?' she said.

I asked who her best friend was. Ten seconds later she replied, 'No, that's a hard one.' Another 20 seconds and she ventured Cheyenne MacLeod or Barbara Hazelton, an aide to former National Party Senator John Stone and now Hanson's personal assistant. 'I haven't had time to get a social life out there,' she said. 'For the past 10 years I've been too busy working 80 to 90 hours a week [in the fish shop]. And when I wasn't working it was like, look after the kids or clean the house or try and get some sleep.'

We then hit the Arctic Circle of her two marriages and two elder children, so we moved to the warmer currents of her shop. I asked her how much she borrowed to buy the business. 'I'm not telling you because it's private, too.' Fair enough, although from what I can judge she is not living in Struggle Town. She has a property worth an estimated $500,000 outside of Ipswich, an apartment in town and the shop, which is on the market. According to one newspaper report, she has assets valued at more than $700,000.

We kept on moving, this time to Morrie Marsden, her former lover, campaign manager and nephew of the man who sold her the shop. 'Where did you get his name from?' she asked. 'Who've you been talking to?'

An ice-breaker was called for. I told her she seemed nervous and suggested continuing the interview over dinner or drinks. She said: 'What I will do is invite you out to my place [tonight] and cook dinner there. You can meet my [two younger] kids [Adam and Lee].'

Pauline Hanson had never really shown much of an interest in — nor aptitude for — politics until the Labor mayor of Ipswich, Dave Underwood, was overthrown three years ago in a coup orchestrated by his fellow Labor aldermen. She had worked as a barmaid and, after her divorce, had bought what must now be the most famous fish and chip shop in the Southern Hemisphere. The shop was to become her political nursery. It was right in the middle of the fifth council division on Blackstone Road. Customers would come in, order their battered snapper, and gripe about the whole place going to the dogs. Hanson was all ears.

At the time she was going out with Rick Gluyas, an ex-policeman and close associate of Dave Underwood. Gluyas was appalled by what the ALP machine had done to his friend. He wanted to run for council and he encouraged Hanson to do the same. They became part of a mini-revolution. At the 1994 council elections Ipswich tossed out a council of 10 Labor aldermen and one Independent and replaced them with 10 Independents and one Labor. Pauline Hanson was one of the Independents.

She wasn't given much time to distinguish herself before the then State Labor government decided, without consultation, to merge Ipswich council with its neighbouring Moreton shire. This forced an election two years early. When Hanson lost by 130 primary votes she became, according to Labor councillor Paul Tully, the shortest-serving council member in Ipswich since 1860. In her brief time on council she gave clues to her eventual tub-thumping on race. She opposed an Aboriginal kindergarten on the grounds that there were already enough kindergartens in the area.

While journalists covering council meetings thought her timid during those first public appearances, she was also revealing a short fuse, the kind that was to become a hallmark of her political persona. Paul Tully recalls a weekend 'bonding' session with fellow councillors where they were asked to talk about themselves and their policies. All was going well until Hanson reportedly said: 'I am Pauline Hanson and if I want anyone to know about me I will speak to them privately.'

When everybody had recovered, the last councillor, Sue Wykes, declared she had taken over from Hanson as a barmaid at the local Booval bowling club. 'Which proves old barmaids never die,' Wykes said. 'They go on to become city councillors.'

'With that, Pauline Hanson stood up and left in a rage and we didn't see her till the next day,' Tully says. 'She was absolutely livid and disgusted that someone had exposed her as a former barmaid.' Asked eventually about this in her parliamentary office, Hanson says, fuming: 'That's their opinion. I didn't storm out of any meeting.'

On August 2 last year, Hanson made her now historic decision to join the Liberal Party. Incredible as it may seem, three months after attending her first Liberal Party meeting she was preselected from a field of three to contest the seat of Oxley, the seat Bill Hayden had held for 27 years until his appointment as Governor-General in 1988. (The ALP's Les Scott was to hold it until this year.)

Steve Wilson, local Liberal heavyweight, staunch church-goer, fierce advocate of corporal and capital punishment, as well as opponent of homosexuals 'and anyone else morally wanting', takes credit for choosing Hanson and cultivating her political ambitions. 'She was a good bit of gear at the beginning of the race,' he tells me. 'She was a small businesswoman who worked hard, had had her fair share of knocks and had a genuine concern for the people. A classic

Liberal ... she was pick of the bunch.' Her preselection speech was all about unemployment and the pain of working-class families.

Within a couple of months she was to become a dilemma for the party because of a bellicose letter she'd written to the local *Queensland Times* deriding Aborigines for their privileges. Phil Nickerson, the newspaper's chief of staff, tried to dissuade her from having it published. 'It was the first time we had ever heard about her preoccupation with Aborigines,' he told me.

The letter was published on January 6 but it was only five weeks later, on February 14, after an angry Paul Tully had written to the Queensland division of the Liberal Party and the Prime Minister himself demanding action over Hanson's views, that she was dis-endorsed. The day after her election victory she caused an uproar when, in claiming victory, she disavowed her black constituents. Denying she was a racist, she said it was unfair that indigenous Australians were getting preferential treatment. She said she was fighting for the 'white community, the immigrants, Italians, Greeks, whoever, it really doesn't matter — anyone apart from the Aboriginals and Torres Strait Islanders'.

Hanson would have won the seat of Oxley whatever the Liberal Party had done, such was the disenchantment with Labor, even in its safest Queensland seat. But how she managed to garner the biggest swing against the government in the country — nearly 23 per cent on primary votes — takes a little more explaining.

According to David Hammill, State ALP member for Ipswich and a former minister in the Goss government, Hanson's stunning victory was aided and abetted by the publicity surrounding her dis-endorsement and the Liberal Party's failure to field another candidate. 'She was still listed as a Liberal on the ballot papers,' he told *Good Weekend*, 'and local (National and Liberal party) activists were working for her on her campaign and in the polling booths handing out how-to-vote cards.'

Morrie Marsden, her campaign manager, dismisses out of hand any suggestion that voters might have been confused about which party Hanson belonged to. 'Look, with the amount of publicity she got everybody knew she wasn't standing as a Liberal candidate,' he said. 'The biggest thing she had going for her was her attitude. She has an attitude that you don't fail.'

Hanson's attitude also allowed her to pass on her preferences to a neo-Nazi named Victor Robb. When asked about this, Hanson says she merely marked the ballot paper according to the order in which the candidates were placed. She was number one, Robb was number three. This, of course, seems naive at best, disingenuous at worst.

The maiden speech that rocked the nation has been picked over now probably more times than any other speech of its kind in Australian political history. So, too, have the explanations for how she ever managed to strike such resonant notes with her call for the abolition of multiculturalism and the Aboriginal and Torres Strait Islander Commission, ATSIC; her denunciation of so-called Aboriginal privileges and her warning that Australia was in danger of being swamped by Asians.

Despite her and her family's claims that she has been grossly misrepresented by the media, it is quite clear from all that she says she has migrants, particularly Asians, and Aborigines clearly in her sights. So, too, has her political adviser, John Pasquarelli.

Her distortion of facts, her reliance on hearsay, her savage and emotional denunciations and over-simplification of complex issues have been glaring.

'I am fed up to the back teeth with the inequalities that are being promoted by the Government and paid for by the taxpayer under the assumption that Aboriginals are the most disadvantaged people in Australia,' she told the House of Representatives on September 10. '[I] challenge anyone to tell me how Aboriginals are disadvantaged when they can obtain three and five per cent housing loans denied to non-Aboriginals.'

She said nothing about the historical and social calamities that have befallen Aboriginal people — nothing about their higher infant mortality rate, shorter adult life expectancy, endemic unemployment, dramatically higher rates of incarceration, disease or poverty. She said nothing about the fact that there would be few Aborigines in Australia today whose parents, grandparents or great-grandparents were not murdered, imprisoned, starved, forcibly removed from traditional lands or wrenched from their mothers and fathers by Europeans.

'I believe we are in danger of being swamped by Asians. Between 1984 and 1995, 40 per cent of all migrants coming into this country were of Asian origin. They have their own culture and religion, form ghettos and do not assimilate.'

'Totally without foundation,' retorts Dr Stephen FitzGerald, former Australian ambassador to China and chairman of the 1988 committee that advised the Federal Government on Australia's immigration policies. 'They don't form ghettos any more than people from Europe did or, in earlier stages of immigration, people from Ireland did. What happens is that in the first stage of immigration people concentrate in a particular area, but once they get established they start moving out.'

Sitting now in her living room of cypress pine and silky oak, the Gene Pitney song *Town Without Pity* (seriously) playing on the stereo, I ask her if she's ever known an Asian person or had an Asian friend. She replies: 'I employed an Asian person [a Laotian] last year in my shop. She worked for me for four months.'

And what about other Asian people you know? Thirteen seconds later, Hanson says through clenched teeth, 'Not a whole lot that I know.'

It would be wrong to suggest that an evening with Pauline Hanson, her children and Cheyenne MacLeod is an entirely unpleasant experience. It is not, although when MacLeod unwrapped a stack of chops for dinner and I informed her I didn't eat meat, I thought momentarily that it was going to be a short-lived one. Hanson raised her eyebrows and shook her head slightly as if I'd just confessed to membership in the Communist Party. But she recovered. 'Spumante or Bundy?' she asked. I opted for Bundy. While the carrots and peas were defrosting I asked Hanson if she always drove so fast. She giggled like a schoolgirl and then poured us two very stiff drinks.

Her son, Adam, 15, walked into the kitchen and asked his mother to explain the last stanza of a Wilfred Owen poem: *And bugles calling for them from sad shires*. Hanson said it was about war, then shrugged her shoulders and suggested he ask me. Adam and I talked for a few minutes before he went off and watched *Braveheart* for what his sister, Lee, 13, claimed was the umpteenth time that month.

For a good part of our interview, Lee sat and listened to us talking. She told me that all her friends agreed with what her mother had been saying. (This squared with my conversation earlier that day with two Year 12 students. They loved Hanson, admitted being racist, claimed that Aborigines were just as racist as them, and said they could express their opinions more freely now because of Hanson's arrival on the political scene.)

Hanson's house is a hacienda of polished floorboards and wood panels on 65 hectares of grazing country boasting 25 head of cattle and a number of Arabian horses. A couple of years ago, when she and Ipswich councillor Rick Gluyas ended their relationship, she bought out his estimated $250,000 share in the house. How she managed to raise the money for that she will not say.

The living room reveals a matching floral lounge and dining suite, a few ornaments over an unused fireplace and a small statue of a Filipino man riding a buffalo. It feels decidedly barren, perhaps because she and her children moved here 'permanently' only a few months ago from their apartment in Ipswich, or perhaps because Hanson is in Canberra all week when Parliament sits, during which time the children are normally looked after by the ever-faithful MacLeod or Barbara Hazelton.

Or perhaps it's because there is a frostiness about Hanson herself which even a Bundy-soaked evening will not penetrate. Her face seldom softens into a smile. When it does, she is transformed: less pinched and paranoid and unforgiving; more like a woman whose heart you might appeal to. But not now; not with me. Her political adviser, former crocodile shooter John Pasquarelli, has been on the phone twice, wanting to know who I am. Good Weekend? Bad Weekend? Hanson doesn't know.

The conversation turns to the Gold Coast where she worked as a cocktail waitress in the early 1970s at the Penthouse Nightclub, the same venue that introduced dwarf-throwing to an unimpressed world 12 years ago and where she was feted like a diva when she returned last month.

'It's just wonderful that it's a tourist destination,' she says, 'but the average Aussie out there is saying, "It's not the Surfers Paradise that we used to know." People are sort of feeling that they're losing something that was theirs. Like you're in your country but it's another world. By all means allow investment into the country, but I think we've got to be selective. If you're not an Australian citizen I don't believe you should be able to own property in this country. We're losing control of this country.'

Hanson talks of her patriotism, her anger at 'inequalities'; the reverse racism of Aborigines, the fear and struggle and pain in her community; the suffering of the Aussie bloke — 'I think the most downtrodden person in this country is the white Anglo-Saxon male,' she says. 'I think they've hit the bottom of the barrel. It's got to the stage where I think the balance has swung too far [in favour of women] and men don't know what to do. "Gee, do I open up the door or don't I? Is she a feminist or is she not?"'

'Are you a feminist?' I ask. 'No,' she replies without hesitation.

I ask Hanson who she most admires. Fifteen seconds later she simply says, 'No.'

Nobody? 'The only person I truly admire is my father.'

No political figure? 'No.'

In history? 'No.'

No musician, actor, writer? 'Got to be alive, eh? That's a tough one . . .'

Eventually, after Cheyenne MacLeod lauds Sir Joh Bjelke-Petersen, Hanson agrees the former Queensland premier would be as close to a political hero as she has ever had. Later on, with Lee by her side, I ask her to tell me the worst thing that's ever happened to her. 'Don't know,' she says.

What's the best thing? 'When I got divorced.'

From the first or second husband? She laughs. 'That's two good things . . .' and an unmistakeable look of forlornness comes over the face of her daughter. Then Hanson says: 'I suppose winning the seat of Oxley, that's been a very high moment for me. I know I'm stirring the pot out there but I honestly believe it needs stirring. We need debate in this country.'

To be Australian today is, for many people, to be deeply insecure about the future. You can't see this trauma in the economic indicators so much as you can in the faces of those in dole queues, in companies being downsized, in work-places of increasing stress and competition, in traffic snarls, in isolated country towns, behind the walls of disintegrating family homes.

It's no secret that the changes in Australian society over the past 15 years have been staggering. No aspect of life has remained unaltered. The catchwords have been globalisation and restructuring. The results have been declining wages, growing job insecurity, changing labour markets, soaring technological advance-ments, altering work practices and a re-definition of leisure. The Australian psyche has taken a pummelling. People are bewildered and apprehensive. They let fly at easy targets — welfare recipients, Aborigines, migrants. It's called the politics of downward envy. The politics of resentment.

Social researcher Hugh Mackay has written extensively on this subject. In an article in the *Australian* recently he tried to assess the Hanson phenomenon by re-visiting an interview conducted in 1939 with the psychoanalyst Carl Jung on the subject of the German people's response to Hitler. Jung said that Hitler was 'the loudspeaker which magnifies the inaudible whispers of the German soul'. Similarly, Mackay wrote, Hanson could be seen as a loudspeaker to the whis-perings of the Australian soul. '[She] might fizzle out in another week or two, as some commentators are suggesting, but I doubt it. She has struck a responsive chord that will resonate for some time.'

In 1984, following historian Geoffrey Blainey's warning about large-scale Asian immigration, the mood turned ugly in a way similar to today. Asians were spat at, attacked in the street; the then Immigration minister Stewart West received death threats and razor blades in the mail and Blainey's reputation, arguably, was never the same.

In 1989, it was headlines again when John Howard said that 'the pace of change of [Asian immigration] has probably been a little too great'. The fol-lowing year he lost the Liberal leadership to Andrew Peacock, partly because of these comments. Now, seven years later, Pauline Hanson has arrived to remind him of his own mixed record on the subject of race, to haunt him with, perhaps, his own unconscious beliefs, his Jungian shadow.

John Howard has been widely condemned for his failure to directly repudiate her. Twelve days after Hanson's maiden speech, he told the Queensland division of the Liberal Party that one of the great changes that had come over Australia in the past six months was that 'people do feel able to speak a little more freely and a little more openly about what they feel. In a sense the pall of censorship on certain issues has been lifted . . . I welcome the fact that people can now talk about certain things without living in fear of being branded as a bigot or as a racist.' Howard had effectively allowed the Hanson genie to stay out of the bottle.

On the day after Federal Parliament has passed its historic joint resolution condemning racism, I visit Pauline Hanson in her parliamentary office. She is kneeling on the floor, shoes off, with the major dailies spread out before her on a long, low table. Each paper carries banner headlines deploring intolerance and noting her absence from the debate the previous day. She seems visibly distressed. This interview is not going to help.

The first thing she says to me is: 'Are you doing a beat-up on me?' I tell her I'm not. She appears unconvinced. She's 'heard on the grapevine' that I am. I want to tell her — but I don't — that it's a journalist's job, particularly in a profile of this sort, to try to win over and extract information from a subject; and that only in rare circumstances does the subject not see betrayal in the result.

The interview goes from bad to worse. Each question is greeted with growing displeasure. What, for example, is her response to the Irish-Chinese National Party Senator Bill O'Chee's passionate speech in Parliament the previous day? He had spoken of the thousands of young Australian schoolchildren who 'know once they leave the safety of their classroom and enter the playground, they will become the whipping boys and girls of the fear and paranoia that Ms Hanson has whipped up. Twenty-five years ago I was one of those children.'

To which Hanson says, 'I think it's dramatising the whole lot.' She shows me her press release which defends her absence from the House the previous day — she had a prior appointment in Melbourne with 'real Australians'. She also says she is 'now being blamed for every misfortune that occurs in Australia. If a farmer's cow has a two-headed calf, it will be my fault.'

On a number of occasions Hanson begins shouting at me, particularly when explanations are sought for why she keeps targeting people on the basis of their race. 'I want a balance brought back into this country,' she yells, as Pasquarelli pokes his big, bald head through her door for what must be the fourth time during our interview. With every new question I see her creeping realisation that it has all spun out of her control — this interview, the headlines, the national and international indignation. Yet the grim determination remains: to keep speaking out on what she insists have been until now 'taboo' subjects.

I ask her whether in giving her maiden speech she had planned this hullabaloo or whether it had caught her by surprise. Finally, the tears and mirth roll together as she says, with dripping sarcasm, 'Yeh, I just love all this controversy. I really do. I just love sitting on a knife's edge with my credibility and integrity and all the rest of it just about down the drain.'

For a brief moment I actually feel sorry for her. I look at Pauline Hanson and see a woman hopelessly out of her depth. I see a media circus and a political neophyte who has lost virtually all privacy. I see, in part, a scapegoat for all the ugly sentiments that gnaw away at the human heart, including those of our more slippery politicians.

But the moment passes and what I see again are the cold, sharp features of bigotry and racism and I am reminded of how far we still have to go to expunge this from our midst. I see the need, more pressing now than ever, for the true story to be told — of how Australia's bold multicultural experiment has actually worked.

Our conversation continues for a while, turning circles on the subject of skin and race. But then Pauline Hanson has had enough. She stands up and, in a white heat, walks me to the door.

Index